Lecture Notes in Computer Science   1411
Edited by G. Goos, J. Hartmanis and J. van Leeuwen

Springer
Berlin
Heidelberg
New York
Barcelona
Budapest
Hong Kong
London
Milan
Paris
Santa Clara
Singapore
Tokyo

Lars Asplund (Ed.)

Reliable
Software Technologies –
Ada-Europe

1998 Ada-Europe International Conference
on Reliable Software Technologies
Uppsala, Sweden, June 8-12, 1998
Proceedings

 Springer

Series Editors

Gerhard Goos, Karlsruhe University, Germany
Juris Hartmanis, Cornell University, NY, USA
Jan van Leeuwen, Utrecht University, The Netherlands

Volume Editor

Lars Asplund
Uppsala University, Department of Computer Systems
P.O. Box 325, S-751 05 Uppsala, Sweden
E-mail: asplund@docs.uu.se

Cataloging-in-Publication data applied for

Die Deutsche Bibliothek - CIP-Einheitsaufnahme

Reliable software technologies : proceedings / Ada Europe '98, 1998
Ada Europe International Conference on Reliable Software
Technologies, Uppsala, Sweden, June 8 - 12, 1998. Lars Asplund
(ed.). - Berlin ; Heidelberg ; New York ; Barcelona ; Budapest ; Hong
Kong ; London ; Milan ; Paris ; Santa Clara ; Singapore ; Tokyo :
Springer, 1998
  (Lecture notes in computer science ; Vol. 1411)
  ISBN 3-540-64536-5

CR Subject Classification (1991): D.2, D.1.2-5, D.3, D.4, C.2.4, C.3, K.6

ISSN 0302-9743
ISBN 3-540-64536-5 Springer-Verlag Berlin Heidelberg New York

© Springer-Verlag Berlin Heidelberg 1998
Printed in Germany

Typesetting: Camera-ready by author
SPIN 10637192   06/3142 – 5 4 3 2 1 0   Printed on acid-free paper

Foreword

The third International Conference on Reliable Software Technologies – Ada-Europe'98 took place in Uppsala, Sweden, from June 8 to 12, 1998. It was the 18th conference organized by Ada-Europe in co-operation with ACM and is the main Ada event in Europe with its counterpart being the SIGAda Conference in the USA in fall.

The programming language Ada with the new standard, Ada 95, is very stable and mature. The language itself provides support for distributed systems, real-time systems, object-oriented programming and design, and the implementation of High Integrity Systems.

The importance of reliable software has grown over the years, and we are today dependent on software in a large number of areas where a malfunction of the software can result in loss of human lives. The programming language Ada may not be the ultimate solution, but it is definitely the best programming language available today for safety critical software. It is not by chance that Boeing decided to use Ada in its fly-by-wire 777 aircraft. The FAA (Federal Aviation Administration) has very strict rules for certifying an avionics system according to the standard DO-178B.

The importance of High Integrity Systems will be more pronounced in the future due to the increased capacity of micro-controllers, and the temptation to use more and more complex software. Other areas where safety is already known to be crucial are systems for nuclear power plants and medical applications.

Ada is being used in real-time systems and with the new abstraction, the protected object, it is now possible to efficiently implement a real-time system using tasks, protected objects, priority inheritance, and the priority ceiling protocol. By the use of these features and methods a system can be guaranteed to meet deadlines, avoid deadlocks, and keep blocking time to a minimum for high priority tasks.

The use of the Internet has exploded over the last few years, and we now see many innovations. We get not only documents with text but also pictures and sound. The documents are also now equipped with programs. The new technology works well with Ada, and the abstract machine for executing the Java byte code can be utilized by an Ada compiler thereby giving us access to a safe programming language for the design and implementation of Graphical User Interfaces.

The three invited keynote speakers, who gave talks about the current and future use of Ada and important aspects on safety critical systems, were:

- *Franco Gasperoni*, E.N.S.T. Paris, France, Embedded Opportunities
- *Pierre Chapront*, GEC Alsthom Transport, Saint Ouen, France,
  Ada+B The formula for safety critical software development
- *Martyn Thomas*, Chairman Emeritus, Praxis Critical Systems Ltd, U.K.,
  Engineering Quality in Software

The technical program of the conference features 23 papers, selected by a program committee of highly qualified researchers in academia and industry in the following sessions

- Ada 95 and Java
- Ada 95 Language and Tools
- Distributed Systems
- Real-Time Systems
- Case Studies and Experiments
- Software Quality
- Software Development Methods and Techniques
- Software Architectures
- High Integrity Systems

The conference also contained an excellent set of tutorials, featuring international experts who presented introductory and advanced material on software engineering:

- Ada 95 as a Foundation Language for Undergraduate Programs,
  Michael B. Feldman
- Java for Ada Programmers, *Ben Brosgol*
- Software Systems Architecture: A Practical Architecture Method,
  David Emery, Rich Hilliard, Timothy Rice
- Distributed Systems Annex of Ada 95 and an Inside Look at the GLADE
  Implementation, *Laurent Pautet, Samuel Tardieu*
- The End of the Age of Miracles, *Richard T. Dué*
- Ada-Based Systems Engineering with O4S, *Ingmar Ögren*
- Building Development Tools for Use with GNAT, *Cyrille Comar, Sergey
  Rybin*
- Ada, Java & GNAT: A Manager's and Developer's Roadmap,
  Franco Gasperoni, Edmond Schonberg
- Guaranteeing Timing Requirements under Real-Time POSIX,
  Michael González Harbour
- SPARK, *John Barnes*

Many people have contributed towards making this conference a success.

Kristina Lundqvist deserves my sincere gratitude for her work as tutorial chair and as a much valued colleague for planning the conference generally. Örjan Leringe has taken care of the practical arrangements, and I am very thankful for his effort with the Web pages, and the printed program. I also would like to thank May-Lill Hansen for her efforts in getting exhibitors to the exhibition.

Last but not least I would like to thank the program committee members, for their hard work during the review process.

The technical program was complemented by a number of social events, the highlight being the musical divertimento by ACT.

March 1998   Lars Asplund

Organization

The International Conference on Reliable Software Technologies – Ada-Europe'98 was organized by Ada-Europe, in cooperation with ACM/SIGAda.

Executive Committee

Program Chair: Lars Asplund, Department of Computer Systems, Uppsala University, Sweden

Tutorials: Kristina Lundqvist, Department of Computer Systems, Uppsala University, Sweden

Exhibition: May-Lill Hansen, Ericsson Radar AS, Norway

Program Committee

Angel Alvarez, Technical University of Madrid, Spain
John Barnes, JBI, U.K.
Lars Björnfot, Ericsson, Sweden
Alan Burns, University of York, U.K.
Dirk Craeynest, OFFIS nv/sa, Belgium
Michael Feldman, The George Washington University, U.S.A.
Mark Gerhardt, Lockheed Martin Corp., U.S.A.
May-Lill Hansen, Ericsson Radar AS, Norway
Michael Gonzáles Harbour, Universidad de Cantabria, Spain
Jan Van Katwijk, Delft University of Technology, The Netherlands
Yvon Kermarrec, ENST de Bretagne, France
Björn Källberg, CelsiusTech Naval Systems AB, Sweden
Doug Locke, Lockheed Martin Corp., U.S.A.
Steve Michell, ORA, Canada
Laurent Pautet, ENST Paris University, France
Erhard Plödereder, University of Stuttgart, Germany
Jean-Pierre Rosen, ADALOG, France
Edmond Schonberg, New York University & Ada Core Technologies, U.S.A.
Alfred Strohmeier, Swiss Federal Insitute of Technology, Lausanne, Switzerland
Joyce Tokar, DDC-I, U.S.A.
Göran Wall, Enator Telub AB, Sweden
Stef Van Vlierberghe, OFFIS nv/sa, Belgium
Brian Wichmann, National Physical Laboratory, U.K.
Daniel Wengelin, CelsiusTech Systems AB, Sweden

Conference Administrator

Mariadata, Box 1085, SE-141 22 Huddinge/Stockholm, Sweden

Table of Contents

Case Studies and Experiments

Software Quality

Software Development Methods and Techniques

Software Architectures

High Integrity Systems

Embedded Opportunities

Franco Gasperoni

École Nationale Supérieure des Télécommunications
46, rue Barrault, F-75634 Paris Cedex 13, France
gasperon@inf.enst.fr

Abstract. This is a modest attempt at unveiling forthcoming opportunities in the embedded computing sector. The final talk will also explain how Ada 95 offers a competitive advantage in the new embedded marketplace.

1 Crystal ball, crystal ball which market will beat them all ?

The last ten to twelve years has seen the PC platform emerge, grow, challenge and finally become the prima donna of computing. A company such as Microsoft which has bet its future on the double digit growth of this market had a 1997 revenue of USD 11.4 billion and a profit of USD 3.5 billions (an average of over USD 500,000 per employee).

Microsoft certainly grabbed the last big computing market as this century is coming to a close. But here is an interesting finding: According to several research firms, the majority of PCs sold in the United States last year were purchased by repeat PC buyers rather than people who never owned a personal computer. This suggests that, at least in the world's largest market for PCs, we may be reaching saturation levels [1].

So, should you be selling your Microsoft shares and look for the next double digit growth company ? Perhaps. But wait just a moment before you call your broker.

Let's look at the other big player in the PC arena: Intel. Intel would certainly be hit more badly than Microsoft if the growth in the PC market stalled. Knowing the motto of Intel's CEO: "only the paranoid survive", you can be assured that Intel is not standing still.

Let's do some first grade mathematics. There are about 50 Million PCs sold world-wide every year. About as many motorized vehicles (cars, trucks, busses, etc.) are also sold yearly on a world-wide basis. With the average price of a motorized vehicle being an order of magnitude above that of the average PC and with increasing demands for intelligence needed in an automobile or a truck, that makes the automotive industry an ideal Intel target. Indeed, last year, Intel started targeting the Pentium to the automotive industry to capture a larger share of its embedded-microprocessor market.

Just as an example of the wonders software can do in an automobile think of the problem Daimler-Benz experienced with its latest Class A model. After 4 curves at 60 Km/h of a particularly winding road, the car would overturn. The problem was solved by adding accelleration sensors, using the breaking system and having software control the whole thing. This is just a simple nuts and bolts example of the importance of computing in the automotive industry. But there is more, much more coming and the automotive industry is just the tip of the iceberg.

2 Did someone say embedded ?

The embedded devices market is hardly a novel one. Indeed, this market has existed for quite some time and has been pretty unglamorous, although companies such as Motorola have successfully bet their future on it.

Here are the figures: In 1995, embedded microprocessors comprised 79 percent of the overall processor unit shipments, or 262.4 million units out of a total 330.8 million [2]. However, in 1995 the embedded microprocessors have generated USD 3.4 billion in revenue compared to USD 14.1 billion for PC microprocessors. This is because, unlike their desktop cousins that are designed for breath-taking performance, embedded microprocessors must be cost-effective and as a result 4 or 8 bit microprocessors are often used.

No wonder this fragmented, assembly language driven industry has so far been unglamorous. Microprocessors have merely been used as cheaper and more reliable replacements for their former mechanical counterparts.

While often written in C and sometimes requiring a relatively sophisticated real-time OS, applications for 16-bit microprocessors represent more of a transition for what is about to unfold rather than a trend in itself.

Certainly 4, 8 and 16 bit microprocessors will be as widely used in the coming years as they are today. But that's not where the opportunities lie.

3 Trends anyone ?

The average price of a 32-bit RISC for the embedded market in 1994 was USD 68. In 1997 this price fell down to USD 26. It is no secret to anyone that processor power is increasing while its price is dropping. Silicon real-estate is getting cheaper by the day and it is now possible to put on a single chip a powerful 32-bit microprocessor along with memory and system microcontrollers. Instead of buying and connecting a bunch of chips manufacturers can get a single module.

Already today, in higher-end tasks such as aerospace, bullet-trains, laser printers, automobiles or sophisticated machine tools, embedded systems often rely on full-blown 32-bit processors. Intel's i960 series has been a big hit in the embedded market, and Sun has versions of its SPARC processors that are widely used as well, not to mention Motorola's 680X0, as well as the PowerPC who have a significant percentage of the high-end embedded microprocessor market at this stage.

The 32-bit embedded microprocessor market has been the safety haven of all the manufacturers who did not make it into the workstation market or who have shied away from it. With Intel targeting the embedded-microprocessor market not only in the automotive, but also in the telecom and other industries, will we see a hardware convergence in the embedded market as we are witnessing in the workstation market with the forthcoming Intel IA-64 architecture ? This is still unclear.

One thing is certain, however. Having amortized its R&D investment by sales in the PC market, PC hardware technologies will be very cost effective in the embedded market and will play an important role in this arena.

4 Don't underestimate human creativity

Whatever the processor, programming 32-bit chips in assembly is not only becoming a performance and in some cases a reliability nightmare (I am thinking of VLIW-type microprocessors such as the Philips Trimedia and the forthcoming IA-64) but is also extremely expensive in terms of manpower. As a result, we will witness a very limited use of assembly in the 32-bit embedded microprocessor market.

This is, to some extend a less fundamental trend than the fact that the array of applications that these processors can accommodate is orders of magnitude more powerful than what most of the embedded systems industry has been used to. Untaught of applications will spread like wild fire offering an array of unheard of capabilities ranging from intelligent door locks, to smart cards and web-phones. Inexpensive, powerful and embedded intelligence will not only result in new opportunities in the already prosperous computing industry, but will, most important, prove an invaluable marketing and product differentiation tool for airlines, car manufacturers, banks while boosting the telecommunications, media and consumer electronics industries at large.

Need an example ? Just think of the latest Japanese gadget: the tomogotchi. Unheard and untaught of only a couple of years ago, here it is sweeping away all your idées reçues.

The richness and complexity of these new applications will not only require high-level languages, but its cornerstone will be real-time programming. Why ? Because the characteristics of an embedded device is that it must respond to multiple, at times conflicting, external unpredictable events in a timely and most important predictable fashion.

5 Where is the beef ?

Real-time programming is hardly a novel concept. It has been used in the industry for the past two decades and the founding papers of the discipline date back to the 70s. The fundamental piece of real-time programming is the underlying, run-time, executive, kernel or operating system that allows the creation of several threads of activities and offers the necessary primitives to synchronize and exchange data between them.

The real-time buyers guide from the Real Time Magazine (http://www.real-time-info.be/encyc/market/rtos/rtos.htm) lists over 80 real-time executives and operating systems products and many more have been built in-house. This shows the level of fragmentation of this market.

An important dimension across which we can divide real-time systems is safety. Safety critical real-time applications are those whose failure can cause catastrophic consequences with losses of human lives or resources such as money (e.g. in the financial industry) or machinery.

Forthcoming embedded applications described below will not be safety-critical. Their malfunctioning may cause customer dissatisfaction and possibly a bad press for their manufacturers, but no short term criticality. On the other hand, as product life cycles are shrinking, there will be an increased time-to-market pressure for these new applications. As volumes will rise, real-time software will morph from an industrial niche to a leading-edge segment of the computing industry.

6 How big is it ?

So how big is this new embedded market ? International Data Corp. (IDC), a research company, has estimated the embedded software market at about USD 700 million in 1995 and expects it to grow to USD 1.6 billion by year 2000. Wessels, Arnold & Henderson, another research firm, estimated the market size at USD 2.5 billions for 1996 and a growth up to USD 5.2 billion by 2001 [4]. The difference in the estimates comes in part from what the different analysts are counting as embedded systems software. Another degree of uncertainty comes from a market that is currently quite fragmented and often hard to define.

There is, however, an agreement in the press about the explosive growth of new embedded applications fueled by the Internet and explosion in networking and telecommunications. For instance IDC forecasts that the number of non-PC Internet devices will grow to more than 48M by 2001, while business opportunities in information appliances will reach USD 6.6 billion by 2005. Key growth areas are the consumer market with an estimated growth rate of 75 percent and 28 percent in the telecommunications/networking market (IDC).

7 May the network be with you

The Internet effect is snowballing into an array of devices and applications that only a few years ago appeared as futuristic. These so-called Internet and generally speaking network appliances include set-top boxes, handheld devices such as personal digital assistants, web-phones, smart cards, automobile guidance and entertainment systems, satellite broadcast receptors, cellular phones, and network computers.

Up to now embedded devices have mostly been isolated and stand alone, with a closed universe of data and applications. Soon these devices will be connected to the network, giving consumers access to a content-rich ever evolving world where the applications running on the embedded device may itself be remotely updated, enhanced or outright reprogrammed.

Because, as previously stated, product life cycles are shrinking and time-to-market is key, it is becoming more important to ship a product quickly even if some less important functionalities are missing while having the ability to download upgrades and fixes over the network. For this your device must be able to connect to some network and the Internet is becoming the cheapest network infrastructure available world-wide.

Does the Internet connected appliance seem a bit far fetched ? Here is something that would have seemed very far fetched 10 years ago: A LAN in an automobile. If that may seem strange, keep in mind that there are around 16 microcontrollers/microprocessors in the average new car, and Motorola, a major player in this market, predicts that by the year 2000 there will be 35 of these in every new car [4]. Some of these processors need to communicate closely, such as those controlling the engine and the transmission. As a result, automakers are working on automotive LAN standards.

8 Good morning, I am your servlet

Servlet is one of the latest buzz words in the embedded arena [5]. A servlet is a small application which allows you to diagnose an embedded system by accessing and monitoring its operations remotely with a standard browser such as Nescape's. This allows connecting to a router to change configurations according to the work load, inquiring the state of a coin-operated food dispenser (how much money is in the machine, how much food is left) or reprogramming the locks on a building.

A servelets is no more than an HTML-cognizant application that listens on a given TCP socket and is capable of accessing data collected by the embedded processor, formatting it for later access by a browser.

With Java enabled servelets, embedded designers can also update, modify or correct the embedded code by downloading a Java applet. The question is of course can Java be used in a real-time environment ?

9 I am on a diet, I am a thin client

If servlet is one of the latest buzz words in the embedded marketplace, thin client is another one [6].

With the advent of very inexpensive LAN solutions and powerful PCs, a new concept is blossoming. The idea is to have inexpensive "thin clients" everywhere connected to some sort of a server (typically a PC).

As an example consider game players. Instead of duplicating the multimedia data handling power of a PC in a game console, why not using a simple game-playing client hooked up to your living-room TV and connected to a PC server using your home network ?

Because the PC can easily be connected to the Internet, a benefit of networked thin clients is the ability to control them remotely through your PC. For instance a home security system that leverages on such thin clients may access the family's schedule stored on the computer or smart phone and automatically turn on various security-enabled gadgets. For instance, the security system may turn lights on and off according to some pattern. From their vacation site the Smiths may use the hotel's Webphone to connect to the home intranet and check the status of security-enabled gadgets and perhaps disable them for the neighbor that will be staying over for a couple of days while they are away. The latest in browsers and networking protocols have made all of this possible.

10 Survival of the richest ?

We have told you how fragmented the RTOS market is at the moment. As this segment of the software industry expands and matures, it is possible that we will witness a number of mergers, consolidations, buy-outs and takeovers.

The main question at this stage is: who will be the software giant of the new embedded software market ? Microsoft has certainly hinted it wants to be a serious player. After moving from desktop domination, to an astounding success in server/network operating systems and Internet browsers, embedded operating systems may be next on the list.

Already today a number of product offerings from companies such as QNX, Wind River Systems, AnnaSoft, Venturecom offer anything from an implementation of the Win32 API on top of a RTOS, to the possibility of running a modified or stripped-down version of Windows NT on the target sometimes in coexistence with their own RTOS [9].

But windows NT is just the beginning. With the diminutive Windows CE Microsoft plans to make Windows the number 1 software platform in the consumer electronics market. The question is how credible is Windows CE in this market ?

The facts speak for themselves. Windows CE is a de facto standard for high-end personal digital assistants (PDAs). Microsoft's recent purchase of WebTV and its agreement with TCI (a cable operator giant) to use Windows CE in TCI's set-top boxes has clearly positioned Windows CE as one of the leading OSes for set-top boxes. That is not all. Microsoft has demonstrated the AutoPC, an in-dash system that uses voice recognition to perform tasks such as dialing a mobile phone, reading e-mail, and activating a GPS. In the second half of 1997, Microsoft invested in Navitel Communications, which has demonstrated a Windows CE equipped telephone with built-in address book, appointment calendar applications and of course Internet browsing capabilities. Last, but not least Microsoft announced a deal with Motorola to include Windows CE in an array of wireless devices [7].

IBM's attitude towards Windows CE is also revealing. Last year, IBM dismissed Windows CE as a simple OS for PDAs, a market IBM is not interested in. Then when Microsoft announced that Windows CE is also for set-top boxes and other embedded devices that could use a RTOS, IBM begun discussions with Microsoft about porting Windows CE to its embedded PowerPC family [8].

11 Windows real-time, are you kidding ?

Windows CE 2.0 provides a rich subset of the well known Win32 API. It also comes with Java and Visual Basic ROM support. Windows CE will include some support for ActiveX. Windows CE is modular, with the ability to include in your application only the necessary modules to minimize memory footprint. In addition, some of the available modules can themselves be custom-built by selecting from a set of available components. A small version of Windows CE can fit in 200 Kbytes of ROM.

The fundamental question is whether the Win32 API upon which Windows NT and Windows CE real-time services are built can indeed be used in a real-time environment.

In short Windows NT is NOT a RTOS while Windows CE is a RTOS for certain categories of real-time problems which have deadline latencies starting at a few milliseconds and up but containing a small number of activities (around 10) that must be responded to in real-time [10, 11].

In [10] are listed some of the requirements needed to consider an operating system a RTOS:

- The OS must be multithreaded and preemptive.
- The OS must support thread priority.
- A system of priority inheritance must exist.
- The OS must support predictable thread synchronization mechanisms.
- The OS behavior must be predictable.

Let's look at each of these points in turn in the context of Windows NT and Windows CE.

Multithreading and preemption. Both Windows NT/CE are preemptive multitasking operating system. Windows CE supports a maximum of 32 simultaneous processes (no such limit exists on NT). The actual number of threads a process can create is limited only by available system resources.

Thread Priorities. Windows NT has a complex notion of priorities with 4 classes of priorities each containing 8 levels. A process chooses the class of priorities and can only change levels within that class. For real-time applications the real-time class has the appropriate semantics. Windows CE has only the real-time class of priorities. Eight levels of priorities (2 of which are used by interrupt handling routines and tasks on Windows CE) is a bit stingy when most

RTOS allow for 256 levels. Why ? Just think of how Rate Monotonic Scheduling (RMS) works. RMS works by assigning a different priority to each different thread according to its periodicity. This means that you cannot have that many concurrent activities on NT and CE, unless you want to handle the scheduling yourself.

Priority Inversion. The problem of priority inversion arises when threads having different priority levels compete for common resources and a thread H of high priority is blocked waiting for a resource held by a lower priority thread L which cannot execute because a thread M with slightly greater priority than L is executing. While NT is NOT priority-inversion safe, Windows CE is.

Thread Synchronization. Windows NT/CE offer a large set of synchronization objects: critical sections, events, mutexes. Windows CE queues synchronization requests in FIFO-by-priority order: a different FIFO queue is defined for each of the eight discrete priority levels. A new request from a thread at a given priority is placed at the end of that priority's list. The scheduler adjusts these queues when priority inversions occur.

Timers. In Windows CE threads can use the system's interval timer which returns a count of milliseconds. For more detailed timing information the OEM must provide the hardware and software support for special higher-resolution timers. In Windows NT there is a lack of programmable timers.

OS predictability. The Windows CE kernel has been inspected to ensure that it can be characterized by a worst-case time that is independent of the number of system objects. This is unlike Windows NT.

12 Windows everywhere or Java on anything ?

Java, the "write once, run anywhere" system introduced only a few years ago by Sun Microsystems promises to be the software development platform of the 21st century, at least that is what Sun is claiming. From browsers, to network computers, to set-top boxes, car navigation and entertainment systems to web phones, and even locks. From reducing the total cost of ownership of a computer system to allowing unprecedented levels of portability Java has it all. Does it ?

Java is really three things: A simple object-oriented programming language, a virtual machine (VM) and an extensive ever-growing API with services ranging from mathematical functions to telephony, electronic commerce and speech recognition.

The programming language is probably the least interesting part of this technology. Several other languages including Ada have been targeted at the Java virtual machine [12, 13].

The Java VM is a fairly conventional, stack based virtual machine which includes late binding, garbage collection, object-oriented, exception handling and synchronization capabilities. While the Java VM does not directly provide threads, the Java API does. It is therefore possible to create multi-threaded applications in Java.

The concurrency model of Java is relatively simple. It has a major drawback: Several key components are undefined. For instance the Java API provides thread priorities, but the use that a programmer can make for them depends on the underlying hardware/software platform. So much for portability.

In a nutshell the current definition of the Java VM and the Java API are such that:

– There is no guarantee that Java be preemptive and supports thread priority.
– The concept of priority inheritance does not exist in Java.

In addition to the above, garbage collection is a real-time scarecrow not to mention the concept of a virtual machine.

Notwithstanding the above, when reading the embedded systems section of computer magazines one finds an awful lot of Java talk, surprising ? Not really.

Given Java's architecture, original excitement about Java came from the ability to run Java applications anywhere where the Java VM and the Java API had been ported. Up to now portability has not been one of the strong points of the embedded systems industry. With a large array of evolving microprocessor architectures, Java is the first glimpse at addressing the portability issue. Also in a context where the target hardware isn't available until late in the design cycle, Java allows the initial phase of software development to take place on a different system.

Java's dynamic linking and loading is also a plus in certain consumer electronics devices as it enables remote updates and patching of software. Java's security and reliability features ensures that malicious unauthorized code cannot harm your system or access information it is not supposed to. Java also saves code storage space, since Java bytecode is more compact than native machine code.

To address Java's current real-time weaknesses and because Sun knows the one-size-fits-all approach is unreasonable in the embedded market, Sun has created a family of Java subsets:

Java Card targets smart cards that are widely used in Europe and Asia. Announced at the end of 1996 it has been adopted by over 95 percent of the manufacturers in the smart card industry. With over 1 billion cards produced in 1997 (not all of them smart) and 3 billion forecasted by the year 2000, smart cards is an appealing business. By comparison, there are over 900 million credit cards in circulation today. Major uses will include providing enhanced financial services, increasing the security and flexibility of cellular phones, recording medical information, securing satellite and cable transmissions in TV set-top boxes, etc. Java Card makes it possible to securely download and run multiple applications on a single card. Furthermore applications written for one card can run on all smart cards implementing the Java Card spec. The specification contains detailed information for building Java virtual machines in memory-tight environments having only 16K of ROM, 8K of EEPROM, and 256 RAM (this is just the memory needed for the Java VM). Note that while current smart cards use 8-bit microprocessor technology, 32-bit processors have already been announced for the Java-enabled smart cards. One last important comment on Java Card: no threads.

EmbeddedJava is targeted at the standalone segment and has been designed for devices that have a character-based display or no display at all. This technology whose spec has not yet been publicly announced, is already been licensed by Motorola, Texas Instruments and Psion among others. Little else is known about EmbeddedJava at this stage.

PersonalJava has been designed for the network-connected devices primarily for those devices with sophisticated displays. Leading real-time operating system vendors such as Lucent Technologies, Microtec, Microware, QNX and WindRiver Systems have been licensed to integrate and sell PersonalJava with their products to deliver a complete Java-based embedded software solution to their customers. Recently Alcatel, Nortel and Samsung announced that they are incorporating PersonalJava into their new webphone products. PersonalJava is targeted at devices with the following characteristics: 32 bit processors running at 50+ MHz with around 2 MB of ROM, between 512 KB and 1 MB of RAM, a network connection and a keyboard or alternate input methods, such as remote control or touch screen.

In addition to the above announcements Sun has bought Chorus a supplier of embedded operating systems for telecommunications and intelligent communications devices. This gives to Sun instant access to proven technologies for highly scalable real-time embedded systems.

In the long run, leading real-time OS vendors will probably be much more on Sun's side than on Microsoft's for one simple reason. While Java piggybacks on the underlying RTOS to offer its real-time services, Windows CE is a complete solution.

If you are wondering whether Java-enabled appliances can run real-time applications the answer really depends of what the future will bring. Several solutions have been announced or are being actively worked upon (see for instance [14]).

Certainly Java has stirred some excitement in the embedded world and there is no doubt in my mind that it will play an important role although, apart from smart cards, it is still unclear which Java-enabled products will hit the stores and when.

Like IBM who got it right in the 60s when it came out with its System 360 line of computers based on an architecture capable of running the same software on a wide range of compatible machines, Sun Microsystems may, with his Java platform, have gotten it rigth in the 90s and perhaps become the IBM of the embedded world. Future will tell.

13 Freedom, freedom at last

An important concept that will gain momentum in the embedded systems market is the notion of "Free Software". Let us first explain this concept and let us then illustrate its underpinnings in the embedded systems market.

Up to the late 60s corporations such as IBM, Burroughs, Univac, and Honeywell manufactured computer hardware based on their proprietary designs and offered software, often with sources, to those who purchased their machines. Users would, at times, modify the original programs to taylor them to their needs. Developers from different companies would freely share opinions and suggestions on a given piece of code. Back then, the cost of a computer system was mainly the cost of its hardware. This situation changed when IBM decided, in 1969, to unbundle software from hardware sales.

With the decreasing costs of computer equipment and the ever increasing complexity of computer applications, the added value of a computer system gradually shifted from hardware to software. By the 80s most software applications had become proprietary and their sources, along with their look and feel, had become fiercely protected.

The Free Software movement began in 1983 at MIT under the impulse of Richard Stallman. This movement aims at reestablishing the spirit of cooperation that prevailed in the computing community before software became proprietary.

So what is Free Software ? Free Software always comes with its sources and allows its users to freely run, copy, distribute, study, change and improve the sources. More precisely users of Free Software have the freedom to study how the program works and adapt it to their needs. They can freely redistribute copies of the sources and have the freedom to improve the program and release the improvements to the public, so that the whole community can benefit from them.

Examples of Free Software include the GNU system, a huge suite of commercial quality software tools and operating systems such as the Emacs editor, the Linux operating system, the multi-platform, multi-language compiler GCC and debugger GDB, the Ada 95 compiler GNAT as well as other GNU unrelated tools such as the source control system CVS, etc. These are just a few of a long list of products available as Free Software.

Free Software is NOT public domain. Free Software is covered by a detailed license agreement called GPL (General Public License) that guarantees the freedom to copy, change and redistribute it. Public domain software has no such license and can be made proprietary.

Free Software is NOT Freeware or Shareware. Free Software always comes with sources; Freeware and Shareware do not. With Free Software you always know what you are installing in your computer. This is unlike Freeware or Shareware.

14   No free lunch

What about price ? Free Software is a matter of freedom, not price. As Richard Stallman likes to say you should think of "free speech", not "free beer."

Whether you have paid to get copies of Free Software, or whether you have obtained copies at no charge, you always have the freedom to copy, change and redistribute the software. This means that a business model based on Free

Software must view software as a service rather than a simple product and any organization developing Free Software products must base its competitive advantage over its software know-how.

A growing number of companies have gone or are going the Free Software route: Cygnus Solutions, Cyclic Software, Ada Core Technologies, etc. Part of Wind River Systems products are Free Software and companies such as Netscape are actively looking at the Free Software model.

15   Support and the embedded market

In a market where complex and reliable software has become an essential component of success, responsive, high-quality support is paramount. In conventional proprietary technology, people mainly pay for the license to use a product. As a result, the emphasis is on selling the product rather than offering good support. Support becomes a cost item and a burden for the software manufacturer.

On the other hand, developers need an increasing amount of help and advice to use effectively the tools at their disposal. The amount of information and the complexity of today's technological reality is daunting. In such a context, support will be one of the essential parameters in the time-to-market equation that will rule the embedded systems arena.

What is the other parameter ? Free Software. And the reason is simple. Reliable, sophisticated, technologically advanced systems that piggy back on other companies technology cannot simply rely on a black-box behavior of such a critical piece of software as the underlying real-time kernel or executive. When speaking about software written in Ada, having the Ada run-time as a black box is very unappealing. Programmers must be able to see how the underlying run-time schedules, synchronizes and all in all orchestrates a program's concurrent activities. Certainly in a number of partnerships or by paying a huge premium, one can indeed have access to the sources of proprietary products. Unfortunately, these sources are very static in the sense that the original manufacturer may not keep up-to-date the sources delivered. Worse yet, the greatest liability with proprietary sources is the attached set of constraints which create a very rigid and uncooperative framework hampering the development of sophisticated software. Free Software is the only license agreement that gives you the freedom to innovate.

References

1. "Embedded rules" by Richard Wallace, Electronic Engineering Times, March 17, 1997, Issue: 945.
2. "Market Focus - Embedded Systems" by Margaret Ryan, Electronic Engineering Times, September 11, 1997.
3. "Motorola To Launch CompactPCI, X86 Boards", by David Lieberman, Electronic Engineering Times, June 9, 1997.
4. "Java embeds itself in the control market", by Rick Cook, Javaworld, January 1998.

5. "Servelets bolster embedded efforts", by Bernard Cole, Electronic Engineering Times, December 22, 1997.

6. "Home server will link smart products", by Ashis Khan, Electronic Engineering Times, October 27, 1997.

7. "Microsoft, Sun Battle For Handheld Market", by Andy Patrizio, TechWeb, January 12, 1998.

8. "Back In Style - Embedded MPUs – Microprocessor makers are descending in droves on the embedded market" by Anthony Cataldo, Electronic Buyer's news, May 12, 1997.

9. "Windows NT Real-Time Extensions: An overview", by Martin Timmerman, Jean-Christophe Monfret, Real-Time Magazine, april/may/june 1997.

10. "Windows NT as RTOS ?", by Martin Timmerman, Jean-Christophe Monfret, Real-Time Magazine, april/may/june 1997.

11. "Real Time Systems with Microsoft Windows CE", Microsoft Corporation, 1998.

12. "Programming the Internet in Ada 95", by Tucker Taft, Ada-Europe'96, Springer-Verlag, 1996.

13. "Targeting GNAT to Java(TM) Virtual Machine" by Cyrille Comar, Gary Dismukes, and Franco Gasperoni, Tri'Ada 1997, ACM press, 1997.

14. "PERC Real-Time API (Draft 1.2)" by Kelvin Nilsen, Steve Lee, NewMonics Inc., July 1997.

15. "Channel Push: Microsoft, Sun take on direct marketers - Battle Over Java Shifts To Embedded Market", by Darryl K. Taft, Computer Reseller News, April 28, 1997.

Ada+B The Formula for Safety Critical Software Development

Pierre Chapront

GEC Alsthom Transport, Saint Ouen, France

1 SOFTWARE AND SAFETY

Railways have the reputation being one of the safest transport means. From the very beginning safety has been the main concern of railway operators, and all possible efforts have been made to avoid accidents, whatever be the failures of the system components. Later on, the required performances, and also concerns of costs, led to the use of software in Railway equipment. In many of these applications there was a need for safety and therefore the software had to be safe.

What is a 'safe' software? It is a software which does not contain an error!

It is always possible to use redundancies in hardware to detect failures and avoid their consequences, for software it is a different matter. The N-programming process where different teams produce different programs is not a definitive solution because there are important common mode which are the specification and the need to obtain, at the end, the same results. And the cost of this process is very high. So, in fact, even when redundancy is used for hardware failure detection, the same program, at least in its functional aspect, is used in the different processors. This program must therefore be error free. Is it possible?

The conditions to obtain such a result are:

- a perfect understanding of the problem to be solved,
- a small size of the program,
- a low complexity,
- a very well defined development process
- and a systematic verification and validation process.

Of course understanding the problem is not a question of software. It is a more general concern, for which some methods exist [1], which do not guarantee systematically the quality of the results but help in this direction. What we can say is that a structured functional analysis continues to be a fundamental part of the process. And whether software is used or not, this understanding is mandatory.

Small size and low complexity are more a matter of design. How to split the solution into parts, as small as possible, with the minimum of coupling between them, is also a process in which some systematic methods can help, but where the skill of the designers is very important.

Then we enter the software development domain. Constructing a program is often considered to be an artistic activity, in which imagination and the sense of aesthetic are very important. For the safety related software design we must reject this viewpoint, and consider it as a scientific activity, in which all the means used by science, including mathematics, must be used... even if this makes it less amusing.

This is why the use of 'formal' methods and structured programming languages are highly recommended in the new CENELEC standards for railway applications.

2 THE B METHOD

The B method was invented by J.R.ABRIAL [2], during the eighties. Working on the Z method, at the Oxford University, J.R.ABRIAL decided that the use of mathematics for software must not be limited to the activity of specification, an area in which Z is very effective, but must be extended to the design process. This is what B offers, which allows to develop programs, from their specification to code, by successive refinements, with a continuous monitoring of the exactness thanks to mathematical proofs at each step.

The first step, after problem understanding, is to express it in a non-ambiguous manner, using mathematical notations, which permits translation of the required safety related properties, as invariant, and verification by proof that the requested actions preserve them. This will constitute, at the upper level of abstraction, the formal specification of the problem.

The problem is then broken down into pieces, reducing the abstraction level, and introducing design decisions, while proving that the obtained result complies with the specification. The B language and the associated tools help in this process by offering automatic provers, and monitored data manipulations. This process is called a refinement.

The last refinement is an 'implementation', that is to say a translation of the problem and its solution in a form which can be translated into a programming language to be compiled for final use.

This progressive process has been studied and documented in 'the GEC ALTHOM B process' published as a deliverable of the European REAIMS [3] project. The purpose of this process is to describe in practice how to start from an engineering problem and through successive phases of design decision making, using the choosen methods, arrive at a formal specification. This involves combined ideas about engineering in the large about key design decisions and engineering in detail with formal descriptions.

The B method implements the basic rules of information hiding and its visibility rules insure that all side effects are avoided. It offers systematic verification that the operations made on the data preserve all the properties of the type they belong to. Set theory, which is the basis of the method, allows representation of all the types we want to construct and, as the invariants are richer than data definition, the proof prescribed by the B method can be considered as a powerful extension of the strong typing principle. Thus all the properties we want to obtain can be expressed as invariants, and the method allows to prove they are effectively obtained.

The important result is that, provided the proof process has been fully performed, the produced program fully complies with its specification. That avoids the need of costly and inefficient unit tests, and allows concentrating the validation on the verification that the needed functionality's are obtained.

Our experience on several projects, corresponding to an important amount of produced safety-related lines of code, shows also that this process is efficient from the cost point of view. Generally speaking the reached productivity is comparable with the productivity of conventionally developed software.

3 Ada

I will not go into details on the Ada features. I will only explain why and how we use Ada for safety related applications. In the next paragraph I shall explain why Ada is a good complement to B.

A first good reason for the use of Ada is that this programming language is highly recommended by the new CENELEC standards for Railway applications. The reason lies in the properties of the language of course, but also in the fact that the compilers are validated. Some suppliers offers validated compilers for a reduced set of the language, specially dedicated to safety related applications. This subset avoids the parts of the language which are too sophisticated and therefore dangerous to use, and allows improvements to run time efficiency.

Another reason is linked with the detection of the hardware failures. Whatever the mean used for that, either hardware redundancy, information redundancy or coding, the software must contain some particularities needed which have nothing to do with the function requested but with run time execution only. For example a simple addition of two integers will be systematically accompanied by another operation to allow the detection of an error in the addition. Or a simple test on a Boolean variable must be completed by some feature to detect a possible error in the branching process. The use of genericity, of the derived type principle, and of operator overloading helps in offering the transparency of these artefacts to the user.

There are some features of the language we avoid to use. Safety related software must be deterministic, that is to say, it must always provide the same results for a certain set of inputs. This reason precludes the use of the Ada real-time features mainly oriented to manage the parallelism. Although these features have been more or less derived from the theory of CSP developed by C.A.R HOARE, the determinism of the tasks execution is very difficult to prove. And we need to prove the correct behaviour of our programs. This is why we use systematically a cyclic process, with a predefined and monitored cycle time, with sampling of the inputs and systematic production of the outputs at predefined moment of the cycle, and interleaving of tasks using a coroutine process. In this case we do not have to use an Ada runtime kernel, the simple scheduler being built by us in assembly language. The capability of Ada to use assembly statements within the main program is very useful for that.

Another feature we do not use is the Exception mechanism. A safety related program must be correctly running or stopped ! There is no place for some error recovery mechanism, which introduce generally a non deterministic behaviour. If, as is generally the case, we have to offer the availability this must be managed at the system level. It may be more expensive to do that than to tolerate incorrect behaviour in some way, but it is the price of safety.

4 Ada and B

As was described in the second section, the B method leads by itself to an errorless program; at the end of the process we have to translate the implementation into a programming language which can be compiled. The properties of the language about correctness, structuration of the algorithm, strong typing... are no more useful because all the work has been made by the B process. So, why use a powerful language such as Ada for the final translation?

A first reason is that reduction of the translation effort. In fact the characteristic of B and Ada are very close, from both the syntactic and semantics point of view. For example the basic construction in B is the abstract machine, which contains the variables and the operations, fully hiding them from the outside. This construction can be immediately implemented in an Ada package. We have also to prove that the properties that exist in the B implementation continue to exist after translation. The fact that Ada is formally specified provides rational about that. And the similarity of B and Ada syntax's facilitates the traceability between B implementations and Ada packages.

The second reason is that the generic abstract machines can be implemented quite directly using Ada genericity. A major interest of B is that, once a machine has been proven, all the derived machines are usable without any complementary proof. This feature encourages reusability, while reducing the verification effort. This property continues to be true in Ada. And this can be used not only for safety related applications but also in other application. For example we can use abstract machines, already proven, and translated into generic package, in Automatic Train Supervision systems, which are applications which are not safety related, but which must be highly reliable.

A third reason is the fact that, inside a safety related application, there are always some parts which are not linked with safety, but works in close co-operation with the fail safe part. This software must be very reliable, and combined with the fail-safe software. Ada offers in this case the features leading to correctness of these parts, and a simpler process to link them with the other parts.

Last but not least several Ada environments offers complementary means for configuration management, tests environments, which can be easily linked with the B Method tools, and simplify the work of software management.

5 CONCLUSION

Based on a fifteen years experience in safety related software design our opinion is that the combination of an efficient formal method and the use of Ada is the best way to reach the total correctness requested by safety. Although these types of methods may appear as grim, they are not very difficult to learn and give finally to their users the satisfaction of producing a high quality work, at the lowest possible cost for this quality. We hope that these methods will find new users for the greatest benefit of the software engineering community.

References

1. See, for example IAN SOMMERVILLE & PETE SAWYER : Requirements engineering, a good practice guide ; (WILEY 1997)
2. J.R.ABRIAL the B Book : Assigning programs to meanings , (Cambridge University Press 1996)
3. REAIMS web pages are available at URL :
   http://www.comp.lancs.ac.uk/computing/research/cseg/projects/reaims

Porting the GNAT Tasking Runtime System to the Java Virtual Machine

Laurent Millet[1] and Ted Baker[2]

[1] Télécom Paris (ENST)
46, rue Barrault
75634 Paris Cedex 13
France
lmillet@enst.fr

[2] Department of Computer Science
Florida State University
Tallahassee FL, 32306-4019
USA
baker@cs.fsu.edu

Abstract. This paper describes an implementation model for porting the tasking portion of the GNAT Ada 95 Runtime Library to the Java environment, and a proof-of-concept implementation. The latter allows one to run multi-tasking applications that are written in Ada and compiled into native machine code, using the thread support of the Java Virtual Machine. The Java Virtual Machine takes care of scheduling the different threads of control, just like any multi-threaded operating system would.

1 Introduction

GNARL is the tasking runtime library of the GNAT Ada 95[1] compiler. GNARL was designed with portability in mind, hence it is structured in two layers, the lower of which (GNULL) isolates dependences on a particular host operating system or real-time kernel. The primary implementation of the lower layer relies on POSIX services, as many systems conform to the POSIX API, at least partially. Yet, other equivalent APIs can be used instead, such as Solaris[1] native threads and OS/2[2] threads.

The Java Virtual Machine[2] (JVM) is the specification of a system with certain characteristics that can be emulated on any existing hardware system or implemented as a specific hardware system. It is the execution platform for Java[3] programs. Java programs use the primitives described in the Java API. These services are platform-independent, so an application written in Java may

---

[1] Solaris is a trademark of Sun Microsystems, Inc.
[2] OS/2 is a trademark of IBM Corp.
[3] Java is a trademark of Sun Microsystems, Inc.

be run on any implementation of the JVM (currently, such implementations exist for SPARC[4] Solaris 2.3, 2.4, 2.5, 2.5.1, 2.6, x86 Solaris 2.5, 2.5.1, 2.6, Microsoft Windows NT/95[5], Mac OS[6] and many other platforms - the latest release of Sun's Java Development Kit is only available on the following platforms: Microsoft Windows 95 / NT 4.0, SPARC Solaris 2.5 and later and x86 Solaris 2.5 and later).

Porting the GNAT compiler to the Java environment would make it easy to run existing Ada applications on a broad range of systems (that is, on every system for which there is a JVM implementation). New applications can take advantage of this port too, benefitting from the strengths of both Ada and Java languages. Indeed, it is perfectly feasible to mix both Ada and Java languages. For example, a company having already developed Ada libraries could port them to the Java environment effortlessly, a Java developer could write some Ada code for critical real-time sections while an Ada programmer could instantly have access to the numerous Java libraries.

This paper describes in general terms how we ported the tasking run-time system of the GNAT compiler to the JVM, which is one part of a larger project to retarget the entire compiler and runtime system to the JVM[3]. Without waiting for the compiler itself to be ported, we have been able to test the runtime system port on the JVM, using the Solaris 2.5.1 SPARC native version of the compiler, and modifying the runtime system to call the JVM instead of the Solaris threads library. In this prototype implementation, an Ada application runs just as usual, except that thread-related actions are performed by the JVM.

The presentation is organized as follows: In Section 2, we give an overview of the Java tasking model. In Section 3, we explain the semantic mapping from GNULL to the JVM. In Section 4, we explain how the prototype JVM port was done.

2 Java Tasking Model

The Java language[4] allows multiple threads of control to run simultaneously. The way this concurrency is implemented is hidden from the programmer, so that it is not easy to determine what the actual mechanism is. Programmers should strictly rely on the Java API[5] to write their programs.

An object is associated with each Java thread. The object must have a run() method. Actually, the Java class describing threads is java.lang.Thread and an object of this class has a run() method (which does nothing by default.) This method will be called by the Java Virtual Machine once the thread is started, after its creation and initialization. The run() method then gets executed. Once it has returned, the JVM takes care of the destruction of the thread.

---

[4] SPARC is a trademark of SPARC International, Inc. Products bearing the SPARC trademarks are based on an architecture developed by Sun Microsystems, Inc.

[5] Microsoft, Windows and Windows NT are trademarks of Microsoft Corp.

[6] Mac OS is a trademark of Apple Computer, Inc.

There are two ways to create such **Thread** objects. One is to create an object of a class that is derived from the class `java.lang.Thread`, and to override its **run()** method. For example, one could write:

```
class MyThread extends Thread {

   //   class fields or instance fields

   public void run() {
      //   this will be run when the start() method
      //   of this object gets called
   }

   //   other methods

}
```

This is maybe the first thing one would think of. However, it prevents a programmer from defining his own new hierarchy of active objects (which have nothing to do with **Thread** objects in general, except the programmer wants them to run concurrently) because Java doesn't allow for multiple inheritance. The solution is to have the object's class implement the **Runnable** interface. This interface specifies only that the class must have a **run()** method. For example, consider the following:

```
class MyClass extends SomeOtherClass implements Runnable {

   //   class fields or instance fields

   public void run() {
      //   code to be run in a separate thread
   }

   //   other methods

}
```

In the previous example, we have created a class of **Runnable** objects. An object of such a class can be passed as an argument of a constructor of class `java.lang.Thread` to specify that Java should call the object's **run()** method upon thread activation.

Once a **Thread** object has been created, its associated thread is started by calling the objects's **start()** method (such a method is associated with each **Thread** object). From then on, the thread may be executing (though execution is actually determined by the scheduler of the JVM).

```
//   create thread objects
MyThread DerivedThread = new MyThread;
MyClass RunnableObject = new MyClass;
Thread  RunnableThread = new Thread (RunnableObject);

//   start threads
DerivedThread.start();
RunnableThread.start();
```

The Java API provides several primitives that affect thread scheduling. First, the `getPriority` and `setPriority` primitives access directly the thread's Java priority. The Java concept of priority is not as precisely defined as the ARM Annex D concept of priority. The specification of `java.lang.Thread` says only: "Threads with higher priority are executed in preference to threads with lower priority." In effect, the priority of a thread is only a hint to the scheduler. The actual effect of thread priority can vary widely between different implementations of the JVM, so it is not a good idea to have a Java program depend too heavily on strict priority scheduling. However, basic scheduling effects can be achieved by manipulating threads' priorities. The Java `yield()` method is more reliable: it makes the current thread temporarily pause execution and give other threads a chance to be scheduled; if other threads cannot resume execution (either because they are waiting to be notified of some event or because of their priority being lower than the thread that is yielding) then the same thread continues running. Its effect should be similar to a `delay 0.0;` Ada statement.

Java has some mechanisms to deal with thread synchronization. The `wait()` method is defined for every Java object. Each Java object has a *monitor* associated with it. At any time, at most one thread can own an object's monitor. The purpose of monitors is to provide mutual exclusion between different threads. In Java, a thread can acquire an object's monitor by executing *synchronized* code, that is either a `synchronized` method (instance method) of the given object, or a synchronized block of statements that synchronizes on the given object. The thread calling the `wait()` method must be the owner of the monitor associated with the object. The effect is to atomically lose ownership of the object's monitor and to wait until another thread notifies on the object or, for the version with timeout, until the timeout expires, whichever happens first. The thread then waits until it can get ownership of the object's monitor again. The `notify()` method can be executed by a thread that is the owner of `this` object's monitor to wake up another thread waiting on the same object. The `notifyAll()` method wakes up all threads waiting on the object. These threads then compete to get the ownership of the object's monitor.

3 Mapping GNULL to the JVM

As far as tasking is concerned, the GNAT compiler works as follows: the code written by the programmer is syntactically and semantically checked, just like any other code. Then the code corresponding to high-level tasking services is expanded by the compiler. That generated code consists of in-line code and calls to subprograms of the GNAT tasking run-time. High-level constructs, such as simple rendezvous, select statements, abortion, etc. are thus reduced to regular non-tasking Ada code and runtime system procedure calls.

The GNAT tasking run-time is divided into two layers. The GNARL layer provides high-level services to the compiler through the GNARL Interface (GNARLI). Typical services include task creation/finalization, rendezvous, protected objects operations, task abortion, etc. Both the interface and the implementation of the GNARL layer are target-independent. At the compiler interface, each task is identified to the GNARL via a reference to a record structure, called the Ada Task Control Block (ATCB).

The GNULL layer provides low-level services to the GNARL through the GNULL Interface (GNULLI), which is target independent. The implementation uses OS or library services, and so is target dependent. For POSIX-compliant targets, the GNULL implementation may use POSIX primitives, but that is not mandatory. For example, the Solaris version of GNULL uses Solaris native threads, and the OS/2 version uses OS/2 threads.

The GNULLI provides the following services:

Task creation, initialization, and termination: The `Create_Task` procedure creates a new thread of control, `Enter_Task` initializes the state of the calling task, and `Exit_Task` destroys the current task. The `Abort_Task` procedure is used to asynchronously abort a target task.

Current task: The `Self` function returns a reference to the ATCB of the current task. As the ATCB of a task contains all the runtime system information associated with that task, this function is of vital importance throughout the GNARL layer.

Task synchronization: The GNULLI defines locks, which are the Ada objects that GNARL uses to provide mutual exclusion between different tasks. `Initialize_Lock` and `Finalize_Lock` initialize and recover the resources associated with a lock, `Write_Lock` makes the current task wait until it can acquire the specified lock, and `Unlock` makes it release the lock.

The `Sleep` procedure makes the current task sleep until another task wakes it up. The `Timed_Sleep` procedure does the same, except that the task wakes up earlier if the specified amount of time has elapsed. The `Wakeup` procedure wakes the specified task up.

Task scheduling: The GNULLI provides priority-related operations: `Set_Priority` and `Get_Priority`. The `Yield` procedure puts the current task at the end of the queue for the task's priority; the current task yields the processor.

Time-related primitives: The `Clock` function returns the current time. The `Timed_Sleep` procedure makes the current task wait for the specified amount of time.

All these primitives and their Java counterparts are covered in more detail in the following subsections.

3.1 Task creation, initialization, and termination

Each Ada task will correspond to a Java thread. Task creation in GNULLI is supported by the `Create_Task` procedure. This can be mapped to one of the constructors of Java class `java.lang.Thread`. The ATCB will be a Java object, derived from `java.lang.Object`, and so will have available the normal Java methods that apply to all objects.

Support for preemptive abort (ATC and whole-task) in GNULLI is via the subprogram `Abort_Task`. There is no corresponding JVM operation: `destroy()` kills the a `Thread` object without any cleanup (in particular, monitors owned by the thread remain locked), `interrupt()` sets only a flag in the target `Thread` object and `stop()` raises an asynchronous exception in the given thread (this exception eventually makes the thread die); `stop()` seems to be close to what we want, but we don't know of a way to defer its effects, as is required by Ada semantics. Not having such a method is not a serious problem. GNARL is designed in such a way that if `Abort_Task` has a null body, aborts will simply take place at the next abort completion point. That is all that is required by the core of the ARM. Thus, it is sufficient for the Java port to simply provide a stub for this operation, since we are not trying to support the preemptive abort feature of ARM Annex D.

The Ada procedure `Exit_Task` is called when a task terminates to tell the underlying threading system that the thread is no longer needed, so that any finalization actions can take place to recover some resources. This is not needed with Java, as the garbage collector does any required cleanup when appropriate. So the Java `Exit_Task` will be only a stub, too.

3.2 Current task

The Java API provides the `java.lang.Thread.currentThread` method. As its name implies, that method returns the `Thread` object associated with the currently executing thread. That method will be used to implement the Ada `Self` function. The idea is to create an object derived from class `java.lang.Thread` with an instance field holding a reference to the ATCB of the `Thread` object. The `currentThread` method returns a `Thread` object. If that object belongs to the class we created, then it is the thread associated with an Ada task, else it is an "alien" (i.e., normal Java) thread. This allows us to create on the fly the Ada record that describes the Java thread as an Ada task (ATCB), so that it is possible to embed Java threads in Ada programs. It would also be possible to have Java threads call Ada code.

3.3 Task synchronization

The GNULLI `Write_Lock` and `Unlock` operations are used to implement protected objects and to protect GNARL internal data structures. These are implemented using the monitor operations that the JVM supports for every Java object. Exclusive access to an object is obtained by executing the `monitorenter` operation, and released via the `monitorexit` operation. Though Java monitors do not have the concept of priority ceiling locking, priority ceiling locking may be emulated by means of GNULL implementation code that manipulates the priority of a thread that is holding a lock, using the `setPriority` operation.

The GNULLI `Sleep` operation allows a task that is holding a lock to atomically release the lock on its own ATCB and block itself until another task calls the

GNULLI `Wakeup` operation for that task. A task that has called `Sleep` cannot resume execution until it is able to reacquire the lock on its own ATCB. Time delay support in GNULLI is via the `Timed_Sleep` operation, which is like `Sleep` except that it has a timeout. The semantics of the `Sleep` operations (with and without timeout) correspond closely to the Java `java.lang.Object.wait()` operations, and the `Wakeup` operation corresponds closely to the Java `notify()` operation. Both of these operations are available on all Java objects, and so they can be applied to ATCBs. It is not possible to use the Java `java.lang.Thread.sleep` method because a thread calling this method does not lose ownership of the monitors that it owns. We cannot release the lock(s) and then call `sleep()` either, because of the timing window that would exist between those method calls: that would allow another thread to become the owner of a just-released lock and then call `notify()` on the first thread before this thread has called `sleep()`, thus making the first thread miss the wakeup (the Java API does not specify what happens when a thread interrupts a non-sleeping thread).

3.4 Task scheduling

As Java priorities are only hints for the scheduler, we will only be able to support the priority task scheduling model of ARM Annex D if the particular JVM platform happens to support a strict priority preemptive scheduling model that is compatible with the Ada model.

The GNULLI `Set_Priority` operation is used to control the priority of an Ada task. This operation can be mapped to the `setPriority` operation in `java.lang.Thread`. The exact effect will depend on the particular Java platform.

The `Yield` operation in GNULLI causes the currently executing task to go to the end of the dispatching queue for its priority. This can be mapped to the Java operation `java.lang.Thread.yield`, though (as with all Java thread scheduling operations) the exact effect is platform dependent.

3.5 Time-related primitives

The `Clock` function in GNULLI is used by GNARL to implement other clocks, such as `Ada.Real_Time.Clock`. This can be mapped to the Java `java.lang.currentTimeMillis` method. This is the closest fit to the Ada requirements for range and precision among the available Java clock interfaces.

4 Prototyping JVM-GNULL Using Native Methods

We wanted to test out this conceptual mapping of GNULL to JVM functionality. Since the Java port of the GNAT compiler was not yet complete, we could not test it out in the context of a version of GNAT that generates JVM code. However, it turned out that there was another way to test it, using the Solaris

SPARC native compiler for the Ada code generation, and interfacing directly to the Solaris implementation of the JVM for thread support.

To implement the GNULL layer using the Java thread operations, we needed to access such Java operations from inside Ada code. In the Solaris environment Java methods are exported to C via the Java Native Interface[6] (JNI). This means we were able to call Java methods from Ada, by interfacing Ada with the C functions of the JNI. We wrote an extra layer of code to do this, called AJI (Ada to Java Interface), which performs several checks to make sure everything worked properly (as far as the JVM is concerned), as explained below.

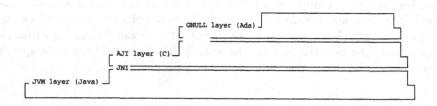

Fig. 1. *Interfaces used to call Java from Ada and vice-versa*

The JNI is a powerful interface that allows one programmer to call any Java method from C code. That includes calls to Java constructors as well, so that it is possible the create Java objects from native (i.e., C) functions. It is also possible access, modify and delete any Java object whose reference is known in C code (either because it is a parameter of the C function, or as a result of creating a Java object from the function itself). The JNI also includes functions that are not part of the Java API, such as direct monitor operations, JVM initialization and creation/destruction, functions to attach/detach a C thread to/from an already running JVM, etc.

Many JNI functions return a value that can be checked to determine whether the function was executed successfully or not. Some functions even throw an exception that has to be caught before further processing.

JNI functions take an "environment" pointer as a parameter. This pointer is valid only in the current thread. It is provided by the JVM upon the JVM's creation (so the pointer is defined for the main thread), or when a native method call is made from Java code (the pointer is defined for the thread the native method call is made inside). This means the pointer can't be stored as a global variable but needs to be maintained on a per-thread basis. We added a field in the Ada structure associated with each Ada task (the ATCB) to store the task's environment pointer. Each time we need to make a "system" call (that is, a call to an AJI function), we have to fetch the value from the current task's ATCB and pass it to the AJI, so that the latter can pass it to the JNI. This is a bit complicated, but won't be needed at all for the actual port of the whole GNAT compiler.

Calling a Java method from C code is not as straightforward as a regular function call, for some other reasons than the one we just discussed (having to pass the environment pointer). A method identification must be computed first, based on the class the function is defined in, the name, and the signature of the function. This means that if you only know the object and not the class, you have to get the object's class. For each of these extra calls, we also have to check their results for possible exceptions. The same checks have to be done for the actual method call.

A wrong result or an exception thrown by a JNI function call is considered a serious failure, so we never try to recover from such errors.

Inside Ada code, AJI primitives are imported from C. As we already said, we also have to pass the environment parameter to the AJI. This means the identity of the current task has to be determined first, in case it is not known when the AJI call is made.

There is an aspect of the port that deserves a little more attention: task creation. Ada has its own mechanism for task creation, and it only requires that an underlying thread be created for each new task. As we have seen above, that is done in Java by creating either a **Thread** object or a **Runnable** object. For this implementation, we chose the first method because it was the simplest, as we could access any Java class from the AJI (through the JNI). For the actual port, it might be more convenient to do it the other way. Here is the code for the Java class that is used to create new threads:

```
package AJI;

public class Wrapper extends Thread {

  private int proc, self_id;

  public Wrapper (int proc, int self_id) {
    this.proc    = proc;
    this.self_id = self_id;
  }

  public void run () {
    wrap (proc, self_id);
  }

  private native void wrap (int proc, int self_id);

  static {
    System.loadLibrary ("wrapper");
  }

}
```

The code is quite simple. The two private instance fields are used to call back Ada code: the **proc** variable holds the address of the procedure that is the body of the newly created thread (that is, the code that will run in that thread), and the **self_id** variable holds the address of the ATCB (it is a parameter of the **proc** procedure). These parameters are set in the constructor. The **run()** method, which is called by the **start()** method of the object, simply calls the native method that does the actual job: calling the proc procedure, passing the proper arguments (the task_id as we already said, and the environment pointer for the new thread). Finally, the static block is used to dynamically link the library that implements the native method when the class Wrapper is loaded.

Conclusion

We have successfully designed and tested a port of the GNAT tasking runtime system to the Java thread environment. This port is currently working well enough to pass all of the basic tasking-related ACVC tests, that is, 189 Ada 83 tests and 49 Ada 95 tests, as well as Annex D tests (it must be pointed out though that the latter results are dependent on the particular implementation of the JVM that we used, whereas basic tests should not fail regardless on the JVM's underlying platfom.) We believe that this demonstrates the fundamental soundness of our semantic mapping. It also demonstrates the possibility of native-code Ada compilers providing pragma Interface support for calls to the Java class libraries. The next step is to see how this will integrate with the Java port of the GNAT compiler, as soon as that is ready.

Acknowledgments

We are grateful to Ada Core Technologies, Inc. for partially funding this work, and to Franco Gasperoni, leader of the GNAT Java port team, for reviewing the design of the GNULL port and suggesting that we use Java native methods under Solaris to test it out in advance of the compiler port.

References

1. ISO/IEC: ISO/IEC 8652: 1995 (E) Information Technology – Programming Languages – Ada (1995)

2. T. Lindholm, F. Yellin: The Java^{TM} Virtual Machine Specification – The Java Series – Addison-Wesley (1997) – ISBN 0-201-63452-X

3. C. Comar, G. Dismukes, F. Gasperoni: Targeting GNAT to the Java^{TM} Virtual Machine – Tri-Ada'97 Conference, Proceedings (1997) – ISBN 0-89791-981-5

4. G. Cornell, C. S. Horstmann: Core Java – The SunSoft Press – Prentice Hall (1996) – ISBN 0-13-565755-5

5. Sun Microsystems, Inc: Java^{TM} Platform 1.1.4 Core API – Java API Packages – http://java.sun.com/products/jdk/1.1/docs/api/packages.html

6. JavaSoft: Java Native Interface Specification – Release 1.1 (Revised May, 1997)

Automating the Ada Binding Process for Java - How Far Can We Go?

David E. Emery[1], Robert F. Mathis[2], and Karl A. Nyberg[3]

[1] The MITRE Corporation 1820 Dolley Madison Blvd., MS W538 McLean,
VA 22102-3481
emery@mitre.org
[2] Pithecanthropus Consulting, Inc., 4719 Reed Rd., #305 Columbus, OH 43220
bob@pithecanthropus.com
[3] Grebyn Corporation, P. O. Box 47 Sterling, VA 20167-0047
karl@grebyn.com

Abstract. This paper describes an automated approach for generating
Ada bindings from Java class files. We start with the set of Java features
that require a visible Ada binding, and an Ada compiler's definition
of how to interface Ada and Java. We discuss how to obtain the Java
definitions from the class file and then translate them into an Ada binding
(using the GNAT binding approach). While it is possible to generate a
technically complete Ada binding from the information in a Java class
file (within the constraints of necessary support from an Ada compiler).
However, we show that such a binding has significant limitations from a
practical usability perspective.

1 Introduction

The Java promise of "write once, run anywhere" [Kramer] (but see [Wragg]) has
generated a lot of excitement and interest in the computing community. This
approach to target-independent computing is achieved by generating intermediate code, which is then interpreted by a target-dependent interpreter, called the
Java Virtual Machine (JVM).

The JVM [Lindholm], [Meyer], [Venners] includes a definition of the format
of a Java Class File (CFF). This file, in Ada terms, contains both the "programming library information" and also the "object file" produced by many
conventional Ada compilation systems. Each class has a separate class file. To
execute a program contained in a specific class file, the JVM loads (on demand)
the class files referred to by the program and interprets the object code accordingly. (This is analogous to the elaboration closure required for Ada packages.)
Java comes with a significant set of library routines, and many software vendors
have produced Java APIs to their products, where all of these services are described by an appropriate CFF. A CFF serves as both the 'object file' for the
class and the 'library file' for separate compilation checking purposes.

Consider the situation where a software vendor provides a Java binding to his product, but provides no Ada binding. The vendor supplies appropriate Java class files for his Java binding, but provides no source code. If we can generate an Ada binding from the Java class file, we can provide access to this product for Ada programmers. This paper describes how we can generate an Ada binding, given a Java class file, and shows the limitations of the Java class file definition for generating such bindings.

The JVM does not place any restrictions on the source language compiler that produces Java class files. Several other languages, in particular Ada, have compilers that target the JVM. [Taft], [Aonix], [GNATJVM]. Thus an Ada programmer can write code targeted to the JVM, but this is not particularly useful unless that programmer can gain access to existing Java libraries. To do this, we need to be able to develop an Ada interface to Java classes, and then develop bindings for the various Java classes of interest. This paper concentrates on the second step.

For this paper, we use the term "Java" to refer to the programming language, including class libraries implemented in that programming language. Thus we make a distinction between "Java the language" that is akin to "Ada the language", and the JVM (which does not imply/require that it execute programs compiled from "Java the language"). Note that our dependence on the JVM format, rather than Java source code, means that our technique will generate an Ada binding for any source language that can be compiled to produce Java class files. However, our focus is on class files where the source language was Java.

2 The Java Model

2.1 Java Virtual Machine

The Java Virtual Machine is an abstract stack-based computational machine with an instruction set generally implemented as an interpreter. (Additional speedups, called Just-In-Time compilers, which actually translate the instructions to concrete instructions on the execution target, are still run under the control of an interpreter.) A JVM interpreter then interprets the byte codes of the class files and updates its internal state according to the execution of the instructions.

2.2 Java Class Files

Java class files are organized collections of variable length records containing information about the class they contain. Those records have an indication of their length and further structured records within them.

At the outer most level a Java class file roughly has the structure:

```
file header
constant pool
class descriptor
```

```
flags
interfaces
fields
methods
attributes
```

The file header has identifying information and the Java version that produced it. The constant pool is similar to the symbol table in a traditional load module, but it is much more comprehensive since other structures within this class file reference it. Much more local information is available. It is in the constant pool that many strings used in the program are recorded: internal and external field, method, and class names; field and method signatures; and actual text strings used within the program.

The class descriptor has the name of the superclass, the name of this class, and any imported interfaces. These names are all stored by providing indexes into the constant pool. The flags provide access information to the class regarding the availability of the methods of the class to other entities (public, final, superclass, abstract, etc.)

The fields are the local variables of the class. They have various attributes including visibility, types, and values among other things. Static fields are shared across all instances of the class, while each class object has a separate copy of the instance (non-static) variables.

The methods have signatures and reference various attributes, such as executable byte code, exceptions that can be thrown, source file location and line number information, referenced out of the attributes section.

The attributes contain information like the source file name and other vendor specific information. This is an extensible section, but our work does not depend on any attributes not guaranteed to be present in all Java class files.

Because Java is dynamically linked, the class file must contain a lot of symbolic and typing information that would have been eliminated in more static systems. The information that enables the JVM to dynamically link classes is the information we use to generate Ada bindings.

3 Binding Technology

There are two problems to be solved in producing a binding for an API implemented in a given programming language. The first problem is the "pragma interface problem", where the solution to this problem ensures that a program written in the source language (i.e., Ada) can access facilities defined by a program in the target language (i.e., C or Java). Solutions to this problem require compiler and linguistic support. Interfacing to C, for example, requires access to C functions and static objects. The details for this interface include topics such as producing values of an arbitrary C type, "by-value" vs "by-reference" parameter modes, passing C struct values (versus struct * values), and handling C functions that both return a value and modify their parameters. In all cases, one issue that must be resolved is the mapping of identifiers from the target language to Ada. (Problems can occur when the target language identifier is an Ada reserved word or when the identifier does not match Ada syntax, including case-sensitive identifiers.)

For Java, we have a similar, but expanded, set of interface issues. The list for Java includes: deriving (inheriting) from a Java class, implementing a Java interface, Java vs Ada exceptions, circular class references and synchronized methods. We are adopting the approach introduced in [GNATJVM] and more completely defined in [GNAT].

The second fundamental problem in binding is to develop a technique or pattern for mapping collections of target language features into the appropriate/best source language representation. Of course, the first requirement on the mapping is that it be feasible, using the solution to the "pragma interface problem" described earlier. The binding solution must take into consideration a somewhat different set of issues, including packaging and aggregation, error handling, binding-wide type models and visibility, and documentation.

Normally, bindings are programming language "syntactic transforms". They start with the expression of the API in the target languages (e.g., C header files or Java class files), and apply a set of transformations (either automated via a bindings-generator tool such as [c2ada], or manually, as in [POSIX].) The target language syntax (and semantics) defines the information that can be used by the binding generator.

Our approach differs from this "classical" approach, since we are not working at the target programming language (Java) syntax level. Instead, we are working with another representation of the target language, the Java Class File. Our approach to working with the Class File is to first define the "classical" Java-to-Ada syntactic transformations, i.e., a Java Class File maps to an Ada package. Then, we obtain the equivalent information from the Java Class File, and transform it into Ada. Thus, instead of parsing Java source code and walking the syntax tree, we instead parse and navigate the Java Class File, searching for specific Java syntactic constructs. The primary advantage of this approach is that we do not require Java source code for the API. All we require is the Java Class Files for that API, which must be accessible for the Java Virtual Machine to use the API. This means that we can generate an Ada binding in situations where the source code is not available, such as reverse-engineering situations or cases where the source code is proprietary.

4 Java Interface Issues

The goal for the binding is to first, extract the 'binding entity' from the Java class file, and second, generate the appropriate Ada text. This section briefly summarizes the GNAT approach as described in [GNAT], with some additional decisions made for our binding.

4.1 Classes Map to Packages

We map each (non-nested) class to a separate package. The package name hierarchy maps well to Java's class heirarchy, i.e., the class java.lang.String maps to the package Java.Lang.String; there is a parent package called "Lang" that itself is a child package of a package named "Java". Nested classes are defined within the package that maps to the non-nested top-level class.

Each class that has instance variables or methods defines a tagged type. An Ada compiler that implements an interface to Java must define the root Object class, along with the rules for how other Java and Ada classes/types are derived from Object. Our binding follows the GNAT approach, and the type representing a class is a child of Java.Lang.Java_Object. See [GNAT] for a description of this approach.

Appropriate Ada95 pragmas (e.g., pragma Convention, pragma Interface, pragma Import) must be placed as defined by the Ada compiler.

4.2 Primitive Types and Variables

The mappings from the basic data types (section 4.3.2 of [Lindholm]) to Ada types are straightforward as described in [GNAT]. (Note that Java has no primitive Enumeration type.)

```
boolean is mapped into Ada's Boolean
char    is mapped into Ada's Wide_Character
byte    is mapped into Ada's Short_Short_Integer
short   is mapped into Ada's Short_Integer
int     is mapped into Ada's Integer
long    is mapped into Ada's Long_Integer
float   is mapped into Ada's Float
double  is mapped into Ada's Long_Float
```

Mapping for arrays of elementary types are nearly as straightforward.

Static instance variables map to objects within the class package. Non-static instance variables are fields of the record type defined in the class. Constructors are defined as functions. Java interfaces are implemented as record fields that point to the interface object.

4.3 Method Modifiers

Java defines the following set of method modifiers. These keywords define specialized semantics for class methods. By default, a method without any modifiers is public, not protected, not abstract, not static and not final.

```
public
protected
private
```

```
abstract
static
final
synchronized
native
```

Public methods are primitive operations in the visible part of the class's package, while protected and private methods are located in the private part of the class's package. Abstract methods match the Ada semantics. Final methods have no direct analog in Ada, and are not treated specially by the binding. Static methods do not have the implicit "self" parameter, and are therefore not necessarily primitive operations of the type defined by the package. Native methods are not currently supported by our binding, but we expect that a native method is no different, from a binding perspective, than any other method.

Synchronized methods require special treatment. Our binding tool marks a class having synchronized methods, and we expect that a type with synchronized methods will need to be based on some combination of tagged and protected types that need to be defined by the Ada compiler vendor.

4.4 Exceptions

Exceptions are defined in the [GNAT] approach as a straightforward binding, consisting of a package containing an object derived from the parent java.lang. Exception_Class.obj with a null record extension, an Ada exception declaration, and the appropriate operations. The GNAT compiler then recognizes this set of declarations and performs the correct mapping to a Java exception.

5 The Binding Implementation

This section describes the implementation of the binding process.

5.1 Parsing the Java Class File

Parsing the Java Class File is rather a straightforward process. The abstract description given in [Lindholm] is sufficiently detailed to permit the direct generation of supporting record types and a recursive descent parser to navigate class files.

5.2 Generating the Package Template

The first task is to generate the package template. A pass through the methods for the class is performed to look for any method that has the synchronized modifier. Code generation for a class with synchronized methods must implement the underlying compiler's approach for dealing with such methods, i.e., including some sort of protected object in the object declaration. Mapping to the Ada package mechanism is straightforward as synchronized methods in Java and protected objects in Ada both commonly have underlying monitors to ensure sequential access.

5.3 Generating the Fields

Each of the non-static fields is placed into the package specification. As the list of fields is traversed, the field name and signature are obtained and mapped into a meaningful name for the Ada compiler.

5.4 Generating Simple Methods

For the simple (public) methods, the list of methods is traversed to find those public methods. Each method's name and parameter list are again mapped into meaningful names for the Ada compiler. All parameters are either mode "in" or an accesstype. Although the parameter's types are available in the underlying class file, the name of the parameters are not always available. This has lead to an instantiation of the parameter list by a simple positional enumeration of their location within the list.

6 Results / Analysis / Discussion

This paper has shown that we can go a long way toward automating the generation of Ada interface specifications for Java class files. We have applied our tool to both the JDK 1.1.4 release, comprising 1611 Java classes and the JDK 1.1.5 release with 1626 Java classes. At the time this paper was written, the tool completely parses all classes, and implements public and static methods and variables, generating the corresponding Ada construct.

One major problem is that the class file does not contain all of the information needed to generate a good binding. The primary limitation is the loss of formal parameter names. The representation of a method descriptor in the Java CFF includes only type information for each formal parameter. The parameter name itself is missing. As an extension to the CFF, it is possible to recompile the Java source using the JDK's "-g" flag. This will retain parameter information for some methods (those that are not abstract) [Taft2]. Unfortunately, we cannot guarantee that any arbitrary Java Class File was generated by the JDK compiler using the -g flag.

In our view, this makes the resulting binding unusable. Consider the following methods from the class Java.Lang.String:

```
public boolean regionMatches (boolean ignoreCase,
        int toffset,
        String other,
        int oofset,
        int len);

public boolean regionMatches (int toffset,
        String other,
        int oofset,
        int len);
```

Here is our generated Ada binding:

```
function regionMatches (this: Java.Lang.String;
          arg_1 : Interfaces.boolean;
          arg_2 : integer;
          arg_3 : Java.Lang.String;
          arg_4 : integer;
          arg_5 : integer) return boolean;

function regionMatches (this: Java.Lang.String;
          arg_1 : integer;
          arg_2 : Java.Lang.string;
          arg_3 : integer;
          arg_4 : integer)  return boolean;
```

For comparison, here is the same method, from the Intermetrics/Aonix binding:

```
function Region_Matches (This : access String_Obj;
          Toffset : Integer;
          Other : String_Ptr;
          Ooff et : Integer;
          Len : Integer) return Boolean;

function Region_Matches (This : access String_Obj;
          IgnoreCase : Boolean;
          Toffset : Integer;
          Other : String_Ptr;
          Ooffset : Integer;
          Len : Integer) return Boolean;

function RegionMatches (This : access String_Obj;
          Toffset : Integer;
          Other : String_Ptr;
          Ooffset : Integer;
          Len : Integer) return Boolean renames
                Region_Matches;

function RegionMatches (This : access String_Obj;
          IgnoreCase : Boolean;
          Toffset : Integer;
          Other : String_Ptr;
          Ooffset : Integer;
          Len : Integer) return Boolean renames
                Region_Matches;
```

Note that the Intermetrics/Aonix binding uses a renames clause that maps the "run-on" Java name to a more Ada-Like name using Underscores. Additionally, since Java is case sensitive and Ada is not, it is necessary to find a mechanism to distinguish between, for example, mappings of AphID and aphid.

The class String points out several other interesting aspects of Java binding. As mentioned in [GNATJVM] the class String refers to the class Object, and vice versa. (String extends Object, while Object contains an operation (toString) that returns a value of the class String.) This circular reference affects both the contents of each individual class, as well as the overall approach to packaging. The Intermetrics/Aonix binding removes this circularity by manual analysis, while the GNAT proposal allows a special pragma that will permit a "forward reference" from one class to another.

Our tool depends on the ability to provide the GNAT-style forward references (see [GNAT] and [GNATJVM]. This simplifies the package structure, and the "withing". Each class maps to a separate package, and the context clause for that package is constructed from the "extends" and "implements" part of the Java class declaration. For example, consider the following extract from the DateFormat class:

```
public abstract class java.text.DateFormat extends
                                  java.text.Format
       implements java.lang.Cloneable {
         ...
       protected Calendar calendar;
         ...
}
```

The generated Ada binding for this class starts out:

```
with Java.Lang.Object; with Java.Lang.Cloneable;
package Java.Text.DateFormat is
  ...

        pragma Import_Access (java.lang.Calendar.ptr);

        type DateFormat is new Java.Lang.Object with
             record Calendar : Calendar.ptr;
          ...
end Java.Text.DateFormat;
```

This approach avoids the problem of determining the circular references, and the even more difficult problem of hand-manipulating the package structure to eliminate such circular references.

The algorithms described in this paper were implemented using Ada 95, consisted of approximately five thousand lines (including blanks and comments) and were ported to a variety of operating platforms (Linux, Solaris and SunOS).

7 Summary and Conclusions

We have demonstrated how an Ada binding can be automatically generated from the information contained in the Java Virtual Machine (JVM) Class File Format (CFF). The resulting binding is functionally complete, but has substantial limitations in usability. The primary limitation is that the JVM class file does not retain the names of formal parameters.

It would be possible to provide formal parameter names through an extension to the JVM CFF. The definition of the CFF allows for implementation-defined attributes, and formal parameter names could be an implementation-defined attribute for methods of a class. But this would not meet our goals of using only the portable aspects of the CFF. A longer-range alternative is for the JVM CFF to define such an attribute. This information would be very useful for a Java debugger, so it is possible, once the issues surrounding Java standardization are settled, that the JVM CFF specification is updated to include such attributes.

The Java language also contributes to usability restrictions on the part of an Ada binding. The Java language permits two classes to be mutually defined. Thus class files do not exhibit the same degree of ordering (they do not form a lattice) as is required by Ada packages, or C/C++ "include" files. Since the Java Language does not provide for user-defined scalar types, nor does it provide an enumeration type, there is no information in the JVM CFF to identify scalar values other than using the predefined Java types such as Integer.

Some of the limitations of the JVM CFF could be mitigated by using Java source code, rather than JVM CFF, as the input to a binding generator tool. This approach requires source code to the Java class, which may not always be available or convenient. Another alternative would be to "revert" to manually developing a more user-friendly binding, that builds on the machine-generated binding derived from the JVM CFF. This approach is time-consuming and there is no guarantee that two bindings authors will generate the same Ada binding from the given Java source. But the human analyst may be able to synthesize information that is not directly available from the Java source or the CFF, such as scalar type information or an appropriate "withing structure".

The most significant restriction with our approach is the loss of formal parameter names. This could be easily rectified through the addition of appropriate attribute values to the JVM CFF. With the addition of formal parameter names, machine-generated Ada bindings to Java class files would not be perfect, but should prove to be usable for Ada developers. Without this information, bindings generated from the Java CFF should be considered only when the Java source code is unavailable.

Another opportunity, as of yet uninvestigated, is to look at the possibility of mapping to a more object oriented binding directly utilizing tagged types in Ada rather than having everything be a subclass of Object (as is done in Java). This might provide additional benefit to the Ada programmer, albeit perhaps at a cost to the bindings implementer.

8 Acknowledgements

The authors would like to acknowledge the contributions of Tucker Taft for the Ada to Java idea and responding to various email questions, the GNAT team for information on their binding approach and Olimpia Velez for last-minute editing and corrections.

References

[AdaBindings] Ada 95 Bindings Report, DASW01-94-C-0054, Task Order T-S5-306, Defense Information Systems Agency Center for Software, 15 August 1995.

[Aonix] "Read me" file for Aonix Ada 95 to JDK 1.1 binding, available from ftp://ftp.aonix.com/pub/web/ada/jdk_1.1.zip

[AppletWriter] Applet Writer's User Guide, available from the AppletMagic home page, http://
www.intermetrics.com/appletmagic/download/appletwriters.guide.txt.

[c2ada] Automated C to Ada binding tool. Available from
http://www.inmet.com/ mg/c2ada.

[Emery] Emery, David and Nyberg, Karl; "Observations on Portable Ada Systems", in Ada: the design choice, Proceedings of the Ada-Europe International Conference, Madrid, Spain, 13-15 June 1989. Cambridge University Press. Also available as MITRE Technical Paper MTP-282, February, 1989, Bedford, MA.

[GNAT] Java to Ada Interfacing, Appendix B of GNAT Ada mapping to JAVA, Ada Core Technologies, in preparation, private communication.

[GNATJVM] Comar, Cyrille; Dismukes, Gary and Gasperoni, Franco; "Targeting GNAT to the Java Virtual Machine", in Proceedings of Tri-Ada 1997, ACM SIGAda, St. Louis, 1997.

[Harold] Harold, Elliotte Rusty Java Secrets, IDG Books Worldwide, Foster City, CA, 1997.

[Intermetrics] Release notes for release 2.0.1 of AppletMagic, available from the AppletMagic home page,
http://www.intermetrics.com/appletmagic/api/index.html

[JNI] The Java Native Interface - available at URL
http://www.javasoft.com/products/jdk/1.1/docs/guide/jni/spec

[Kramer] Kramer, Douglas; The Java Platform,
available at http://java.sun.com/docs/white/platform/.

[Lindholm] Lindholm, Tim and Yellin, Frank; The Java Virtual Machine Specification, Addison-Wesley, Reading, MA, 1997.

[Meyer] Meyer, Jon and Downing, Troy; Java Virtual Machine, O'Reilly & Associates, Sebastopol, CA, 1997.

[POSIX] IEEE Standard IEEE STD 1003.5-1992, POSIX System Interfaces Ada Binding, IEEE, Piscataway, NJ, 1992.

40

[Taft] Taft, S. Tucker, "Programming the Internet in Ada 95", in Proceedings of the Ada-Europe International Conference, 1996. Cambridge University Press; also available as: http://www.inmet.com/štt/adajava_paper/.

[Taft2] Taft, S. Tucker, private communication.

[Venners] Venners, Bill, Inside the Java Virtual Machine McGraw-Hill, New York, 1998.

[Wragg] Wragg, David; Drossopoulou, Sophia and Eisenbach, Susan; "Java Binary Compatibility is Almost Correct", available as http://outoften.doc.ic.ac.uk/projects/slurp/papers.html#bincomp

Synchronizing Multiple Clients and Servers

Mordechai Ben-Ari

Department of Science Teaching, Weizmann Institute of Science
Rehovot 76100 Israel
ntbenari@wis.weizmann.ac.il, benari@acm.org
http://stwi.weizmann.ac.il/g-cs/benari/

Abstract. This paper presents a programming paradigm for synchronizing multiple clients and servers. The solution is flexible and efficient and shows how class-wide types and protected objects can be used to achieve the effect of dispatching on entry calls.

1 Introduction

The Ada rendezvous is asymmetric in that the calling task must know the name of the accepting task but the accepting task does not know the name of the calling task. This construct is exactly what is needed to implement passive servers; the server task uses a selective wait to wait simultaneously on a set of entries, one for each service. The client tasks call the server as needed.

However, there is no construct for a multi-way select where a calling task waits simultaneously for one of a set of entry calls to be accepted. Synchronizing multiple waiting callers and acceptors is deemed to be inefficient. This topic is discussed in Section 9.9 of [4], where several less-than-satisfactory workarounds are presented. One uses variant records which results in an inflexible program structure, and the other suffers from too much tasking overhead. Burns and Wellings conclude their discussion with the sentence:

> More radical solutions to this problem such as those using concurrent receiving tasks, the OOP facilities or nested asynchronous select statements could be explored. (p. 234)

This paper presents a flexible, efficient programming paradigm for coordinating multiple clients and servers using the Ada 95 constructs for class-wide types, dynamic dispatching and protected objects. The paradigm can also be adapted for other applications where a multi-way select would seem to be needed.

The idea is that an access to a task or protected type is encapsulated in a tagged record, and the entry calls are themselves embedded in a primitive operation of the type. A heterogeneous data structure of objects of the class-wide type is maintained, and entry calls are 'dispatched' as each object is removed from the structure. Synchronization is done using protected objects which can be efficiently implemented using ceiling priorities as described in detail in Section D.3.2 of the *Rationale* [2].

The paper will present a solution to the mailbox problem exactly as described in [4], p. 230–231.[1] Then I will discuss modifications to the program for other versions of the problem, and the relation of the paradigm to multi-way select. The emphasis is more on solving specific client-server problems than on a direct implementation of multi-way select. For this reason, I am careful to distinguish segments of the program that an applications programmer is expected to write, from implementation details that would be assigned to an Ada tasking specialist on a project.

Full source code for several versions of the program is available from the author's web site and by e-mail.

2   Previous Work

I originally developed this technique of 'dispatching' on entry calls in order to implement occam-style channels in Ada 95 [3].

Multi-way select was discussed during the Ada 9X language design. The User-Defined Procedure Mechanism was suggested by Kamrad and Hassett [5], and worked out in more detail by Baker and Pazy [1]. The problem with these solutions is that the applications programmer must use a case-statement upon return from the procedure that implements the wait, making maintenance difficult. Furthermore, the detailed implementation given in [1] supports the most general semantics of a select-statement in that for each execution of the 'select' it processes a data structure containing all the entry calls. Our approach is more application-oriented and more efficient.

Other solutions have been proposed that use asynchronous transfer of control to simulate multi-way select, but this construct is too 'heavy' for the relatively simple problems involved.

Taft [6] gave a sketch of a solution to multi-way select using dispatching rather than a case-statement. Since a complete solution was not given, a full comparison with my proposal is not possible. The proposed solution differs in many respects from the one in [6]: the use of two queues for flexibility, extensive use of requeue for efficiency, and the preference for indefinite types over pointers.

3   The Mailbox Problem

The techniques will be demonstrated using the example of a server that serves one of a set of mailboxes filled by clients with messages. Rather than passively

---

[1] Note that the terminology in [4] is not consistent; on pages 226–229, the client is the task that is waiting to call one of a set of servers, while in the example, it is the server which is calling the clients! Our terminology follows the example, not the preceding discussion.

waiting for a call, the server can provide service to a pending requests on its own initiative.

A mailbox has two entries; each client calls the **Send** entry of its mailbox, while the server can choose to wait for one of the mailboxes to be filled:

```
protected type MailBox is
   entry Send(D: in Data);
   entry Receive(D: out Data);
end MailBox;

MailBox1.Send(D1);                -- Client one

MailBox2.Send(D2);                -- Client two

MailBox3.Send(D3);                -- Client three

loop                              -- Server loop
   -- Do something then decide to serve
   select
      MailBox1.Receive(D);        -- Not Ada
      Serve1(D);
   or
      MailBox2.Receive(D);
      Serve2(D);
   or
      MailBox3.Receive(D);
      Serve3(D);
   end select;
end loop
```

To implement this in Ada 95, a queue of pending requests must be maintained. For flexibility, the (protected) data structure used to store identification of the pending requests is separated from the (protected) data structures used to store the messages themselves, one for each message type. While I have chosen to use a generic data structure and to instantiate it for each message type, different data structures could easily be used, perhaps to impose different priority schemes among objects of the same message type.

The solution will be presented, first from the point of view of the applications programmers, and then from the point of view of the programmer implementing the underlying support software. While reading the solution, refer to the figures as needed. The data structures are shown in Fig. 1, where double-walled rectangles represent protected objects. The program structure is shown in Fig. 2,[2] and Fig. 3 shows a portion of the program structure with dataflow superimposed.

---

[2] Almost all other units 'with' package **Root**; arrows are not drawn to avoid clutter.

44

3.1 Creating Clients and Servers

Package Root contains the declarations of abstract and access types.

```
with Ada.Unchecked_Deallocation;
package Root is
   type Message is abstract tagged null record;
   procedure Serve(M: in Message) is abstract;
   type Message_Class_Ptr is access all Message'Class;
   procedure Free is
      new Ada.Unchecked_Deallocation(Message'Class, Message_Class_Ptr);

   type Request is abstract tagged null record;
   function Get_Message(R: Request) return Message'Class is abstract;
   type Request_Class_Ptr is access all Request'Class;
   procedure Free is
      new Ada.Unchecked_Deallocation(Request'Class, Request_Class_Ptr);
end Root;
```

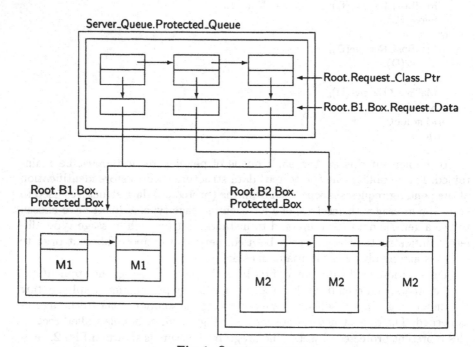

Fig. 1. Queue structures

The server maintains a queue of requests. A request is just an access to the protected object containing the message associated with the request. **Request** is an abstract tagged type; each time you create a new message type, you extend Request with an access to the protected type encapsulating the queue for the new message type, though this is hidden from the applications programmer. Since the data fields of the queue elements can be of any type derived from Request, they must be of type Request'Class, and since they are indefinite, they are stored indirectly using Request_Class_Ptr, an access to the class-wide type.

Similarly, type Message is an abstract tagged type from which specific message types are derived. Upon removing an object of type Message'Class from the queue, the server performs the service by dispatching on the primitive procedure Serve.

For each specific message type, a child package, such as Root.B1 shown below, is declared. The child declares the extension Root.Message1 with the message-specific fields, and a protected data structure for messages of the type; here, it is obtained by instantiating Root.Generic_Box with the specific message type as a formal parameter to obtain Root.B1.Box.

```
with Root.Generic_Box;
package Root.B1 is
   type Message1 is new Message with
     record N: Integer; end record;
   procedure Serve(M: in Message1);
   package Box is new Root.Generic_Box(Message1);
end Root.B1;
```

The generic package exports two subprograms. Procedure Get_Message, called by the server, is primitive for the type Request_Data and returns a class-wide message value; similarly, Send_Message, called by the client, takes a class-wide message parameter. Each instantiation of the package also declares Request_Data which *privately* extends the abstract type Request.

```
generic
   type Message_Type is new Message with private;
package Root.Generic_Box is
   type Request_Data is new Request with private;
   function Get_Message(R: Request_Data) return Message'Class;
   procedure Send_Message(M: in Message'Class);
private
   . . .
end Root.Generic_Box;
```

The code for a client is extremely simple; it just creates an object of the specific message type and sends the message.

```
Root.B1.Box.Send_Message( Root.B1.Message1'(N ⇒ I) );
```

The server obtains a message from the server queue and dispatches to the version of Serve corresponding to the message tag. (The requirement for the explicit pointer is explained below in Section 3.5.)

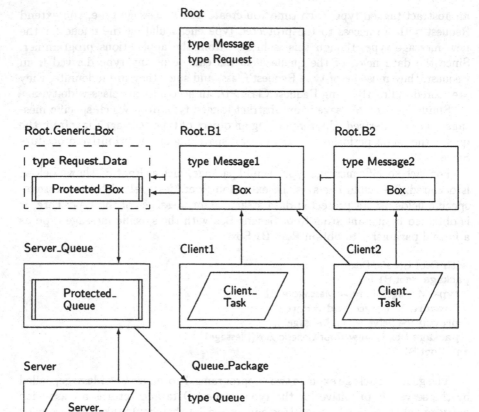

Fig. 2. Program structure

```
with Server_Queue; with Root; use Root;
package body Server is
  task body Server_Task is
    M: Message_Class_Ptr;
  begin
    loop
      Server_Queue.Protected_Queue.Get(M);          -- Get message
      Serve(M.all);                 -- Dispatch !
      Free(M);                      -- Free temporary object
    end loop;
  end Server_Task;
end Server;
```

The specification of the package Server_Queue follows. The applications programmer need only see entry Get, so it would be better to encapsulate it in a procedure and hide the protected object. However, the protected object must be exported for reasons to be described shortly.

```
with Root; use Root;
with Queue_Package;
package Server_Queue is
  protected Protected_Queue is
    entry Put(M: in Message'Class; R: in Request'Class);
    entry Get(M: out Message_Class_Ptr);
  private
    ...
  end Protected_Queue;
end Server_Queue;
```

Before moving to the details of the implementation, note that the applications programmer works only with *messages* not with requests, whose implementation is hidden.

3.2 Implementation

Let us return to package Root.Generic_Box and repeat its specification including the private part. Request_Data is extended with an access to Protected_Box which maintains a queue (implementation not shown) for objects of generic formal type Message_Type.

```
generic
  type Message_Type is new Message with private;
package Root.Generic_Box is
  type Request_Data is new Request with private;
  function Get_Message(R: Request_Data) return Message'Class;
  procedure Send_Message(M: in Message'Class);
private
  protected type Protected_Box is
    entry Put(M: in Message'Class; R: in Request'Class);
    procedure Get(M: out Message_Type);
  private
    ...
  end Protected_Box;

  type Box_Ptr is access all Protected_Box;
  type Request_Data is new Request with
    record
      Which_Box: Box_Ptr;
    end record;
end Root.Generic_Box;
```

In the package body, a protected box My_Box is declared. Send_Message creates a *request* containing an access to the protected box, and sends both the request and the message to the box. Get_Message is dispatching; when a version is called, it dereferences the box access to call the correct Protected_Box.Get. Note the requeue statement in Protected_Box.Put: after the message has been placed on the internal queue, the request is sent to be placed on the common server queue.

```
with Server_Queue;
package body Root.Generic_Box is
    My_Box: aliased Protected_Box;

    procedure Send_Message(M: in Message'Class) is
        R: Request_Data :=
            Request_Data'(Request with Which_Box => My_Box'Access);
    begin
        My_Box.Put(M, R);
    end Send_Message;

    function Get_Message(R: Request_Data) return Message'Class is
        Temp: Message_Type;
    begin
        R.Which_Box.Get(Temp);
        return Message'Class(Temp);
    end Get_Message;

    protected body Protected_Box is
        procedure Get(M: out Message_Type) is
        begin
            -- Get message from queue and assign to M
        end Get;

        entry Put(M: in Message'Class; R: in Request'Class)
            when Count < Index'Last is
        begin
            -- Put message M on queue
            requeue Server_Queue.Protected_Queue.Put with abort;
        end Put;
    end Protected_Box;
end Root.Generic_Box;
```

Server_Queue encapsulates the Protected_Queue of requests. Protected_Queue is declared in the *visible* part of the package so that calls from the client can be requeued on its entry. Since types cannot be declared within the specification of a protected object, the data structure itself is split off into an additional package Queue_Package (see Fig. 2), so that implementation of the queue is not exported. Note the allocation of a temporary object for the returned message in entry Get.

```
with Root; use Root;
with Queue_Package;
package Server_Queue is
  protected Protected_Queue is
    entry Put(M: in Message'Class; R: in Request'Class);
    entry Get(M: out Message_Class_Ptr);
  private
    Q: Queue_Package.Queue;
  end Protected_Queue;
end Server_Queue;

package body Server_Queue is
  protected body Protected_Queue is
    entry Put(M: in Message'Class; R: in Request'Class)
        when Queue_Package.Not_Full(Q) is
    begin
      Queue_Package.Put(new Request'Class'(R), Q);
    end Put;

    entry Get(M: out Message_Class_Ptr)
        when Queue_Package.Not_Empty(Q) is
    R: Request_Class_Ptr;
    begin
      Queue_Package.Get(R, Q);
      -- Dispatch to message queue for this type of request
      M := new Message'Class'(Get_Message(R.all));
      Free(R);
    end Get;
  end Protected_Queue;
end Server_Queue;
```

3.3 Transaction Dataflow

The dataflow of a transaction can be followed in Figure 3.

The client creates a message of some specific type (say Message1), and calls Send_Message for this type. Send_Message creates a request pointing to the protected box for this type, and calls Protected_Box.Put to enqueue the *message*. The call is then requeued on Server_Queue.Protected_Queue.Put, which placed the *request* on the server queue. Successive executions of this sequence will lead to a state where messages are queued on type-specific queues, and for each message a request has been placed on the common server queue. Because requeue is used, the entire sequence involves just one protected action.

The server calls Server_Queue.Protected_Queue.Get which removes a request from the head of the queue. The request is of type Request'Class, so if it is used as the controlling (actual) parameter of a call to the primitive procedure Get_Message, the call will be dynamically dispatched to the overridden procedure corresponding to the specific type of the request. Get_Message will use the access to the protected box in its parameter to call Protected_Box.Get for this message

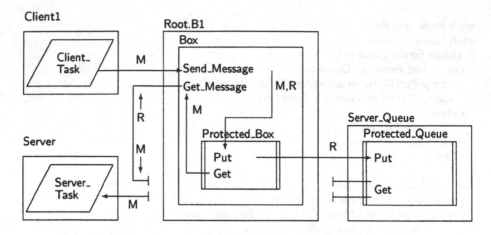

Fig. 3. Dataflow

type. Protected_Box.Get will remove a message from its queue and return it up the chain to the server. Finally, the server dispatches procedure Serve for this message type.

There are two technical problems that had to be solved with the server; these are discussed in the following subsections.

3.4 Requeue Parameters

Requeue is permitted only if the parameter profile of the new entry is the same as that of the original entry, or if the new entry has no parameters. For the client, this is not a problem: *any* version of Protected_Box.Put simply passes the message of type Message'Class to Protected_Queue.Put which ignores it. For the server, this is not possible because the call from Protected_Queue.Get must be dispatched via a primitive *subprogram* to the correct Protected_Box.Get, but requeue is only permitted *directly* within an entry body.

The solution is to note that if a request exists on the server queue, then the corresponding message queue will necessarily be non-empty, so Protected_Queue.-Get need never block and can call the protected *procedure* Protected_Box.Get (indirectly through Get_Message). A procedure of another protected object is not considered to be a potentially blocking operation (ARM 9.5.1) which should not be invoked within an entry body.

Despite the inconvenience, I do not suggest a future language change here because there are cogent technical reasons for the rule (see 9.2 of [2]).

3.5 Returning from an Entry

An entry does not have a result; conversely, only a function result—not an out parameter—can return an arbitrary object of class-wide type. The workaround is to allocate a dynamic message object upon return from Get_Message and let Protected_Queue.Get return an access to this object.

I suggest that a future version of Ada allow a function syntax for entries so that class-wide types can be returned. This was rejected during the design of Ada 95 because the workaround of access types is always available.[3] However, I believe that one of the advantages of Ada is that indefinite types can be used to avoid exporting to the applications programmer the pointers that are necessary for implementing heterogeneous data structures. Thus, I recommend that this design decision be reconsidered in a future version of Ada.

4 Analysis, Modifications and Extensions

In this example, you do not actually need to store an access to the protected boxes. Since there is only one protected object associated with each message type, the requests can be null records and the primitive function Get_Message can simply call the entry of the protected object in its instantiation. The present solution is more flexible; for example, it would allow multiple queues for a single message type.

Server_Queue.Protected_Queue should define a function that checks if the queue is empty. This is needed to create a truly active server that could perform other computations while waiting for requests.

As programmed, the clients do not block. This can be achieved by requeuing the client on an additional entry Block_Client after queuing the request in Server_Queue.Protected_Queue.Put. The barrier of Block_Client is opened at the end of the server call to Server_Queue.Protected_Queue.Get. Alternatively, the client can be blocked until after the service is completed by having Server_Task call a protected procedure.[4] This gives the transaction the flavor of a rendezvous and is essential if the result of the service is to be returned.

The mailbox program only requires in-parameters. I have written a version of the program that has both in- and out-parameters. The modifications were not difficult, however, there is additional overhead because the messages in the mailboxes are now pointers to a parameter block.

The program can support multiple servers without modification since Server_-Queue.Protected_Queue is already protected. It would not be difficult to combine single entry calls with this paradigm for multi-way select: the server queue package would need an additional entry that would search the request queue for a request with a matching tag. The full semantics of multi-way select would need to support several such statements with different sets of entry calls. This would require more complex programming similar to that in [1]; for most applications, this is probably not necessary.

---

[3] Tucker Taft (personal communication).
[4] I have programmed both these variants and the source code is available.

5 Conclusion

This paper has presented a programming paradigm in Ada 95 for message-passing in the presence of multiple clients and servers. The program is also a useful case study in the interaction of class-wide types and protected objects, and points out that future versions of Ada could benefit from a closer integration of the two constructs. The proposed solution to the problem posed by [4] shows that you need not simulate the full semantics of multi-way select; rather, you can use existing Ada constructs to create flexible software that can be specialized for a specific application.

6 Acknowledgements

I would like to thank the referees for their incisive comments which materially improved the paper. I would also like to thank Tucker Taft and Stef Van Vlierberghe for pointing me to the material on the Ada 95 language design.

References

1. T. Baker and O. Pazy. Doing without the multi-way select. Language Study Note 035-DR, file LSN_035_ in directory /ada/ajpo/standards/95com/lsn, Walnut Creek Ada CD-ROM, 1992.
2. J. Barnes, editor. *Ada 95 Rationale: The Language, The Standard Libraries*, volume 1247 of *Lecture Notes in Computer Science*. Springer-Verlag, 1997.
3. M. Ben-Ari. Using inheritance to implement concurrency. In *Twenty-Seventh SIGCSE Technical Symposium*, volume 28 of *SIGCSE Bulletin*, pages 180–184, 1996.
4. A. Burns and A. Wellings. *Concurrency in Ada*. Cambridge University Press, 1995.
5. M. Kamrad and J. Hassett. Applying Ada9X to two real time applications: A case study. In M. Gauthier, editor, *Ada-Europe '93*, volume 688 of *Lecture Notes in Computer Science*, pages 79–94. Springer-Verlag, 1993.
6. S. T. Taft. Standard event queue package. Language Study Note 1032, file 92.07/92.0702 in the archive 9207mrt.zip in directory /ada/ajpo/standards/95com/mrtcomments, Walnut Creek Ada CD-ROM, 1992.

How to Avoid the Inheritance Anomaly in Ada

Guido Schumacher, Wolfgang Nebel

Carl von Ossietzky University Oldenburg, Department of Computer Science, Postfach 2503
D-26111 Oldenburg, Germany
e-mail: {Guido.Schumacher, Nebel}@Informatik.Uni-Oldenburg.de

Abstract. Object-oriented techniques such as inheritance promise great benefits for the specification and design of concurrent systems. To exploit these benefits appropriate techniques for object-oriented programming within a concurrent programming language context are required. Especially a concept how to support the inheritance of synchronization constraints is necessary to avoid what is called the inheritance anomaly. We present a modelling style of Ada which allows the integration of concurrency into object-oriented programming and which offers a solution to the inheritance anomaly.

1 Introduction

Ada 95 includes a concept for object-oriented programming with run-time polymorphism as well as a tasking concept. It is thus a concurrent object-oriented programming language. If both language concepts are used in a program it is necessary to use communication and synchronization mechanisms which allow the interaction of inheritance and tasking, object-oriented programming and tasking.

One of the basic problems in such an interaction is to make the inheritance of synchronization constructs in form of synchronization code possible. The synchronization code defines synchronization constraints which the objects must meet to perform communication. Typically each operation has a corresponding piece of synchronization code which interacts with the synchronization code of other operations. If an object inherits synchronization code it is difficult to add new synchronization code to the object's operations without re-analysing or modifying the existing one. However, re-analysing or modifying means to break encapsulation which goes directly against the object-oriented paradigm. This problem is discussed in several publications, e.g. in [1][2][6] and there still is ongoing research to find appropriate solutions, e.g., [4],[7] just to mention two proposals. The problem is known as the inheritance anomaly.

In this paper we investigate two techniques to define synchronization constraints which can be found in variants in several proposals to solve the anomaly.

The first is to use guard expression to determine when an object's method has permission to run [5]. The second technique is to trace the invocation history of an object's methods by defining a state machine with transitions depending only on a method's execution. The actual state of the state machine determines which methods have permission to run [8].

The technique to solve the inheritance anomaly presented here consists of a combination of both techniques. It can be regarded as a modelling style to specify synchronization constraints in Ada which makes inheritance possible. It does not introduce any non-standard language features but is purely based on existing language constructs.

The remainder of the paper presents a modelling style which allows mutual exclusion synchronization of an object's methods. The modelling style then is extended and slightly modified to allow user defined synchronization which can be inherited by derived objects without breaking encapsulation. Synchronization has the quality of fairness in the modelling style.

2 Synchronization of Tagged Types

Object-oriented programming especially inheritance is supported in Ada by a type extension mechanism. It is possible to extend an existing tagged type incrementally by creating a new type which inherits features from the existing type including its primitive operations. The following section describes how tagged types can be designed so its objects can be used in a concurrent execution environment if they require mutually exclusive access to their data for synchronization. The concept described in this section is taken from [3]. It provides the synchronization which performs the mutually exclusive access by the base (root) object type.

As the Ada language does not allow a tagged type to be at the same time a protected type it is necessary to introduce a lock object as part of the tagged type. The lock object provides a simple mutual exclusion lock.

The lock object has a lock operation which blocks all the following invocations of lock until an unlock operation is performed. Such an object becomes a component of a base type in a hierarchy of tagged types:

```
package lockable_package is

    type lockable_type is tagged limited private;
    procedure protocol_op (object : in out lockable_type'class);

private
    type lockable_type is tagged limited
    record
        -- lock object to provide mutual exclusion synchronization
        -- protected object with entry lock and procedure unlock:
        lock_handler : mutex;
    end record;

    procedure op (object : in out lockable_type); -- actual operation

end lockable_package;
```

The primitive operations implementing the actual operations of the tagged types are declared private. The protocol which guarantees the mutual exclusive access is implemented by procedures declared in the visible part of the specification. Protocol procedures perform a lock on the lock object which has become a component of the tagged type invoke the actual operation and unlock the object:

```
package body lockable_package is

    procedure protocol_op (object : in out lockable_type'class) is
    begin
        object.lock_handler.lock;
        op (object);          -- dispatch to actual operation
        object.lock_handler.unlock;
    end;

    procedure op (object : in out lockable_type) is
    begin
        ...
    end;

end lockable_package;
```

As the actual operations are private, the only way to extend the tagged type is to use a child package. It is then no problem to derive a new tagged type, add new primitive operations to it, or override existing ones if necessary:

```
package lockable_package.child is

    type lockable_with_extensions is new lockable_type with private;

    procedure protocol_new_op (object : in out lockable_with_extensions'class);

private
    type lockable_with_extensions is new lockable_type with record
        ...
    end record;

    procedure op (object : in out lockable_with_extensions); -- override operation
    procedure new_op (this : in out lockable_with_extensions);

end lockable_package.child;
```

By using the same synchronization mechanism in the original and the new operation with the class-wide parameter a mutual exclusive access to an object of the tagged type is guaranteed:

```
procedure protocol_new_op (object : in out lockable_with_extensions'class) is
begin
    object.lock_handler.lock;
    new_op (object);
    object.lock_handler.unlock;
end;
```

The protocol is only used for implementing mutual exclusion synchronization and it will not change for derived types. The further pros and cons of this modelling style in which the synchronization is provided by the base (tagged) type are discussed in more detail in [3]. The protocol does not implement what is called condition synchronization which might be necessary when a caller wishes to perform an operation that can only be performed if another object has itself taken some action or is in some defined state.

3 User Defined Synchronization

The previous section explains a modelling style which provides synchronization for objects of tagged types in form of mutually exclusive access to an object's data. What is missing is a technique to design user defined synchronization in form of condition synchronization. In other words, the approach does not solve the inheritance anomaly.

Synchronization constraints described by synchronization code for condition synchronization typically consist of a state space which describes the object's relevant states for synchronization, a set of conditions which must be met before a method has permission to run, and some state transitions which are performed on the state space after a method's execution. Each single condition of a constraint which depends on the attributes' values of an object divides them into two sets. One set of attribute values which fulfils the condition and the complement set which does not fulfil the condition. Thus, a set of conditions defines the state space which is relevant for condition synchronization.

3.1 Compatibility of Synchronization Constraints

In the context of inheritance a derived object should impose the synchronization constraints of the parent's type even if the synchronization code is modified or extended by overriding methods. New synchronization constraints should only be a kind of refinement of the parent's constraints. This view on synchronization constraints motivates the following definition of compatibility:

Definition 1. *Assuming a synchronization constraint C defines the conditions which must be met to allow an overridden method M of a derived object to be executed and assuming it defines the state transitions which are performed after the method's execution, we then define C to be compatible to the synchronisation constraint B of the parent's method M if the following conditions are met:*

i) *The fulfilment of the conditions of C implies the fulfilment of the conditions of B.*

ii) *Each state in the parent's state space can be described as a set of states of the derived object and thus, the state space of the derived object can be embedded in the parent's state space.*

iii) *The synchronization code of the overridden method M causes the same state transition as the parent's operation M with respect to the parent's state space.*

We now can say that if we are able to modify or extend synchronization constraints in a derived type so that they are compatible to the parent's constraints without breaking encapsulation then we have solved the inheritance anomaly.

The remainder of this section describes a technique to write synchronization code in Ada. It presents rules how to modify the synchronization code guaranteeing the compatibility of the modified constraints with the parent's constraints by construction without breaking encapsulation.

The technique uses tagged types. Like in the modelling style of the previous section, the mutual exclusion synchronization is included in the root type definition.

```
package concurrent_tagged_type_package is

   type concurrent_tagged_type is tagged private;

   procedure op_protocol (this : in out concurrent_tagged_type'class);
   -- protocol guarantees mutual exclusive access to object
   -- protocol invokes actual operation

private
   reschedule : exception;
   type concurrent_tagged_type is new event_driven_type with record
   -- event_driven_type provides the synchronization
   ...
   end record;

   procedure op (this : in out concurrent_tagged_type);   -- actual operation
end;
```

Declaring the derived type (concurrent_tagged_type) private hides the lock and unlock operations of the base type (event_driven_type) from the client. A client only has access to the protocol operations of the derived type[1]. The actual operation is also declared private. It is invoked in the protocol implementation:

```
package body concurrent_tagged_type_package is

   procedure op_protocol (this : in out concurrent_tagged_type'class) is
   begin
      lock(this);        -- guarantee exclusive access to object (this)
      loop
         begin
            op (this);   -- call actual operation
            signal_event_and_unlock (this);
            -- signal successful execution of operation to callers
            -- which are queued for rescheduling
            -- unlock the object
```

---

[1] This version of the protocol does not properly handle bypassing the unlock by raising an exception different from reschedule in an operation.

```
                return;
            exception
                when reschedule =>
                -- guard evaluation in operation failed, rescheduling of op required
                unlock_and_wait_on_event (this);
                -- queue caller for rescheduling, caller waits until a possible
                -- change of the object's state is signalled
                -- unlock the object
            end;
        end loop;
    end;


    procedure op (this : in out concurrent_tagged_type) is
    begin
        ...
    end;
    end;
```

The protocol implements mutual exclusion synchronization with its invocations of the lock/unlock operations (lock, signal_event_and_unlock, unlock_and_wait_on_event).

The important improvement compared to the approach presented in the previous section is the possibility to stop the execution of the actual operation and to re-schedule it for a time in the future. The re-scheduling can be performed in the actual operation by raising the exception reschedule. This re-schedule mechanism can be regarded similar to requeuing. It allows to check conditions depending on the internal state of the object and to suspend the execution until the conditions are met.

If a primitive operation is terminated by an exception the parameter will have been updated because tagged types are always passed by reference. Therefore, the modelling style requires the checks to be performed in the actual operation before any write access to an object to ensure consistency of any object in case of re-scheduling. Thus, guards can be modelled in the actual operation in the following way:

```
    procedure op (this : in out concurrent_tagged_type) is
    begin
        if condition then raise reschedule; end if;              -- guard
        if another_condition then raise reschedule; end if;      -- another guard
        -- operation implementation follows
        ...
    end;
```

After re-scheduling an attempt to re-execute an operation is only useful if the conditions probably have changed. The conditions may change if the object's internal state changes after the successful execution of an actual operation (op). To signal such an event an event driven scheduling mechanism is part of the synchronization. The mechanism is provided by the root type (event_driven_type). The invocation of the procedure unlock_and_wait_on_event in the protocol implementation suspends a caller and delays the re-execution of the operation until the object's internal state might have changed. Such a possible change is signalled to all suspended callers by invoking the procedure signal_event_and_unlock after an successful execution of an actual operation. The re-execution causes the re-evaluation of all guards modelled in an operation.

The re-scheduling mechanism allows to call an operation within another operation of the same object. Then, the rule that the guard evaluations have to be performed before any write access to the object requires that there is no such access before the call because there might be guard evaluations inside the called operation. It is not necessary for the calling operation to know anything about the synchronization constraints of the called operation nor is any compatibility between the synchronization constraints of the calling and the called operation required. If rescheduling is raised inside the *called* operation then the exception is handled in the protocol operation of the *calling* operation so the guards of both operations are re-evaluated during the re-execution.

3.2 Event Driven Re-Scheduling Mechanism

We now briefly sketch the required event driven re-scheduling mechanism which is used in the protocol. It is provided by the base (root) type. The base type (event_driven_type) contains the procedures which are used in the protocol to implement the mechanism.

```
package event_driven_package is

    type  event_driven_type is tagged limited private;

    procedure lock (object : in out event_driven_type);
    procedure unlock_and_wait_on_event (object : in out  event_driven_type);
    procedure signal_event_and_unlock (object : in out event_driven_type);

private
    type event_driven_type is tagged limited record
        event_handler: event_handler_package.event_handler_type;
    end record;
end;
```

A protected object is included in the root type which provides the mutual exclusion synchronization and the actual event mechanism. We call this object event handler.

```
protected type event_handler_type is

    entry lock;
    entry unlock_and_wait_on_event;
    procedure signal_event_and_unlock;

    private
    entry wait_on_event;
    entry inner_lock;
    number_of_unblocked_waits : integer range 0..integer'last := 0;
```

```
        tasks_to_requeue_at_inner_lock : integer range 0..integer'last := 0;
        event_handler_is_locked : boolean := false;
        event_handler_inner_lock_is_locked : boolean := false;
    end;
```

The base type event_driven_type simply uses the entries and procedures of the protected object (event_handler) to implement the primitive operations:

```
    procedure lock (object : in out event_driven_type) is
    begin
        object.event_handler.lock;
    end;
```

In the same way the other primitive operations unlock_and_wait_on_event and signal_event_and_unlock are implemented:

```
    procedure unlock_and_wait_on_event (object : in out event_driven_type) is
    begin
        object.event_handler.unlock_and_wait_on_event;
    end;

    procedure signal_event_and_unlock (object : in out event_driven_type) is
    begin
        object.event_handler.signal_event_and_unlock;
    end;
```

The event handler provides a simple lock and unlock mechanism with the entries and procedure in its visible part. A call to lock is suspended if there has been a previous call to lock without a corresponding call to either unlock_and_wait_on_event or signal_event_and_unlock. If there is a call to the signal mechanism then first the signalling is executed and then the unlock is performed. The protected type is implemented as follows:

```
    protected body event_handler_type is

    entry lock when (not event_handler_is_locked and
                    number_of_unblocked_waits = 0 and
                    tasks_to_requeue_at_inner_lock = 0) is
    begin
        event_handler_is_locked := true;
        requeue inner_lock;
    end;

    entry unlock_and_wait_on_event when true is
    begin
        event_handler_is_locked := false;
        event_handler_inner_lock_is_locked := false;
        requeue wait_on_event;
    end;
```

```
entry wait_on_event when (number_of_unblocked_waits > 0) is
begin
    number_of_unblocked_waits := number_of_unblocked_waits - 1;
    requeue inner_lock;
end;

entry inner_lock when ( not event_handler_inner_lock_is_locked and
                        number_of_unblocked_waits = 0) is
begin
    if tasks_to_requeue_at_inner_lock > 0 then
        tasks_to_requeue_at_inner_lock := tasks_to_requeue_at_inner_lock - 1;
        requeue inner_lock;
    else
        event_handler_inner_lock_is_locked := true;
    end if;
end;

procedure signal_event_and_unlock is
begin
    number_of_unblocked_waits := wait_on_event'count;
    if number_of_unblocked_waits > 0 then
        tasks_to_requeue_at_inner_lock := inner_lock'count;
    end if;
    event_handler_is_locked := false;
    event_handler_inner_lock_is_locked := false;
    end;
end;
```

A call to lock is blocked if there was a previous call to lock without corresponding unlock or if there is an event caused by a signal which is not yet completely processed. The invocation history of the lock/unlock operations is traced by the private variable event_handler_is_locked. If a call to lock is performed this variable is set to true. The lock then is requeued at an inner lock.

The invocation history of the inner lock is traced by the private variable event_handler_inner_lock_is_locked. It might be necessary to re-arrange some tasks in the entry queue of the inner lock from the head of the queue to its tail to make the re-schedule mechanism fair. In this case a certain number of tasks are just requeued at the inner lock.

An unlock is performed by calling unlock_and_wait_on_event. This causes both locks (lock and inner_lock) to be released by setting the corresponding variables to false. Before the unlocks take effect the caller is requeued on the entry wait_on_event. The caller is suspended on the entry until an event is signalled. The caller then is requeued at the inner lock. By requeuing at the inner lock the caller precedes entries queued at the (outer) lock when the locks are released.

Such an event needed by the entry wait_on_event is signalled in the procedure signal_event_and_unlock by assigning the number of waiting callers in the entry queue of wait_on_event to the private variable number_of_unblocked_waits.

The procedure signal_event_and_unlock is used to signal that the object's state might have changed. Each suspended caller becomes a candidate for re-scheduling. The candidates are queued at the entry wait_on_event, at the entry inner_lock, and at the entry lock. To perform the re-scheduling all these callers are (re-)queued at the inner lock. The inner lock then is released so that all callers can try to execute the actual operation in a protocol operation.

To make the re-scheduling fair the queuing at the inner lock has to be done in a certain order. The oldest callers are queued in the entry queue of wait_on_event in a first-in-first-out-order. They are requeued by assigning the numbers of entries in the queue to the private variable number_of_unblocked_waits. The callers are requeued at the tail of the entry queue of the inner lock. As the requeued callers are older than previously existing entries in the queue of inner_lock they should be at the head of the queue. To become head of the queue the previously existing entries of the entry queue of the inner lock are shifted from the head to the tail by requeuing. The number of (younger) entries to be requeued is stored in the private variable tasks_to_requeue_at_inner_lock. The guard condition of the entry inner_lock which checks the variable number_of_unblocked_waits to be zero assures that the shifting of the entries from the head to the tail is performed after the requeuing from the entry wait_on_event to inner_lock.

Finally, the most recent callers which are queued in the entry queue of the entry lock are requeued at the inner lock by releasing the lock (event_handler_is_locked). The guard conditions which checks the variables number_of_unblocked_waits and tasks_to_requeue_at_inner_lock to be zero guarantees that the requeuing from the lock to the inner lock is performed after the other requeuing steps to the inner lock. All the requeuing happens in a first-in-first-out order. This makes the callers to be re-scheduled in the order of their original call.

3.3 Modelling of Synchronization Constraints

The presented modelling style allows to design guards which are evaluated when the change of an object's state is signalled by the event mechanism. Such guards as part of the actual operation can be used to implement the condition synchronization code. A state space which describes the relevant states for synchronization can be modelled by state variables. A state variable is implemented by a component of the tagged type. The relevant states for the synchronization of an operation are distinguished by a guard which checks the value of the state variable. A state transition at the end of an operation can be modelled by an assignment statement to the state variables:

```
procedure op (this : in out concurrent_tagged_type) is
begin
    if not (this.state_variable = relevant state) then raise reschedule; end if;
    ...
    this.state_variable := next state;
end;
```

If the tagged type is incrementally modified by deriving a new type and the modification affects the synchronization code of existing operations then synchronization constraints can be added to existing operations. The additional constraints are modelled as described above by using the guard modelling technique. It can not be allowed to replace existing constraints. To ensure this, additional synchronization code of an inherited operation must not assign a value to an inherited state variable. Write access is only allowed to new state variables of the derived type. The additional constraints of an existing operation are encapsulated in a new implementation of the actual operation which invokes the original operation after checking the additional constraints:

```
procedure op (this : in out derived_concurrent_tagged_type) is
begin
    if not (this.new_state_variable = new relevant state permitting execution) then
        raise reschedule; end if;
    -- new additional guards for existing operation:
    if new condition then raise reschedule; end if;
        op (concurrent_tagged_type(this));
        -- encapsulates inherited synchronization code
    this.new_state_variable := new next state; -- refinement of state transition
end;
```

The effects of incremental modifications according to the presented modelling rules are as follows. Each new state variable partitions each state in the inherited state space into sub-states. A guard classifies relevant (sub-)states for the synchronization of an operation. An assignment to a new state variable after a method's execution is a refinement of an existing state transition.

The invocation of the original operation within the new implementation of the operation ensures that all conditions checked in the original operation are checked in the new implementation too. Thus the fulfilment of the conditions in the new implementation with the extended synchronization constraints implies the fulfilment of the conditions in the original operation. The introduction of new state variables and additional conditions to distinguish relevant states for the synchronization without removing existing ones creates a new state space which can be embedded in the existing one by simply ignoring the new state variables and the additional conditions. The state transitions after a method's execution do not change with respect to the state space of the original operation because this state space is formed by the inherited state variable and there must not be an assignment to an inherited state variable in the additional synchronization code. Thus, the modelling style guarantees the compatibility of the synchronization constraints of a derived type with the parent's constraints.

As compatibility is guaranteed by the modelling rules it is not necessary to analyse existing synchronization code of an inherited operation before adding new synchronization constraints to it and thus the desired encapsulation is provided.

The modelling style presented in this section allows incremental modification of objects containing synchronization code without violating the object's encapsulation, in other words, it is an approach to solve the inheritance anomaly.

4 Conclusion

It is an interesting idea to integrate object-oriented concepts into concurrent programming. In Ada such an integration is possible by providing a modelling style which allows inheritance of synchronization code. The modelling style uses existing communication concepts of Ada to implement an event-driven synchronization mechanism. It provides guards to program synchronization code and it allows the refinement of existing transitions between the internal state of an object without breaking its encapsulation. The main idea of the modelling style is to partition each operation into two parts. The first (protocol) part provides the basic event-driven synchronization mechanism which includes a mutual exclusion synchronization. The second private part of the operation provides the user defined synchronization in form of condition synchronization. The second part of the operation also contains the functionality. Additional synchronization code can be added to an operation by extending the second part of the operation which then contains the new synchronization code and invokes the original inherited second part of the operation.

Thus, the presented modelling style allows the inheritance of synchronization code without suffering from the inheritance anomaly.

References

1. America, P.: Inheritance and Subtyping in a Parallel Object-Oriented Language. in Bézivin, J.; Hullot, J-M.; Lieberman, H. (eds.): European Conference on Object-Oriented Programming ECOOP '87, Lecture Notes in Computer Science, Vol. 276, Springer-Verlag (1987)
2. Atkinson, C.: Object-oriented reuse, concurrency and distribution: an Ada-based approach. ACM Press (1991)
3. Burns, A.; Wellings, A.: Concurrency in Ada. Cambridge University Press (1995)
4. Ferenczi, S.: Guarded Methods vs. Inheritance Anomaly Inheritance Anomaly Solved by Nested Guarded Method Calls. ACM SIGPLAN Notices, Vol. 30, Number 2, (February 1995)
5. Frølund, S.: Inheritance of Synchronization Constraints in Concurrent Object-Oriented Programming Languages. in Lehrmann Madsen, O. (ed.): European Conference on Object-Oriented Programming ECOOP '92, Lecture Notes in Computer Science, Vol. 615, Springer-Verlag (1992)
6. Matsuoka, S.; Yonezawa, A.: Analysis of Inheritance Anomaly in Object-Oriented Concurrent Programming Languages. in Agha, G.; Wegner, P.; Yonezawa, A. (eds.): Research Directions in Concurrent Object-Oriented Programming, MIT Press (1993)
7. Mitchell, S., E.; Wellings, A. J.: Synchronization, Concurrent Object-Oriented Programming and the Inheritance Anomaly. Technical Report 234. Department of Computer Science, University of York UK (1994)
8. Tomlinson, C.; Singh, V.: Inheritance and Synchronization with Enabled-Sets. in Meyrowitz, N. (ed): Object-Oriented Programming: Systems, Languages and Applications. OOPSLA'89 Conference Proceedings. ACM Press (1989)

Inside the Distributed Systems Annex

Laurent Pautet and Samuel Tardieu

École Nationale Supérieure des Télécommunications
46, rue Barrault
F-75634 Paris Cedex 13, France

Abstract. The current Ada revision tries as much as possible to provide the programmer with an easy way to build distributed systems; in many cases, the programmer can easily modify its monolithic application and transform it in a very short amount of time into a distributed one. However, there is a huge amount of work involved in the compiler and in external tools and libraries to build and run a distributed application without loosing Ada semantics and strong type checking. This paper describes how such a task has been achieved in the current implementation of GNAT, the GNU Ada compiler, and in GLADE, GNAT's companion package for building and running distributed programs.

1 Annex E: a short overview

This section describes the key features of the distributed systems annex. The reader interested in the other features should read the full text in [12].

1.1 Distributed systems

A *distributed system* is a computer program that executes on several processing units at the same time. This partitioning across several processors and hosts may be necessary because of the following points (non exhaustive):

CPU power requirements: if the program is computation intensive, then a single processor may not be sufficient to achieve its goals in a timely fashion

CPU specialization: some processors may be unable to perform efficiently complex mathematic computations while some others will be unable to directly access certain devices

Fault tolerance: it may be required that some parts of the program be duplicated, in order to provide an uninterrupted service despite computer crashes and network temporary unavailability

Repartition of the application on various sites: a travel agency for example will use large databases replicated on several secondary servers that are not too far from terminals located across the country to ensure a decent response time

In Ada 95, a distributed program is a regular computer program in the sense that it has one entry point (the main procedure) but may be separated in a semi-transparent way into *partitions*. The partitions will then communicate with each other by exchanging data, using remote subprogram calls and distributed objects, a much more powerful mechanism than the traditional message-passing mechanism used in client/server applications (message-passing is equivalent to *goto*s in non-distributed applications while remote subprogram calls are similar to regular subprogram calls).

1.2 Streams manipulation

Basic distributed systems are easily built using the facilities offered by the underlying operating system, e.g. BSD sockets (see [11]). However, these tools operate only on arrays of bytes without any consideration of their content. To write portable distributed programs that can run on heterogeneous architectures, the programmer must carefully choose the byte ordering (big-endian *vs.* little-endian), the word size and the floating point format.

In order to work around this difficulty, Ada provides the user with the possibility to define four attributes (*Input*, *Read*, *Output* and *Write*) that control how a value will be transformed into and from a freely chosen "stream format". All the standard types already have implementation-defined subprograms for these attributes, but there is no guaranty that the default values are suitable for heterogeneous processing. These attributes are inherited by types derived from the standard types unless they are overloaded by the user. Also, these attributes do have pre-defined values for compound types such as records or arrays.

To build a distributed system that will run on different architecture, one can adopt an encoding method such as XDR (see [6]). However, this does not solve the problem of access values, that are meaningful only on one partition since this is likely that another partition will have a completely different object space filled in with different objects. The user still needs to define its own Read and Write attributes to read and write the designated value rather than the pointer itself.

Also, some data structures do not need to be transmitted as-is. For example, transmitting a complete graph to another partition only requires that the vertices be transmitted; since the full structure can be rebuilt at the other end, sending the edges would add zero information (using the definition from [10]). Some other data structures require extra care too, for example doubly linked lists, not to run into an infinite loop while flattening the elements.

1.3 The remote subprogram call paradigm

As we wrote in section 1.2, it is possible to write a distributed system based on low-level communication primitives. However, even if we consider the endianness problem and friends as solved, the programmer still faces the slight incompatibilities between various interfaces to the low-level routines. For example, reading or writing several file descriptors at a time may require that the user uses "select" on some systems and "poll" on some others.

The distributed systems annex allows the programmer to forget about these details. Strong data typing is preserved, including types of class-wide objects that can still control dispatching operations after being transmitted across partitions; the exception model is not modified in any kind and localizing and contacting other partitions as needed is taken care of at run time. The *remote subprogram call* paradigm which is the most intuitive one for the programmer is being used, while basic communication systems provide the user with a message-passing only mechanism. A remote subprogram call is no more no less than a regular subprogram, except that it may require that the network be accessed. It is a two way process from the caller's point of view: it makes a call and waits for the answer or the exception to come back.

As an extension, some procedures may be tagged as *asynchronous* (using the "Asynchronous" pragma). An asynchronous procedure is a procedure which has only "in" or "access" parameters. These kind of procedures do not respect the Ada semantics because they have two properties:

1. They may return before the completion of the procedure
2. Any exception raised during the procedure execution is lost (this property is a side effect of the first one)

Using asynchronous procedures, it is very easy to build an application that is deterministic when executed in non-distributed mode and non-deterministic in distributed-mode, by using for example nested asynchronous procedures whose execution path can follow different network links with different speeds. However, these procedures are very useful in some types of applications. For example, sending an informational message to a user's terminal need not raise an exception if the user's partition is unreachable, and the operation of sending such a benign message should not block the whole application for a long time, even if the underlying network is slow.

1.4 Categorization pragmas

Annex E of the Ada Reference Manual (see [12]) introduces three new categorization pragmas whose goal is to identify packages that must have a "remote-aware" property. These pragmas are:

pragma Remote_Types: a package containing this pragma will be used to define types that can be called remotely. These types must have some characteristics ensuring that they can be transmitted between partitions running on various nodes without loosing their semantic meaning. Basic types such as Integer, Character, Float do have an intrinsic meaning that cannot be loosed while exchanged between partitions. On the other hand, pointers may be meaningless outside of the partition where they have been built; if the user wants to transmit a pointer type across partitions, he has to provide *Read* and *Write* attributes that will encode the information in a meaningful way. For example, if a linked list is to be transmitted between partitions, the user can define attributes that will flatten the list and build an array before the transmission, while a linked list structure will be rebuilt from the array on the receiver side

pragma Remote_Call_Interface: this pragma identifies a package that will offer remote subprograms to the rest of the application. Any subprogram defined in the visible part of such a package will result in a network access if necessary. The user needs not be aware of whether such an access will occur or not; its effect must be transparent and semantically equivalent to a regular procedure call[1]. Also, *remote access to subprogram* types can be defined in these packages to define dynamically bound remote subprograms

pragma Shared_Passive: packages that are said to be Shared_Passive contain data that can be shared amongst partitions running on the same processing node. This data can be seen as regular shared memory

1.5 Distributed objects

The concept of *distributed objects* is a very popular paradigm; the well-known CORBA technology, amongst others, uses them as the basis for building distributed systems. The power of dynamic dispatching combined with the Distributed Systems Annex makes distributed objects an appropriate solution for highly dynamic and evolutive distributed systems.

With distributed objects, existing code can be extended without modification or recompilation since calls to primitive operations ("methods" in some non-to-be-cited programming languages) will automatically dispatch on the new object's code if needed.

In Ada, a special class of pointers are dedicated to distributed objects; they designate any object in a hierarchy rooted by a (possibly abstract) tagged limited private type. These pointers are called *remote access to class-wide types* (or *RACW*).

The declaration of the designated type and of its primitive operations, which must occur in the visible part of a Pure or Remote_Types package declaration, looks like this:

> **type** Object **is tagged limited private**;
> **procedure** Primitive (O : **access** Object);

while the declaration of the remote access to class-wide type reads:

> **type** RACW **is access all** Object'Class;

and must be located (paragraph E.4 (18) of the Reference Manual) into the visible part of a Remote_Types or Remote_Call_Interface package declaration.

---

[1] The semantic equivalence cannot always be strictly guaranteed given that the subprogram body can have access to low-level information concerning the partition it is running on; also, some characteristics such as the time used to perform the subprogram call will not be identical.

Thereafter, if a statement "Primitive (R);" appears with R being of type RACW, the call is not only dispatching on the tag of the object designated by R, but also on the partition where the access value has been created.

1.6 A standardized interface

As the vast majority of operating systems do not include transparent distributed processing, a *Partition Communication Subsystem* interface has been specified in the reference manual by means of a language-defined package named *System.RPC*. This package defines useful types such as *Partition_ID* which represents a partition identifier in a distributed program, as well as key subprograms such as *Do_RPC* which is the entry point for a remote subprogram call.

Despite this standardization effort, a lot of things have been left up to the implementation, for example the way a distributed application is divided into partitions or where and how the various partitions are launched. In the rest of this paper, we will try to show how the annex specification and much more were implemented; for example, some of the concepts defined in CORBA (see [8]) or in RMI (see [5]) have been mapped onto corresponding features, to take the best side of every world.

2 GLADE: an implementation

GLADE (see [1], [4] and [7]) is an implementation of the distributed systems annex for GNAT. It is jointly developed by Ada Core Technologies and the ENST in Paris, France. It comes with its own implementation of System.RPC, which fulfills the requirements of the reference manual. That is, another compiler implementing correctly the Distributed Systems Annex should be usable with GLADE.

2.1 Structure of GLADE

GLADE is divided in two major parts:

GARLIC is the partition communication subsystems. It is made of:
- **System.RPC**, a compliant implementation of the package described in the Reference Manual
- **System.RPC.***, child packages of System.RPC, that provide additional services such as message passing, as allowed by the Reference Manual
- **System.Garlic** and child packages, the heart of the partition communication subsystem, which takes care of network-related system calls, concurrent requests, partition localization and launching, error handling and recovery, etc., used by System.RPC
- **System.Stream_Attributes**, a XDR implementation of standard stream attributes (see section 1.2) to adapt streams to an heterogeneous environments[2]

---

[2] GLADE 2.02 will offer a choice between XDR, CDR (see [8]) and possibly other encoding methods such as DER/ASN.1 (see [2]).

GNATDIST is the partitioning tool, responsible for:
- checking the consistency of a distributed system before building it
- calling GNAT with the appropriate parameters to build the needed stubs
- configuring the filters that will be used between different partitions
- linking the partitions with GARLIC and building the initialization sequence
- building the main program that will launch the whole distributed application on the right hosts

2.2 Compilation model

Since some subprograms can be called remotely in a distributed system, the traditional compilation model which consists of the generation of an object file from a source file cannot be applied anymore. At least two object files must be generated, one for the calling side and the other for the receiving side. This model is very close to what is done in CORBA and RMI, except that in Ada the user does not need to write extra code or use another IDL[3] (Ada is used as the IDL) to describe the signatures of the remote subprograms or objects.

Up to version 3.10, GNAT was generating two files (called stubs files) containing legal Ada code, one for the calling stubs, one for the receiving stubs. These stubs files had to be compiled to produce object files. However, this model, despite its simplicity and ease of use, was not suitable for all the constructs; some complex structures could not be expressed in legal Ada without using lots of unreadable code. As of version 3.11, GNAT generates object files directly thus decreasing the processing time since only one pass is necessary whereas two passes were required in the past. The user interested in reading the content of the stubs can still use the appropriate compiler flags to see the expanded re-generated Ada-like tree.

3 Implementing remote calls

3.1 General case

Let's consider a function Add with the following profile:

function Add (X, Y : Integer) **return** Integer;

We will examine what needs to be done to perform this function call, in both non-distributed and distributed cases.

Non-distributed case The various steps performed by the executable when this function is called in the non-distributed case are listed below:

---

[3] Interface Definition Language

1. Put X on the stack[4]
2. Put Y on the stack
3. Call function Add
4. Read the return value from a dedicated hardware register

If an exception has been raised in the function's body, then the execution will never reach point 4, but will be redirected onto the exception handler instead.

Distributed case: caller point of view The calling stubs will contain some code looking like the following:

1. Look for the partition containing function Add and put the RPC_Receiver corresponding to the package containing Add in the stream
2. Put the index of the function Add in a stream
3. Put X in the stream
4. Put Y in the stream
5. Send the stream to the receiving partition
6. Get the result stream back
7. Get the exception occurrence from the result stream
8. If it is not Null_Occurrence, then re-raise the exception occurrence
9. Read the result (sum of X and Y) from the result stream, it is the return value of the function

Distributed case: receiver point of view The receiving stubs will include:

1. Get the RPC_Receiver from the stream, and jump to the corresponding dispatching procedure (which will execute stages 2 to 5 below)
2. Get the function index from the stream
3. This function takes two integers, so read two integers X and Y from the stream
4. Call the Add function (which is present on the current partition) with parameters X and Y
5. If an exception occurred, put the exception occurrence into the result stream and send it back; otherwise, put Null_Occurrence then the return value in the result stream and send it back

These steps are not performed by the environment task of the receiving side. Instead, a new task called "anonymous task" is created to serve the request. That way, a potentially unlimited number of requests can be handled at the same time.

---

[4] "stack" is a general term here, since on some architectures the first parameters are passed in registers that emulate a stack.

This scheme shows that the Ada model has been completely preserved. If an exception is raised during the execution of Add, then it is re-raised in the calling partition, thus interrupting the right flow of control. Also, the user does not have to take care of putting the parameters with the correct format in the stream, because the compiler itself will generate the right sequence using its knowledge of argument and return types.

While this example looks trivial, it may become much more complicated when unconstrained or tagged objects are considered. Also, "out" and "in out" parameters must be handled as if they were return values, possibly with an additional size or discriminant constraint. For these values, it is necessary to transmit the bounds of the objects while performing the call, so that the callee may check that it does not try to write past the bounds of an array for example. Also, the fact that an object that has discriminants is constrained or not must be given to the callee before it can process the request.

3.2 Asynchronous remote procedure calls

Asynchronous procedures are implemented in a straightforward way: after having put the parameters in the stream and sent the request, the caller does not wait for the result stream. The receiver will throw away any exception raised during the execution of the procedure, and will never send any stream back to the caller.

3.3 Handling remote abortion

The Ada Reference Manual states that if a construct containing a remote subprogram call is aborted, whether the processing is also aborted on the receiver end or not is implementation-defined. If we consider large applications with heavy computations, it seems desirable to abort a computation as soon as we know that its result will not be used because the caller has been aborted. For this reason, we chose to implement remote job abortion to release the CPU when possible.

To do this, GLADE associates a *request id* with every non-asynchronous remote call. This identifier is bound to the request and transmitted to the receiver side along with the request itself. Also, a controlled object is declared in GLADE within the scope of the call. If the caller is aborted, the *Finalization* procedure of the controlled object will be executed anyway, thus suspending the abortion for the time of the finalization. Then this finalization subprogram sends an abortion request to the receiver partition with the right request id. Upon reception of this abortion command, the receiver side aborts the task that was bound to this request, thus achieving the propagation of the abortion undergone by the caller to the receiver.

4 Implementing distributed objects

Because we consider distributed objects as being a very important feature for building distributed systems, we have tried to make them as efficient as possible in GNAT. One strong requirement was to avoid any overhead for objects located on the partition on which the call is made.

In order to achieve this, GNAT does not use a wrapper for all objects, but instead create a new derived object type to designate remote objects. Also, GNAT creates a wrapper for all primitive operations of the original type, hence catching all attempts to use the object[5].

```
type Remote is new Object with record
    Partition : System.RPC.Partition_Id;
    Receiver  : System.RPC.RPC_Receiver;
    Addr      : System.Address;
end record
procedure Prim (Object : access Remote);
```

The three fields respectively correspond to the partition on which the object has been created, the address of the subprogram which will handle the incoming remote calls to the object's primitive operations, and the address of the object on its own partition. Note that what is presented here is only a functional equivalence. In fact an access discriminant on such a structure is added to the object.

Read and Write attributes for the remote access to class-wide type are also defined by the compiler. The Write attribute transmits the Partition, Receiver and Addr fields of the structure (if the object is local, these fields are built dynamically at run time, otherwise they are copied from the existing ones). The Read attribute works the other way around: it reads the three fields, and check the local partition ID against the object's one. If they match, then the Addr field is used and a pointer on the real local object is returned. If they don't, then a new object containing these fields is built and returned.

5 Efficiency concerns

5.1 Anonymous tasks

In section 3.1, we wrote that anonymous tasks were created to handle incoming calls in order to serve several requests at the same time. However, this mechanism was too costly to be used as-is, and has been reworked in order to avoid dynamic creation of tasks as much as possible.

In the new model, the concept of *task pool* has been introduced. Some tasks (the exact number can be set in the configuration file) are created by a low-priority background task and put themselves in a global task pool. Whenever a request arrives, a task is extracted from the pool and assigned to this request. When the request terminates, the task inserts itself back into the pool and waits for another job.

---

[5] Since the object is of a tagged limited private type, the only possibility to access the object's fields is to call a primitive operation on this object.

If the number of tasks is insufficient to handle all the incoming requests, then more tasks will be dynamically created and destroyed. For this reason, it is important to have an idea of how many incoming requests may occur at the same time; a number too high will require memory space that could be used for something else, while too low a number may cause frequent dynamic task allocation.

5.2 Storage handling

Up to GLADE 1.03, all the structures used for communicating were created on the stack, as local variables. This became a problem when some users needed to transmit very large arrays which caused repetitive (and fatal) stack overflows.

The safe and low computation cost method adopted in GLADE 2.01 is to dynamically allocate the arrays of bytes needed to communicate using a special storage pool. This storage pool reserves a fixed number of data structures of a fixed size at elaboration time. Whenever an array of byte is needed, the allocator corresponding to this storage pool gets called automatically and first tries to return a pre-allocated block if the required size is not greater than the pre-allocated size, thus avoiding "real" dynamic allocation.

When such a pointer gets freed, the deallocator corresponding to the storage pool is called and if a pre-allocated block had been used, it returns to the list of free block without calling the system deallocation routine. With these constructs, dynamic memory allocations occur only at elaboration time, when no more pre-allocated blocks are available or when a request for a huge block is made, thus reducing dramatically the costs of heap allocation while guaranteeing the safety of the application by not using the stack for potentially huge allocations anymore.

5.3 Name server, location server and communication

GLADE uses two different services to locate partitions on the network:

1. A name server that maps the package name on a partition id and checks for the coherence of the versions of the various packages used in the distributed application (using a checksum-based mechanism)
2. A location server that maps the partition id onto a host

These services are separated because they will be independent in the future; in our fault-tolerant model, partitions will be replicated and the location server will get new locations for the new replicas, while dead partitions will be removed from its database. However, the distributed application structure will not change and the data on the name server will not be modified.

To avoid frequent useless exchanges between those two servers and other partitions, the results returned by these servers are cached onto each partition. If a location becomes unavailable, then the location server will either send an invalidation request to any partition that knows anything about the dead partition, or wait until the partitions ask for the new location of the dead partition.

Once a partition knows where another partition is located, it connects directly to it using a common protocol such as TCP. This direct connection model implies that there is no need to transmit partition information along with each request, unlike IIOP (see [8]), because the link is dedicated to a pair of partitions. Also, no forwarding needs to be done since the different partitions can talk together directly. Also, the user does not need to know what a name server or a location server is since everything is done in a transparent way by the compiler and the run time libraries.

6 Configuring the system

As explained in section 1.6, the Reference Manual does not describe how a distributed application should be configured; this feature is implementation-dependent. For this purpose, we have designed a tool called GNATDIST and its associated configuration language to ease the build of a distributed application (see [3] for an exhaustive description of GNATDIST functionalities).

The configuration language looks like regular Ada declarations and is intuitive for the Ada programmer. It is parsed and analyzed by GNATDIST which then builds various executables (one executable for each partition) after producing Ada packages enabling the features that have been selected by the user in the configuration file. Since GNATDIST reuses some sources from GNAT, it can access the information usually available only to the binder. In particular, it can compute the closure of the main unit and then explore the list of Remote_Call_Inte face packages to check that they have been assigned to exactly one partition, as required by Ada semantics, and that child Remote_Call_Interface packages belong to the same partition as their parent.

GNATDIST provides the user with a way of using specific services, such as filters (see [9]) or alternate termination modes. For example, it is possible to specify that an encryption filter will be used between every partition, that a compression filter will be used to communicate to one particular partition located at the end of a slow link, and that an authentication filter will be used between two important partitions of the distributed application.

Also, GNATDIST tries to minimize the number of recompilations during the development cycle by using a private subdirectory to store the stubs object files and handles the coherency of this cache. Partial compilations are also possible by specifying the name of the partitions to be compiled on the command-line.

7 Work in progress and future work

We are continuing to implement new features in GNAT and GLADE and to improve the efficiency of the system. Amongst other topics of research, we can cite (by decreasing order of importance):

- Fault tolerance partition communication subsystem; this system will support crash faults as well as byzantine failures (failures that can result in a partition

sending a wrong result, opposed to no result at all for crash faults) using replication and voting mechanisms
- Enhanced distributed debugging facilities
- Very light run-time for client-only partitions, without any tasking involved
- Statistical and optimization tool to help in placing partitions while respecting the constraints given by the user.
- Graphical partitioning tool
- Distributed compilation in GNATDIST.

8   Contact and software availability

- The authors can be reached using electronic mail in ENST at addresses `Laurent.Pautet@inf.enst.fr` and `Samuel.Tardieu@inf.enst.fr`
- GNAT and GLADE are both free software and can be obtained via anonymous FTP respectively at
  `ftp://cs.nyu.edu/pub/gnat/` and `ftp://cs.nyu.edu/pub/gnat/glade/`
- Related tools and components for GLADE and network programming in general are available for free at `http://www-inf.enst.fr/ANC/`
- Ada Core Technologies is selling support contracts for both GNAT and GLADE.
  You can get more information on this support at `http://www.gnat.com/`

References

[1] Anthony Gargaro, Yvon Kermarrec, Laurent Pautet, and Samuel Tardieu. PARIS: Partitionned Ada for Remotely Invoked Services. In *Proceedings of Ada-Europe'95*, Frankfurt, Germany, March 1995.

[2] JTC 1/SC 33. *Specification of Abstract Syntax Notation One (ASN.1)*. 1990. ISO 8824:1990.

[3] Yvon Kermarrec, Laurent Nana, and Laurent Pautet. Gnatdist: a configuration language for distributed ada 95 applications. In *Proceedings of Tri-Ada'96*, Philadelphia, Pennsylvania, 1996.

[4] Yvon Kermarrec, Laurent Pautet, and Samuel Tardieu. GARLIC: Generic Ada Reusable Library for Interpartition Communication. In *Proceedings of the Tri Ada conference*, Anaheim, California, 1995. ACM.

[5] Sun Microsystems. *Remote Method Invocation – Documentation*.

[6] Sun Microsystems. *xdr – library routines for external data representation*.

[7] Daniel Neri, Laurent Pautet, and Samuel Tardieu. Debugging distributed applications with replay capabilities. In *Proceedings of Tri-Ada'97*, Saint-Louis, Missouri, 1997.

[8] OMG TC Document 97-09-01. The Common Object Request Broker: Architecture and Specification Revision 2.1. September 1997.

[9] Laurent Pautet and Thomas Wolf. Transparent filtering of streams in GLADE. In *Proceedings of Tri-Ada'97*, Saint-Louis, Missouri, 1997.

[10] Claude E. Shannon and Warren Weaver. *The Mathematical Theory of Communication*. University of Illinois Press, 1963.

[11] Richard W Stevens. UNIX *Network Programming*. Prentice Hall, 1990.

[12] Tucker Taft. *Ada 95 Reference Manual: Language and Standard Libraries*. February 1995. ISO/IEC/ANSI 8652:1995.

Integrating Groups and Transactions: A Fault-Tolerant Extension of Ada*

Marta Patiño-Martínez, Ricardo Jiménez-Peris and Sergio Arévalo

Universidad Politécnica de Madrid, Facultad de Informática,
28660 Boadilla del Monte, Madrid, Spain

Abstract. We present Transactional Drago a language that implements *Group Transactions*, a new transaction model we have developed. This model integrates the group communication paradigm with the nested transaction model. Transactional Drago extends Drago, a distributed fault-tolerant extension of Ada implementing the group paradigm. In this paper we describe the linguistic features added to Drago to support group transactions and how they are integrated with the existing mechanisms in Drago, particularly with group communication.

1 Introduction

Transactions [4] are a mechanism to provide data consistency in the presence of concurrent activities and system failures. Transaction systems were first developed for banking applications, but today they are used in many areas such as communications, finance, flight reservations systems, manufacturing, ...

Transactions have four properties (known as ACID properties) that are useful for constructing reliable distributed applications:

1. Atomicity guarantees that the effect of the transaction is all or nothing.
2. Consistency ensures a correct transformation of the state.
3. Isolation (serializability) ensures that other transactions will not interfere.
4. Durability ensures that once a transaction has finished its effect will remain.

To deal with isolation, concurrency control mechanisms are used, while to preserve atomicity and durability recovery mechanisms are employed.

Transactions that involve several servers located in different nodes in the network are called distributed transactions. Commit protocols are used to ensure the atomicity of a distributed transaction.

Clients and servers in a transaction traditionally interact via remote procedure call (RPC) [8, 16]. RPCs are executed as subtransactions of the client transaction. Thus, transactions can be nested. Nested transactions [10] are useful for

---

* This work was partially supported by the Spanish Research Council, CICYT, under grant TIC94-C02-01.

two reasons: they allow additional concurrency within a transaction (particularly in distributed systems) by running concurrently nested subtransactions and the failure of a subtransaction does not force the parent transaction to fail, providing in this manner a kind of firewall against failures. However, the concurrency allowed inside a transaction is very limited, as concurrent subtransactions cannot cooperate due to the isolation property. There are several languages [8] and systems [3, 16] that implement the nested transaction model providing transactions as high level primitives. In [13] it is proposed an Ada implementation of atomic actions. An ad-hoc Ada implementation of transactions for air-traffic control systems is presented in [17].

On the other hand, process groups, a collection of processes, have been used to perform a distributed computation. Process groups and the group communication model, in particular Causally and Totally Ordered Communication (CATOCS) have also been proposed as an adequate way to build reliable distributed applications [2] such as cooperative and replicated ones. Causal and total ordering ensures that all the messages sent to a group are delivered in the same order to all the group agents, preserving its causal order. This kind of communication is required for a variety of applications like management of replicated data, observation of a distributed system, multimedia systems, mobile computing environments and teleconferencing. The *Isis* toolkit [2] provides a collection of libraries to manage process groups that communicate using CATOCS primitives.

According to [11] a current important topic of research is the integration of these two models, i.e., group communication and transactions. [14] studies the relationship between group communication primitives and the isolation property of transactions. Our opinion is that both models are complementary and a system offering both mechanisms, in an orthogonal way, will improve the availability, throughput and reliability of the system. As a result, our approach is to integrate both models.

We have developed a new transaction model, *Group Transactions* that integrates both approaches. We have followed a linguistic approach starting from *Drago* [9] a group oriented fault-tolerant distributed language. Transactional mechanisms have been incorporated in a new version of the language called *Transactional Drago*.

Our goal is to introduce as few new mechanisms as possible, with the simplest semantics. In this extension, there will be Drago groups (non-transactional ones) and transactional groups (providing atomic services). We are interested in the following goals:

1. The behavior of transactional groups should be as close as possible to non-transactional ones.
2. The interaction with transactional groups must be atomic, so its effect will be all or nothing.
3. Due to uniformity reasons (with Drago), the interaction with transactional groups should be based on rendezvous as non-transactional groups do.
4. Transactional and non-transactional boundaries must be well defined.

5. Non-transactional groups will be able to interact with transactional groups from a transaction.
6. Non-transactional applications must be as efficient as they were previous to the introduction of transactions.

In the next section, we present Drago. In Sect. 3, our model of transactions, *Group Transactions*, is introduced. Section 4 presents *Transactional Drago*, the extension of Drago (and thus of Ada) that implements the Group Transaction model. Some details on the implementation of Transactional Drago are presented in Sect. 5. Finally, we present our conclusions.

2   Drago

Drago [9] is a language to program fault-tolerant distributed applications that supports the group paradigm. It has been implemented as an extension of Ada. Drago provides two group abstractions: replicated groups and cooperative groups. Groups are composed out of *agents* that are the distribution unit of Drago. Group communication in Drago is based on the client-server model. Groups interact using group remote entry calls (GREC).

Replicated groups provide fault tolerance by means of modular redundancy (via a replicated set of deterministic replicas), that is, Drago supports the active replication model [15]. They behave as a single agent tolerating failures of its agents in a transparent way both in front of clients and servers. For this reason, this kind of group returns (sends) a unique answer (request) to the client (server), as all the answers (requests) will be the same.

Cooperative groups allow programmers to express parallelism writing distributed applications and so increase throughput. In these applications agents of a group cooperate to achieve a common goal. A cooperative group can reduce the latency of the service, as well as tolerate partial failures, working in a degraded mode. When a service is requested to a cooperative group, the result is the set of answers of all its agents.

The group specification provides the common interface of all the agents of a group. It contains declarations of constants, types and remotely callable operations (entries), which must be implemented inside every agent of the group. Entries correspond to the services provided by the group.

There are two sections within the group entry specification. The first section is public (intergroup declaration) and it is used by clients of the group. The second one is only visible to the agents of the group (intragroup declaration) and it is only applicable to cooperative groups. Agents of a cooperative group interact by means of calling intragroup entries.

Agents have an internal state, not accessible from outside, and a flow of control; they are similar to Ada tasks. When an agent calls one of the entries specified in a group by means of a GREC, the call is multicasted to all the agents of the target group. It is a natural extension of remote entry calls. GRECs implemented in Drago [5] are atomic, total and causally ordered, and uniform. Uniformity ensures that if a message is delivered to any agent of the group (even if it dies immediately after), it will be delivered to all live agents. Once all (live) agents finish the service requested by the GREC, the result and control is returned to the client.

3 Group Transactions

Our model is an integration of the group communication and transaction paradigms, that extends the nested transaction model [10] by means of *transactional cooperative and transactional replicated groups* that provide atomic services.

The integration of the group and transaction models in a single model has several advantages:

1. It improves transaction latency, because distributed servers may run concurrently, probably cooperating, to provide a transactional service.
2. Available transactions. Our integration allows the replication of both clients and servers, that is, a transaction can be initiated by a replicated group. This increases the availability of the transaction because it will survive node failures.
3. Isolation of a sequence of group calls. A set of group calls (total and causally ordered operations) can be serialized with respect to other sequence of operations encapsulating them within a transaction.
4. Failure atomicity of a sequence of group calls. It is possible to undo the effect of a whole set of operations in case some kind of exception arises.
5. Transactions ease recovering from a network partition of a group during a client/server interaction.

One of the main features of our model is that it allows concurrency within a transaction without starting concurrent subtransactions. This *intra-transactional concurrency* allows decreasing the latency of transactions. Some database management systems add intra-transaction concurrency, but it is limited to execute in parallel fragments of a query and it is imposed by the compiler, it cannot be expressed at application level. We present two kinds of intra-transactional concurrency:

1. *Multi-thread transactions.* A transaction can have several threads, that is, several (concurrent) flows of execution can act on the behalf of a transaction. This allows taking advantage of multiprocessor and multiprograming capabilities.
2. *Multi-process transactions.* A transactional service requested to a cooperative group will be provided by all the agents of the group. This service is executed as a single multi-process (distributed) subtransaction of the client transaction. Due to all the agents of a group participate in the transaction, they will be able to cooperate using intragroup communication or calling other groups.

We have called *fingers*[1] the flows of execution of a transaction, concurrent or distributed. Fingers of the same transaction are called *sibling fingers*. Sibling

---

[1] This name was inspired by a tale of the Asimov's book "I robot".

fingers are not concurrent subtransactions, but part of the same transaction (they share the transaction identifier). A finger can initiate a subtransaction anytime; that subtransaction will be atomic with respect to its sibling fingers. A transaction ends when all its fingers have finished.

Because a transaction can be made up of several fingers, if a finger initiates a subtransaction, its sibling fingers will continue running. In this sense, the parent transaction and a child of it will be running concurrently, unlike in the nested transaction model, where a parent transaction with concurrent children subtransactions will be blocked waiting for the end of its children.

Group transactions are serialized in the traditional way. The final effect of the concurrent execution of two transactions must be the same as if they were executed sequentially in any order; as if all the fingers of the transaction serialized in the first place were executed first and then all the fingers of the other transaction.

In the traditional transaction model, transactions are automatically serialized; concurrency control among transactions is implicit and based on data, and there is no other concurrency than the concurrent execution of different transactions. On the other hand, in a concurrent/distributed language concurrency control is explicit, but there are no transactions. However, in our model we have to deal with both kinds of concurrency control: transactions must be serialized (**inter-transactional concurrency control**) and threads and processes of groups within transactions (i.e. sibling fingers) must synchronize and communicate among them (**intra-transactional concurrency control**). One of the difficulties to be solved is how to prevent interference between both types of concurrency control, keeping inter-transactional concurrency control implicit and intra-transactional concurrency control explicit.

There is an additional kind of synchronization to take into account: **client and server transactions synchronization** [1]. Client and server transactions usually synchronize using RPC. That is, the client transaction triggers the server subtransaction and waits for its end. A thread is created in the server to provide the requested service. This thread executes the server subtransaction and when the service finishes, it commits and returns the results to the client. Then, the client continues its execution. This type of synchronization between client and server transactions is also known as single-request [18]. It must be noticed that in this case the synchronization is explicit, but it is not the same than intra-transactional synchronization due to the synchronization is between two different transactions (one is the parent of the other). Client and server transactions synchronization can also be conversational [18], that is the client transaction issues a set of requests to the server and then decides whether to commit or abort that transaction. During the conversation control changes between client and server, each time the client transaction issues a request, the server transaction is responsible for generating an answer. Conversational synchronization is the one used in our model.

Replication is traditionally used to provide highly available data. In our model, replicated groups not only provide highly available data, but also highly available transactions. A transaction can be initiated in a replicated group; the failure of a process of the group does not abort that transaction. Replicated groups (transactional or not) can also act a servers, providing available services in spite of node failures.

4 Transactional Drago

Transactional Drago is the extension of Drago, and thus of Ada, that supports the Group Transaction model incorporating new linguistic features.

4.1 Transactional Groups

Transactional Drago provides two new kinds of groups: *transactional cooperative groups* and *transactional replicated groups*. Both kinds of groups provide atomic services to clients. Their services must be called within a transaction and they can only call to other transactional groups in order to keep the service atomic. The syntax of these agents is similar to their corresponding non-transactional agents. To distinguish them, the specification and body of transactional groups are prefixed with the word **transactional**.

Data declared in transactional agents are atomic. Locks are used to perform inter-transactional concurrency control. Locking is automatically (implicitly) performed by the system. Before a datum is used in a transaction, a lock is automatically acquired in the appropriate mode (read, write). The usual locking rules apply: multiple readers are allowed, but readers exclude writers and writers exclude writers and readers. Strict two-phase locking is applied to prevent cascading aborts. Persistency is necessary to achieve permanence of effect of transactions. Global data (the outermost scope) of an agent can be persistent if its declaration is prefixed with **persistent**. In this case data are backed-up in non-volatile memory, surviving node failures.

The code of a transactional agent is written as if there were a single client, while the code of non-transactional agents is organized to deal with several clients. Transactional agents are passive in the sense that their execution does not start until a client makes a request (see Sect. 4.4).

4.2 Transactions

Any agent (transactional or not) can initiate a transaction using the predefined statement **begin transaction/end transaction** (*transactional block*). All the code comprised within that statement will be executed as a transaction. A transactional block can be used in any place where a block statement can be placed. It has the same structure that the block statement in Ada, that is, it has a declaration part and some statements and also creates a new scope. Calls to other groups within a transaction are restricted to transactional groups, otherwise isolation of transactions could not be guaranteed.

Data declared inside a transaction are atomic (failure atomicity) and have concurrency control. In the declaration section there can be tasks; they will be part of the transaction (sibling fingers) and they will synchronize (intra-transactional concurrency control) via Ada synchronization mechanisms (e.g. rendezvous). The transaction will finish when all its fingers have finished. As it was mentioned in Sect. 3 the effect of serializing two transactions is equivalent to execute all the fingers of one transaction first, and then the ones of the other transaction.

4.3 Nested Transactions

Top level transactions are those that are not enclosed by another transaction. They ware always initiated by agents of non-transactional groups, because transactional groups must be called within a transaction. *Nested transactions* (subtransactions) are initiated within another transaction. There are several ways to achieve transaction nesting in Transactional Drago:

1. Transactional blocks can be nested, that is, there can be new transactional blocks within a transactional block, in which case the inner transaction will be a subtransaction of the enclosing (parent) transaction.
2. Any task declared inside a transaction can also use the begin/end transaction statement, starting a new subtransaction of the enclosing transaction. This subtransaction will be executed concurrently with the sibling fingers of its parent transaction.
3. When a transaction issues a call to a transactional group a new subtransaction is created. Those subtransactions, *remote subtransactions*, are created implicitly (there is no begin/end transaction statement) and dynamically, and they are executed in a different group.

4.4 Remote Transactions and Client-Server Transaction Synchronization

Agents of a non-transactional group deal with calls from different clients. In transactional groups it is not possible to deal with different clients (transactions) in a single thread because if there is no concurrency control inside an agent of a transactional group, serialization could not be guaranteed[2]. If there is concurrency control, deadlocks would be very likely to happen [12]. So, the main thread of the agent should deal with a single client transaction. If this approach is used, an agent will only serve a client at a time, reducing concurrency. In order to allow different transactions to execute concurrently in an agent, a thread will be created in each agent of the group the first time a client transaction calls to that group. These threads will execute concurrently an instance of the code of the corresponding agent and will only deal with calls of its associated client transaction (see Fig. 1). This is a natural extension of RPC to

---

[2] After accepting a call from a client transaction the thread should delay calls from other transactions until the first transaction finishes.

rendezvous; if there were a single call to that group on behalf of a transaction, it would be equivalent to RPC. When there are more calls, rendezvous helps servers (transactional groups) to impose a protocol of calls to their clients.

Threads created in the agents of a group on behalf of a transaction are *distributed sibling fingers* of the client transaction (see transaction T1 in Fig. 1).

Each **accept** statement in the agents of a transactional group is considered a distributed subtransaction of the client transaction that is executed concurrently by all the agents of the group (see transaction T1.1 in Fig. 1). After finishing that sub-subtransaction, data can be communicated to its parent (client transaction) through the parameters of rendezvous. If an accept subtransaction aborts, client and server fingers can cooperate to prevent the propagation of the abort, thus tolerating partial failures.

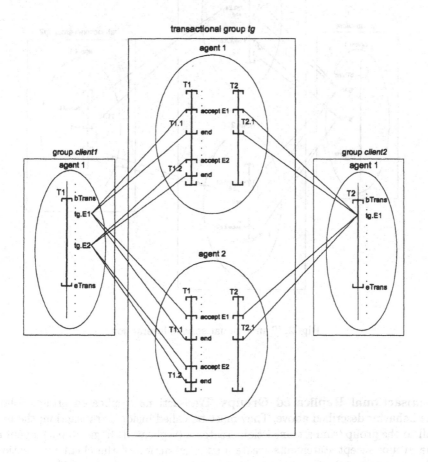

Fig. 1. Two clients interacting with a transactional server

The code of accepts are implicit transactional blocks in the sense that they do not have a begin/end transaction statement. They start a new subtransaction and have declarative and statements parts. So, there can be tasks declared inside of an accept statement, in that case, these tasks will be sibling fingers of the accept subtransaction.

Any agent of a transactional group can initiate new subtransactions: explicitly, using the begin/end transaction statement, or implicitly, calling another transactional group within the accept statement (see Fig. 2).

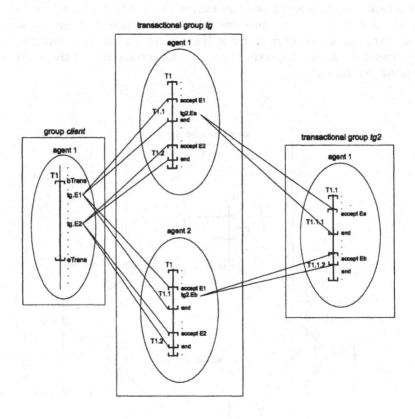

Fig. 2. Transactional servers interaction

Transactional Replicated Groups Transactional replicated groups follow the behavior described above. They must be called inside a transaction; the first call to the group from a transaction creates a (replicated) finger in each agent of the group; accept statements create a subtransaction of the client transaction. They can initiate new subtransactions explicitly or implicitly inside an accept statement. In either of those cases the group behaves as if there were a single agent. The crash of an agent does not abort running transactions; only crashes of all agents of a group will abort running transactions, what increases transaction availability. Despite the creation of a thread per transaction replica consistency is guaranteed by a deterministic scheduling.

Transactional Cooperative Groups When the group is called from within a transaction for the first time sibling fingers of the agents are created. There will be at least one of those fingers per agent (executing the code of that agent) and possibly additional ones corresponding to tasks declared in the agents of the group.

Accepts of cooperative groups create a distributed subtransaction of the client transaction, that subtransaction is the same transaction for all the sibling fingers executing the accept statement.

Intragroup communication is allowed when all the fingers are in the same (sub)transaction; otherwise there would be information smuggling between subtransactions loosing serializability.

Any sibling finger can also initiate new subtransactions explicitly or implicitly. If two or more fingers initiate explicitly subtransactions, they will be different subtransactions. But if the subtransaction is created implicitly (calling another transactional group within an accept) all the sibling fingers of that finger that are executing the same accept statement can call to that group and they will share the new subtransaction (see Fig. 2). The same situation happens when a non-transactional client starts a transaction explicitly with several fingers. If two or more of those fingers call a transactional group, they will be attended by the same set of sibling fingers at the server, as they act on behalf of the same transaction. Failure of an agent of a cooperative group causes the abortion of all active transactions in the group, what helps to handle partitions.

4.5 Aborts and Exceptions

Transaction aborts have been integrated with the Ada exception mechanism. Transaction implicit aborts (crashes, deadlocks, logging problems, ...) are propagated as the predefined exception, *Transaction_Abort_Error*, and they can be handled like any other exception. Explicit aborts are achieved by raising an exception. An unhandled exception inside a transaction forces the abortion of the enclosing transaction (undoing its effects) and the propagation of the exception outside of the transaction.

If there is an unhandled exception within the accept statement, the accept subtransaction will be aborted (undoing its effects) and the exception will be propagated to the client finger and to the ones that executed the accept statement, like Ada tasks. If all the fingers handle that exception, the client transaction will not be aborted, otherwise it will.

5 Implementation of Transactional Drago

Drago code is translated into Ada via a preprocessor [9]. We have extended the Drago preprocessor to contemplate Transactional Drago extensions. In Transactional Drago a transactional agent is translated into an Ada main program which executes at its outermost level a main task that is in charge of creating tasks for new transactions and forwarding requests to them. These tasks have the same interface and behavior than their corresponding transactional agents.

As in Drago and Ada 95 protected objects, there is a two-level scheme for entry calls. There is an external queue where stable[3] messages are total and causally ordered. Additionally, there is an internal queue per entry and active transaction in the agent. The main task of a transactional agent keeps a table with active transactions and their associated tasks (server transaction). Each time a task is ready to accept a message, it takes a message from the internal entry queue of its transaction. If the queue is empty then messages are extracted from the external queue and queued in their corresponding internal entry queue. Certain messages require an extra work; when the first message from a client transaction is extracted, a new server transaction task must be created to serve the new client.

6 Conclusions

We have presented Transactional Drago, an Ada extension that integrates the group and transaction models. With this integration we provide three dependable services proposed in the literature: data consistency (transactions and transactional groups), data availability (transactional replicated groups) and process availability (replicated groups). Furthermore, the integration of both models has enabled us to obtain additional benefits such as improving the transaction performance (transactional cooperative groups) and availability (transactional replicated groups). In addition, transactions provide a good framework to handle group partitions.

We have shown how Group Transactions can be introduced in Drago with a small set of new mechanisms. In addition, we have integrated in a natural way the Ada exception mechanism with the abort mechanism of transactions. Despite the details of the model, the semantics is as simple as transaction and multicast semantics.

Currently, a prototype of the system is already running. It consists of a preprocessor (an extension of the Drago preprocessor) that generates code that uses a library implementing our model, *TransLib*. We have used alex, ayacc, gnat, linux and standard sockets in our prototype. We plan to provide support to access files and databases within Transactional Drago programs.

---

[3] Stable messages are those that have been received in all the destination nodes, and there is no other message, still non-received, that may be before it.

7 Acknowledgments

We wish to thank to Ángel Álvarez, Mikel Larrea and the members of the Distributed Systems Seminar (GSOD) at UPM for their help and comments.

References

1. N. S. Barghouti and G. E. Kaiser: Concurrency Control in Advanced Distributed Database Applications. ACM Computing Surveys, 23(3), Sep. 1991, 269–317
2. K. P. Birman and R. van Renesse: *Reliable Distributed Computing with Isis Toolkit.* IEEE Computer Society Press, 1994.
3. J.L. Eppinger, L.B. Mummert, and A.Z. Spector: *Camelot and Avalon.* Morgan Kaufmann Publishers, 1991
4. J. Gray. *Operating Systems: An Advanced Course.* LNCS 60. Springer, 1978, 393–481
5. F. Guerra, S. Arévalo, Á. Álvarez, and J. Miranda. A Distributed Consensus Protocol with a Coordinator. In *ICDDS'93.* Elsevier, Sept. 1993, 85–96
6. F. Guerra, J. Miranda, Á. Álvarez, and S. Arévalo. An Ada Library to Program Fault-Tolerant Distributed Applications. In *Ada-Europe'97*, LNCS 1251. Springer, 230–243
7. L. Lamport. Time, Clocks and the Ordering of Events in a Distributed System. *CACM*, 21(7), Jul. 1978, 558–565
8. B. Liskov. Distributed Programming in Argus. *CACM*, 31(3), Mar. 1988, 300–312
9. J. Miranda, Á. Álvarez, S. Arévalo, and F. Guerra. Drago: An Ada Extension to Program Fault-tolerant Distributed Applications. In *Ada-Europe'96*, LNCS 1088. Springer, 235–246
10. J. E. Moss. *Nested Transactions: An Approach to Reliable Distributed Computing.* PhD thesis, MIT, 1981.
11. G. D. Parrington, S. K. Shrivastava, S. M. Wheater, and M. C. Little. The Design and Implementation of Arjuna. TR-65, BROADCAST Project, Oct. 1994.
12. M. Patiño, R. Jiménez, and S. Arévalo. Synchronizing Group Transactions with Rendezvous in a Distributed Ada Environment. In *ACM Symposium on Applied Computing.* ACM Press, 1998.
13. A. Romanovsky, S.E. Mitchell, and A.J. Wellings. On Programming Atomic Actions in Ada 95. In *Ada-Europe'97*, LNCS 1251. Springer, 254–265
14. A. Schiper and M. Raynal. From Group Communication to Transactions in Distributed Systems. *CACM*, 39(4), 1996, 84–87
15. F. B. Schneider. Implementing Fault-Tolerant Services Using the State Machine Approach: A Tutorial. *ACM Computing Surveys*, 22(4), 1990, 299–319
16. S. K. Shrivastava, G. N. Dixon, and G. D. Parrington. An Overview of Arjuna: A Programming System for Reliable Distributed Computing. *IEEE Software*, 8(1), Jan. 1991, 63–73
17. C. J. Thompson and V. Celier. DVM: An Object-Oriented Framework for Building Large Distributed Ada Systems. In *TriAda Conference.* ACM Press, 1995.
18. B. Walter. Nested Transactions with Multiple Commit Points: An Approach to the Structuring of Advanced Database Applications. In VLDB'84, 161–171

Implementing and Using Execution Time Clocks in Ada Hard Real-Time Applications

By: M. González Harbour, M. Aldea Rivas, J.J. Gutiérrez García,
and J.C. Palencia Gutiérrez

Departamento de Electrónica y Computadores
Universidad de Cantabria
39005 - Santander
SPAIN
email: {mgh, aldeam, gutierjj, palencij}@ctr.unican.es
phone: +34 42 201483 - fax: +34 42 201402

Abstract[1]. Off-line analysis techniques for hard real-time systems are all based on the assumption that we can estimate the worst-case execution time of the different tasks executing in the system. In the traditional cyclic-executive schedulers, execution time limits were enforced for each task by the scheduler. Unfortunately, in concurrent hard real-time systems such as those using the tasking model defined in Ada, no bound on the execution time of tasks is enforced, which may result in a system timing malfunction not detected by the analysis techniques. In this paper we explore the implementation of execution time clocks within the task scheduler, and we describe methods to detect execution time overruns in the application, and to limit their effects. We also discuss the use of execution time clocks to enhance the performance of sporadic server schedulers implemented at the application level.

Keywords: Scheduling, Hard Real-Time, Ada 95, Execution Time, Sporadic Server

1 Introduction

All the hard real-time analysis techniques used to get off-line guarantees on the schedulability of the system, such as Rate Monotonic Analysis (RMA)[5][1], rely on the estimation of the worst-case execution times of the different tasks and actions that execute in the system. Although there are techniques to measure or calculate these execution times [9][10], this is always a difficult task because of the unpredictability of the different execution paths within the program. Today's computer architectures with superscalar processors [11] and caches [8] make the prediction of execution times even more difficult, specially in the context of concurrent programs in which cache misses are frequent after interrupt service routines or context switches. If the worst-case execution time is underestimated, severe timing errors may occur, causing the system to fail. These faults are not always detectable during testing, because they may only happen under particularly improbable circumstances. Besides, an overrun of the execution time of a particular task may not cause that task to miss its deadlines, but

---

1. This work has been funded in part by the *Comisión Interministerial de Ciencia y Tecnología* of the Spanish Government under grant number TAP97-892

perhaps it will be a lower priority task the one missing them. In systems with a large number of tasks, the problem of finding the task that overrun its execution time may be practically intractable.

Traditional real time systems were built (and still are) using cyclic executive schedulers [1]. In these systems, if a particular task or routine exceeded its budgeted execution time, the system could detect the situation. Basically, whenever the minor cycle interrupt came in, it could check whether the current action had completed or not. If not, that meant an overrun. Unfortunately, in concurrent real-time systems built with multitasking preemptive schedulers, there is no equivalent method to detect and handle execution time overruns. This is the case for systems built using the Ada tasking model and the associated Real-Time Annex.

As part of the development of the real-time extensions to POSIX [3], the standard for open operating system interfaces, execution time clocks and timers have been proposed as a new extension within the POSIX.1d standards project [2]. The purpose of this extension is precisely to provide a way to measure the execution time of real-time processes and threads, and to be able to detect and handle execution time overruns. If the POSIX.1d standard is approved, real-time systems built using a concurrent threads model will have the same capabilities that are available in traditional systems based on the cyclic executive approach.

In this paper we present an implementation of the POSIX execution time clocks and timers within an implementation of threads that follows the real-time POSIX standard very closely. We have used the Florida State University (FSU) threads implementation [7] because it is free software and the sources are available. The GNAT compilation system uses threads to implement the Ada tasks, and it can work on top of FSU threads. This means that we can access the thread/task execution time clocks and timers from the Ada application.

We will use execution time timers to detect execution time overruns. We have created a software package to encapsulate the use of the low-level POSIX primitives that are needed to handle the execution time timers and associated signals. Using this package, periodic or aperiodic hard real-time tasks written in Ada 95 can detect and limit the effects of execution time overruns in various ways, that will be described here.

In this paper we also show how to improve the throughput of sporadic server schedulers built at the application level [4]. If execution time clocks are not available, the scheduler must assume that each response to an event consumed an amount of execution capacity equal to the estimated worst-case execution time. By consuming only the actual execution time used, if the variability in execution time is large a fair amount of extra execution capacity is made available to schedule new events.

The paper is organized as follows. First, in Section 2 we present the POSIX model for execution time clocks and timers and we give details about their implementation. In Section 3 we present the design of the software package CPU_Time that provides operations to detect and limit execution time overruns. We also show four schemes for using this package from real-time application tasks. In section 4 we show how to take advantage of execution time clocks to implement application-level sporadic servers. In Section 5 we discuss implementation issues and we give performance metrics that help in evaluating the overhead associated with the execution time clocks. Finally, Section 6 gives our conclusions.

2 Execution Time Clocks and Timers

2.1 The Proposed POSIX Model

The execution time clocks interface defined in the proposed standard POSIX.1d [2] is based on the POSIX.1b [3] clocks and timers interface used for normal real time clocks. The new interface creates two functions to access the execution time clock identifier of the desired process or thread, respectively: *clock_getcpuclockid*() and *pthread_getcpuclockid*(). In addition, it defines a new thread-creation attribute, called *cpu_clock_requirement*, which allows the application to enable or disable the use of the execution time clock of a thread, at the time of its creation. Once the thread is created, this attribute cannot be modified. Therefore, if we want to use CPU-time clocks for threads, we must set the *cpu_clock_requirement* attribute to the value CLOCK_REQUIRED_FOR_THREAD.

An execution time clock "id" can be used to read or set the time using the same functions *clock_gettime*() and *clock_settime*() that are used for the standard CLOCK_REALTIME clock, which measures real time. In addition, timers may be created using either the CLOCK_REALTIME or a CPU-time clock as their time base. A POSIX timer is a logical object that measures time based upon a specified time base. The timer may be armed to expire when an absolute time is reached, or when a relative interval elapses. When the expiration time has been reached, a signal is sent to the process, to notify the timer expiration. The timer can be rearmed or disarmed at any time. In addition, it is possible to program the timer so that it expires periodically, after the first expiration.

If a timer is created using a CPU-time clock of a particular thread, and a relative expiration time is given, it can be used to notify that a certain budget of execution time has elapsed, for that thread. If the timer is armed each time a thread is activated, and the relative expiration time is set to the thread's estimated worst-case execution time (plus some small amount to take into account the limited resolution and precision of the CPU-time clock), then the timer will only expire if the thread suffers an execution time overrun.

2.2 Implementation Details

The implementation of CPU time clocks and timers within the FSU threads requires on the one hand modification of the data structure that defines each thread, the thread control block, and on the other hand modifying the scheduler code to include the necessary steps to update each thread's CPU-time clock and to operate the associated timers.

The information that must be added to the thread control block consists of:

- *cpu_clock_requirement*: a boolean that indicates whether the thread has a CPU-time clock enabled; it is set at the time of thread creation using the value specified in the thread attributes object used to create the thread.

- *cpuclk*: a structure with the information needed for the CPU time clock, including the clock identifier, the time of the last activation of the thread, and the total CPU-time consumed by that thread.

- *associated_timers*: an array with the information needed for each of the timers associated with that thread's CPU-time clock; this includes the timer identifier, a boolean indicating whether the timer is in use, a boolean indicating whether the timer is armed, and the timer's expiration time.

The FSU scheduler does not operate on a periodic basis, as it is invoked only at the points when the running task gets blocked or when a blocked task is activated. Thus, the modification required to support CPU time clocks and timers consists of adding code at the point where a new thread becomes the running thread. This code must: read the real-time clock storing the value as the "current time", perform the "actions for previous thread" if there was one running, and perform the "actions for new thread":

- *Actions for previous thread*: update the value of the CPU time clock by adding the difference between the current time and the activation time to the total CPU time of that thread; in addition, disarm any associated timers that were armed and had expired.

- *Actions for new thread*: store the current time as the activation time of the thread. In addition, if there are armed timers associated with this thread, calculate the time remaining until the nearest timer expiration as the difference between the minimum of the expiration times of the associated timers and the total CPU time of that thread. In this case, program an operating system timer to send a signal to the process when the calculated remaining time elapses. If there are no armed timers associated with the new thread, disarm the operating system timer. The operating system timer that we have used in our implementation is the "virtual time" timer that is accessible through the *setitimer()* OS function.

In addition, it is necessary to add the following actions at the point where a thread becomes blocked and there are no more active threads in the ready queue: read the real-time clock storing the value as the "current time", perform the "actions for previous thread", and disarming the operating system timer.

The implementation described above only works when there is just one active process in the system. It would be necessary to have a process cpu-time clock available (like the one defined in POSIX.1d) to create an implementation that would work with multiple processes.

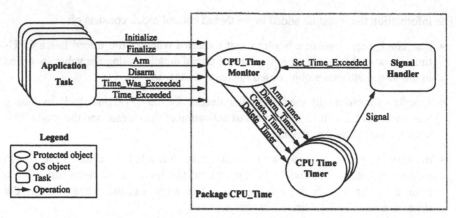

Fig. 1 Architecture of package *CPU_Time*

3 Execution Time Limits

3.1 Package CPU_Time

We have created an Ada package to encapsulate the internal aspects of the use of the POSIX interface for clocks and timers, including the use of signals to notify the occurrence of timer expirations caused by an execution time overrun. This package, called *CPU_Time*, contains the objects and operations that appear in Fig. 1.

The central part of package *CPU_Time* is a protected object called Monitor. This protected object has visible operations for the application tasks to initialize or finalize a CPU-time timer, to arm or disarm a timer, and to determine whether a timer has expired or not (*Time_Was_Exceeded*). In addition, *Monitor* has a family of entries (*Time_Exceeded*), one entry per timer, which can be used by application tasks to block until an execution time overrun is detected or, as we will see later, as an event that triggers the abortion of the instructions of a select statement with an abortable part.

Task *Signal_Handler* is a very high priority task that takes care of accepting all the signals generated by the different timers, identifying the particular timer, and notifying the *Monitor* protected object through operation *Set_Time_Exceeded*. This follows the recommended way of handling signals in multithreaded POSIX applications, using threads to accept signals with a *sigwait()* operation, instead of using signal handlers. The advantage is that the thread executes in a well-defined context, with well-defined scheduling behaviour, while a signal handler executes in a much more unspecified context.

3.2 Usage Schemes for CPU-Time Timers

Using package *CPU_Time*, described above, we can design different usage schemes, that depend on the particular needs of the application task whose execution time is being monitored. We have identified four major schemes:

- *Handled*: This is the case in which an execution time overrun is detected, but the task is allowed to complete its execution. This is applicable to systems under testing, or for tasks that have a high degree of criticality (and thus cannot be stopped) or for which an occasional execution time overrun can be tolerated, but needs to be reported.

In this scheme, the application task arms the execution-time timer at the beginning of its regular execution (after initialization). At the end of its execution, it uses function *Time_Was_Exceeded* to determine whether the execution time was exceeded or not. If an overrun is detected, the error can be reported. Table 1 shows the pseudocode of the application task under this scheme.

Table 1. Periodic task under the "handled" scheme.

```
task body Periodic_Handled is
   Timer_Id : CPU_Time.Monitor_Id;
begin
   CPU_Time.Monitor.Initialize(Timer_Id);
   loop
      CPU_Time.Monitor.Arm(Timer_Id, Worst_Case_Exec_Time);
      Do Task's Useful Work;
      if CPU_Time.Monitor.Time_Was_Exceeded(Timer_Id) then
         Handle the Error;
      end if;
      CPU_Time.Monitor.Disarm(Timer_Id);
      delay until Next_Start;
   end loop;
end Periodic_Handled;
```

- *Stopped*: This is the case in which if an execution time overrun is detected, the associated task execution is stopped, to allow lower priority tasks to execute within their deadlines. The whole instance of the stopped task is aborted and is never repeated. The task itself waits until its next activation and then proceeds normally.

The implementation of this scheme consists of executing the regular instructions of the task inside the abortable part of an asynchronous select statement. The event that triggers abortion in this case is a call to the entry *Time_Exceeded* of *CPU_Time.Monitor*. As a consequence, if an execution time overrun occurs, the task instructions are aborted for that instance of the task execution. The pseudocode of the application task under this scheme is shown in Table 2.

- *Imprecise*: This scheme corresponds to the case in which the task is designed using the imprecise computation model [6], in which the task has a mandatory part (generally short and for which it is easier to estimate a worst-case execution time), and an optional part that refines the calculations made by the task. Since the worst-case execution time of this optional part is usually more difficult to estimate, this part will be aborted if an execution time overrun is detected. This allows us to use

Table 2. Application task under the "Stopped" scheme

```
task body Periodic_Stopped is
   Timer_Id : CPU_Time.Monitor_Id;
begin
   CPU_Time.Monitor.Initialize(Timer_Id);
   loop
      CPU_Time.Monitor.Arm(Timer_Id, Worst_Case_Exec_Time);
      select
         CPU_Time.Monitor.Time_Exceeded(Timer_Id);
         Handle the Error;
      then abort
         Do Task's Useful Work;
      end select;
      CPU_Time.Monitor.Disarm(Timer_Id);
      delay until Next_Start;
   end loop;
end Periodic_Stopped;
```

fixed priority scheduling in applications in which the optional part has an unpredictable execution time. The technique is also valid for cases in which the optional part continuously refines the quality of the results; we can let the optional part run until it exhausts its execution time budget, and then use the last valid result obtained. The implementation of this scheme consists of using the "handled" approach for the mandatory part of the task, and the "stopped" approach for the optional part. After the optional part, whether it is aborted or not, another mandatory part may exist to cause the outputs of the task to be generated. Table 3 shows the pseudocode of the application task under this scheme.

Table 3. Application task under the "Imprecise" scheme

```
task body Periodic_Imprecise is
   Timer_Id : CPU_Time.Monitor_Id;
begin
   CPU_Time.Monitor.Initialize(Timer_Id);
   loop
      CPU_Time.Monitor.Arm(Timer_Id,Worst_Case_Exec_Time_I);
      Do Task's Mandatory Part I;
      select
         CPU_Time.Monitor.Time_Exceeded(Timer_Id);
      then abort
         Do Task's Optional Part;
      end select;
      CPU_Time.Monitor.Disarm(Timer_Id);
      Mandatory Part II: Generate Task's Outputs;
      delay until Next_Start;
   end loop;
end Periodic_Imprecise;
```

- *Lowered*: This scheme can be used to limit the effects of an execution time overrun of a particular task, on lower priority tasks, when asynchronous select statements are not allowed or are not available for an application task. In this case, when the overrun is detected, the priority of the task is lowered to a background level, lower than the priorities of all real-time tasks. When the task that overrun its execution time has the opportunity to finish its execution, it can determine that it overrun by invoking *Time_Was_Exceeded*, and then it can take a corrective action or report the error; if it wishes so, it can raise its priority back to its normal level.

This scheme requires a different implementation of package *CPU_Time*. In the new implementation, operation *Initialize* must store the task identifier of the calling task. This identifier is then used to lower the priority of the task when an execution time overrun is detected. This is done by the signal handler task (see Fig. 1) by using the facilities of package *Ada.Dynamic_Priorities*.

4   Enhancing Sporadic Server Schedulers

In [4] we presented a number of application-level implementations of the sporadic server scheduling algorithm. This algorithm is designed to schedule aperiodic activities in hard real-time systems, while bounding the effects of these activities on lower priority tasks. The sporadic server scheduler is based on keeping record of the amounts of execution time consumed by the aperiodic activities, and allowing them to consume only a certain execution time *capacity* during an interval of time called the *replenishment period*. In the implementations presented in [4] we always assumed that the consumed execution time for processing one event was equal to the worst-case execution time. In addition, we would only allow the aperiodic task to run at its normal priority level if the available execution capacity was at least equal to the worst-case execution time. Now, we can take advantage of execution time clocks and timers to enhance the performance of the sporadic server schedulers by eliminating both restrictions, as we describe in the following two subsections. Both enhancements increase the throughput of the sporadic server scheduler, while still preserving the schedulability of lower priority tasks in the system.

4.1   Accounting for the Execution Time Spent

In this first enhancement, we account for the actual execution time spent, instead of assuming that the worst-case execution time was spent. This makes sense in the sporadic server schedulers that allow *multiple* events per replenishment period. The sporadic server implementations do not need to change; we only need to change the application task to use a CPU-time clock to measure the execution time spent during the response to each event, and to pass the actual time spent to the sporadic server scheduler, as a parameter to the *Schedule_Next* operation. In tasks that have a high variability of their execution time, this approach allows the scheduler to save execution capacity for processing future events. The pseudocode of the application task for this case is shown in Table 4.

Table 4. Aperiodic task under a sporadic server scheduler

```
task body Application_Task is
   SS : Sporadic_Server.Scheduler;
   Last_Time, Now : POSIX.Timespec;
begin
   Sporadic_Server.Initialize(SS);
   Last_Time:=POSIX_Timers.Get_Time(pthread_getcpuclockid);
   loop
      Sporadic_Server.Prepare_To_Wait(SS);
      Wait for Event;
      Sporadic_Server.Prepare_To_Execute(SS);
      Do Task's Useful Work;
      Now:=POSIX_Timers.Get_Time(Thread_CPUtime_Clock);
      Sporadic_Server.Schedule_Next
           (SS, Spent=> Now-Last_Time);
      Last_Time:=Now;
   end loop;
end Application_Task;
```

4.2 Detecting When the Execution Capacity Gets Exhausted

In this second enhancement, we create one execution time timer per sporadic server scheduler, to measure the consumption of execution time, and to detect the case in which the sporadic server runs out of execution capacity. This is particularly useful in the schedulers using a replenishment manager like the *background* manager, that allows the application task to run at a background priority level when it does not have enough capacity available. Each time the aperiodic task is activated, we arm the timer with an expiration time equal to the available execution capacity. The aperiodic task is allowed to execute at its normal priority level. If the application task consumes all of the available capacity, the execution time timer expires, sending the associated signal. A signal handler task shared by all the schedulers, similar to the one shown in Fig. 1, accepts this signal and invokes the sporadic server protected manager to lower the priority of the application task, and schedule the corresponding replenishment operation. The advantage of using the execution time timer in this case is that we can use all of the available capacity; before, we could only use it if at the activation of the task the available capacity was larger than or equal to the worst-case execution time of the task.

Fig. 2 shows the basic architecture of the new replenishment manager called *CPU-time* manager. This manager is derived from the *Queued* manager and has the same attributes as the *Background* manager, except for a different *Protected_Manager* and with the addition of a new attribute to hold the CPU-time timer. The new *CPU-time* manager can be used by the *Simple*, *High_Priority*, and *High_Priority_Polled* sporadic server schedulers, giving way to three new implementations.

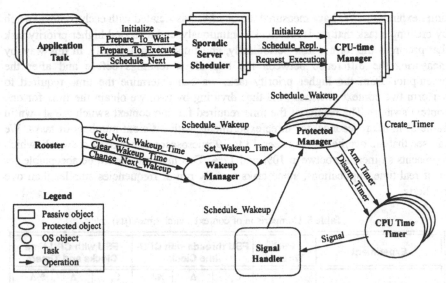

Fig. 2. Basic architecture of the new implementations using the *CPU-time* manager

5 Performance Considerations

The use of execution time clocks affects the performance of the system because it adds a fixed overhead to each context switch. There are two different classes of thread scheduler implementations that must be considered:

- *Ticker implementation.* In this implementation a periodic signal or interrupt activates the task scheduler. A simple way to count execution time in this case is to have an integer value counter for each thread and, each time the tick interrupt comes in, increment the counter associated to the task that was running. The resolution of such clock is one tick, but it is relatively cheap, since it only involves an addition operation during each tick.

- *Alarm clock implementation.* In this implementation, each task is allowed to run until it gives up the processor. A time-ordered delay queue is used to store the next activation time for timed tasks that are currently blocked. An alarm clock is set to invoke the task scheduler when the first task of the delay queue needs to be activated. In this case, the scheduler is not invoked periodically, and thus at each invocation it must read a hardware clock to determine how much time has elapsed since the last scheduling operation. This time must be added to the execution time of the task that was just running. Execution time clocks may be expensive in this implementation, depending on how much time it takes to read the hardware clock.

The FSU threads that we have used in our implementation of CPU-time clocks and timers follow the "alarm clock" model, and thus at each context switch we need to read the real-time clock and to program an operating system timer to take care of CPU-time timer expirations. We have measured the overhead associated with each context switch by creating a task that reads the clock continuously, and a second higher priority task that preempts the former task periodically, and finishes immediately. In this way, by measuring the difference between the two clock readings before and after the preemption from the higher priority task, we can determine the time required to perform two context switches (and thus dividing by two, we obtain the time for one context switch). The results of the time required for one context switch are shown in Table 5, in microseconds, for three experiments with different numbers of tasks. We can see that the overhead is between 13 to 19 microseconds per context switch, which represents an increase between 10% and 17%. This increase should be acceptable for most real-time applications, since tasks usually run at frequencies smaller than one kilohertz.

Table 5. Comparison of context switch times (μs)

Experiment	FSU Threads	FSU threads with CPU-time Clocks			FSU with CPU-time Clocks and Timers		
	C_s	C_s	Δ	%Δ	C_s	Δ	%Δ
2 tasks	110	128	18	14%	129	19	17%
2+10 tasks (low priority)	117	130	13	10%	132	15	13%
2+10 tasks (high priority)	115	130	15	12%	131	16	14%

Table 6 shows the results of average execution time measured for the different POSIX CPU-time clock services that we have implemented, as well as the times for the operations of package *CPU_Time*. All results have been obtained in a Pentium-133 CPU running under Linux.

Table 6. Execution times of the different operations (μs)

Posix_Timers	μs	CPU_Time	μs
Get_Time(pthread_getcpuclockid)	4	Monitor.Arm	62
Get_Time(CLOCK_REALTIME)	4	Monitor.Disarm	55
Arm_Timer	12	Monitor.Time_Was_Exceeded	12
Disarm_Timer	12	Monitor.Set_Time_Exceeded	35
		Monitor.Time_Exceeded	84

6 Conclusion

We have discussed the importance of enforcing the worst-case execution estimates in hard real-time systems. In an application designed under a concurrent tasking architecture, such as in the Ada tasking model, detecting and limiting execution time overruns may be achieved by using the proposed POSIX model for execution time clocks and timers. In this paper we describe how to implement these CPU-time clocks in the context of a POSIX threads implementation.

We have also described an implementation scheme that allows application tasks to use the POSIX execution time clocks to detect execution time overruns and limit their effects. We have also described how to take advantage of execution time clocks to enhance the behaviour of application-level sporadic servers. As a guide to users of these clocks, we have discussed some performance considerations that allow the application developer to determine the amount of overhead that he or she will suffer by using execution time clocks, for a particular application.

References

[1]   A. Burns and A. Wellings. "Real-Time systems and Programming Languages". 2nd. edition. Addison-Wesley, 1997.

[2]   IEEE Standards Project P1003.1d, "Draft Standard for Information Technology -Portable Operating System Interface (POSIX)- Part 1: Additional Realtime Extensions". Draft 10. The Institute of Electrical and Electronics Engineers, January 1997.

[3]   ISO/IEC Standard 9945-1:1996. "Information Technology -Portable Operating System Interface (POSIX)- Part 1: System Application Program Interface (API) [C Language]". The Institute of Electrical and Electronics Engineers, 1996.

[4]   M. González Harbour, J.J. Gutiérrez García, and J.C Palencia Gutiérrez. "Implementing Application-Level Sporadic Server Schedulers in Ada 95". Proceedings of the 1997 Ada-Europe International Conference on Reliable Software Technologies, in Lecture Notes in Computer Science, Vol. 1251, Springer, June 1997.

[5]   M.H. Klein, T. Ralya, B. Pollak, R. Obenza, and M. González Harbour. "A Practitioner's Handbook for Real-Time Analysis". Kluwer Academic Pub., 1993.

[6]   J. Liu, K.J. Lin, W.K. Shih, A. Chuang-Shi Yu, J.Y. Chung, and W. Zhao. "Algorithms for Scheduling Imprecise Computations". IEEE Computer, pp. 58-68, May 1991.

[7]   F. Mueller. "A Library Implementation of POSIX Threads under UNIX". 1993 Winter USENIX, January, 1993, San Diego, CA, USA.

[8]   F. Mueller. "Generalizing Timing Predictions to Set-Associative Caches". Proceedings of the 9th Euromicro Workshop on Real-Time Systems, pp. 64-71, Toledo, Spain, June 1997.

[9]   C.Y. Park. "Predicting program execution times by analyzing static and dynamic program paths". Real-Time Systems Journal, Vol. 5, No. 1, pp. 31-62, 1993.

[10] P. Puschner and A.V. Schedl. "Computing Maximum Task Execution Times: A graph-based approach". Real-Time Systems Journal, Vol. 13, No. 1, pp. 67-91, July 1997.

[11] N. Zhang, A. Burns, and M. Nicholson. "Pipelined Processors and Worst-Case Execution Times". Real-Time Systems Journal, Vol. 5, No. 1, pp. 31-62, 1993.

Programming Hard Real-Time Systems with Optional Components in Ada

Agustín Espinosa, Vicente Julián, Carlos Carrascosa, Andrés Terrasa, and
Ana García-Fornes

Universidad Politécnica de Valencia,
Departamento de Sistemas Informáticos y Computación,
Camino de Vera s/n, 46071, Valencia, Spain

Abstract. Flexible and adaptive behavior is seen as one of the key characteristics of next generation hard real-time systems. Within the context of fixed priority pre-emptive scheduling, existing approaches deal with optional components and provide kernel mechanisms to schedule effectively such components when spare processor capacity is available. This paper describes a framework that provides a task programming model with optional components, and the appropriate mechanisms for supporting it, by using the main results of existing research in computing spare processor capacity. The paper shows how these ideas can be adapted for being used from an Ada application. The concurrency and real-time programming features of Ada allow an elegant and efficient implementation of a model where hard real-time tasks, optional unbounded components and optional firm tasks coexist.

1 Introduction

Hard real-time systems are characterized by the fact that severe consequences will result if logical as well as timing correctness properties of the system are not satisfied. They are commonly control systems, on which some kind of interaction between the system and the environment is carried out. More specifically, the system must control certain variables from the environment, and to do so, it must read incoming information from sensors, compute the appropriate outcome values, and then write them to the actuators, affecting the environment. Usually, these actions are done periodically, in order to maintain the environmental variables in a right range of values. A hard real-time application is then formed by a number of critical periodic tasks, each of which is characterized by its period, its deadline and its worst-case execution time (or wcet). These tasks must be guaranteed by an off-line schedulability test in order to proof all tasks to always meet their deadlines. This test assumes a particular scheduling policy at run time.

On the other hand, the requirement to support flexible, adaptive and intelligent behavior whilst also providing the 100% guarantees needed by hard real-time services, has been identified as one of the key challenges presented by the next generation of real-time systems [9]. One method of improving flexibility is via the incorporation of optional components into tasks with hard deadlines. These components are not provided with off-line guarantees, but they may be executed at run-time if sufficient resources are available.

Within the context of fixed priority scheduling, mechanisms which are required to effectively schedule optional components have been developed by Audsley and others [2],[3]. The mechanisms described there are incorporated to the kernel for run-time monitoring of spare processor capacity and its subsequent assignment to requesting processes.

Conversely, the focus of this paper is upon providing such a framework within the application level using Ada. The paper shows how the concurrency and real-time features of Ada can be used to provide a task programming model with optional components, which will run when spare capacity is available. Within this approach, the application tasks themselves (as opposed to the kernel) are responsible for the identification and assignment of spare capacity at run-time. Further, the model allows the existence of optional tasks with firm deadlines that have a 0/1 constraint (if it commences execution, it must complete). This kind of tasks are guaranteed on-line. This task model is offered to the programmer as an Ada package, which encapsulates all the related real-time mechanisms.

In the next section, the task model and assumptions used are outlined. The remainder of the paper is organized as follows: in section 3, a package that implements this task model is presented, showing its specification and how the programmer must use it. Section 4 discusses the implementation issues, and finally section 5 presents the conclusions of this work.

2 The Task Model and Assumptions

We consider a real-time system comprising a fixed set of hard periodic tasks and a set of optional firm tasks.

Each periodic task has a period, worst case execution time (wcet), deadline and is assigned a unique priority. Further, each task is formed by three parts: the first one is the initial part, which is a mandatory part that reads information from sensors and computes a primary solution for these values. The second one is the optional part, which refines the solution computed by the initial part, but only executes if spare capacity is available when initial part ends. The third one is the final part, which is a mandatory part in charge of accessing the environment to write the outcomes computed by either the optional or the initial part. The initial and final parts have bounded computation requirements with known wcet. The optional part can have unbounded computation, but if it exhausts the assigned time for its execution, then it is terminated.

A set of scheduling techniques have been developed to efficiently determine the processor spare capacity at run time. In particular, slack stealing algorithms [4] are used to know at run time the amount of time the critical tasks can be delayed without loosing its timing constraints. This time is known as *slack time*. The task model presented here uses the the Approximate Dynamic Slack Stealing Algorithm [5], which computes at run time the available slack time at each priority level and then uses it to safely execute optional components.

The hard periodic task set (initial + final parts) is supposed to be schedulable according to an exact feasibility test [1], which assumes a fixed priority preemptive dispatching following the deadline monotonic priority ordering. Tasks deadlines are assumed to be less than or equal to their periods.

On the other hand, optional firm tasks have a bounded amount of computation that needs to be completed by a given deadline. Further, they have a 0/1 constraint: if one of them commences execution, it must complete. These tasks are created dynamically by any periodic task. Priority assignment and acceptance testing of optional firm tasks is carried out on-line by following the methods proposed in [7] and [6] respectively. Upon arrival, each optional firm task is assigned the highest priority level such that every task of a lower priority level has a later absolute deadline. Once it has been assigned a priority, the acceptance test given in [6] determines if this new task can be guaranteed. Only optional tasks which have been given a guarantee are allowed to execute, and they are said to be accepted.

Both optional parts of periodic tasks and optional firm tasks are only executed if slack time is available. The main difference between them is that optional firm tasks are guaranteed and optional parts are not. This means that when an optional firm task is accepted the slack time available is reduced at that moment, so the needed computation time is reserved. In fact, once guaranteed, optional firm tasks are treated in exactly the same way as hard periodic tasks with off-line guarantees. In contrast, when an optional part becomes active, the maximum deadline at which its execution must end is calculated. This deadline is computed by using the slack available and the interference of the higher priority level tasks. The slack time consumed is not decreased until the optional part has been executed. This way of maintaining slack leads to more flexible approaches as discussed in [8].

3 The Task Model in Ada

A real-time application following the task model depicted above may be constructed by using the package Real_Time_Tasks implemented here. This package provides the user two simple task types -one for periodic tasks and another for optional firm tasks-, and a procedure for starting the whole application.

Within this approach, a real-time application is divided into two parts. The first one is to program the task model itself, including all the involved techniques such as support for hard and optional real-time tasks, slack stealing management, and on-line guarantee test for optional firm tasks. Designing and implementing this part is quite a hard labour, and so debugging. The second part is concerned in implementing a solution to the application problem. The package presented here fully implements the first part. Then, when programming a real-time application using this package, the user must only consider aspects related to the problem being solved.

The package Real_Time_Tasks specification will now be shown, as well as the way the user must use it.

```
pragma Task_Dispatching_Policy(Fifo_Within_Priorities);
pragma Locking_Policy(Ceiling_Locking);

package Real_Time_Tasks is
   subtype Microseconds is Natural;
   type Access_To_Simple_Procedure is access procedure;

   task type Hard_Periodic_Task
      (Initial_Code, Optional_Code, Final_Code: Access_To_Simple_Procedure;
      Period, Deadline: Microseconds;
      Initial_Code_Wcet, Final_Code_Wcet: Microseconds)
   is
      entry Initialize;
   end Hard_Periodic_Task;

   task type Optional_Firm_Task
      (Code: Access_To_Simple_Procedure;
      Deadline,Code_Wcet: Microseconds)
   is
      entry Initialize(Accepted: out Boolean);
   end Optional_Firm_Task;

   procedure Start_Real_Time_Tasking;
end Real_Time_Tasks;
```

This package uses the well defined task dispatching policy Fifo_Within_Priorities and locking policy Ceiling_Locking, both necessary to provide a deterministic system response.

Hard periodic tasks must be declared in the main subprogram, at the beginning of the application. Real-time attributes (Period, Deadline,Initial_Code_Wcet and Final_Code_Wcet), and the actions the task executes (Initial_Code, Optional_Code, Final_Code) are passed to the task via discriminants. An example of this declaration is shown below.

```
Task_1: Hard_Periodic_Task
   (Initial_Code       => Initial'Access,
   Optional_Code       => Optional'Access,
   Final_Code          => Final'Access,
   Period              => 200_000,
   Deadline            => 200_000,
   Initial_Code_Wcet   => 3_000,
   Final_Code_Wcet     => 70_000);
```

Once the periodic tasks are declared, the user must initialize them by calling the Initialize entry. This is an internal initialization, and no user code is executed. At this stage, each task is registered by the underlying implementation, and the task's execution is temporally delayed until all tasks are ready to begin.

```
Task_1.Initialize;
---
Task_N.Initialize;
```

When all the periodic tasks which conform the application are initialized, Start_Real_Time_Tasking must be called in order to instruct the underlying implementation to start tasking. At this moment, tasks' base priorities are assigned by means of the Deadline Monotonic ordering, initial slack time is calculated at each priority level and all the tasks are awakened. Then, the application starts running.

Once the application has started, no more periodic tasks may be created. Conversely, optional firm tasks may be declared by any periodic task, within the code of its initial, optional or final part. This declaration is quite similar as the one explained above. In this case, the task type Optional_Firm_Task is used, as shown in the following example.

```
Task_New: Optional_Firm_Task
  (Initial_Code     => Optional_Firm'Access,
   Deadline         => 130_000,
   Final_Code_Wcet  => 23_000);
```

Again, the new task must be initialized before its execution may begin, by calling Task_New.Initialize(Accepted). When the initialization call is done, the underlying implementation checks if the new task can be accepted. This check is returned to the caller task and, if the check is successful, the base priority of the new task is calculated and assigned by using the Earliest Deadline First (EDF) ordering.

4 Implementation

The core of the implementation is a protected object called The_Manager. The main functions of this object are the following:

- Task registration at the initialization stage. Real-time attributes are stored and an internal identifier is generated for each task.
- Priorities assignment for hard periodic tasks, by using the Deadline Monotonic ordering approach.
- Keeping the slack time available in a per-priority level basis.
- Computing the time at which an optional part must be aborted.
- Acceptance of optional execution requests.
- Assignment of priorities for optional firm tasks execution requests, by using the EDF ordering.

The **The_Manager**'s protected operations are called by the bodies of the task types **Hard_Periodic_Task** and **Optional_Firm_Task** at specific points in its implementation. Several of these calls permits **The_Manager** to keep track of the state of each task and also to perform all the necessary operations in order to maintain the available slack time at each priority level. The other calls are used to synchronize the execution of tasks at the initialization stage or when a new task must be accepted. The specification of **The_Manager** will now be shown, as well as the way the tasks will use it.

```
subtype Real_Time_Task_Identifier is Integer range
                                    1..Max_Real_Time_Tasks;

protected The_Manager is
   entry I_Am_A_New_Task
               (With_Period:        in  Real_Time.Time_Span;
                With_Deadline:      in  Real_Time.Time_Span;
                With_Initial_Wcet:  in  Real_Time.Time_Span;
                With_Final_Wcet:    in  Real_Time.Time_Span;
                Id_Assigned:        out Real_Time_Task_Identifier);

   entry I_Am_A_New_Optional_Firm_Task
               (With_Deadline: in  Real_Time.Time_Span;
                With_Wcet:     in  Real_Time.Time_Span;
                Id_Assigned:   out Real_Time_Task_Identifier;
                Accepted:      out Boolean);

   entry Wait_For_Begin
               (Time_Launched:  out Real_Time.Time);

   procedure Initial_Code_Starting
               (The_Task:            in Real_Time_Task_Identifier;
                Current_Activation:  in Real_Time.Time);

   procedure Optional_Code_Starting
               (The_Task:    in  Real_Time_Task_Identifier;
                Time_To_Die: out Real_Time.Time);

   procedure Final_Code_Starting
               (The_Task: in Real_Time_Task_Identifier);

   procedure Final_Code_Ended
               (The_Task: in Real_Time_Task_Identifier);

   procedure Optional_Firm_Code_Ended
               (The_Task: in Real_Time_Task_Identifier);

   procedure Startup;
end The_Manager;
```

```
task body Hard_Periodic_Task
is
   My_Id: Real_Time_Task_Identifier;
   Next_Activation: Real_Time.Time;
   Time_To_Die: Real_Time.Time;
begin
   accept Initialize do
      The_Manager.I_Am_A_New_task
                 (Real_Time.Microseconds(Period),
                  Real_Time.Microseconds(Deadline),
                  Real_Time.Microseconds(Initial_Code_Wcet),
                  Real_Time.Microseconds(Final_Code_Wcet),
                  My_Id);
   end Initialize;
   The_Manager.Wait_For_Begin (Next_Activation);
   loop
      The_Manager.Initial_Code_Starting (My_Id,
                                         Next_Activation);
      Initial_Code.all;

      The_Manager.Optional_Code_Starting (My_Id,Time_To_Die);
      select
         delay until Time_To_Die;
      then abort
        Optional_Code.all;
      end select;

      The_Manager.Final_Code_Starting (My_Id);
      Final_Code.all;

      The_Manager.Final_Code_Ended (My_Id);

      Next_Activation := Next_Activation
                         + Real_Time.Microseconds(Period);

      delay until Next_Activation;
   end loop;
end Hard_Periodic_Task;
```

The first action executed by a hard periodic task is to accept the entry
Initialize -called from the main subprogram-, which calls the operation I_Am_A
_New_Task to register itself in the The_Manager. The The_Manager creates a task
descriptor for this new task, takes note of its real-time attributes and assigns it
a identifier, which will be used by the task in the rest of calls.

After registering itself, the task must wait until the whole application starts
running (Wait_For_Begin). This event occurs (once all hard periodic tasks have
been created and initialized) when the main subprogram calls the Start_Real_Ti-
me_Tasking procedure, which tells the manager to start the application. The
The_Manager assigns priorities to tasks (by using the Deadline Monotonic or-

der), calculates each tasks' initial available slack time, and allows all tasks to proceed. Note that this call will also return to the task the Next_Activation time, which will act as the base of its periodic releases.

Each (hard periodic) task consists of an endless loop, on which each loop corresponds to a release of the task. In particular, this loop contains some calls to run each part of the task, being these parts delimited by special invocations to The_Manager. These special invocations are used by The_Manager to keep track of the current state of the task, and also to compute the CPU consumed time of the task, and to maintain the amount of slack time available at each priority level.

Each time a task is released, it first calls theInitial_Code_Starting operation, in order to notify the The_Manager that it is about to start running its initial part. The The_Manager calculates and registers then the CPU time consumed by a potential (lower priority) interrupted task, if any. It also updates the available slack time for higher priority tasks, registers the next activation time point of the newly released task, and switches the task's state from *dormant* to *initial*.

When the initial part of a task has been finished, the Optional_Code_Starting operation is called. Then, the available slack time for all the hard tasks is updated, and the task's state is switched from *initial* to *optional*. This operation calculates and returns a time point which denotes the latest moment at which the task's final part may start without loosing its deadline. This time point is used in an ATC construct, which will abort the optional part execution if necessary. In this way, the execution of the optional parts will not jeopardize the timing constraints of any hard real-time task.

When the Final_Code_Starting is called, again the available slack time for all the tasks is updated and the task's state is switched from *optional* to *final*.

Finally, when the task ends its current release, the Final_Code_Ended operation is called. Now, the task state is switched from *final* to *dormant*, and the avaliable slack time at the task's priority level is calculated.

```
task body Optional_Firm_Task
is
    My_Id: Real_Time_Task_Identifier;
    Ok: Boolean;
begin
    accept Initialize(Accepted: out Boolean) do
        The_Manager.I_Am_A_New_Optional_Firm_Task
                    (Real_Time.Microseconds(Deadline),
                     Real_Time.Microseconds(Code_Wcet),
                     My_Id,
                     Accepted);
        Ok:= Accepted;
    end Initialize;

    if Ok then
        Code.all;
```

```
        The_Manager.Optional_Firm_Code_Ended (My_Id);
    end if;
  end Optional_Firm_Task;
```

When an optional firm task begins execution, it waits until it is initialized. At this moment, it calls **The_Manager** to be accepted. The **The_Manager** assign it the highest priority level such that every task of a lower priority level has a later absolute deadline. Then, the new task is tested in order to know if it can be guaranteed. To do so, the **The_Manager** first checks if the interference of more priority tasks will permit the new task to meet its deadline. Then it must also check if there is enough slack time available at each lower priority level. This test is returned to the optional firm task, which in its turn returns it to the creator (periodic) task. If the test is successful, the user-provided code for the optional task will be executed.

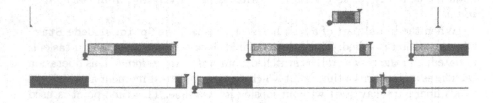

Fig. 1. *Quivi*'s execution display.

To illustrate how the tasks run, Fig. 1 shows a display of an application's real execution. The figure has been generated by a graphical tool, called *quivi*. This tool interprets a text file generated at run time by the application, on which some kind of events (like the release or the execution of a task) are registered. In the display shown, the execution of each task is placed in an horizontal line, and all lines are ordered by priorities (corresponding the top line with the highest priority). Also, a circle denotes a task release, a vertical line denotes a deadline, a grey box denotes the execution of an initial or final part, a black box denotes the execution of an optional part, and finally a black triangle denotes the end of a task release.

5   Conclusions

In this paper, some of the more recent results in real-time scheduling have been revised and adapted in order to provide a flexible and coherent task model to hard real-time programming. This task model permits hard real-time guarantees whilst providing optional components to improve response quality.

On the other hand, Ada's wide set of real-time features has been showed to be apropriated for implementing such a complex task model. In particular, the standard dispatching policy, the ceiling lock policy, dynamic priorities and protected objects have been used, and they have resulted to be excellent building blocks.

Another key issue in our implementation is efficiency. No supporting tasks have been necessary, and only a single protected object have been used to synchronize all tasks. This leads to a minimum context-switch overhead, also considering that protected objects may be implemented in a very efficient way. It must be noted that there is some overhead due to the synchronizing calls included into the body of tasks. However, most of these calls executes just a few instructions, and only two of them have a cost which is linear with the number of the application tasks.

All these features have been encapsulated into a single Ada package with a quite simple interface, in such a way that programmers will only have to implement aspects related with the solution of the application problem.

References

1. Audsley, N.C., Burns, A., Davis, R., Tindell, K., and Wellings, J. (1995). "Fixed priority pre-emptive scheduling: an historical perspective". *Real-Time Systems*, **Volume 8**, 173–198.
2. Audsley, N.C., Burns, A., Davis, R., and Wellings, J. (1994). "Apropiate Mechanisms for the Support of Optional Processing in Hard Real-Time Systems". *Proc. IEEE Real-Time Operating Systems and Software Workshop* , 23–27.
3. Audsley, N.C., Davis, R., and Burns, A. (1994). "Mechanisms for Enhancing the Flexibility and Utility of Hard Real-Time Systems".*Proc. Real-Time Systems Symposium*, pp. 12–21, IEEE Computer Society Press.
4. Davis, R.I., Tindell, K.W., and Burns, A. (1993). "Scheduling Slack Time in Fixed Priority Preemptive Systems". *Proc. Real-Time Systems Symposium*, Raleigh-Durham, North Carolina, December 1–3, pp. 222–231, IEEE Computer Society Press.
5. Davis, R.I. (1994). "Approximate Slack Stealing Algorithms for Fixed Priority Preemptive Systems".Real-Time Systems Research Group. Department of Computer Science. University of York, UK. Report number YCS-93-217.
6. Davis, R.I. (1994). "Guaranteeing X in Y: On-line Acceptance Tests for Hard Aperiodic Tasks Scheduled by the Slack Stealing Algorithms".Real-Time Systems Research Group. Department of Computer Science. University of York, UK. Report number YCS-94-231.
7. Davis, R.I. (1994). "Optimal Priority Assignment for Aperiodic Tasks with Firm Deadlines in Fixed Priority Pre-emptive Systems". Real-Time Systems Research Group. Department of Computer Science. University of York, UK. Report number YCS-94-239.
8. Garcia-Fornes A., Crespo, A., and Botti, V. (1995). "Adding hard real-time tasks to artificial intelligence environments". *Proc. of the 20th IFAC/IFIP Workshop on Real-Time Programming*, Fort Lauderdale, Florida, USA.
9. Stankovic, J. and Ramamritham, K. (1993). "Advances in Real-Time Systems". IEEE Computer Society Press. ISBN 0-8186-3792-7.

Object Oriented Abstractions for
Real-Time Distributed Systems
Foundation steps of Ada 95 Purity and Generics

Scott Arthur Moody

Boeing Information Space & Defense Systems
P.O. Box 3999, M/S 87-37, Seattle, WA 98124
scott.a.moody@boeing.com

As software development and maintenance costs rise, providing higher architectural language abstractions is an effective tool. This paper describes a key set of object oriented abstractions developed using the Ada 95 toolset, and discusses their applicability to distributed real-time command and control systems under development at Boeing. The abstraction concepts described build upon each other and eventually become high level tools. This helps to increase the leveraged development of real-time systems, especially as the product and customer configurations vary. This papers particular emphasis is on how to migrate to the new Ada 95 package (purity) categorization rules, and describes their use in the distributed Annex-E. A strongly typed, possibly remote, data subscription concept is described and then shown in it's use of the advanced Ada distributed generics capabilities. Client-server and distributed-object abstractions are also contrasted.

1.0   Introduction

As real-time system architectures increase in scale, a valuable abstraction tool involves decreasing the static coupling of components and systems, while maintaining strong compile time checks[13]. Ada 95 provides an elegant and effective toolset as it supports the de-coupling concepts shown throughout this paper, and provides an important concurrency and distribution model. Concurrency abstractions are important, especially in real-time systems, to model the real-world processing, while distribution is another important tool for migrating concurrent systems to parallel systems. Concurrency and distribution tools are most powerful if one can focus mostly on the system architectural concepts with the lower level implementation constraints minimized. One finds that correct phased introduction of the object-oriented capabilities described here allows distribution to become just another concurrency tool, with near seamless introduction.

This paper describes foundation steps for using the Distributed Annex-E, especially the package purity and categorization rules. A set of diagrams are also presented which introduce a new concept of showing the categorization of the packages. Real-Time architectures must deal with various data and execution processing demands. These building blocks will support decreased development and maintenance for large long lived systems by decreasing the known coupling between clients and servers. Because of space considerations, this paper describes two main abstractions to highlight the use of the package categorization and to show how data intensive systems can make use of the extensive typing available within Ada. In the Boeing work these abstractions are also incorporated with many other building blocks, such as protected types and tasks, to help in the modeling of sub-systems as data and processing flows throughout the system. The two abstractions include:

- Remote Simulated Time Server - an extension once time purity is solved
- *Typed* Customer Data Subscription (data *push* model) without modifying framework software

These low and medium building blocks can then be extended with the extensive Ada 95 *generics* capabilities, providing additional dimensions of static compilation. Large scale system (as well as small scale) can benefit from maximal interface checking. The Ada compiler is still one of the most important tools in this role for supporting system developers (of Ada systems), as it consistently checks every line of code against an international ISO standard[14]. This is possible because of a key set of abstractions supported directly in the Ada Language without having to step out to API libraries. API libraries, on the other hand, do have types but the semantics are not guaranteed and usually conveyed only via comments.

Most of the concepts presented are applicable for implementation in other languages, but are described here in terms of the available Ada 95 language constructs. Making them as seamlessly available in any language can be difficult, but API middleware libraries can easily be developed after the original object based Ada 95 system has been tested.

As distribution becomes just another tool, the designer is free to determine the best use of distributed processes. For example, this may range from utilizing multiple processors, to just being able to shorten development time by dynamically connecting to pre-built components. The interfaces are described in the native Ada language and enforced like they would be for a re-usable linked in library. Thus, the development mindset is not changed just to introduce distribution. The same compiler enforcement concepts are extended to the *gnatdist* configuration language of the GLADE implementation. To put these abstractions together, especially to include distribution, this paper concludes with a sample application from the Boeing command and control domain.

1.1   Project Context and Tool Utilization

This research work deals with examining an existing full-scale Boeing project as they develop a COTS-based Open System Architecture for various Command and Control System applications of the AWACS variety[1][2]. As the system migrates from Ada 83 to Ada 95, this effort has examined the viability of commercial distributed processing capabilities, such as CORBA[4] and Ada 95's DSA Distributed Annex-E[6], while determining the best uses of object oriented concepts in these new architectures.

The runtime environment consists of both Sun-Solaris and DEC-Alpha Digital-Unix platforms of varying and increasing performance characteristics. Ada 95 is supported by the GNAT[7] production compiler and runtime system. DSA is implemented in the GNAT tool called GLADE (GNAT LIbrary for Ada Distributed Execution) and it's runtime infrastructure called GARLIC (GNU Ada Reuse Library for Inter-partition Communication)[5]. GNAT/GLADE were wavefront versions and may not be generally available. The CORBA/Ada-95 product (ORBexpress) is provided by OIS (Objective Interface Systems). A goal of the project is to have totally portable Ada 95 systems running on most Unix based platforms and communicating with local and remote networks.

2.0   Data Definition and Large System Issues

Real-Time system of the command and control variety are very data intensive. As these systems are very large, strong static type definition and type checking is an important maintenance characteristic. Adding Object-Oriented techniques to these systems provides more tools to help the type definitions, especially as they evolve over time. In particular, dealing with various provider and consumers of different portions of data leads to using extensible types. A framework and maintenance goal is to minimize the re-specification of information in duplicate locations, and to support system and data type growth.

Some issues and Ada 95 tools for defining and maintaining large evolving data definitions include[1]:

- Hierarchical Types are useful to support various product configurations demands.
- Strong Typing: A major software cost deals with data structure interface matching, and user type comments don't provide adequate compiler checking. Subtyping through ranges is also valuable.
- Stream-IO is used as a tool to ease describing the passing of subset data.
- Mix-in Inheritance allows for flexible global datatype definitions based on product demands. This is supported by strong compile checking, and very efficient runtime support.
- Children Packages for providing compiler enforcement for Read-Only Information

Once there is a good handle on the data definitions, adding multiple threaded access requires some kind of Data Hiding, provided effectively with protected types. As threads and tasking are introduced, efficient access to shared data is important. There seems to be change in philosophy with newer (distributed) object technology. Instead of the traditional Client/Server approach, where you somehow "know" both sides, the new approach is to manipulate "Objects" via their known "methods". The actual physical location of the objects is not known until runtime, and implementation dependencies are isolated from users code. Protected Buffers, and Shared Data(bases) are two useful abstractions to protect information and increase the concurrency.

Protected Types modeled in "protected buffers" are used in various Boeing architectures to act like a mail-box of related information. These perform the action of moving data from one thread to another, without being coupled into knowing the end user, modeling the real-world running at various runtime rates. For example, one project is investigating the varying effectiveness of different data fusion algorithms, both in-house and commercial. Distributed interfaces are defined that must support passing of various data. An abstraction was built that wraps, via an Ada generic, both the protected buffer and the *task* used to empty the buffer. This task can be configured for periodic flushing, and most importantly is receives an event if the buffer is full so it can be emptied, to decrease the blocking of the external supplier. This is supported by the Ada 95 *protected type* abstraction. The runtime efficiency and latency issues have been examined under various loads and this abstraction works effectively once the periodic rates are set correctly.

The other main use of protected types deals with the random storage and retrieval of data structures. The difference from protected buffers is that there is no pipeline of flowing information. Instead, their use is more like a database. Ada 95 provides support for at least two abstractions to support this: (1) Entry-Families, where the array is built into the object, and (2) Arrays of Protected Types. There are various costs associated with using these two abstractions including what the syntax is for external use.

---

[1]. Publication space considerations limit a more in-depth description of these valuable foundation real-time large scale Ada 95 abstractions.

3.0 Purity and Package Categorization

Ada 95 has introduced a number of categorization *pragmas* to help constrain the type of valid information contained in packages[6]. In particular, the *Pure* categorization limits the content of a package to only contain stateless information. This includes most types and procedures or functions without global state changes[2]. This is enforced by the compiler, since the body or specification of a pure package cannot define global variables. A major advantage of categorizing packages and their resulting types, such as pure, is their ability to support distribution across partitions using an implementation of the Distributed Annex-E.

Outside of distribution, an important reason to take the state (e.g. *globals*) out of the type definitions, and have it compiler enforced, is when dealing with code that may end up anywhere in the system. For example some code may just *with* a types package and create a couple instances. Without the purity rules, any global state would have been copied with the type, and the user would be getting a possibly large storage hit, even though they didn't use it. And if they did reference the global, there is no guarantee it is the same global as what is desired (if your code is really in a different executable partition)[3]. The same goes with procedures that have an implementation that requires *with-ing* in large sub-systems, and the user never intended calling the procedure since they only wanted the type information.

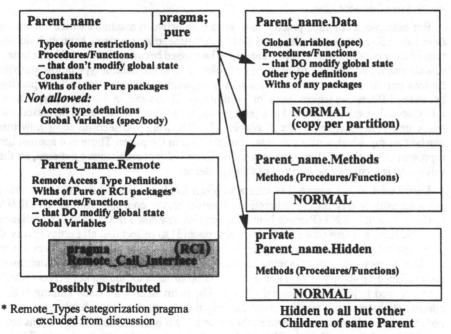

Figure 1   Example Package Purity Graphic Convensions for Types and Data

---

[2.] Utility Procedure and Functions are allowed if the only side effects are to the parameter objects. This code is replicated on each partition. In contrast, CORBA[10] cannot support this concept since it would have to be language neutral code.

[3.] Pragma shared_passive, should be used if the global requires accessible (see section 8.3.)

Ada 95's purity rules solve these issues, but it takes some re-work and re-organization (especially for the state variables). Figure 1 gives an example convention for package names, and describes what should be contained in those packages. For example, the *Parent_Name* contains all the pure type information. Then a sub child package, with the name "data" is used to contain the global state and possibly additional methods. An alternative is to have another sub child package called "methods" which contains the utility methods. In addition, "private" children can also be defined that are made visible only to other descendents of the same parent. Ada 95 can also support the distribution of particular routines by classifying the package as *remote_call_interface*, or RCI for short. The other pragmas, such as *shared_passive* and *remote_types* are not mentioned.

As a concrete example, the following section will describe the issues of time purity, and motivate a solution technique. It will also show the difference between a client-server approach, and distributed-objects.

4.0 Remote Time Capabilities - Purity Architecture Pattern

The designers of Ada 95 have determined that the *Ada.Calendar* and *Ada.Real_Time* packages, and in particular the type *time*, are not valid pure packages or types. There are many valid reasons behind this decision since distributed machines can not be forced to keep a global time. Because of this restriction, any data type defined in a pure package can not use this *time* type.

For example, a common practice is to send data between machines which contains a *time* value. Since Ada provides good tools to get time, many systems have include this type in their data structures. Unfortunately to be passed between distributed boundaries, this structure and the time value must be broken into some neutral type before transfer (unless one uses unchecked conversion, a dangerous technique especially if passing between different machine types or compilers). If instead, a new *time* type were introduced that was categorized in a pure package, then the ease of use is increased and many new Ada 95 solutions are available. The following two sections show how this can be accomplished, with a concrete example later in the paper. These two approaches represent examples of client-server and distributed-object architecture patterns, so the following is a cursory description of these patterns.

Distributed object approaches take a step out in abstraction while implementation portions usually rely on the indirection of name_server concepts such as a CORBA ORB or Ada 95's RNS (Remote Name Server) implemented in GLADE. The reliance on static names is termed a client-server approach[3] to reflect that all parties involved have statically determined the capability name, but resolve the physical location at runtime. Various projects at Boeing has determined that architectures should minimize their reliance on static names. Their use should be isolated to finding key servers which are then used to provide additional objects. The main issue with static naming is that additional abstractions, which extend the original abstraction through inheritance, are not available unless statically named the same known name. Extensibility is thus hard to achieve and very in-flexible. This model is almost identical to the static and inflexible procedure call binding.

The alternative pattern is called a distributed-object approach[3]. It models the object-oriented design principles relying on inheritance and polymorphism, and are vital to realizing the goals of extensible and adaptable architectures. This approach involves designing key abstractions to support the goals set out by framework architectures. Clients then rely on the abstraction, represented by types, and not on the name of instances. This non reliance on the physical implementation, but rather the abstraction, allows various objects of different inherited types to reside anywhere, and physically created over time. When clients need instances, they are retrieved by various server capabilities, but usually not relying on instance names. Finding these object instance servers is another issue. The client-server pattern is best when used for managing collections of these similar abstract objects. This concept is sometimes called a *factory server* or *abstract factory*[16].

4.1 Initial Client-Server Approach

The following is a discussion on developing a capability that provides a *pure* time type. This package is based on an existing real/simulated time package. The first section describes a new package where this pure time type is defined. The rest of the routines are implemented as per the original requirements. Figure 2 shows the Client-Server approach where the simulated time services can also be made available across distributed boundaries (provided in *mission_time.remote*).

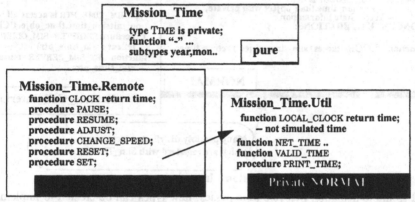

Figure 2   Client-Server Mission Time

Now, other pure data structures can include the *mission_time.time* data type, and the resulting type is still *pure*. Objects of this type can then be passed across distributed boundaries. An example of using this time service is described later in Section 8.0. Actual representation of the time type is not shown here, as there are various solution techniques with different portability constraints.

4.2 Later Distributed Objects Mission Time

An Object-Oriented approach to the same problem can be useful to decrease the static coupling of a known package name (e.g. mission_time). In this concept, there is a "simulation" object type with the same operations defined in the previous packages. Thus one could have different simulations running around, with a time source stored on the different machines. Basically the object oriented approach allows many simulators to be running anywhere in the network, with clients asking a central server for the best simulator in a particular class. The user then has a set of abstract operations at their disposal, with a guarantee that there will be concrete instances behind the objects. This approach is called *Distributed Objects*, as a contrast to *Client-Server*[3], and shown graphically in Figure 3. This abstraction allows implementations to occur anywhere,

118

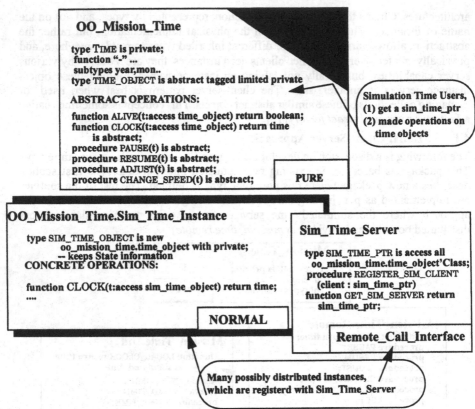

Figure 3   Object Oriented Mission Time

and as implementation lifecycle time passes, new types can be created to implement different types of simulators. One motivation for a distributed time object is described in Section 8.2.

5.0   Strongly Typed Data Subscription Capability (Possibly Remotely Accessable)

One technique available to increase concurrency is to provide some form of de-coupled data subscription capability[4]. This de-coupling is required in a physically distributed system. Protected objects exhibit this capability in a multi-threaded system, but they are not as effective for distribution. In the subscription pattern shown in Figure 4, important state information is made available to desired users through a registration scheme. As important state is modified, updates are pushed to those registered. In keeping with the de-coupling theme, this can be accomplished through the RACW (Remote Acess to Class Wide types) pattern, where abstract objects define an abstract *push* operation, which is later utilized by the supplier. At runtime, various instances of those abstract

---

[4.] The Ada 95 *Shared Passive* concept (E.2.1 of Ada 95 LRM[6]) is under investigation as a possible solution technique. In this approach, the data passing version of the code described here would be hidden by the underlying implementation, and this code would instead be used by applications to inform subscribed users when the data is valid. A multi-cast mechanism could be used for efficient implementation[12][8].

object definitions are created and registered with the appropriate instance server. If distribution is involved, instances may exist in different runtime partitions, but that is handled by the lower level distributed infrastructure, outside any layer of the application.

An important attribute of this concept is that the data being manipulate is statically typed, and thus compiler enforced. When combined with generics (see Section 7.0) this entire data subscription capability can be built once and instantiated many time, again with strong compiler enforced type checking.

In contrast, other technologies, such as the CORBA *EventChannel*[10], provide similar subscription concepts, but they are usually generic and therefore require dynamic type checking (using a construct called *any*). This involves reading the input stream for both the transmitted type information, as well as the actual data. Getting unexpected data types at runtime is interesting and must be accounted for in users application software. Large, long lived real-time systems can directly benefit from strong static typing in all phases of the software.

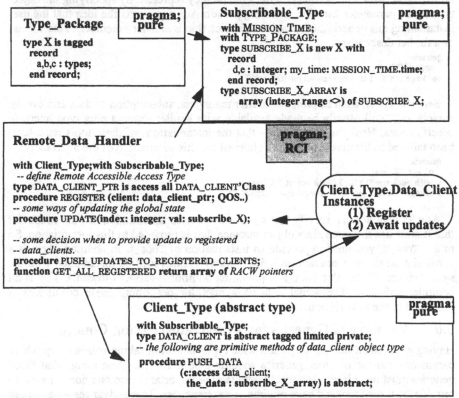

Figure 4   Remote Data Subscription Concepts

6.0   Generics: A New Typed Component Composition Dimension

Barns[9] uses the term *static polymorphism* when describing the *generics* Ada language construct. This tool is widely used but the real power is vastly under evaluated. Other languages don't come close to Ada's ability for defining so many levels of typed connection. It is important to know why these are basically only allowed in Ada; strong typing permeates every construct and require exhaustive enforcement by Ada compilers. With this foundation, adding more layers of checks was a natural extension.[5]

Generics provide a very powerful plug connectivity "language". Basically new dimensions are added which are not available with one dimensional interface specs. As "components" are made more available, inter connecting them is the next phase. Various graphical tools try to help with this but they all must step outside the language constructs, which decreases the coupling and cohesion of the feature with the descriptive mechanisms, namely the language constructs. A desired component may be valuable by itself, but will usually be more powerful if additional tools are provided for it's use. These tools are essentially abstract objects, and to be used must have been pre-instantiated. Two important language defined and compiler enforced dimensions added by generics were introduced in Ada 95.

First: the objects you provide on instantiation can be required to meet specific interface requirements, and the generic is built to manipulate objects of a known object family/class. Ada 95 can constrain the subtype they represent by specifying the object type in the parameter list. The following pseudo Ada represents the idea that the user instantiating this generic must provide an object, that is *at least* a member of the Y class or a further descendent.

```
generic
    object Y'Class;
package TOOL_1 is -- operations on "Object Y"
```

Second: Tools, such as protected buffer managers, subscription to data and events, parsers, etc., will usually be made available with similar abstract plug type interface specifications. How can one describe that the instantiations of these tools must have been tailored to the class of objects of interest for this incarnation of the interface?

```
generic
    object Y'Class;
    with package TOOL_1 (with object Y'Class);
package TOOL_2 is -- new operation on "Object Y"
```

Ada 95 generics can specify that a previous generic instantiation has the constraint that it must use the same class object instance that is provided to this instantiation. So to use TOOL_2, you must to provide an instantiation of TOOL_1. In addition, there is a constraint on the instantiation provided, namely it must also be instantiated with the same "object Y" that this TOOL_2 is providing additional services towards. This is all compiler enforced. The actual Ada 95 syntax for describing these constraints is described in the next section.

7.0   Example of Generics for Typed Subscription Concept

Having established that passing class wide types is useful, taking another step where parameters consist of other generics shouldn't be a stretch. Describing what those generics must have been instantiated with is now important since one doesn't want to provide the wrong tool and have runtime in-consistencies. These advances generics can take a system to a new and attractive distributed dimension: describing entire

---

[5]   By contrast, a C++ Template provides at best only untyped class parameters. This code cannot know until runtime whether objects provided are what is desired (for one reason there is no description of this requirement). Stepping down another level, languages like Java or IDL don't provide templates. There are various attempts at adding Generics to Java - a feature deemed important even in the non Ada community[15].

distributed systems as type enforced stamped instantiations of useful tools. As an example, take the typed subscription described in Section 5.0 to the next dimension, basically a physically generic RCI unit is available. The Typed Subscription can now be taken off the component shelf and installed with the desired types. As this abstraction involves numerous other tools (e.g. servers, clients, providers) the entire suite must also be instantiated. This is an important reason for package parameters as a building blocks.

```
-- The abstract type package
generic
    type BASE_TYPE is tagged private;
package GEN_SUB_TYPE is
    pragma pure;
    type SUBSCRIBE_DATA is new base_type with
private;
    type DATA_ARRAY is array(integer range <>)
of subscribe_data;
end gen_sub_type;

-- The "future Remote object definition" (which
will be using the gen_sub_type)
with gen_sub_type;
generic
    with package P is new gen_sub_type(<>);
package GEN_CLIENT is
    pragma pure;
    type DATA_CLIENT is abstract tagged limited
null record;
    procedure PUSH_DATA
        (client : access data_client;
                the_data: P.subscribe_data)
        is abstract;
end gen_client;
```

```
with gen_client;
with gen_sub_type;
generic
    type X is tagged private;
    with package G    is new gen_sub_type(X);
    with package CLIENT is new gen_client(G);
package GEN_REMOTE is
    pragma remote_call_interface;

    type DATA_CLIENT_PTR is access all
            Client.data_client'Class;
    procedure REGISTER_DATA_CLIENT
        ( client : data_client_ptr);
end gen_remote;
```

Figure 5   Generic Typed Configuration Showing 3 Generics

The code in Figure 5 shows this concept of the 3 generics, building on each other. Assuming the data definitions shown elsewhere, an instantiation of this code is then easily accomplished as shown in Figure 6.

```
with trks;
with gen_sub_type;
with gen_remote;
with gen_client;

package TRK_SUBSCRIBE is new gen_sub_type (Base_Type ⇒ trks.trks);
    pragma pure(TRK_SUBSCRIBE);
-- similar with's
package TRK_CLIENT   is new gen_client(P    ⇒ trk_subscribe);
    pragma pure(TRK_CLIENT);
-- similar withs'
package TRK_REMOTE    is new gen_remote(X    ⇒ trks.trks,
                    G    ⇒ trk_subscribe,
                    Client ⇒ trk_client);
    pragma remote_call_interface(TRK_REMOTE);
-- Now the type clients use is:
-- trk_remote.data_client
```

Figure 6   3 Generic Instantiations (At the Library Level)

Note that the generic instantiations must be at the library level and they must have the correct package categorization applied to this instantiation. If the pragma was not used then the resulting instantiation would be categorized as a *normal* package. The first generic (gen_sub_type) is only needed to make the rest of the code totally stand-alone. Another approach is to base all the subscribable data on a core type, and associated data array, which constrains the generic to a known set of types.

These instantiations would be repeated for all subscribable types. This shows the minimal amount of code needed, leading to decreased maintenance and allowing users to focus on their application issues without worrying about framework issues. It is also important to note that if a subscriber object ends up in the same runtime partition as the supplier, then the efficiency is down to procedure call overhead. Also, this abstraction can be used without any distribution at all, but if these steps are followed then eventual distribution is easily accomplished.

8.0   Distribution to Put the Entire Application Together

With the current and vast research in distributed processing, one shouldn't underestimate the power of compiling and integrating a single Ada system before distributed allocation is performed. Once the former is completed, the later is almost trivial. Thus the engineers don't need to learn many new concepts to make distributed components.

A valuable system description language, allocating subsystems to partitions is embodied in the *gnatdist* configuration file from GLADE. A cursory description of this language is presented, but more as a comparison to other approaches. As with the patterns work, these abstractions could be valuable to system architects as a set of toolbox options. Providing inter component connectivity modeling the extra dimensions is achievable with any technology, but having the descriptive capability ingrained in the language and more importantly having this checked by the compilers extensive syntactic and semantic checkers is very valuable.

Ada 95's Distributed Annex-E provides a powerful capability for distributing Ada programs to different processors. Moreover, this can be accomplished without changing any user code. Integration of external distributed mechanisms usually require various levels of code modification making portability to other capabilities harder. Is should be noted that this Ada 95 capability only supports inter-Ada communication and is not directly compatible with CORBA's communication model. That said, the code in Figure 7 is about the simplest distributed program a user could write in any language:

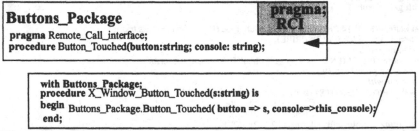

Figure 7   Simplicity of Ada 95 Distribution (Simple Client-Server Model)

This simple program has one extra line of code to categorize the package, and relies on external tools and a configuration language, both of with are similar to other distributed processing tools. In this approach, there are no runtime user issues with object name spaces (e.g. finding objects) since the program is treated like a single Ada program. In contrast, the distributed objects approach, such as shown in Section 4.2, requires some form of runtime name resolution. The later is the only method available in most other distributed capabilities (such as CORBA).

An external language, like IDL[10], has limitations that are more severe to Ada programmers. For example, IDL is missing a Generics Model, is weak in typing and overloading, and misses the object type extensions supporting the passing of large extensible data arrays as shown in Section 5.0[6]. The final resolution is that all users in any language have to draw a line between their own languages syntactic constructs and that of a foreign language like IDL (and provide the associated conversion software). This is the handicap required for *possible* future language independent interfacing.

With the new distributed processing capabilities being developed, distributed processing can be left to a later design decision, while the syntax for programming is shielded as much as possible (if the original system was designed to be multi-task safe).

8.1   Configuration Files to Describe Partition Layout

Most Real-Time systems will be closely coupled, in that all components are built with some knowledge of each other. This means that even with the best language neutral description and connection mechanism, there is still work molding of an existing component to a different interface specification. That said, use of inheritance and polymorphism are important to keep the coupling knowledge at the type/class level, while reducing the amount of predetermined object names, the basic difference between a client-server model and distributed objects.

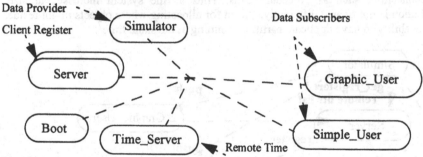

Figure 8   Partition Allocation Layout (Not Connectivity)

To put the abstractions described throughout this paper together, Figure 8 is a graphic representation of a set of partitions built with some of these abstractions. Figure 9 shows the corresponding *gnatdist* configuration file.

This examples shows a simulator providing information to two external users, one presenting the data graphically (graphic_user) and the other showing the information textually (simple_user). The information is pushed to these users since they have subscribed to this data. The Simulator also relies on the simulated time provided by time_server. It is important to note that the pushing to the subscribed users is not know until runtime, and subscribers can join or leave dynamically.

---

6. The Object-by-Value RFP from the OMG is trying to solve this issue in a very ambitious manner (www.omg.org).

```
configuration test is                        Simple_User : Partition;
   pragma Boot_Server ("tcp", "localhost:5");   for Simple_User'Main use TIME_MANAGER;
   Boot : Partition;
   procedure BOOT_PARTITION is in Boot;        Graphic_User: Partition;
     -- Lead Partition                         procedure YANOTHER;
                                               for Graphic_User'Main use yanother;
   Simulator : Partition;
   procedure GEN_SIM_TARGETS;                  begin
   for Simulator'Main use Gen_Sim_targets;r       Time_Server := (remote_sim_time);
                                                  Server    := (remote_dsp_targets);
   Server    : Partition;                       -- simulator := (dsp_targets_user); Implied
                                                  Simple_User:= (dsp_targets_user);
   Time_Server : Partition;                      Graphic_User := (dsp_targets_user);
   procedure TIME_MANAGER;                     end test;
   for Time_Server'Main use TIME_MANAGER;
```

Figure 9   Example GNATDIST Configuration Language

It is also important to note that this GNATDIST configuration file does not describe inter object connections. Instead, subsystems are described as they are allocated to executable partitions. This will even support replicated partitions and capabilities (such as package *dsp_targets_user* in the example). This reflects the minimal layout of key remote categorized packages, and not the entire system. Packages will be incorporated based on the outcome of the transitive closure of all required packages, a normal Ada feature. In contrast, Figure 10 shows one network connectivity runtime configuration.

Distributed module interconnections are described in Ada itself, just like any other interconnection, such as procedure calls. Thus as the system increases in size, distribution is not treated differently, except for allocating where objects might reside, and the ability to have duplicate partitions running at the same time[7].

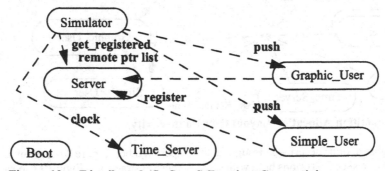

Figure 10   Distributed (Or Local) Runtime Connectivity

There are still open design questions with describing a Broadcast/Multicast capability, but as mentioned previously, the *Shared Passive* may be the best hope for a seamless language solution.

As a useful exercise, how would one provide a user control for the *pause* and *resume* timer_server operations, and could this be accomplished without taking down the already running system? The quick answer is that one would just write another package

---

7. There has been some discussion on creating a single executable that represents the same (or close to the same) layout as described in the configuration file, with *tasks* being used to implement the partitions[12].

which made calls on those operations. Then define a new partition where that package is allocated and then build just that partition. After that, it can be started, duplicated, killed without effecting the rest of the (possibly still running) system, other than side effects such as pausing or resuming the time. This is an un-obtrusive capability and is similar to the concept of Network Objects[11].

8.2   Partition ID and Quality of Service Usage

A new attribute for Ada 95 is *Partition_ID*. A user can query any package or procedure to determine the partition they have been allocated. This will be a universal integer, and only useful for the configuration and runtime instance being executed. This value could become useful when filling a runtime *Quality of Service* role. Basically once distributed objects are floating around, finding the best object implementation may involve querying for an object that is somehow "nearest". When an object resides inside the same partition, distributed execution is magnitudes faster.

Implementation of this can be as easy as providing your Partition_ID along with the object registration. Then when objects are queried, the user provides their own partition. The server (running anywhere) can then try to match known objects for identical partitions. If none are found, then other objects could be returned, or errors returns.

In this case, there may be two types of time object: simulated or real-time. A real-time version of the time object would reside locally with each partition, and either provide direct *Ada Calendar* functionality, or some other global synchronized time. In the simulated mode, a single time object would reside somewhere in the network which presented the simulated time. The registration of the objects would then denote their mode (simulated or real-time) and then their own partition_ID.

Users then query for time objects based on the simulated mode, and then when in real-time mode the registration routine would utilize the additional partition_ID parameter to find the time server within the same partition.

8.3   Shared Passive Design Concepts

The Ada 95 language added a categorization feature called *Shared_Passive*. In general this states to the compiler that all uses of this type of data are guaranteed that the data is shared and kept consistent. When this is stretched across distributed boundaries various implementations are available. In a single process, or shared memory cluster, a hardware shared memory mechanism can be used. Other distributed environments require some lower level framework to keep these consistent. The GLADE developers[12] have proposed that an implementation could use a multi-cast/broadcast capability. Subscribers are determined by inclusion (*with*-ing) of the shared data type in the users code.

Once this is available, there are other issues that any shared memory system must deal with, namely guarding against updates while in the middle of reading or writing, much like transactions. The user display of an air traffic control symbol, for example, would use this sharing to represent the current location. Without transactions, the software may be reading the x-location and before reading the y-location, it's content is modified by the underlying shared memory system. Then the x-y displayed shows the old x and the new y. This is rather annoying to the display users. The current proposal involves user insertion of pragmas to denote transaction areas (where updates can not be made, or conversely when updates can not be sent out). This is similar to Ada 95 GNAT (www.gnat.com) extensions that restrict when *task aborts* are allowed (i.e. pragma abort_deferred).

126

9.0 Summary

The choice of programming languages and distribution mechanism could change as the vast programming force starts to deal with their next set of problems: modeling interactions between concurrent and distributed systems, especially as they find out that language abstraction is important. The missing pieces are available within the constructs of the Ada Language, as it was designed from the ground up for these real-time problems. Software is becoming a more expensive commodity, and shortages are happening. Ada can help support these next set of abstractions within the language itself, allowing programmers to express and manager their complex problem space, instead of worrying about implementation technology (such as threads, mutexes, distribution).

Once distributed Ada is understood, one learns this capability is more seamless than having to decide when to use external languages like IDL and how to interface to AdaIDL, as the weaknesses in IDL are well know. The entire issues for any language developers of distributed systems, is when to express in IDL and when to express in their native language.

Ada programmers in most cases will initially want to express their internal object designs in Ada, unless they need to integrate external capabilities. Then over time, exposing some of the interfaces to other languages can be accomplished (like IDL or even C++). If this exposure were automated (e.g. auto or semi-auto IDL generation) then maybe the only time Ada programmers have to worry about IDL is for interfacing to external services. Also for Ada, using the categorization pragmas are a great new tool regardless of the Distributed Annex. Keeping "state" out of packages can be very valuable. There is still work needed to get this integrated, as mentioned in this paper. The steps to integrate a CORBA (or other external language) capability should not be under estimated. This is particularly true for data structures, and less true for simple method calls.

Developing and integrating complex real-time systems is highlighting that the Ada 95 language comes close to the magic line between too much language and too little. Witness the rush to build API libraries to implement features ingrained in Ada from day-1, circa 1979. Hopefully the Ada community can continue to show the effective use of the Ada language and especially target the younger generation to let them know there are some great elegant and effective alternative computing capabilities available.

Acknowledgments

This research could not have been performed without Boeing commitment and recognition that advanced object-oriented architectures are vital in the ever changing business climate, as they best support reuse concepts of extensible and adaptable systems. Ada 95 has been recognized as one of Boeing's vital object-oriented real-time tools to support Reuse. The OSA project must also be acknowledged as they let the reuse work absorb enough of the key personal to gain the knowledge for migrating key functionality while learning how to best use these new technologies. The Mission Information Processing Technology group has been providing focused research to help apply these advanced technologies, and as Boeing expands it will continue this important research. Also various engineers at ACT-E in Paris have helped with some of these concepts, as well as building the infrastructure capabilities inside GLADE.

References

[1]   S. Moody, "Objected Oriented Real-Time Systems Developed with a Hybrid Distributed Model of Ada 95's Built-in DSA capability and CORBA", Proc IRTAW8, April 1997 and *Ada-Letters* Vol XVii, Num 5, September/October 1997, Also a revised version in *Proceedings of 1st IEEE International Symposium on OO Real-Time Distributed Computing*, April 1998.

[2]   S. Moody, "The Ada Language; An Elegant and Effective Real-World Toolset", Proc. *Workshop on Methods and tools for Ada 95 Distributed and Real-Time Systems*, September 1997.
       Available at: http://www.seanet.com/~moody/papers

[3]   A. Burns and A.J. Wellings, "Concurrency in Ada", 2nd Edition, Cambridge University Press, 1997

[4]   DEC, HP, et al. "The Common Object Request Broker: Architecture and Specification". Technical Report OMG 91-12-1, Object Management Group and X Open, December 1991.

[5]   Y. Kermarrec, et al, "GARLIC: Generic Ada Reusable Library for Interpartition Communication", Proc. TRI-Ada'95, ACM Press

[6]   Ada 95 Reference Manual, ANSI/ISO/IEC-8652:1995, January 1995.

[7]   E. Schonbert et al. "GNAT: The GNU-NYU Ada translator, a compiler for everyone". Proc. TRI-Ada'94, Nov 94. ACM Press

[8]   Kermarrec, L. Pautet. "Integrating page replacement in a distributed shared virtual memory". In Proceedings of the 14th International Conference on Distributed Computing Systems, Poznan, Poland, June 1994. IEEE.

[9]   Barns, "Programming in Ada 95", Addison Wesley.

[10]   Siegel, "CORBA: Fundamentals and Programming", John Wiley & Sons inc., 1996

[11]   Kinzel, Jorg, "Network Applications in Ada95", Proc Tri-Ada 97

[12]   Sam Tardieu, Laurent Pautet, - Personal Coorespondence, Nov 1997.

[13]   Kempe, Magnus. "The Design of Interfaces and Connectors for the Composition of Abstraction", Proc Tri-Ada 97.

[14]   Taft, Tucker, "High Integrity Object-Oriented Programming with Ada 95", Tri-Ada 97

[15]   Myers, Bank, Liskov, "Parameterized Types for Java", POPL 97, France, 1997

[16]   Gamma, et al., *Design Patterns: Elements of reusable object-oriented software*, Addison Wesley, 1994.

(Astro)Physical Supercomputing: Ada95 as a Safe, Object Oriented Alternative

Martin J. Stift

Institut für Astronomie, Türkenschanzstr. 17, A-1180 Wien, Austria

Abstract. Due to a variety of policy errors of the guardians of Ada in the past, the scientific community has never come to appreciate Ada83; Fortran still holds virtually absolute sway over computational (astro)physics. The advent of Ada95 may have changed this unhappy situation. Extensive exploration of the potential of Ada in the field of spectral line synthesis over the past years has revealed its suitability for numerically intensive (astro)physical modelling. Genericity, hierarchical libraries and programming by extension are among the most attractive features, facilitating code maintenance and extension and achieving a high degree of software reuse. In addition, Ada tasking together with protected objects allows straightforward parallelisation with very few modifications to sequential code, yielding linear scaling of performance with the number of processors, and almost perfect load balance, whereas the data-parallel approach of High Performance Fortran turns out to be of little use. Numerous code examples illustrate how easy it becomes to write safe, reusable and massively parallel scientific codes in Ada95 without incurring the "abstraction penalty".

1 Introduction: Ada and scientific computing

If Ada has had little if any impact so far on scientific programming, the reasons for this are manifold: about everything, from the original language design and the DoD policy to the prevailing culture of scientific programming have conspired against the use of Ada. It is not unjust to consider Ada83 too rigid in its countless restrictions, in not providing even the most elementary mathematical functions, in tantalisingly offering parallel constructs while at the same time making them inaccessible to anyone but the system programming specialist. Ada was developed at a time when even mainframes could barely handle such a sophisticated compiler and it was prohibitively expensive. Even those university people who had cheap access to a commercial compiler such as DEC-Ada were discouraged by the library system and by the near endless compilation times prior to the advent of the Alpha chips.

The cultural barrier between the respective worlds of the computational (astro)physicist and of the software engineer did the rest. In a Fortran dominated lost world of traditional, almost prehistoric programming practices even students quickly adopt the age-old practices of established researchers. Modern software engineering techniques do not appeal to the innate programming conservatism of most astrophysicists but when in addition they are presented and illustrated with examples taken from a universe far outside the scientist's horizon (you remember all those defence and commercial applications) the result is wholly negative. The many wonderful books on Ada do little to convey the message to the average scientific programmer that Ada is well suited for scientific programming and I must admit, having perused most of the books in question, that I frequently found the presentation biased towards those features least pertinent to scientific problems. No wonder that even the most acute awareness of the shortcomings of Fortran is rarely if ever translated into affirmative action; in utter despair a few scientists even try C++!.

To make things worse, supercomputing – in science invariably associated with High Performance Fortran (HPF) – has started to largely mask the basic weaknesses of Fortran: HPF can make badly designed codes run very fast. Who is prepared to complain about the difficult maintenance and lack of transportability of a really fast code? "Supercomputing" as a simple synonym for massively parallel number-crunching? In my opinion this concept has to encompass sound software engineering practices and OOP techniques in addition to massive and efficient parallelism. In the present contribution I want to develop such a wider view. Not only do I find innumerable advantages of Ada95 over Fortran90 both in daily scientific life and in large scale projects, but Ada95 also proves a most attractive and powerful alternative to HPF while the "abstraction penalty" turns out to be by far not as heavy as found in previous studies.

2 Spectral synthesis and stellar atmospheres

In astrophysics, the theory of radiative transfer and of stellar atmospheres play a central role. The photons created deep in the interior of a star slowly diffuse outwards through innumerable absorption, re-emission and scattering processes, modifying their energy distribution according to the various contributions to the stellar opacity. Millions of atomic transitions (bound-bound, bound-free and free-free) and of molecular transitions give an extremely complex run of opacity with frequency, reflecting among others the run of temperature in the outer layers of a star and its chemical composition. Wavelength resolutions of about 10^{-12} meters are required to adequately sample the opacity in order to compare synthetic spectra with high-resolution observed spectra.

There are also stars which display surface magnetic fields of the order of 0.1-3 Tesla; Zeeman splitting of the atomic lines in these fields leads to observable linear and circular polarisation. Periodic variations in the observed magnetic fields are ascribed to the time-dependent aspect of a fixed dipolar field structure in the course of the rotation of these stars (the dipole axis is assumed to be almost perpendicular to the rotation axis, the so-called Oblique Rotator Model). Even though even in the most powerful telescopes these stars remain point-sources, modelling of the full phase-dependent polarisation spectrum allows the reconstruction of the magnetic field geometries.

2.1 Computing a spectrum: the algorithm

A code capable of synthesising – over a finite spectral region – a polarised spectrum consisting of a large number of Zeeman split lines must execute the following steps:

1. Read and store data defining the atmosphere of the star such as temperature and pressure structure and the run of continuous opacity with depth and with frequency;
2. determine the ionisation balances of the elements considered;
3. read and store atomic transition data such as level energies, J-values, Landé factors and broadening constants (van der Waals, Stark, radiation damping), and determine Zeeman patterns;
4. determine central line opacities and opacity profile widths (including thermal Doppler broadening);
5. sample the opacity at a given frequency by summation over all lines, for the σ^-, σ^+ and π subcomponents separately, taking into account the local field strength and the angle between the magnetic field vector and the line-of-sight;
6. solve the equation of polarised radiative transfer;
7. repeat (4) and (5) over the whole frequency range.

2.2 Computing requirements

As far as unpolarised line synthesis is concerned, a number of codes have been written in the past – mainly in Fortran but also in Algol68 – for the purpose of synthesising intensity spectra over moderate to large wavelength intervals. Even on a modest PC synthetic spectra covering several nanometers can be calculated within a time span of minutes. In rotating and non-radially pulsating stars calculations become substantially more expensive because we have to carry out a two-dimensional spatial integration of the duly Doppler shifted individual local spectra to obtain the observable integrated spectrum. Cpu times may increase by factors of 10-100!

The inclusion of magnetic effects drastically increases the complexity of the problem. The simple equation of radiative transfer changes to a vector equation in terms of the Stokes vector $IQUV$ where I stands for the intensity, Q and U describe the linear polarisation and V the circular polarisation; in discretised form it is written as a block tri-diagonal system with 4x4 submatrices. For each transition sampled in the nonmagnetic case, there are now between 3 and some 20 Zeeman subcomponents. In addition, the spatial integration grid has to become denser than for the nonmagnetic case. To synthesise a polarised stellar spectrum becomes very expensive indeed!

No wonder that Stokes codes (as I shall call them) do not abound; in fact, I am aware of only a handful of them throughout the world. Apart from my family of Stokes codes there presently exist no other codes capable of synthesising realistic polarised stellar spectra over large wavelength intervals. This is not due to untractable physics: the difficult administration of the line data and the prohibitive execution times on single-processor machines constituted the major obstacle to the systematic exploration of stellar magnetic polarisation. Apparently nobody so far has found a solution to these difficulties within a Fortran context. The extensive investigation and modelling of solar and stellar polarisation had to wait for Ada95.

3 A full Stokes code in Ada

A feasible software design solution in Ada83 for such a code has been presented by Stift [1][2]; it solved the problem of adminstrating the data, but did not implement concurrency. However, even the most superficial analysis of the steps involved in the synthetisation of a spectrum as given above immediately reveals that the concurrent constructs as provided by Ada95 are ideally suited for the purpose of writing parallel line synthesis codes for unpolarised or polarised light: both (3)-(4) and (5)-(6) can be executed in parallel by an arbitrary number of tasks with just minimum synchronisation. In fact, it does not matter in which order we read line data, determine whether the line really contributes to the total line opacity, and finally store the relevant line data. Similarly, one can calculate the frequency points in any order; in both cases one simply has to ensure that there is no redundancy. In the following I shall present the salient features of the family of Stokes codes I have developed so far. Emphasis is put on the implementation of parallel execution of large program segments, on synchronisation, the successful strive for software reuse, and performance.

3.1 Implementing parallelism

A very straightforward approach to parallelisation of the spectral line synthesis code involves the simple conversion of the procedure that controls the step by step synthetisation of the spectrum to a task (of course with some provisions for synchronisation, the details of which will be discussed later). An auxiliary procedure allocates an array of these worker tasks, attaching them to the different processors of the system. On an Origin200 4-processor system there would be 4 such worker tasks. In the example below the function Profile_point calculates one point of the spectrum by opacity sampling at a given wavelength Pos and subsequent solution of the transfer equation. In Profile_task the synthetisation proceeds towards smaller and then larger wavelengths until the spectrum has been calculated over the desired interval; Establish_Profile creates and distributes the worker tasks. The function New_Bound_Thread_Attributes is SGI specific; it creates an *sproc* (share group process) and attaches it to a particular Cpu.

Parallelised in this way, the resulting code is perfectly suited for the calculation of a *small* number of spectra during one run of the program. No more than a few dozen lines of code have to be modified to convert a sequential code

Table 1. Partial listing of (generic) packages with protected types and operations used for synchronisation in parallel Stokes codes, together with the procedure which allocates the worker tasks and attaches them to specific processors in a simple parallel solution

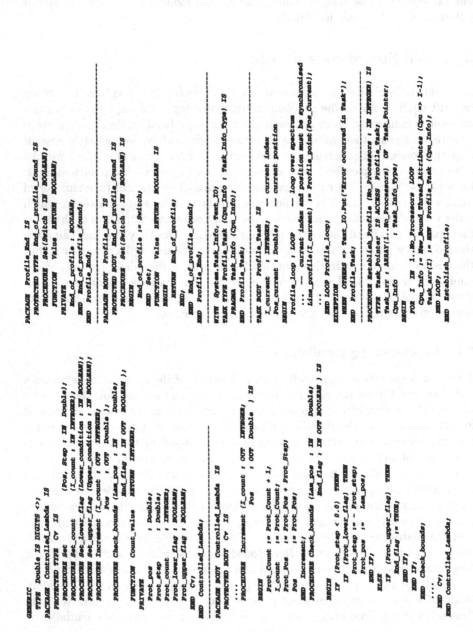

Table 2. Partial listing of tasks and subprograms used in a rendezvous based parallel solution

```
PACKAGE BODY Syn IS
....
TASK BODY Profile_Task IS
BEGIN
  Task_loop : LOOP
    SELECT
      ACCEPT Start;      -- start spectral synthesis run
    OR
      ACCEPT Stop;
      EXIT Task_loop;
    END SELECT;
    Proc_Info.ALL;       -- line synthesis routine
    ACCEPT Done;         -- spectral synthesis finished
  END LOOP Task_loop;
END Profile_Task;

TASK BODY Distribute_to_tasks IS
  Cpu_Info : Task_Info_Type;
BEGIN
  FOR I IN 1..Iproc LOOP   -- allocate worker tasks
    Cpu_Info := New_Bound_Thread_Attributes (Cpu => I-1);
    Profile_Loop_Task(I) :=
                NEW Profile_Task (Cpu_Info, Proc_Info);
  END LOOP;
  Task_loop : LOOP
    SELECT
      ACCEPT Synthesise_Spectrum DO
        FOR I IN 1..Iproc LOOP
          Profile_Loop_Task(I).Start;  -- start worker tasks
        END LOOP;
        FOR I IN 1..Iproc LOOP
          Profile_Loop_Task(I).Done;   -- wait for tasks
        END LOOP;                       -- to finish
      END Synthesise_Spectrum;
    OR
      ACCEPT Stop DO
        FOR I IN 1..Iproc LOOP
          Profile_Loop_Task(I).Stop;   -- stop worker tasks
        END LOOP;
        Stop;
      END Stop;
      EXIT Task_loop;
    END SELECT;
  END LOOP Task_loop;
END Distribute_to_Tasks;
END Syn;
```

```
PACKAGE BODY Syn.mg IS
.... -- line synthesis for magnetic case (Stokes profiles)
  PROCEDURE Profile IS
    I_current   : INTEGER;
    Pos_current : Double;
    End_flag    : BOOLEAN := FALSE;
  BEGIN
    Profile_loop : LOOP
      EXIT WHEN End_of_profile_found.Value = TRUE;
      EXIT WHEN (Cv.Count_value >= Iprofil);   -- array full
      Cv.Increment (I_count => I_current, Pos => Pos_current);
      Line_lambda(I_current)  := Pos_current;
      Line_profile(I_current) := Determine_point (Pos_Current);
      -- exit if array is full now
      IF (I_current = Iprofil) THEN
        End_of_profile_found.Set(TRUE);
        EXIT Profile_loop;
      END IF;
      -- check whether line is disappearing in the continuum
      IF ( Line_profile(I_current).S(I) <= 0.001 ) AND
         ( Line_profile(I_current).S(V) <= 0.0001 ) THEN
        Cv.Set_lower_flag (Lower_condition => TRUE);
      END IF;
      IF (Pos_current < Min_pos) THEN
        Cv.Set_lower_flag (Lower_condition => TRUE);
      END IF;
      IF (Pos_current > Max_pos) THEN
        Cv.Set_upper_flag (Upper_condition => TRUE);
      END IF;
      -- check whether lower and upper flags are set; if both are set,
      -- communicate end-of-profile-found to other tasks and exit
      Cv.Check_bounds (Lam_pos => Lam_pos,
                       End_flag => End_flag );
      IF (End_flag) THEN
        End_of_profile_found.Set(TRUE);
        EXIT Profile_loop;
      END IF;
    END LOOP Profile_loop;
  END Profile;
END Syn.mg;
```

134

to a parallel code. However, each time a new model is calculated, new tasks are created whereas the terminated tasks do not disappear, but continue to use resources (at least on SGI machines). After some time – typically with 256 tasks created – the program will crash. Needless to say that one can easily avoid this situation by resorting to a more advanced sort of parallelism.

3.2 Synchronisation

Protected objects have to be declared for synchronisation purposes. There are not many objects that have to be updated in mutual exclusion: *Prot_lower_flag* and *Prot_upper_flag* which are set to TRUE when the respective line intensity shortwards or longwards of the central wavelength becomes equal to the continuum intensity, the point count *Prot_count*, the step size *Prot_step*, and the wavelength position *Prot_pos*. After every wavelength step, the line intensity relative to the continuum intensity is checked and the flags set if the necessary conditions are met. The protected procedure *Check_bounds* determines whether the direction of the spectrum synthesis has to be reversed or whether the spectrum is already complete upon which the protected *End_of_profile* flag is set. If the spectrum synthesis is not finished yet, the position is incremented and everything repeated. Point count and position of course have to be incremented at the same time; the same is true for changing the sign of *Prot_step* and resetting *Prot_pos*.

With these protected objects, procedures and functions as listed in Table 2 one can achieve synchronisation between the different worker tasks with comparatively little overhead.

3.3 Advanced, rendezvous-based parallelism

Excessive task creation as encountered in the simple parallel solution discussed above can be avoided by using the classical rendezvous mechanism. The worker tasks, which are created at an early stage of program execution, have 3 entries, viz. Start, Done and Stop; the task distribution is done by another task with 2 entries, viz. Synthesise_Spectrum and Stop.

```
WITH  System.Task_Info;  USE System.Task_Info;
WITH  Controlled_Lambda, Profile_End, Text_IO;
GENERIC
  TYPE Real    IS DIGITS <>;
  TYPE Double  IS DIGITS <>;
  Iproc : IN  INTEGER := 4;   -- number of processors
PACKAGE Syn IS
  .... -- common definitions for magnetic and nonmagnetic cases
  PACKAGE CoLam IS NEW  Controlled_Lambda(Double);
  Cv                    : CoLam.Cv;
  End_of_profile_found : Profile_End.End_of_profile_found;

  TYPE Proc_Access IS ACCESS PROCEDURE;  -- procedure to be passed to task
  TASK TYPE Distribute_to_Tasks (Proc_Info : Proc_Access ) IS
    ENTRY   Synthesise_Spectrum;
    ENTRY   Stop;
  END Distribute_to_Tasks;
```

```
    TASK TYPE Profile_Task (Cpu_Info  : Task_Info_Type;
                            Proc_Info : Proc_Access   ) IS
      PRAGMA  Task_Info (Cpu_Info);
      ENTRY   Start;
      ENTRY   Done;
      ENTRY   Stop;
    END  Profile_Task;
    TYPE  Task_Pointer  IS ACCESS  Profile_Task;
    Profile_Loop_Task : ARRAY(1..Iproc)  OF  Task_Pointer;
END  Syn;
-------------------------------------------------------------
GENERIC
    Iprofil : IN INTEGER := 10000; -- max. no. of profile points
PACKAGE  Syn.mg  IS
    .... -- data types for magnetic case
    TYPE Line_lambda_type   IS ARRAY (1..Iprofil) OF Double;
    TYPE Line_profile_type  IS ARRAY (1..Iprofil) OF Stokes_Vector;
    Line_lambda  : Line_lambda_type;
    Line_profile : Line_profile_type;

    ....
END  Syn.mg;
```

The structure of the respective task bodies is very simple (see Table 3). In both the distributer task and the worker task there is a SELECT alternative between Start and Stop enabling a graceful exit from the indefinite loops. Having initiated execution of the worker tasks, the distributer task waits for the rendezvous at entry Done; it is then ready for a further spectral synthesis run.

The structure of the main procedure is not overly complicated either. With the elaboration of the declaration of *Task_Distributer* the worker tasks come into existence and are ready for the spectral line synthesis by means of the procedure Profile_actual – an appropriate instantiation of the generic procedure Profile – passed to the distributer task and the worker tasks in the respective discriminants.

```
PROCEDURE Sysolm IS
    ....
    Delta_lam, Lam_pos : Double;    -- step size and wavelength position
--  declare the worker tasks
    PROCEDURE  Profile_actual  IS NEW  Profile (Determine_point);
    Task_Distributer : Distribute_to_Tasks (Profile_actual'ACCESS);
BEGIN
    ....
    Model_loop : LOOP
        ....  -- initialise protected objects
        Cv.Set          (Pos => Lam_pos + Delta_lam, Step => -Delta_lam );
        Cv.Set_lower_flag(Lower_condition => FALSE);
        Cv.Set_upper_flag(Upper_condition => FALSE);
        Cv.Set_count     (I_count => 0);
        End_of_profile_found.Set(FALSE);
        Task_Distributer.Synthesise_Spectrum;
        ....
    END LOOP  Model_loop;
    ....
    Task_Distributer.Stop;
END Sysolm;
```

3.4   Parallelism with Ada: execution time and load balance

How do the parallel Stokes codes written in Ada perform, how does execution time scale with the number of processors, what about load balance? Not surprisingly, in view of the simple synchronisation mechanism based on protected objects, the synchronisation overhead is negligible as compared to the time required for opacity sampling and for executing the formal solver. Extensive tests have revealed that the sum of the execution times on the different processors remains constant to within 1% for up to 30 processors, i.e. total execution time of the code goes inversely with the number of processors.

Gratifyingly enough, almost perfect load balance is achieved in a natural way without any additional sophisticated algorithms. The calculation of a new spectral point is distributed in virtually exact correspondence to the available Cpu resources.

Of course, spectral line synthesis – as scores of other astrophysical problems – is "embarrassingly parallel" as some people like to call it, but try to use HPF for this purpose! Ada's control-parallel paradigm turns out to be ideally suited for any kind of stellar atmosphere work.

4 Families of line synthesis codes and software reuse

Whatever kind of spectral line synthesis one chooses to carry out, the calculations always closely follow the steps outlined in section 2.1. Whether opacity sampling is done over all Zeeman subcomponents or over unsplit lines, whether the formal solver deals with a simple differential equation or a vector differential equation, whether one considers a single point on the solar surface or the integrated flux over the visible stellar hemisphere, the various codes all have a common structure.

Taking advantage of the OOP features of Ada one can fully exploit this common structure. There are astrophysical applications where we are solely interested in the normalised (to the continuum) intensity I or in normalised the Stokes parameters $IQUV$ in the magnetic case. Sometimes however it becomes necessary to have absolute values for the Stokes parameters and the continuum. The algorithm for the calculation of the spectrum in Profile remains unchanged whether or not the final output contains normalised or absolute intensity or Stokes profiles, so it makes sense to declare a type $Basic\_Line\_Type$ as a tagged null record (when the continuum is not needed) or with a component of floating type (otherwise) from which we derive the type $Actual\_Line\_Type$ by adding for example a component of type $Stokes\_Vector$. The generic procedure Profile must now be instantiated with a function Determine_point which returns a result of type $Actual\_Line\_Type$. This simple software design solution obviates the use of separate subprograms for identical spectral line synthesis algorithms.

Similarly, the distribution of the worker tasks over the available processors is of course the same for polarised and unpolarised spectra, whether or not the normalised or absolute Stokes profiles or intensity profiles are printed. By passing Profile_actual as a discriminant to $Distribute\_to\_Tasks$ and thence to $Profile\_Task$, one can use these task types for all kinds of spectral line synthesis calculations.

Regrettably, neither inheritance, nor hierarchical libraries and task discriminants were available in Ada83, so this elegant way of developing and maintaining closely related families of codes had to wait for Ada95. These new facilities can rightfully be considered a major attraction for computational astrophysicists programming in the large; they are among the best arguments in favour of Ada as compared to Fortran90 and HPF, but also to C++.

```
WITH  Syn_start.mg, Stokes_Package.Polar_formal_solver.Standard;
GENERIC
   Iprofil : IN  INTEGER  := 10000;
   TYPE  Basic_line_type  IS TAGGED PRIVATE;
PACKAGE  Syn.mg  IS
PACKAGE  Synstart  IS NEW  Syn_start   (....); -- instantiate packages
PACKAGE  Syns      IS NEW  Synstart.mg (....); -- and make Stokes operations visible
USE  Syns.Stokes_Pack, Syns.Stokes_Pack.Stokes_Operations;
   PACKAGE  Solver_Standard  IS NEW  Syns.Solver.Standard; -- instantiate formal solver

   TYPE Line_lambda_type  IS ARRAY (1..Iprofil) OF Double;
   TYPE Actual_line_type  IS NEW  Basic_line_type
     WITH RECORD
       S : Stokes_Vector;      -- Stokes parameters (vector)
     END RECORD;
   TYPE Line_profile_type  IS ARRAY (1..Iprofil) OF Actual_line_type;
   Line_lambda  : Line_lambda_type;     -- resulting wavelength list
   Line_profile : Line_profile_type;    -- resulting Stokes spectrum

   GENERIC -- routine to be supplied for calculating a single point of the spectrum
     WITH FUNCTION Determine_point (Position : Double) RETURN  Actual_line_type;
   PROCEDURE  Profile;
END  Syn.mg;
```

5   Performance issues: the "abstraction penalty"

Much has been written about the "abstraction penalty" with which the brave Ada (and the C++) programmer are faced but not the cautious and conservative Fortran programmer. An extended investigation into this problem has been presented by White [6] but in my view it completely misses the point by analysing artificially contrived cases.

Why for example should a computational scientist ever consider employing dispatching calls in the most critical parts of the program? A straightforward analysis with simple profiling tools easily reveals the most time consuming parts of the code. Extensive optimisation pays in these parts, even at the price of resorting to Fortran style and it would be utter folly to trade performance for elegance (unless demanded by the complexity of the problem). Elsewhere in the program one does not have to worry about the potential cost of OOP features. Thus, in the Stokes codes discussed above which spend up to 70% of the total time in the routine that calculates the Voigt and the dispersion functions and another 5-10% in the formal solver routine there is no point in not using all those wonderful OOP features elsewhere. Sometimes the world is not hostile to the scientific programmer and the good and the bad can be well distinguished.

It is amazing that Fortran freaks (and also White, 1897) never dwell on abstraction penalties in Fortran77 as encountered when using complex variables. Take an example: the Voigt function is best calculated by means of a rational expression involving two complex polynomials and can be either coded by using the Fortran COMPLEX data type or more primitively with REAL variables. Depending on the compiler and the platform (DEC, SGI, SUN) the complex version can be a staggering 126% slower than the real version. Even the best compiler tested led to a difference of 36% and one wonders how many such similar cases in Fortran have gone undetected so far. For comparison, my first Stokes code in Ada was only about 10% slower than a nearly identical Fortran code. This appears to indicate that the comparison between Ada and Fortran performance respectively should be carried out in a more realistic way than what has been done up to now.

Notwithstanding theses findings, it must be admitted that there can be spectacular differences between compilers. Concerning more specifically GNAT, we find very satisfactory performance with respect to Fortran on some popular platforms, but at least in one case GNAT can be devastatingly slow. It is not unreasonable to assume that Ada is at best of peripheral interest to all the big companies and it appears that the poorest relative Ada performance is coming from the world leader in Fortran supercomputing.

6 Conclusions

Ada is in principle and often even in practice (when compilers create efficient code) ideally suited for scientific computations on any scale, the larger the better. The major attractions are to be found in the packaging concept, in genericity, in hierarchical libraries and programming by extension, and in tasking. Only towards the end of the first decade of the next millennium will Fortran possibly boast similar features. A Fortran programmer of course needs some time to get used to strong typing but there is always the joy of easy interfacing with the cherished old programs.

In accord with the findings of the Zeigler paper [7] development times have dropped sharply as compared to my previous 20 years with Fortran. The pleasure of successful major modifications of large codes in the shortest of possible times is in stark contrast to boundless frustration in the FortranIV and Fortran77 times. And once the scientific programmer has understood the mechanisms of task allocation and of the rendezvous, the parallelisation of code segments is quite easy to achieve, although "parallel thinking" as required for correct synchronisation proves more difficult. In all parallel applications ranging from simple line synthesis codes to Doppler Imaging codes (which reconstruct non-homogeneous stellar surface structure from time-dependent line profiles) near perfect load balance has been routinely achieved by simple use of protected objects as discussed above.

Having worked for 2 years with Ada83, I very much appreciate the increased power and flexibility of Ada95. As outlined in the beginning, some of the Ada83 features served as a most effective repellent for anyone but the most intrepid; fortunately the Ada95 revision process has removed all these obstacles to the enjoyable use of every single aspect of Ada in the scientific community. An introduction to object-orientation in astrophysics [3] and an overview of scientific programming with Ada [4] are taylored to the needs and interests of computational scientists. They are available, together with countless packages, whole (parallel) line synthesis programs and many more pages of lecture notes on the use of Ada in science on the Web [5]; information is spreading that Ada is good for you.

With increased funding for high quality optimising compilers, Ada could become the first choice in many fields of computational physics and all our efforts should be directed towards lobbying for such funding.

Acknowledgements Generous support has come from the Austrian *Fonds zur Förderung der wissenschaftlichen Forschung* under project P12101-AST. Additional funds from the *Hochschuljubiläumsstiftung der Stadt Wien* are gratefully acknowledged.

References

1. Stift, Martin J.: Spectrum synthesis in polarised light: software engineering issues and serendipitous results on broadband circular polarisation. In: Adelman, S.J., Kupka, F. and Weiss, W.W. (eds.): Model Atmospheres and Spectrum Synthesis. ASP Conference Series, Vol. 108, San Francisco (1996) 217-222.
2. Stift, Martin J.: Astrophysical software engineering in Ada. Irish Astron. J. **23** (1996) 46-48.
3. Stift, Martin J.: Object-Orientation in Astrophysics. In: Strohmeier, A., Barbey, S., Eckert, G., Stift, M.J.: Analyse, conception et programmation par objets pour physiciens, Troisième cycle de la physique en Suisse Romande. Ecole Polytechnique Fédérale de Lausanne (1996) 29 pp.
4. Stift, Martin J.: Scientific programming with Ada95: object oriented, parallel and safe. Computers in Physics (1998), **12**, in print
5. Stift, Martin J.: High Performance Ada in Astrophysics: The HPAda Homepage. `http://amok.ast.univie.ac.at/~stift/stift_home.html`
6. White, J.B., III: Performance issues of scientific programming in Ada95. Tri-Ada '97
7. Zeigler, S.F.: Comparing Development Costs of C and Ada. `http://sw-eng.falls-church.va.us/AdaIC/docs/reports/cada/cada_art.html`

Ada 95 for a Distributed Simulation System

Helge Hagenauer and Werner Pohlmann

Institut für Computerwissenschaften und Systemanalyse
Universität Salzburg
Jakob-Haringer-Straße 2
A-5020 Salzburg
Austria
hagenau@cosy.sbg.ac.at, pohlmann@cosy.sbg.ac.at

Abstract. In the distributed discrete event simulation area, Jefferson's time warp algorithm initiated a lot of research and practical work. We proposed a generalisation, split queue time warp, that allows lazy message reception and thus may reduce rollback frequency. The present paper contains a brief description of our algorithm and then describes an implementation that uses Ada 95 and its capabilities for distributed programming.

1 Introduction

In distributed discrete event simulation (for an introduction see [10], [5] and [4]), the traditional concept of a central simulation clock and its event-list implementation are replaced by a very different approach. One now views a system under study as composed of loosely coupled "physical processes", PPs, and simulates them by "logical processes", LPs, that interact exclusively by sending and receiving timestamped messages. The problem then is to maintain causal correctness. There are two main solutions, the "conservative" and the "optimistic" one, and the second, well-known as "time warp", [9], is our subject here. Time warp combines a no-wait strategy with an error detection and recovery scheme. LPs never wait for possible further messages but proceed on the basis of whatever has been received so far. This "optimistic" behaviour runs the risk of getting ahead of its input and thus producing errors. So if and when a LP receives input that should have been considered earlier, it must rollback to a former state and cancel its unjustified interim output (thus possibly inducing rollbacks elsewhere). Clearly, rollbacks and especially cascades of them form a major cost and reduce the advantage of having work done in parallel.

In standard time warp, henceforth called TW, all messages sent to a LP are inserted into and read from a single input queue that is maintained in ascending timestamp order, and corrective actions are triggered by "time faults", i.e. by the arrival of a message whose timestamp is smaller than the receiver's already achieved temporal level. This strategy is safe but possibly overcautious since the causality relation is covered by temporal order but usually much sparser than it: Many real-world processes are "active" in the sense of choosing, in relation to current state, what kind of information is relevant for their next move and what can be postponed.

Example: A typical case is a LP that models synchronisation of model entities; consider e.g. taxi-cabs and customers arriving at a taxi-stand. If there already is a customer present, the next output of the taxi-stand LP depends on the availability of a free taxi and not on the arrival of more customers. Consequently, in this state, the LP may ignore incoming messages denoting customer arrivals and instead look for a returning taxi.

Processing messages in strict timestamp order has two drawbacks: First, the LP has to copy currently unwanted information from the input queue and temporarily save it in its internal state. Second, the premature reading and copying of not-yet-needed messages inflates the past of the LP with event messages that, in time warp, may be erroneous or still subject to time faults; consequently, the LP runs a superfluously increased risk of rollbacks.

We therefore proposed to furnish the LPs with several input queues each of which corresponds to a message type and is read only when necessary for progress, i.e. message processing is now "lazy" or "by need". Figure 1 illustrates this for the taxi-stand example. The basic no-wait/error-recovery approach of time warp can be generalised to work with the new arrangement; the need for rollbacks is now discovered by comparing changes in the input queues against how far the queues were already read. We call the new algorithm split queue time warp or SQTW ([6]).

```
LOOP
  IF customer_is_present
  THEN
    get(message, taxi_channel);      -- seize taxi
    local_time := max(message.timestamp, local_time) ;
    send((taxi, local_time + some_travel_delay), somewhere);
    customer_is_present := false;
  ELSE
    get(message, customer_channel);      -- next customer
    local_time := max (message.timestamp, local_time);
    customer_is_present := true;
  END IF;
END LOOP;
```

Fig. 1. Taxi-stand model for SQTW

We first tried out our idea in a pseudo-parallel one-processor prototype written in Ada 83 [7] and found that SQTW can indeed lead to a decrease in rollback numbers. In the present paper we describe a new and more adequate implementation that is based on Ada 95 and its capabilities for programming distributed systems; we used the GNAT/GNATDIST tools (cf [1], [8]). Section 2 describes the basic functioning of and requirements for SQTW-LPs. Section 3 and Sect. 4 describe the structure of the system and then add some programming details; we here assume that the reader is familiar with Ada 95 and its Annex E. In Sect. 5 we sum up and indicate open issues and future work.

2   Logical Processes

The "asynchronous iteration" paradigm of parallel programming (cf [3]) provides a convenient way of viewing and designing distributed simulators (cf [12]). We accordingly characterize each LP by a sequential, deterministic and always properly terminating piece of program that is executed (virtually) infinitely often and in fair but otherwise unconstrained conjunction with other LPs. For message-based communication, LPs have input buffers with get and put operations. – We next describe the workings and requirements in more detail. As usual in this area, the goal is to provide a framework which the user (simulationist) can and must complete according to his specific modelling purpose. As a first design decision in this direction, we here lay down that the to-be-iterated computation of an LP consists of a model-specific part, called the LP step, and a preceding more technical part, called the LP prologue, that serves error-recovery needs (see Fig. 2).

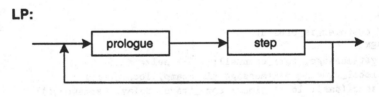

Fig. 2. LP diagram

Input Buffers. LPs may own several input buffers (or channels or queues) each of which is kept and used in timestamp order. Incoming messages are mapped to the diverse buffers by type, which is the responsibility of the receiving LP (and requires corresponding definitions by the modeler). Buffers are unbounded so that a put operation never fails. Conversely, a get attempt on exhausted buffer makes a LP abandon its current step and enter a "terminated" state, which is rollbackable. – For error recovery purposes, input buffers are not actually consumed (shortened) by a get operation but subdivided into an already covered initial part and the yet unread rest. For the same reason, a LP must be able to cancel (unsend) a formerly sent message; we use the classic technique of antimessages together with a correspondingly extended (viz. destructive) semantics of the put operation. – In addition to simple put and get operations on input buffers, it is consistent with SQTW to look for the earliest message in a group of buffers or the existence of any message in a given time horizon, but we have not yet implemented this facility.

LP steps. The purpose of LP steps is to simulate, i.e. to provide an equivalent of PP behavior, and to this end they fetch and interpret messages from input buffers, update local state and send messages to other LPs; the body of the loop in Fig. 1 gives an example. Programming LP steps is the main obligation of the modeler. A sufficient condition for SQTW to function correctly is model causality: the timestamp of messages sent in a LP step should not be smaller than the maximum timestamp of messages the LP read so far, and any cycle of send-receive relationships in the model should include proper temporal progress.

LP prologue. Prior to each step, a LP examines itself for consistency and saves its present state for later recovery (if consistent) or rolls back to a suitable earlier stage (otherwise). Consistency relates to input buffer content: An inconsistency exists iff, in the meantime and through the actions of other LPs, an input buffer has gained or lost (via message cancellation) an entry in the already read part, i.e. the "past" of the LP has undergone some change. Repeatedly applying the same criterion, the LP then searches for and returns to the most recent consistent state in its recovery stack, and in this rollback across earlier steps the LP cancels all then sent messages, i.e. invalidates the exterior effect of the discarded computation. Consistency checks and rollbacks are relevant for terminated LPs too; particularly, a terminated LP unterminates after a message is inserted into a buffer that was formerly found exhausted. – For more details on recovery data see Sect. 4. – SQTW also allows other and sometimes more efficient state saving techniques like incremental state saving or longer/changing intervals, but we have not yet implemented such alternatives.

Since continuous accumulation of recovery data leads to memory overflow, it is important to discover and discard obsolete ones. This requires a superimposed distributed computation that provides systemwide lower temporal bounds on possible inconsistencies. Matters are similar for TW and SQTW (with slightly more indirect memory reclamation for the diverse input queues), and we adapted Mattern's algorithm (cf [13]) and made it a responsibility of LP prologue. For lack of space we cannot go into details here.

3 System Structure

LPs are the main building blocks of a SQTW system, but we need some structural additions and refinements. LPs can be realised as processes (tasks) or as passive objects whose operations are executed in the control flow of callers; we choose the

144

second alternative for reasons apparent below. Our implementation is intended for the cheapest and most common parallel machine, viz. workstations on a network, and we expect the user to allocate several or even many LPs to the same processing node; let us call such a group of LPs a submodel.

LPs as Objects. For scope and flexibility of use (the simulationist may e.g. want to set up communication relationships at system start and not freeze them in program text) we need the "distributed objects" approach, which allows remote calls to be dispatching. Since Ada separates tasking and OO concepts, one has to form combinations. So we use LP objects together with driving tasks. The two main operations of a LP object are "write" (-me-a-message) and "go" (= prologue; step;); the first is invoked by other LPs for communication and the latter is repeatedly called by the driving task.

Submodels. Though asynchrony is the very idea of distributed simulation, the user may wish to exercise some control on the relative temporal progress of LP objects on the same processor to e.g. improve efficiency. This is most easily done by having a single task, the submodel manager, drive all these LP objects. The submodel manager and its LPs are packaged into an active partition (see Fig. 3).

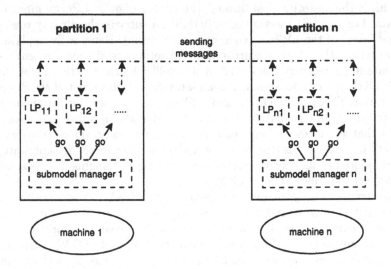

Fig. 3. Implementation structure

In addition to this basic functionality, the submodel manager has responsibilities in system start and close-down and to this end cooperates with a main program (the interface to the experimentator) and an adress server, see Fig. 4.

In a two-phase protocol, the submodel manager first creates, initializes and registers (with address server) its LP objects and then, conversely, supplies them

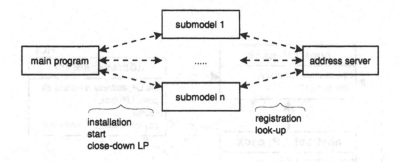

Fig. 4. Collaboration structure

with addresses of remote partner LPs obtained from address server. It then exercises its LP objects by repeated calls of their go operations until some termination criterion is met, extracts results and reports back to the main program, see Fig. 5.

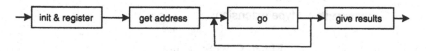

Fig. 5. LP life cycle

4   Implementation Details

Figure 6 shows the core of our class model together with package dependencies and categorizations according to Annex E. The packages without categorization are normal packages whose definitions are used in every submodel partition but only locally.

The Type pure_lp. This is the root type in the class structure and introduces the abstract procedure **write** for sending messages to a LP. This operation is for remote calls so that we need a pure package. In the same package (Fig. 7) we have the type **abstract_message**. It contains attributes common to all messages like timestamp, sign (for marking positive and anti messages) and ordering by timestamp. For use in a concrete modeling context, specific message types have to be derived. This needs another pure package to make universal communication possible.

146

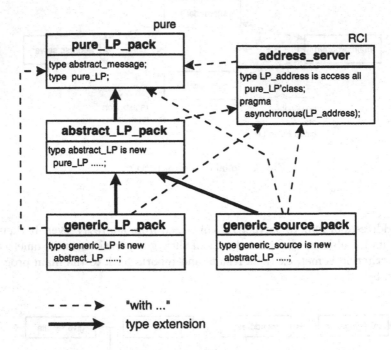

Fig. 6. Class Structure

```
PACKAGE pure_lp_pack IS
  PRAGMA pure;
  .....
  TYPE abstract_message IS ABSTRACT TAGGED RECORD
    sign : sign_type := positive_sign;
    timestamp : float := infinity;
  END RECORD;

  FUNCTION "<" (m1, m2 : abstract_message'class) RETURN boolean;
  .....
  TYPE  pure_lp IS ABSTRACT TAGGED LIMITED PRIVATE;
  PROCEDURE write (lp_adr: ACCESS pure_lp; d: abstract_message'class)
    IS ABSTRACT;
PRIVATE
    TYPE  pure_lp IS ABSTRACT TAGGED LIMITED NULL RECORD;
END pure_lp_pack;
```

Fig. 7. Package pure_lp_pack

The Package address_server. This remote call interface package (Fig. 8) provides the already mentioned LP registration and look-up services. It furthermore defines the necessary general access type for `pure_lp'class`, which is made asynchronous so that a caller of the `write` operation is not delayed until completion of its call.

```
WITH pure_lp_pack; USE pure_lp_pack;
PACKAGE address_server IS
  PRAGMA remote_call_interface;

  TYPE lp_address IS ACCESS ALL pure_lp'class;
  PRAGMA asynchronous(lp_address);
  .....  -- registration and address information
END address_server;
```

Fig. 8. Package `address_server`

The Type abstract_lp. In simulation models one often needs LPs that only produce output and do not depend on input themselves. Consequently, such source LPs have no use for the rollback mechanism and allow a simpler implementation . (They still must participate in the overlaid computation for memory reclamation and therefore need the write operation of `pure_lp`.)

To obtain a convenient interface to submodel managers, we create (in a normal package `abstract_lp_pack`) the type `abstract_lp` (Fig. 9) as a common ancestor for ordinary and source LPs. It is derived from `pure_lp` and introduces additional operations:

1. Installation procedures
2. **go**-operation (= prologue; step;)
3. **send**-operation: write a message to another LP and remember it for possible cancellation

The implementation of these operations is done at the next hierarchy level.

The Type generic_lp. Defined in the generic package `generic_lp_pack` (see Fig. 10), this type implements the basic components of an ordinary LP, viz. input buffers, state stack and the operations

1. **write**-operation
2. Installation procedures
3. Operations for sending and receiving messages (elementary operations plus bookkeeping)

```
WITH pure_lp_pack, address_server, ...; USE ...;

PACKAGE abstract_lp_pack IS

   TYPE abstract_lp IS ABSTRACT NEW pure_lp WITH NULL RECORD;
   TYPE abstract_lp_class_pointer IS ACCESS ALL abstract_lp'class;

   .....                  -- Installation procedures

   PROCEDURE go (who : access abstract_lp) IS ABSTRACT;

   PROCEDURE send (who  : access abstract_lp;
                   whom : positive; -- index of communication partner
                   what : a_message_pointer) IS ABSTRACT;
END abstract_lp_pack;
```

Fig. 9. Package abstract_lp_pack

4. **go-operation**: prologue and (placeholder for) step
5. Some auxiliary operations

This implementation must anticipate information that is only supplied later by a modeler who uses our system, and we chose Ada's generic mechanism as a convenient and safe (esp. in connection with the various container types) means for this purpose. Examples are the number and element types of input buffers or the model-specific descriptive state of a LP (e.g. the Boolean variable customer_present in the taxi_cab illustration of Fig. 1).We called this latter item, usually a record, small_state to distinguish it from the more comprehensive big_state that additionally contains the more technically recovery-related information like how far input queues have been read or what messages have been sent to whom in which step. Naturally, the production of such bookkeeping information is made a side effect of communcation operations. One further point is worth mentioning: since write and go operations are concurrent, some control is necessary. To give go undisturbed possession of the input buffers, we made a mailbox (a protected object) the immediate target of write.

5 Conclusion

In this paper we described an implementation of SQTW, a variant of the time warp algorithm for distributed simulation. Our work relies on the Ada 95 model of programming distributed systems, and we used the GNAT/GNATDIST tools. It was our first experience with Ada 95, but language and tools allowed quick and rather smooth progress. Our system shows plausible behavior, but we still need more experimentation and measurements for a proper assessment of what was achieved. Some implementation details will be reconsidered and perhaps

```
WITH pure_lp_pack, abstract_lp_pack, address_server, ...; USE ...;

GENERIC
  .....
  TYPE small_state IS PRIVATE;   -- state of a concrete LP
PACKAGE generic_lp_pack IS

  TYPE generic_lp IS NEW abstract_lp WITH PRIVATE;

  PROCEDURE write (whom : access generic_lp;
                   m    : abstract_message'class);
  .....
  PROCEDURE go (who : access generic_lp);

  PROCEDURE receive (who   : access generic_lp;
                     where : in_range;
                     mp    : out a_message_pointer);
  -- reads the next message from the denoted input queue
  -- and does bookkeeping

  PROCEDURE send (who : access generic_lp;
                  whom : positive;
                  what : a_message_pointer);
  -- writes a message to a LP; does bookkeeping

  PROCEDURE step (who : access generic_lp;
                  s    : in out small_state;
                  rs   : in out positive);
PRIVATE

  TYPE big_state IS RECORD
    s_state : small_state :=  initial;    -- model specific information
    ...              -- general information
  END RECORD;

  PACKAGE  my_state_stacks IS NEW state_stacks(big_state); USE ...;

  TYPE generic_lp IS NEW abstract_lp WITH RECORD
    .....   -- identification, input queues, data report
    my_mailbox : mailbox;
    my_state_stack : my_state_stacks.state_stack_type;
    my_state : big_state;
  END RECORD;
END generic_lp_pack;
```

Fig. 10. Package generic_lp_pack

revised, and we have to add appropriate support for data gathering, reporting etc. (till now, we rather monitor the behavior of our system and not the simulated model) to make the implementation useful to practising simulationists. Our design strictly keeps to the distributed simulation paradigm of LPs interacting via messages and use Ada's remote procedure calls just to implement this (the `write` operation of LPs). But instead of having to think and program in terms of timestamped event messages, a modeler might prefer to work with timed remote invocations of operations that are meanigful at model level. This is an interesting question for future work.

References

1. Barnes, J.G.P. 1994. *Programming in Ada*. Addison-Wesley, Reading, Ma.
2. Burns A. and A. Wellings. 1995. *Concurrency in Ada*. Cambridge University Press, New York.
3. Chandy, K. N. and J. Misra. 1989. *Parallel Program Design*. Addison-Wesley, Reading, Ma.
4. Ferscha A. 1996. "Parallel and Distributed Simulation of Discrete Event Systems". *Parallel and Distributed Computing Handbook* (A.Y. Zomaya ed.). Mc Graw-Hill.
5. Fujimoto, R. M. 1990. "Parallel Discrete Event Simulation". *Communications ACM* 33(10), pp.31-53.
6. Hagenauer, H. and W. Pohlmann. 1996. "Making Asynchronous Simulation More Asynchronous". Proc. 10th European Simulation Conference, Budapest.
7. Hagenauer H. and W. Pohlmann. 1996. "Prototyping a Parallel Discrete Event Simulation System in Ada". Proc. ACM TRI-ADA'96 (S. Carlson ed.). Philadelphia.
8. Kermarrec Y., L. Nana and L. Pautet. 1996. "GNATDIST: A Configuration Language for Distributed Ada 95 Applications". Proc. ACM TRI-ADA'96 (S. Carlson ed.). Philadelphia.
9. Jefferson, D. R. 1985. "Virtual Time". *ACM TOPLAS 7*, pp.404-425.
10. Misra, J. 1986. "Distributed Discrete Event Simulation". *ACM Computing Surveys* 18(1), p.39-65.
11. Pohlmann, W. 1987. "Simulated Time and the Ada Rendezvous". Proc. 4. Symposium Simulationstechnik. Zuerich. J. Halin ed., pp.92-102.
12. Pohlmann, W. 1991. "A Fixed Point Approach to Parallel Discrete Event Simulation". Acta Informatica 28, pp.611-629.
13. Mattern, F. 1993. "Efficient Algorithms for Distributed Snapshots and Global Virtual Time Approximation". Journal of Parallel and Distributed Computing 18, no 4.

PINROB: A Portable API for Industrial Robots

M. González Harbour[1], R. Gómez Somarriba[1], A. Strohmeier[2] and J. Jacot[2]

[1]*Departamento de Electrónica y Computadores*
Universidad de Cantabria
39005 Santander, Spain
email: mgh@ctr.unican.es, gomezr@ctr.unican.es

[2]*Swiss Federal Institute of Technology*
Department of Computer Science &
Department of Micro-Engineering
1015 Lausanne, Switzerland
email: alfred.strohmeier@di.epfl.ch, jacques.jacot@epfl.ch

Abstract: This paper describes a software architecture for industrial robots used in manufacturing equipment. In order to achieve software portability, the application software is dissociated from the low-level robot controller software. The interaction between these two pieces of software is achieved by a portable application programming interface (API) for industrial robots. We discuss the requirements for such an API, and propose a design called PINROB.

Keywords: Robot, Manufacturing Cell, Production Cell, Robot Programming Language, Application Programming Interface, API, Software Portability, Ada.

1   Introduction

Industrial robots are in large use in manufacturing equipment. Production cells are designed around one or several robots. In a typical simple system, a robot sits in the middle of a cubicle surrounded by "peripherals". One of the "peripherals" is usually a buffer store, containing pieces to be worked on, and the others are "dumb" machines. Their kinds depend on the manufacturing process: measuring and marking, assembly by gluing, insertion of parts, adjusting mechanical pieces, polishing, etc. Production cells are usually custom-made, the specifications being defined by the customer. Little design work is required to tailor the mechanical components to the intended use. The provider of the manufacturing cell is used to only a few number of robots, with the right physical characteristics, and the design and selection of the peripheral machines is largely based on past experience. However, the application software is usually developed from scratch, which is expensive, time-consuming and error prone. Software appears to be on the critical path of quality, but also for the time-to-the-customer. It should be noticed that the customer in turn sometimes adapts the application software, with or without the help of the vendor. Up to three months might be needed for such an adaptive maintenance operation. The loss of the corresponding production cycles has a major negative impact on the profitability of the equipment.

1. Supported in part by the *Comisión Interministerial de Ciencia y Tecnología* of the Spanish Government under grant number TAP97-892

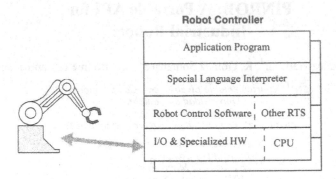

Fig. 1. Layers in a Robot Computer System

The robot integrates a computer system (see Fig. 1), usually called a robot controller, which not only controls the robot, but also runs the application program specific to the production cell. The robot vendor provides all the hardware, but also the robot control software, and some kind of programming environment. This environment is usually built around a proprietary interpreted programming language. Technical details about the robot control software, especially the so-called servo loop, and other pieces of the run-time support system are not disclosed by the robot vendor to his customers.

The robot control programming language varies therefore with the robot vendor (or the kind of robot controller), and also over time, because robot vendors improve constantly their programming languages. Production cell specialists explained us that all the robot control programming languages were very similar in purpose and functionality, but quite different in form. Different software development teams are therefore needed if several different robots are used.

As in other fields of software, we thought it should be possible to use a single high-level programming language, together with an application programming interface (API) for robots. Such an API would provide the basis for writing portable application programs. The purpose of this paper is to discuss the requirements and design of such a portable API, that we are currently implementing for several industrial robots. We call it PINROB, for Portable API for INdustrial ROBots.

In a first step, we examined the following robot control programming languages: Adept V and V+ [3], Adept SILTOOLS [4], ABB-IRB 200 S3 programming language, ABB S4 Rapid programming language [2], AUTOMELEC Lucie [5], Siemens SIROTEC ACR-20 [10], and Demaurex Delta95 [6]. All of them support the normal programming language constructs such as conditional and loop statements, input and output statements, data types and variables, expressions and assignment. In addition, they provide robot-specific operations, such as the ability to move the robot to a particular point, or through a specified trajectory, or to read the position of the robot.

Some of these languages allow for some degree of multitasking, i.e. concurrent execution of different tasks or programs.

We believe that the features to be considered in the API are basically the union of the features found in these robot controllers, rather than their intersection. Otherwise, all robots would become functionally alike, and any competitive advantage would be lost. The chosen approach implies that sometimes a feature cannot be implemented on a particular controller. In that case, we define the acceptable behaviour that the robot application must tolerate.

We have chosen to use the Ada language as the programming language for the robot applications. In this way we can use all the normal constructs of a high-level language without having to implement them ourselves (such as data types, variables, expressions, conditional and loop statements, etc.). In addition, we can exploit the advantages of Ada over other standard languages, such as packaging in modules, data abstraction, encapsulation, object-oriented features, and well-defined real-time multitasking. What is missing is a set of robot-specific operations, similar to those of the robot programming languages, such as moving the robot to a particular point or reading its position. These operations together with the necessary data types are integrated into the PINROB API.

It might appear that the Ada language is more difficult to learn and use than a conventional robot programming language. However, it is always possible to describe a small subset of the Ada language that, together with the robot API, would be no more complex than an average robot programming language. Of course, advanced programmers could always make use of all the advanced features of the Ada language.

2 Architecture of the Robot Programming Environment

Because the robot controller is usually a special-purpose computer with a proprietary operating system, it is not possible to integrate Ada programs into it. Consequently, the programming environment that we have designed consists of an external computer linked to the robot controller through a communications channel (e.g. serial line or network). The application program written in Ada and using the PINROB interface runs in the external computer and sends commands to the robot controller. A command executive program written in the controller's special-purpose language, and running in the robot controller, receives the commands, and interprets them. Then, if the command is a request to execute an action, it performs it by invoking the appropriate operations in the controller; if the command is a request for information about the robot, it obtains this information and returns it.

Fig. 2 shows a diagram with the basic architecture. The execution of the robot application at one end and the subsequent execution of the associated commands at the controller end are synchronized by an acknowledge message that the command executive sends back for every command processed.

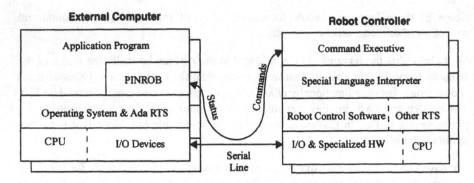

Fig. 2 Basic architecture of the robot programming environment

The advantages of this approach are that we reuse all the robot controller software without having to interact with internal aspects of its implementation. In addition, the remote computer can be any general-purpose computer, and both the robot application and most of the PINROB implementation will be portable. The non portable part of this architecture is the command executive, that has to be rewritten for every special controller, and part of the PINROB implementation.

3 Basic Requirements

The requirements for the PINROB API have been inspired by different robot programming languages. All the systems that we investigated were capable of controlling one robot with its arm and gripper, a control pendant keyboard and display used by the robot operator to program and supervise the robot operations, as well as digital input and output, analog input and output, and independent axes. In addition, some systems were capable of controlling several secondary robots, each with its arm and a gripper. Among the requirements, we have included the capability to control and monitor all of these objects.

Some other systems have image processors, conveyor belts, welding tools, and many special tools that can be controlled from the controller. Since these are too system-specific, we have not included them in the PINROB interface, although they can be included in particular systems as extensions.

All of the robot controllers that we have checked have the capability to execute robot movement operations in parallel with instructions that use other objects such as digital or analog I/O, or the control pendant. We have required this behaviour as the default for the PINROB API, to increase the level of concurrency, which can then be exploited by the application program using Ada tasking. Also required are operations to synchronize the execution of the task controlling the robot movements with their finalization. In this way the program may be synchronized with the robot movements.

Another important requirement derived from most robot controllers is the ability to create "interrupt service routines" that are triggered by a digital input. In the PINROB API this is accomplished by requiring a *Wait_Until_Signal* operation, that blocks the calling task until a given digital line changes its state. In this way, that task itself becomes the "interrupt service routine".

In order to take full advantage of the learning capabilities of the robot (to learn about the position of objects, the size and orientation of its tools, etc.), we also require operations to read the values of variables defined in the robot controller. Another way of learning about positions of objects is accomplished through a requirement for the robot program to be able to stop temporarily, passing control to the robot controller. In this situation, the operator can move the robot to the desired position using the manual movement operations provided by the robot controller. Once the robot has been moved, the robot application program can resume its execution right after the point where it stopped. At that point, it can read the new position of the robot and store it for future reference.

The requirements for the PINROB robot library [7] as well as the PINROB specification [8] are available from the authors upon request.

4   PINROB Software Architecture

One of the first design criteria for the robot library has been the simplicity of the interface, to make it easier for robot programmers to use it for writing robot application programs. We think that this is an extremely important criterion because if the interface is complex it will not be used.

The simplicity criterion has driven us to avoid using advanced features of the Ada language. In this way, the interface is simpler to understand by robot programmers. Among such unused features, we can mention unconstrained data types, generics, and object-oriented features, such as inheritance and polymorphism. This limits the extension of the library in the sense that it will be necessary to recompile it and perhaps make slight changes to the applications when new features are added, but still we want to give more importance to simplicity.

In the design of the architecture we have used encapsulation techniques to make the library interface implementation-independent. We have used private types for those data structures that are usually implemented in different ways in different robots (e.g. position frames). However, some other common data types have been defined as visible types because, traditionally, they are always used in the same way (e.g. joint coordinates as an array).

We have also used the Ada 95 hierarchical library facility, to make the interface modular. However, we have kept the hierarchy to mostly two levels, in order to keep the simplicity. Fig. 3 shows the hierarchy of modules in the robot library.

156

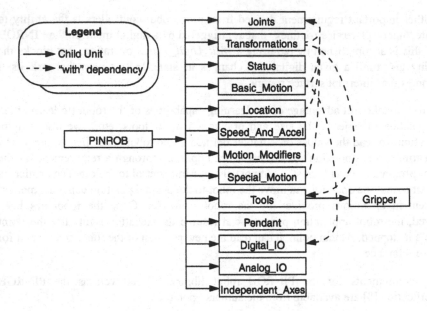

Fig. 3 Hierarchy of the PINROB API

A short description of the modules of the robot library appears next. A complete description can be found in [8].

- *PINROB*: It is the parent unit of the robot library. It defines the basic data types, the elementary operations for these basic data types, the geometrical operations, and also defines all the exceptions that may be raised by the different operations of the robot library.

  The elementary data types used in addition to the predefined Ada data types are angle, angular speed, length, linear speed, weight, and robot identifier. Some arithmetic operations are provided to allow operations between some of the elementary data types (for example, angular speed times duration, returning angle).

  For geometry, PINROB specifies the data types cartesian position (X, Y, Z) and orientation (yaw, pitch, roll). In addition, it defines the type *Frame* that represents an absolute or relative position and orientation of an object in space. This type is defined as private, because different systems may prefer to use different representations of the orientation, such as yaw-pitch-roll or Euler angles. Operations are provided to build a frame from position and orientation data, and vice versa. In order to allow different coordinate systems and geometrical transformations, PINROB defines operations to calculate the absolute position of a position that is specified relative to a given coordinate system; to calculate the relative position, relative to a given coordinate system, of an absolute position; and to invert a relative position. These operations give PINROB full capabilities for performing geometrical transformations and for using different coordinate systems. For example, this may be used to handle a robot that is upside-down and located at a particular point in space, or to manipulate objects whose coordinates are given relative to some particular frame.

- *Joints*: It defines the robot-dependent location data types, which are the joint coordinates and the robot configuration. The names of these types are portable, but their internal structures are robot-dependent. Operations are provided to set or retrieve the limits for each joint.

- *Transformations*: It defines the operations required to operate robots with different coordinate basis, and different tools with different sizes. It also provides operations to perform direct and inverse transformations between the two basic location types: joint coordinates and frames.

- *Status*: The operations in this module allow the application to read the current status of the robot and the controller, attaching or detaching robots to or from the application program, setting and reading the power status of each robot, determining whether communications with the robot are OK or not, stopping the program temporarily to allow the robot controller to move the robot, and stopping the robot under a panic situation.

- *Basic_Motion*: It contains the operations that allow absolute or relative movements in straight-line, circle, or joint coordinates. All the motion instructions are asynchronous, i.e. the actual movement is performed concurrently with the execution of the program, up to a system-dependent number of pending movement operations. For each of the basic movement instructions there are two versions: one that accepts positions in joint coordinates, and one that accepts positions in frame units.

The module also defines operations to allow the program to synchronize with the movement operations, by waiting until all the previously issued movement operations have been completed. Defer-movement operations are provided to specify an interval of time during which the robot movement needs to be stopped. The time interval may be fixed, or may depend on a signal condition (i.e. the state of a digital input). A *Brake* operation is provided to allow the application program to stop the robot, even if there are pending movement operations. Usually this operation is invoked after an abnormal condition. The *Brake* operation may be unconditional, or conditional depending upon a signal condition (i.e. the state of a digital input). In this latter case, the brake operation is asynchronous to the program.

- *Location*: It defines functions that allow the application program to read the robot's current position or its current target position, in different units. The target position is the final position of the current movement instruction.

- *Speed_and_Accel*: It provides operations to set and read the different speed and acceleration factors that are used in all subsequent movement operations.

- *Motion_Modifiers*: The motion modifier operations allow the application program to manipulate and read the conditions under which other movement operations work. Continuous path enables a set of subsequent robot move operations to be considered as a continuous trajectory in which the robot does not stop at each point, but rather it approximates the trajectory to follow a smooth path between the different points. Continuous path may be broken explicitly, with the *Disable_Continuous_Path* operation, or implicitly (and only temporarily) with the instructions that require synchronization such as *Wait_Until_Stopped*.

  The stopping mode determines when a movement operation is considered to have been finished. There are different criteria to establish whether the robot is or not stopped, and operations are provided to specify the stopping mode desired by the application. Singular points are points in which the angular position of one or more joints may be arbitrary. Some systems provide different motion modes to deal with paths that come close to singular points, and thus operations are provided for the application to specify the desired behaviour. In some systems the servo control parameters may be adjusted to accommodate for different payloads, or different precision and force requirements. Consequently, this module defines operations that affect the servo control parameters. Finally, an operation is provided to adjust the advanced run setting, which allows the program to control the maximum number of simultaneously pending movement operations.

- *Special_Motion*: It defines operations that imply moving the robot to perform some special action. A special operation is provided for moving the robot in a single drive mode. A calibration move operation is necessary in some systems to initialize relative position encoders. In those systems in which this operation is not required, calibration move may be a null operation. This module also provides operations to change the robot configuration, which can be used when the target position of a movement is unreachable in the current configuration, or when movements in the current working area would become more comfortable.

- *Tools*: It defines the type *Tool* and its associated basic operations. This type is defined as a private type because different implementations may have different parameters associated with a tool. The operations associated with the tools are setting and reading its dimensions and weight. Other operations that control the tool are tool-dependent, and thus are not provided in this module.

- *Gripper*: The gripper operations initiate an action (open or close) on the gripper. This action starts after the last issued movement operation has been completed and it may proceed in parallel with the execution of the program and subsequent movement operations. If the system does not have a gripper attached, these operations fail silently.

- *Pendant*: Some robot applications may need to interact with a human operator. For example, the robot application may have to wait until the operator changes a tool in the robot and then presses a button. This kind of communication with a human operator is best accomplished through the control pendant. The pendant is assumed to have a small display, and a keyboard. In addition, it may have other devices such as a potentiometer, joystick, or beeper. Operations are provided to control all such devices. In addition, there are functions to check for the presence of the pendant and of some of its devices.

- *Digital_IO*: Most controllers support digital I/O, and thus this module provides operations for reading from and writing to individual digital input or output lines, or ranges of them. It is also possible to wait for a digital input to reach a given state, or to set the outputs to default values. There are two interrogation functions to determine whether the system supports digital I/O, and whether it is concurrent with the program operation or not.

- *Analog_IO*: It defines operations for reading or setting analog inputs and outputs.

- *Independent_Axes*: Some systems have one or more independent axes that may be moved independently of the robot without coordination with it. In other systems, independent axes may be moved in a coordinated motion with the robot. This module defines a constant that specifies how many independent axes are present. It also defines operations for moving an independent axis, reading its position, and moving one or more independent axes together with the robot in a coordinated manner.

5 Operating Procedures

Programming in the PINROB architecture is different than the usual approach with most industrial robots, because the language is not interpreted, but compiled. This means that the execution and debugging of the program need different approaches. Usually, when a robot operator is using a program, he or she uses the robot to learn the positions of the different objects it has to manipulate. These positions are stored into variables defined in the controller, which are then read and used by the program itself. In the PINROB environment, we can take a similar approach, but we must also program the learning phase into the application. We can define a number of variables, and ask the robot operator to move the robot manually, with the application program temporarily stopped, and store different robot positions into the variables defined. After this learning procedure finishes, the application program may continue at the point where it was stopped. Alternatively, if we do not wish to use robot variables, the position of the robot may be "learnt" by the application program, by invoking the *Current_Position* operation.

Since the external computer used to program the robot is a general-purpose computer, it can have a nice windows-based user-interface, which can be used to implement user-friendly communication with the robot operator, during the learning or configuration phase, as well as for monitoring the robot during its productive operation.

One of the advantages of interpreted robot programming languages is that debugging the program is very easy. The programmer can run the program step by step, or manually insert breakpoints (stop instructions) without having to recompile the application. However, debugging technology for high-level language compilers is pretty mature, and thus we can use a conventional debugger to execute the Ada application program step by step, or manually insert breakpoints and read the values of variables. Of course, any modification of the program will require recompilation, but since the compiler will usually reside in the same machine as the Ada application, this should not represent any major difficulty.

6   Robot Application Example

In this section we will present a simple example of a typical robot application, to give a flavour of the PINROB interface and how it can be used. The system consists of a robot whose job is to pick up objects from a conveyor belt and put them in another one. Each object is picked up at a fixed position but, since it is moving, we use an optoelectronic sensor to determine when the object is ready to be picked up. This sensor is connected to digital input channel number one, which can be read by the application program. When the object is ready, the robot closes its gripper, moves up by 200 mm, and then moves in straight line to a point positioned 200 mm above the dropping position. There, the robot moves down by 200 mm and opens the gripper to drop the object. Finally, the robot moves back along the same trajectory to begin a new cycle. Table 1 shows the application code that performs this task.

We can see that the application is self-configurable, because it includes operations to learn the positions of both the pick-up and the drop points, prior to the start of the normal operation cycles. This is achieved by making two calls to procedure *Learn_Point*, to learn each point. This procedure displays a message asking the operator to move the robot manually to the desired point, and then stops the program execution. When the operator resumes the application program, the current robot position is learnt. For convenience, before the two points are learnt, the robot's orientation is changed to make the gripper point down.

After the two points are learnt, the robot is moved to its initial position (200 mm above the pick-up point) and the gripper is opened. For the main cycle we select the continuous path mode, which does not require the robot to stop after every movement. We break continuous path temporarily both at the pick-up point and at the drop point, with the *Wait_Until_Stopped* command.

7   Conclusion and Future Work

In this paper we have shown the design of a portable API for industrial robots. This interface is based on the use of Ada as the robot programming language. It can be implemented on top of existing robot controllers from different manufacturers, and thus it provides for application program portability, which is not possible today because of the different programming languages used for each robot. We have described the main features of this API, and through a simple example we have shown that it is easy to use and yet very powerful. The use of the Ada language makes the

```
with PINROB,                PINROB.Status,
     PINROB.Transformations, PINROB.Basic_Motion,
     PINROB.Speed_And_Accel, PINROB.Tools,
     PINROB.Tools.Gripper,   PINROB.Motion_Modifiers,
     PINROB.Digital_IO,      PINROB.Location,
     PINROB.Pendant;
use PINROB;
procedure Move_Objects is
   Pick_Up_Pos, Above_Pick_Up_Pos,
      Drop_Pos, Above_Drop_Pos : Frame;
   The_Tool   :Tools.Tool:=Tools.Gripper.Gripper_Parameters;
   Height     : constant Length := 200.0; -- millimeters
   Object_Ready: constant Digital_IO.Input_Channel:=1;
   Timeout    : constant Duration:= 300.0; -- seconds
   Vertical   : constant YPR_Orientation :=
                     (Yaw=> 0.0, Pitch=> 180.0, Roll=>0.0);

   procedure Learn_Point (Message: in String;
                          Point : out Frame) is
   begin
      Pendant.Write_To_Display (Message);
      Status.Stop; -- The robot is now driven with the robot
                   -- controller to the desired position
      Point:=Location.Current_Position;
   end Learn_Point;

begin
   Status.Attach;
   Motion_Modifiers.Enable_Continuous_Path;
   Transformations.Set_Tool(The_Tool);
   Basic_Motion.Move_To (To_Frame(
      Position_Of(Location.Current_Position), Vertical));
   Learn_Point("Drive robot to pick up position",Pick_Up_Pos);
   Learn_Point("Drive robot to drop position", Drop_Pos);
   Above_Pick_Up_Pos := Retract (Pick_Up_Pos, Height);
   Above_Drop_Pos := Retract (Drop_Pos, Height);
   Speed_And_Accel.Set_Linear_Speed_Factor (40.0); --percent
   Basic_Motion.Move_To (Above_Pick_Up_Pos);
   Tools.Gripper.Open;
   loop
   Basic_Motion.Move_To_Straight (Pick_Up_Pos);
      Basic_Motion.Wait_Until_Stopped;
      Digital_IO.Wait_Until_State (Object_Ready,
            Digital_IO.Asserted, Timeout);
      Tools.Gripper.Close;
      Basic_Motion.Move_To_Straight (Above_Pick_Up_Pos);
      Basic_Motion.Move_To_Straight (Above_Drop_Pos);
      Basic_Motion.Move_To_Straight (Drop_Pos);
      Basic_Motion.Wait_Until_Stopped;
      Tools.Gripper.Open;
      Basic_Motion.Move_To_Straight (Above_Drop_Pos);
      Basic_Motion.Move_To_Straight (Above_Pick_Up_Pos);
   end loop;
end Move_Objects;
```

Table 1. Moving objects from one conveyor belt to another one

application code almost self-explaining and the compiler helps in eliminating many programming errors.

We are currently implementing PINROB for several robot controllers, including self-developed robots as well as commercial ones. When these implementations are finished, we will know to what extent the API is portable. We also intend to translate production cell software into Ada and PINROB. The first goal is to assess the difficulty of the translation process. The second goal is to measure the time-behaviour of the new software. We will then port the Ada production cell software to a "foreign" robot in order to evaluate the level of portability of an application, rather than of the API.

Acknowledgements

The authors would like to thank Mr. *Fernando Gómez Estefanía*, of *Equipos Nucleares S.A.*, for his many contributions to the definition of the requirements of the PINROB API.

References

[1]   A. Aasten, G. Elia, G. Menga. "G++: A Pattern Language for Computer Integrated Manufacturing"; Proceedings PLOPS'94, (J. Coplien and D. Schmidt, eds.), Addison-Wesley, Reading, Mass., 1995, pp. 91-118.

[2]   ABB Robotics Products AB. "ABB S4 Rapid programming language. User's Guide".

[3]   Adept Technology Inc. "V and V+ Reference Guide", Vol. 1/2, Version. 10.1, Oct. 1990.

[4]   Adept Technology Inc. "SILTOOLS Developer's Guide.", 1996.

[5]   AUTOMELEC. "Lucie. Description des Instructions."

[6]   Demaurex. "Logiciel Delta95: Fonctionnalités de la couche haut niveau", Version. 4.0.

[7]   M. González Harbour and A. Strohmeier. "Requirements for Portable API for Industrial Roâots. Version 2.1". Internal report, February 1998.

[8]   M. González Harbour and A. Strohmeier. "PINROB Specification. Version 2.1". Internal report, February 1998.

[9]   H. A. Schmid. "Creating Applications from Components: A Manufacturing Framework Design" in IEEE Software, Nov. 1996, pp. 75.

[10] Siemens. "SIROTEC ACR-20. Software Version 4. Programming, parts 1-3".

Quality-for-ASIS: A Portable Testing Facility for ASIS

Alfred Strohmeier[1], Vasiliy Fofanov[1], Sergey Rybin[2], and Stéphane Barbey[1]

[1]*Swiss Federal Institute of Technology*
Department of Computer Science
Software Engineering Laboratory
1015 Lausanne, Switzerland
{alfred.strohmeier, stephane.barbey}@epfl.ch, fofanov@bigfoot.com

[2]*Scientific Research Computer Center*
Moscow State University
Vorob'evi Gori
Moscow 119899, Russia
rybin@gnat.com

Abstract: This paper describes the project Quality-for-ASIS, aiming at the development of an extensive testing facility for ASIS implementations. First the specific problems and requirements are presented. After a section about the basic concepts of ASIS and after a short introduction to testing, the designs and implementations for testing important subsets of ASIS are described. Finally, adequacy coverage statistics for a test set based on the ACVC compiler validation suite are provided.

Keywords: Ada, ASIS, Testing, Black-Box Testing, Specification-Based Testing.

1. Introduction

The Ada Semantic Interface Specification (ASIS) [1] is an interface between an Ada environment, and any tool or application requiring statically-determinable information from this environment.

This paper reports about Quality-for-ASIS, a project aiming at the development of a portable testing facility for ASIS implementations. The facility is composed of test drivers, test sets and test coverage measurement tools. Quality-for-ASIS is developed in a joint project of Moscow University and the Swiss Federal Institute of Technology in Lausanne, within the ASIS-for-GNAT project [3, 4, 5, 7]. It is used for testing ASIS-for-GNAT, the ASIS implementation for the GNAT compiler [6].

Here are some of the specifics of the project:

- ASIS is a large library. ASIS is composed of 21 packages, two of which are optional. These packages define 349 queries.
- ASIS is a library and not a program. To exercise an ASIS query, a driver calling the query must first be implemented. In the case of ASIS, such a driver is called an ASIS application.

Paper accepted for publication in the proceedings of the International Conference on Reliable Software Technologies - Ada-Europe'98, Uppsala, Sweden, June 8-12, 1998, Lars Asplund (Ed.), LNCS (Lecture Notes in Computer Science), Springer, 1998.

- As usual testing cannot be exhaustive. Therefore coverage criteria must be defined, and the testing facility must be able to measure coverage in order to assess the quality of test sets.
- The input to an ASIS application is not just some simple data, but an Ada compilation unit, or a set of such units. So the test "data" are costly to develop. By using the ACVC test suite, we try to solve this problem.
- The results of many queries are not directly observable, because they are of some private type. Ways must therefore be find to observe indirectly the results of such queries, e.g. in order to compare them with expected results.
- The procedure Traverse_Element in the package Asis.Iterator is generic, which raises the problem of testing generic units.
- The testing facility should be as portable as possible.
- The test drivers should be self-checking, in order to provide for low-cost automatic regression testing.

The paper starts with a presentation of the basic ASIS concepts. A short introduction to testing follows. In some length, we then show how this testing "theory" can be applied to the generic procedure Traverse_Element. Some testing criteria for ASIS implementations are then defined. The designs of drivers and oracles for different classes of ASIS queries are then described. Finally, adequacy measurements obtained for the ACVC-based test set are reported for the ASIS structural queries.

2. Basic ASIS Concepts

The Ada Semantic Interface Specification (ASIS) [1] is an interface between an Ada environment, as defined by the Ada language reference manual [2], and any tool or application, called an ASIS application, requiring statically-determinable information from this environment. ASIS itself is defined as a set of self-documented Ada package specifications providing the types and operations, called ASIS *queries*, used to retrieve and to deal with this information.

Consider the following small Ada program:

```
with Text_IO;
procedure Demo is
    A : Integer := 1;
    B : Integer := 2;
    C : Integer;
begin
    C := A + B;
    Text_IO.Put_Line (Integer'Image (C));
end Demo;
```

Element is the term used by ASIS for a valid Ada syntax construct. The procedure body is an element. It can be decomposed by calling *structural queries*. The query Body_Declarative_Items will return the list of declarations, each declaration being an element in turn. The result of the query Body_Declarative_Items is therefore of type

Element_List. The query Body_Statements will return a list of elements, each being of the *kind* A_Statement, as defined in the enumeration type Element_Kinds. For any of these statements, it will be necessary to determine its so-called *subordinate kind* before continuing top-down parsing. For the first statement in the list, the call to the function Statement_Kind will yield the value An_Assignment_Statement. The statement can then be processed by calling an appropriate structural query, in this case Assignment_Variable_Name or Assignment_Expression for retrieving the left-hand and right-hand parts of the assignment. As soon as we know that the left-hand side of the assignment is a simple name, we can get its string image by calling Name_Image, which is one of the queries returning the image of a terminal. In order to find out about the type of the left-hand part of the assignment, it is possible to call the *semantic query* Corresponding_Expression_Type, which will return the element corresponding to the type declaration. What we said so far, can be summed up by this (correct, except for unconstrained array handling) piece of code of an ASIS application:

```
declare
    Unit: Asis.Compilation_Unit;
    Procedure_Body: Asis.Element;
    Declaration_List: Asis.Element_List;
    Stmt_List: Asis.Element_List;
    First_Stmt: Asis.Element;
    Declaration: Asis.Element;
begin
    -- initialize Unit
    Procedure_Body := Unit_Declaration(Unit);
    Declaration_List := Body_Declarative_Items(Procedure_Body);
    Stmt_List := Statement_List(Procedure_Body);
    -- Get the list of statements of the body.
    First_Stmt := Statement_List(1);
    -- Select the first statement.
    if Statement_Kind(First_Stmt = An_Assignment_Statement then
        Put(Name_Image(Assignment_Variable_Name(First_Stmt)));
        Declaration := Corresponding_Expression_Type
                        (Assignment_Variable_Name(First_Stmt));
    end if;
    -- etc.
end;
```

The generic iterator Traverse_Element is defined in the package ASIS.Iterator. It is a generic procedure used to traverse the syntax tree corresponding to an element. Here is its specification:

```
generic
    type State_Information is limited private;
    with procedure Pre_Operation
        (Element : in     Asis.Element;
         Control : in out Traverse_Control;
         State   : in out State_Information) is <>;
    with procedure Post_Operation
        (Element : in     Asis.Element;
         Control : in out Traverse_Control;
         State   : in out State_Information) is <>;
```

```
procedure Traverse_Element
   (Element : in      Asis.Element;
    Control : in out  Traverse_Control;
    State   : in out  State_Information);
```

Elements are traversed in top-to-bottom order, and at a given level from left-to-right following the textual order of the component elements within the parent element. For each element, the formal procedure Pre_Operation is called when first visiting the element. Each of that element's children are then visited recursively, and finally the formal procedure Post_Operation is called for the element.

3. Short Introduction to Testing

This section defines some terminology related to testing and provides a short overview of the theory behind testing. The interested reader may refer to [12] for a more comprehensive introduction.

Testing is the most popular verification technique. It aims at answering the following question:

> "Does a program P correctly implement a model M?"

In order to do so, it tries to find counterexamples showing that it does not [11]. This question is named the *verification requirement*.

A *test case* is an input on which the program under test is executed during testing. A *test set* is a set of test cases. After execution of a test case, the result generated by the program is compared with the one expected by the model. The means used to perform this comparision, be it a program or human inspection, is called an *oracle*.

The answer to the verification requirement is undecidable in the general case. Already in the mid-70s, Goodenough and Gerhart [13] pointed out that the central question was therefore to find a *test criterion*, i.e. a criterion that states what is an adequate test set. A great number of such critera have been proposed and investigated. The criterion is often defined by *sampling* the input domain of the program to exercise it with interesting cases only. Thus, the verification requirement becomes:

> "How well does a program P implement a model M
> according to a sampling criterion C?"

Sampling criteria are an essential part of any testing approach. There are two kinds of sampling criteria: correctness and fault hypotheses. The aim of a correctness criterion is to show that the program satisfies its model (that it is correct), whereas the aim of fault hypotheses is to show that particular classes of faults are not present. Test selection based on a correctness criterion should include test cases that represent the essential features of the model, and should establish that the test cases are feature-sufficient, i.e. that they are sufficiently representative for giving confidence that the program implements its model.

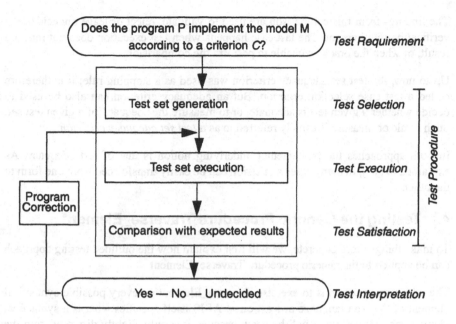

Fig. 1. Test process for specification-based testing

The quality of a test set is measured by its *adequacy*, which needs appropriate measurement techniques [9, 12]. Adequacy is usually a function of the coverage of the sampling criteria by a test set, but can also be a function of hypotheses set on the program [8]. The classical mutation analysis is an example of such a measurement [10]. In this approach, faults are injected in a program, and the quality of a test set is defined by the number of detected faults. For *program-based testing*, also called *white-box testing*, coverage measures include the percentage of called subprograms, executed statements, or followed simple paths. For *specification-based testing*, also called *black-box testing*, adequacy might be measured by coverage of axioms as found in the formal specification, or coverage of the input domain after partitioning in equivalence classes.

The test process (see figure 1) usually involves three steps:

- A test selection step, in which a test set is generated that will validate the test requirement, according to the previously chosen sampling criterion. The test selection procedure should also decide what the expected results of the test cases are.

- A test execution step, in which all the test cases in the set are executed.

- A test satisfaction step, in which the results obtained during the test execution phase are compared with the expected results. This last step is commonly performed by the help of an oracle.

The findings from this comparison are used to validate, reject or leave undecided the verification requirement. The last case happens when test execution does not return a result, or when the oracle is unable to perform the comparision.

Up to now, the test set adequacy criterion was used as a stopping rule; it is therefore called a test case selection criterion. But an adequacy criterion can also be used to decide whether a given test is adequate, or to measure the adequacy of a given test set. Such a rule or measure is usually referred to as a *test set adequacy criterion.*

In both approaches the fundamental underlying notion is that of test adequacy. As explained in [12], in many cases a criterion can be easily transformed from one form to the other.

4. Testing the Generic Procedure Traverse_Element

To make things more concrete, we will first explain how the outlined testing approach can be applied to the generic procedure Traverse_Element.

The adequacy criterion is to exercise Traverse_Element on every possible syntactical element of the Ada language at least once. ASIS itself specifies what is a syntactical element, and its definition will be used, because it is only slightly different from the one defined in the Ada language reference manual [2]. For the time being, elements corresponding to implementation-dependent Ada constructs, e.g. implementation-specific attributes and pragmas, will not be included in the adequacy criterion, because one of the goals is to develop a portable testing facility.

Traverse_Element is not a main program, so a test driver must be devised. Because Traverse_Element is a generic procedure, the test driver will have to instantiate it, and then call instantiations.

The only syntactical element that can be a direct input to an ASIS application, and therefore to the driver, is a compilation unit. For any other syntactical element, it is necessary to create an *execution context*. Such a context is formed by the sequence of enclosing elements, starting from the compilation unit. This approach provides a path from a test data input to a call to an instantiation of Traverse_Element on some actual syntactical element. To implement it, it is sufficient to call Traverse_Element iteratively for all the elements in the context, starting from the compilation unit.

However, traversal of a given element cannot be observed directly, and an observation context must therefore be created. The idea is to use traversal for reconstructing the source code of the traversed element. As a result, the driver will rewrite the source code.

Finally, it must be decided if the generated source code is equivalent to the original one. This is the task of the oracle. Requiring that the source codes must be the same would be too much. Indeed, extra blank characters might be suppressed, formal parameters of subprograms might be normalized: "X, Y: Integer" becoming "X: in

Integer; Y: in Integer", etc. Comparing the textual representations taking into account all these variations would be quite difficult. The idea is therefore to ensure their operational equivalence, by compiling the source codes and comparing the generated object codes. If they are the same, the oracle will decide that the test case passed successfully. Even though the comparison itself might be somewhat tricky, e.g. in the presence of a time stamp inside the object code, we think this approach can be adapted to many compilation systems. Its use with GNAT [6] is straightforward.

Let's put it all together. A test case is a compilation unit. Traverse_Element is instantiated with appropriate pre- and post-operations for writing out the source code of the element passed as a parameter. The test driver rewrites the source code of the test case by traversing it recursively by means of calls to the instantiation of Traverse_Element. The oracle finally checks if the two source codes are equivalent.

In the case of ASIS-for-GNAT, Traverse_Element is in fact implemented by recursive calls to itself. The source code of Traverse_Element itself can therefore be used for implementing the driver.

The rewriting instantiation of Traverse_Element was exercised on the ACVC test suite. This suite contains all possible syntactic elements (but no implementation-dependent constructs), and therefore satisfies the coverage criterion fully at 100%.

The implementation of Traverse_Element in ASIS-for-GNAT passed successfully this test.

5. Testing Criteria for ASIS Implementations

The goal is specification-based testing of an ASIS implementation. Following figure 1, the program P is an implementation of ASIS, e.g. ASIS-for-GNAT, and the model M is the specification of ASIS, as defined in [1]. "P implements the model M" means that for all legal Ada compilation units all the ASIS queries yield correct results as defined by their specifications. Because ASIS is a library, test drivers must be built.

Since the test unit is a library, sampling or adequacy criteria are to be expressed in terms of coverage of the library. Only correctness criteria will be proposed.

ASIS queries are completely defined in the sense that they *always* produce a result, either by returning a result value or by raising a well-defined exception.

Criterion 1

To meet the first criterion, any ASIS query must be called with a return result, at least once. Exception raising is therefore not covered by this criterion.

Criterion 2

Many ASIS queries have one of the following profiles:

Element -> Element

Element -> Element_List

Element × Boolean -> Element_List

Element -> some classification enumeration type

As already explained, elements are language constructs, and are classified, e.g. A_Declaration or A_Statement. There are 10 different element kinds, not including the so-called Not_An_Element. These different element kinds are in turn subdivided into a hierarchy of so-called subordinate kinds. On the overall, there are about 300 subordinate kinds. But usually, a query can validly be called only for a selection of subordinate kinds. Otherwise, an exception is raised.

To achieve criterion 2 coverage, any query must be called with all possible valid combinations of parameters and results.

Criterion 3

Sometimes a query cannot return a meaningful result. It then raises an exception, as defined by the ASIS definition. To fulfill criterion 3, any query must be exercised with all its possible exceptions raised.

Although coverage of criterion 3 is certainly desirable, Quality-for-ASIS does not yet take it into account.

6. Drivers and Oracles

The figure 2 shows the current state of the Quality-for-ASIS project, especially the availability of drivers and oracles for different sorts of queries.

Structural queries and images of terminals

For structural queries (except Enclosing_Element) and the queries yielding the image of a terminal, the test driver is the same as for the Traverse_Element generic procedure: it rewrites the source code of the Ada unit serving as an input, by parsing it top-down, and making calls to the structural queries for decomposing the encountered syntactical elements. The context of the call to a query is in some way top-down parsing of a compilation unit. The observation context is built by producing a textual representation of the element processed by the query. Finally, the same oracle as the one described for testing the Traverse_Element generic procedure is used for comparing the generated source code with the original one.

Semantic queries

The test driver for semantic queries also performs a traversal of the compilation unit submitted as an input. For any visited element, all applicable semantic queries are

Total ASIS queries			349	100%
Tested				
	Structural queries	125		
	Images of terminals	6		
	Traverse_Element	1		
Subtotal			132	38%
Implemented				
	Semantic queries	31		
Subtotal			31	9%
Designed				
	Classification queries	35		
	Enclosing_Element	1		
Subtotal			36	10%
Done			199	57%
To be done			150	43%

Fig. 2 State of the Quality-for-ASIS project

called. The oracle works as follows: for each semantic query, it is first checked that the kind of the result is an allowed one. For queries having a complementary query, such as Corresponding_Body and Corresponding_Declaration, it is checked that composing the calls, e.g.

```
Corresponding_Body (Corresponding_Declaration (Element))
```

correctly returns the original Element. The check itself is performed by calling the ASIS query Is_Identical. Finally, for elements representing a named construct related to the same entity, a check is made that the names are the same.

The driver for this kind of queries is already implemented.

Classification queries

Once again, the test driver is based on top-down parsing of a compilation unit. For every visited element, the results returned by all classification queries are recorded sequentially in a text file. The conversion to a string is simply performed by applying the 'Image attribute to the enumeration value returned by the query. The generated file must then be manually reviewed, but can further on be used as a reference file, e.g. for non-regression testing or for testing another ASIS implementation, because top-down parsing of a given compilation unit will almost always yield the same sequence of elements. Possible exceptions are due to implementation permissions granted by the ASIS specification.

The driver for this kind of queries is not yet implemented and reference files are not yet available.

The Enclosing_Element query

The Enclosing_Element query is in fact a structural query, but unlike all other structural queries used for top-down parsing, it performs a bottom-up step.

The implementation of a test driver, including an oracle, is straightforward. It is again based on top-down parsing of a compilation unit, implemented by instantiating Traverse_Element. At each step down in traversal, the pre-operation pushes the current element on the stack. Enclosing_Element is then called for all its children and the results are compared with the element at the top of the stack by calling the Is_Identical query. Finally, when coming back to an element, the post-operation will pop it off the stack.

7. Use of the ACVC Test Suite as a Test Set

The Ada Compiler Validation Capability, ACVC, now in version ACVC 2.1, provides an extensive set of Ada programs used to validate Ada compilers. This test suite is supposed to cover quite well the full language. It is therefore a good starting point for a test set. The so-called B tests must however be eliminated, because they correspond to illegal Ada units raising compilation errors; therefore they cannot be the input to an ASIS application. What remains are about 4'057 Ada compilation units.

At the time being, ASIS-for-GNAT is not able to deal with library-level instantiations of generic subprograms and with some kinds of static expressions that are transformed into values by the GNAT compiler. As a consequence, 61 compilation units belonging to the ACVC suite, i.e. about 1.5%, could not be included in the test set. In some sense, only partial correctness of ASIS-for-GNAT will be demonstrated by this test set.

8. Measurement of Adequacy

In ASIS-for-GNAT, the generic Traverse_Element procedure is a plain ASIS application, and its source code is publicly available. In order to gather statistics about test cases, its source code was modified by adding a logging mechanism: immediately before a query is called, its name is recorded. This generic procedure is called Traverse_Element_And_Log.

First, the Traverse_Element_And_Log procedure was instantiated with empty pre- and post-operations. This Gather_Query_Names procedure was then applied to the ACVC-based test set. The result is shown in figure 3. All structural queries are called except Enclosing_Element, with which we deal separately, and Body_Block_Statement, which is deprecated. The adequacy criterion 1 is therefore fully satisfied by the ACVC-based test set for the structural queries.

Total structural queries		126	100%
(except Enclosing_Element)	Called	125	99%
	Not called	1	1%

Fig. 3 Adequacy criterion 1 for structural queries

Traverse_Element_And_Log was further extended to track parameter-result combinations, whenever a structural query is called. Results were then gathered in a file for the ACVC-based test set.

Manually, by inspection of the ASIS specification, the legal combinations were entered in a reference file. The two files were then compared. The results are shown in figure 4. The total number of legal combinations is 1212, 883 of which are exercised by the test set. For 82 structural queries, all combinations are exercised. Although all not called profiles correspond to syntactically correct constructs, most of them will never be found in "useful" Ada programs; e.g. a goto or raise statement does not make sense immediately within a loop statement (without being part of a compound statement). As a consequence, the ACVC suite does not contain these combinations, because it tries to avoid idiosyncratic constructs. However, the question remains open if an ASIS implementation should be tested on such combinations. Indeed, it would be perfectly possible, and perhaps even desirable, to have a tool implemented as an ASIS application, which searches for undesirable combinations, either for helping the programmer write better code, or for assessing code quality.

In conclusion, the ACVC-based test set fulfills criterion 2 at a level of 83% for structural queries.

If needed, the test set could be extended. For instance, the following test case:

```
package addon is
    type t is null record;
end addon;
```

can be used to check the Record_Definition query for a parameter of kind A_Record_Type_Definition and the result of kind A_Null_Record_Definition.

Total number of profiles		1212	100%
	Called profiles	883	83%
	Not called profiles	329	27%
	Completely covered queries	82	65%

Fig. 4 Adequacy criterion 2 for structural queries

The adequacy criterion statistics for the Enclosing_Element query are the same as for the set of the other structural querie, because it is in some way the inverse function.

For the semantic queries and the classification queries, we have not yet measured the adequacy of the ACVC-based test set.

9. Conclusions and Future Work

A testing approach, including adequacy criteria and a test set, was defined for an important part of ASIS. Testing facilities have been implemented for the structural queries, queries yielding the image of terminals, the semantic queries and the Traverse_Element query. Testing approaches were designed for the classification queries and the Enclosing_Element query. These 199 queries count for 57% of all the queries found in ASIS.

It was shown that the ACVC-based test set fulfils quite well the adequacy criteria for the structural queries, the queries yielding the image of terminals, and the Traverse_Element query. Adequacy for the semantic queries, the classification queries, and the Enclosing_Element query will be investigated in the future.

Work has still to be done for the other kinds of queries, e.g. those working with ASIS Contexts, Compilation_Units, etc.

However, structural queries together with Traverse_Element are used whenever a tool needs parsing of Ada source code. The current state of Quality-for-ASIS testing facility therefore comprises testing of a very important subset of ASIS.

Acknowledgements

The first version of the source rewriting tool was implemented by Jean-Charles Marteau and Serge Reboul, then working for Sema Group in Grenoble.

The ASIS-for-GNAT project is partially funded by a grant from the Swiss Federal Government, grant no 7SUPJ048247.

References

[1]   ASIS documents are available electronically on the World Wide Web:
             http://www.acm.org/sigada/WG/asiswg/asiswg.html
       or by anonymous ftp:
             ftp:// sw-eng.falls-church.va.us/public/AdaIC/work-grp/asiswg

[2]   S. Tucker Taft, Robert A. Duff (eds.) Ada 95 Reference Manual: Language and Standard Libraries, International Standard ISO/IEC 8652:1995(E). Lecture Notes in Computer Science, vol. 1246, Springer-Verlag, 1997, ISBN 3-540-63144-5.

[3]   S. Rybin, A. Strohmeier, E. Zueff: ASIS for GNAT: Goals, Problems and Implementation Strategy. In Marcel Toussaint (Ed.), Second International Eurospace - Ada-Europe Symposium Proceedings, Frankfurt - Germany, October 2-6 1995, LNCS no 1031, Springer, 1995, pp. 139-151.

[4]   S. Rybin, A. Strohmeier, A. Kuchumov, V. Fofanov: ASIS for GNAT: From the Prototype to the Full Implementation. In Alfred Strohmeier (Ed.), 1996 Ada-Eu-

rope International Conference on Reliable Software Technologies Proceedings, LNCS no 1088, Springer, pp. 298-311, 1996.

[5]   ASIS-for-GNAT is available electronically from LGL-EPFL by anonymous ftp: ftp://lglftp.epfl.ch/pub/ASIS.

[6]   E. Schonberg, B. Banner; The GNAT Project: A GNU-Ada 9X Compiler; TRI-Ada'94 Proceedings, ACM Press, 1994; pp.   48-57. See also http:// www.gnat.com.

[7]   V. Fofanov, S. Rybin and A. Strohmeier, "ASIStint: An Interactive ASIS Interpreter", in Susan Carlson (Ed.), Proceedings of TRI-Ada'97, St. Louis, USA, ACM Press, 1997, pp. 205-209.

[8]   Stéphane Barbey. *Test Selection for Specification-Based Testing of Object-Oriented Software Based on Formal Specifications*. PhD thesis, Swiss Federal Institute of Technology in Lausanne (EPFL), December 1997. Ph.D. Thesis 1753.

[9]   Robert V. Binder. Testing object-oriented software: a survey. *Journal of Testing, Verification and Reliability*, 6:125–252, September 1996.

[10] Muriel Daran and Pascale Thévenod-Fosse. Software error analysis: A real case study involving real faults and mutations. In *Proceedings of 3rd International Symposium on Software Testing and Analysis (ISSTA-3)*, pages 158–171, San Diego, California, USA, January 1996.

[11] Glenford J. Myers. *The Art of Software Testing*. Business Data Processing: a Wiley Series. John Wiley & Sons, 1979.

[12] Hong Zhu, Patrick A. V. Hall, John H. R. May. Software Unit Test Coverage and Adequacy. In ACM Computing Surveys, Vol. 29, No. 4, Dec 1997. pp. 366-427.

[13] John B. Goodenough, S. L. Gerhart. Toward a theory of test data selection. In IEEE Trans. Softw. Eng. SE-3, June 1975.

Ten Years of Tool Based Ada Compiler Validations
An Experience Report

Michael Tonndorf

IABG
Ada Validation Facility
D-85521 Ottobrunn Germany

Tel.: +49 89 6088 2477
Fax: +49 89 6088 3418
tonndorf@iabg.de

Abstract: This paper summarizes IABG's experience as an Ada Validation Facility from the last decade. The paper puts an emphasis on the improvement of the validation process by evolving tool support.

Keywords: Ada Compiler Validation, Ada Standardization, Ada Policy, Ada Language Maintenance

1 Introduction

The programming language Ada was first standardized by ANSI in 1983. This standard was confirmed by ISO in 1987. A test suite was developed as a means for conformance testing according to the standard. The US DoD, language sponsor and largest user of Ada products, accepted only the code generated by validated compilers as project deliverables. The test suite, called Ada Compiler Validation Capability (ACVC), was developed and continuously improved from versions 1.0 through 1.11 for Ada 83. For Ada 95 ACVC 2.1 is in effect since July 1997. ACVC 2.0 and ACVC 2.0.1 were transition phase versions which did not yet cover the full Ada 95 language.

IABG was accredited as an Ada Validation Facility in September 1984 and performed its first validation in November 1984. After three years of manual validations IABG started in 1988 to develop a set of tools to support and facilitate the process of validating Ada compilers. The development of the toolset went along with the evolution of portable computers and the Internet. Meanwhile IABG performed 145 validations until the end of 1997 and is one of the two active Ada Validation Facilities (AVFs).

This paper is structured as follows: In Chapter Two the principles of Ada Compiler Validation are summarized. Chapter Three contains the history, ideas, and actual status of IABG's tool environment used for Ada validations. In Chapter Four a summary and outlook on the future of Ada validations is given.

2 Principles of Ada Compiler Validation

2.1 General

The intention of Ada compiler validation is to demonstrate that the compiler implements the language as defined in the Ada Language Reference Manual. It is obvious that this goal cannot be reached to its full extent. Limitations must be accepted, which is a true statement for every quality management system.

In order to verify conformance to the Ada standard with realistic effort and affordable costs a validation system was established by the AJPO. This system consists of

- the organizations involved in the validation process (the certification body),

- the suite of test programs and documentation (the Ada Compiler Validation Capability, ACVC),

- the set of rules defining the roles of the organizations, the steps of the validation process and the acceptance criteria. The Ada Validation Procedures (see [5] for the actual version as of January 1998) and AVF Operation Manual are the most relevant documents.

In November 1997 the DoD announced that it is seriously planning to close the Ada Joint Program Office in September 1998 and to withdraw from all standardisation and validation related activities then. The future of the Ada validation system after the end of AJPO's authority is outside the scope of this paper. Until January 1998 an authority replacing the role of the AJPO did not exist. There is an expressed interest in the Ada world to have some validation system in effect in the future. However no sponsor for the maintenance of the testsuite and for an integrating role like the AVO is identified. Although ACVC 2.1 is a milestone there is a consensus in the certification body of today that the ACVC needs further maintenance.

2.2 Outline of the Validation Process

The Ada Compiler Validation Capability (ACVC) is the official test method used to check conformity of an Ada implementation with the Ada programming language standard ANSI/ISO/IEC 8652:1995, FIPS PUB 119-1 [4].

The ACVC tests do not check or report performance parameters (e.g., compile-time capacities or run-time speed). They do not check or report for characteristics such as the presence and effectiveness of compiler optimization. They do not investigate or report compiler or implementation choices in cases where the standard allows options.

Compliance of Ada implementations is tested by means of the ACVC. The ACVC contains a collection of test programs structured into six test classes: A, B, C, D, E, and L. The first letter of a test name identifies the class to which it belongs. Class A, C, D, and E tests are executable. Class B and class L tests are expected to produce errors at compile time and link time, respectively.

Table 1 below summarizes definitions for the terms used in this paper:

Term	Meaning
Test result	the result of one test (in general a data file with either a compiler/linker listing, and/or the output of an executable test)
Validation result	the complete collection of all test results of one validation
Grading category	one of the catagories *PASSED, FAILED, UNSUPPORTED, NOT APPLICABLE* (see below)
Result grading	the assignment of a test result to exactly one of the grading categories
Evaluation result	the collection of gradings of all test results

Table 1

The executable tests are written in a self-checking manner and produce a PASSED, FAILED, or NOT APPLICABLE message indicating the result when they are executed. Three Ada library units, the packages REPORT and SPPRT13, and the procedure CHECK_FILE are used for this purpose. The package REPORT also provides a set of identity functions used to defeat some compiler optimizations allowed by the Ada Standard that would circumvent a test objective. The package

SPPRT13 contains constants of type SYSTEM.ADDRESS. These constants are used by selected chapter 13 tests and by isolated tests for other chapters. The procedure CHECK_FILE is used to check the contents of text files written by some of the Class C tests for the Input-Output features of the Ada Standard, defined in Annex A of [4]. The operation of REPORT and CHECK_FILE is checked by a set of executable tests. If these units are not operating correctly, validation testing is discontinued.

Class B tests check that a compiler detects illegal language usage. Class B tests are not executable. Each test in this class is compiled and the resulting compilation listing is examined to verify that all violations of the Ada Standard are detected. Some of the class B tests contain legal Ada code which must not be flagged illegal by the compiler. This behavior is also verified.

Class L tests check that an Ada implementation correctly detects violation of the Ada Standard involving multiple, separately compiled units. Errors are expected at link time, and execution is attempted.

For some tests of the ACVC, certain implementation-specific values must be supplied. Two insertion methods for the implementation specific values are used: a macro substitution on the source file level of the test, and linking of a package that contains the implementation specific values. Details are described in [1] In addition to these anticipated test modifications, additional changes may be required to remove unforeseen conflicts between the tests and implementation-dependent characteristics. For the validation of each Ada implementation, a customized test suite is produced by the AVF.

The number of tests in the six test classes A, B, C, D, E, L changed over time. The largest number of tests in an ACVC version was reached for ACVC 1.11 with 4.071 tests. As an order of magnitude the following number of tests in the respective test classes of ACVC 1.X versions can be given:

- 2500 executable tests (class A, C, D, E),

- 100 linker tests (class L),

- 1500 compiler tests (class B). Altogether more than 12.000 intentional errors have to be matched against the actual error messages of the compiler.

For the current version *ACVC 2.1,* in effect since July 1997, Table 2 next displays the relevant counts:

ACVC 2.1	Total	Core Tests	Specialized Needs Annexes	Foundation	Docu-ments	Sup-port
Number of Files	4242	3919	245	44	11	23
Number of Tests	3662	3474	188	-	-	-

Table 2

This is not the right place to present the techniques of Ada validation in detail. The principle ideas on the method were first presented at the Ada Europe Conference 1993 [2].

Table 3 gives an overview on the six steps that make up a validation. These steps are described in more detail in The Ada Validation Procedures [5]. The validation authority DoD does not define nor require a specific method how an AVF has to conduct a validation. However its practice can be subject to an audit at any time.

Step	Activity	Meaning
1	Validation Agreement	Contractual regulations between the implementer (customer) and the AVF
2	Prevalidation	• Self-testing of the implementer • Resolution of open test issues • Results evaluation and grading by the AVF • Preparing a results base for validation testing
3	Validation Testing	Testing of the implementation with the customized testsuite under supervision of the AVF
4	Declaration of Conformance	A signed statement of the implementer where he confirms that the implementation does not violate the Ada Standard deliberately and that no rights of a third party are infringed
5	Validation Summary Report	A report in a uniform structure which identifies and describes the validation process and all validation results that are not *PASSED*
6	Validation Certificate	Issued by the validation authority; identifies the implementation, the ACVC version, awardees, and the expiration date of the validated status

Table 3

The motivation for *prevalidation* was to minimize the risk for an on-site visit of the validation team in times when it took two weeks or more to run a validation. But at least one prevalidation for a series of validations is still good practice. With the clarifications and results of a prevalidation the AVF is able to build a comparison base for tool supported evaluation (see Chapter 3) and thus reduces the on-site time as much as possible.

3 The Development of the Tool Environment CANDY

IABG's development of its tools for Ada compiler validation support started in 1988. Currently IABG is working with a version which is in use since March 1997.

3.1 Tool Development: Requirements and Principles

The following requirements guided the tool development:

- the tool shall be easy to understand and use,

- the tool shall be portable to be used on every platform for which an Ada compiler is available,

- the tool shall be customizable in order to tolerate differences in result layout and compiler features,

- the tool shall provide increased trust into the correctness of the evaluation result compared to manual evaluation,

- for B- and L-tests the tool has no authority to decide whether a test is passed,

- the tool shall provide reporting and bookkeeping facilities.

The intended use of CANDY is not primarily to automize the grading of test results; this is only done for executable tests. The real advantage is the comparison of B-test results with previously obtained test results, reducing the evaluation effort on essentially mismatching results. This process is described in more detail in section 3.4. CANDY always needs two sets of test results to work: this may be a prevalidation result and a validation result from the same platform, but also a validation result on platform A and a validation result on platform B. Experience has shown that the comparison of validation results between different ACVC versions is difficult: often the implementer improved compiler passes along with an ACVC version change. As a consequence an automatic comparison of test results had no real benefit.

A validation (prevalidation or validation testing) is done in two phases which can be executed interleaved:

- production of the validation result,
- evaluation of the validation result.

The responsibility of producing the validation result is on the implementer's side. He runs the tests under his control using his command scripts, with the AVF monitoring the process. The evaluation of the test results is done as a separate activity after parts of the test suite have been processed and material has been made available for evaluation.

In contrary to possible other approaches IABG's method deliberately does not provide automatic B- or L-test grading. *Automatic grading* means to let the tool decide whether a test is passed, at least in „obvious" cases. This idea was discussed in depth during the development phase but rejected in the end as being too risky.

The principles as presented here remained unchanged over the development of CANDY; what improved over time was the user interface, portability, reporting facilities, and of course speed.

3.2 Manual Test Result Analysis

For each test result the decision must be made whether the test objective is met and the result is in accordance with the language. This is done by inspecting the

- test output for an executable test,
- compiler listing for a B-test,
- linker listing for an L-test.

Then the result of each test is assigned to one of the grading categories (se section 2.2).

Within the first three years Ada compiler validations were evaluated completely by hand. An *ACVC logbook* was part of the ACVC distribution. The grading of each test result and additional evaluations for some more than 200 tests were documented in the logbook. The logbook was the relevant evidence for the progress and status of the validation.

This was the initial situation in the early phases of Ada validation. The manual evaluation of a validation result is a time consuming effort. For a full result evaluation of one validation at least eight person workdays are required, including bookkeeping effort. If prevalidation is performed (which is the normal case) the effort is doubled.

A complete validation however is more than that. The manpower-consuming activities of the six validation steps (see Table 3 and [5]) are

- customizing and delivering the testsuite,
- preparing, including and evaluating modified tests,
- discussing, resolving and realizing test issues (*disputes*)
  with the implementer and the AVO,

- monitoring the test installation and test processing,
- production of the Validation Summary Report (VSR).

For an evidence and trace of the test processing all logfiles are kept. Logfiles are however not processed by CANDY.

3.3 The Development of CANDY

3.3.1 CANDY 1: Monolithic Comparison Routines

The use of the manual *logbook* inspired the initial plans for automating the process. As one could expect prevalidation results and validation results of one implementation differed only marginal. So why not save the manual effort and have a customizable routine which compares previously obtained *base* validation results with recently produced *candidate* validation results and marks the differing lines. That's where *CANDY* got its name from. An OS routine like *diff* did not provide the required flexibility to serve validation purposes. The tool had to be able to cope with varying error message layouts, different formatting elements like page breaks or time stamps. The information about ignorable output differences had to be provided by string patterns.

The first version of the tool was designed in a way that all relevant informations like the patterns, error conditions, path and file name information had to be in the source code of the tool. Therefore for each validation a new tool had to be compiled and built. Especially an Ada compiler for the tool platform had to be available. Also the validation results had to be moved to that platform on which the tool was installed, which might have required a transfer of magnetic media. Note that the functionality of the tool was restricted to pure string comparisons. Every mismatching candidate result had to be examined manually. The first real use of the tool was in 1988, for a European Ada vendor.

3.3.2 CANDY 2: A Host-Based Tool with Limited Evaluation Capabilities

In 1990 the AVF started a complete redesign of the toolset. The added requirements were portability and adaptability. Also the bookkeeping facilities had to be improved. For all results of normal executable tests the type of result was captured and the result profile statistics were computed. This toolset was a major implovement and made Ada compiler validations a predictable, economic enterprise. The tool was available in mid-1991 running on Sun/Unix and DEC VAX/VMS.

3.3.3 CANDY 3: Installation of CANDY 2 on a Portable PC

With the evolving of laptops and notebooks the idea became obvious to install CANDY on a portable computer. Re-installing of CANDY on different host systems of the implementer was no more needed. Connection to the host systems was now established through TCP/IP networking directly. Therefore a notebook PC was configured for „plug-in" validations. Now the AVF was ready to conduct validations wherever appropriate. As a side effect of the port CANDY was recompiled using an

Ada 95 compiler without any problems. However it still runs in a DOS Window under Windows 95.

Also with the growing availability and speed of the Internet file transfers were simplified considerably, making the business of tape handling obsolete. The Internet now is the preferred data transfer medium. In cases where security barriers or availability restrictions do not allow a direct file transfer between the implementer and the AVF the well known *AJPO host* can be used as an intermediate storage buffer.

The migration to portable computing and Windows involved further simplifications: a couple of support tools like tape manager, unpacker, and archiver were no longer needed and could be abandoned.

3.3.4 CANDY 4: An Integrated Validation Environment

The remaining domain for further development is an overall optimization, using database functions. This database shall contain all relevant data about Ada vendors, Ada compilers, and validation specific information. Work in this area has begun and can be accomplished within few months. The fascinating aspect is that all relevant data can be kept on one portable PC, including up to 20 validation results. This is more than sufficient for one round of on-site validations.

The plans for CANDY 4 were presented at the TRI-Ada conference 1993 [3]. With the exception of database integration the implementation is completed.

3.4 Functional Description of CANDY 3

The chapter on CANDY concludes with a summary of the functional description of CANDY 3. [2] gives a more detailled specification which is still accurate and valid. Especially the grading rules are listed there.

The essential functionality of CANDY is reporting the states of pairs of test results (base and candidate). For each test in the testsuite the findings on a pair of base and candidate results as listed in Table 4 are possible:

CANDY Status	CANDY Report
Base and candidate results exist and match modulo the acceptable differences specified by the patterns	*match*
Base and candidate result exist but differ in aspects not covered by the patterns	*mismatch*
A result file is missing or incomplete	*no base, no candidate, none, incomplete*

Table 4

These reports are possible for all test results; for executable test results the grading (see Table 1) is reported in addition. So for all *matching* test results the grading of the base result is extended to the candidate result. In case of a matching result therefore no manual effort is required for grading the test result. Experience from more than 80 validations with CANDY showed that 85% to 99% of the results of one validation are matching the base results, depending on the degree of relationship of between the test results.

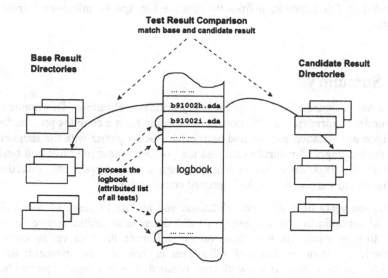

Pic. 1: CANDY's Operations

The graphic in Pic. 1 shows the principal operation of CANDY: for each of the test listed in the logbook the corresponding base and candidate results are tested for the *match* condition, depending on the ignore patterns.

A typical CANDY session looks like this:

1. Prepare the required data for CANDY (base and candidate test results residing in different subdirectory structures on the CANDY host);

2. Start the CANDY program;

3. Set the options required to run CANDY :
   - link to the base and candidate results,
   - select the part of the validation result that is to be processed,
   - set or verify the error and ignore patterns;

4. Launch the *compare loop*, in which all selected pairs of base and candidate results are compared and the resulting validation book is written;

5. Compile listings, logfiles, summaries, and statistics which display CANDY's findings; print the lists as necessary;

6. Save and archive the validation results, CANDY's listings and logfiles as part of the validation material.

What remains is the manual examination and grading of all test results that are not matching. Moreover there is a number of tests which always must be graded individually because there is more information to consult than only the regular test result (e.g. OS information from the runtime log, special information from Annex tests).

4 Summary

Ada was designed as a language for safety-critical applications. This implies that the compiler requires special attention. An Ada compiler is a complex product for which a rigorous validation process had been established together with the standardization of the language. If manually executed the process is cost intensive and tends to be unreliable. Experience has shown that using tool support the effectivity and reliability of the process can be improved considerably.

After ten years of tool based validations and almost 14 years of Ada validations IABG has optimized the efficiency of validations. Some administrative functions are left to implement, which do however not influence the core validation activities. Experiences from the last real validations endorse this achievement: ten on-site validations were done in six workdays, preceeded by one regular prevalidation. So compared to an eight days average for one validation (yielding 88 days for ten plus one prevalidation) we have now eight for the prevalidation, plus six on-site plus three for administration, resulting in a total number of 17 days compared to 88, which is roughly 20% of the original effort. These are rough estimations of elapsed times; more convincing of course are the cost reductions. The price of a validation can now be less than 10% compared to the initial costs, depending on the number of validations done in parallel.

It should be mentioned that IABG's activities had never been subsidized by anyone. The tool development was always sponsored internally from the validation fees. IABG honors the excellent contributions of students from Staffordshire University GB from the last decade. Without them CANDY would not be what it is today.

IABG's experience demonstrated that Ada compiler validations can be optimized and integrated smoothly into the development cycle of the implementer. The proposed closing of the AJPO in fall 1998 will enforce new directions for Ada validations. At the end of this development an increased autonomy for the AVF and more competence on issuing validation certificates is expected. IABG is prepared for this development.

5 References

Note: The URLs of the documents [1] and [5] are dated February 1998 and may change over time.

[1]   The Ada Compiler Validation Capability (ACVC) Version 2.1 User's Guide, CTA Incorporated, Dayton, OH 45431, March 1997 (*http://www.sw-eng.falls-church.va.us/AdaIC/compilers/acvc/95acvc/acvc2_1/index*)

[2]   An Efficient Compiler Validation Method for Ada 9X, Michael Tonndorf, Proceedings of the Ada Europe '93 Conference, Springer Verlag LNCS 688, Berlin Heidelberg, 1993.

[3]   An Integrated Tool Environment for Ada Compiler Validations, Michael Tonndorf, Proceedings of the TRI-Ada '93 Conference, ACM SIGAda, New York, 1993.

[4]   Reference Manual for the Ada Programming Language, ANSI/ISO/IEC 8652:1995, FIPS PUB 119-1.

[5]   Ada Compiler Validation Procedures, Version 5.0, 18 November 1997, Ada Joint Program Office , Center for Computer Systems Engineering, Defense Information Systems Agency (*http://www.sw-eng.falls-church.va.us /AdaIC/compilers/val-proc/val5_0fin.shtml*)

A Two-Level Matching Mechanism for Object-Oriented Class Libraries

S. Araban and A.S.M. Sajeev

School of Computer Science and Software Engineering (CSSE)
Monash University
Caulfield East, VIC 3145
Australia
{araban, sajeev}@insect.sd.monash.edu.au

Abstract. Providing an effective search/retrieval mechanism is essential for supporting software reuse. Such a tool can help both software designers and developers in finding, understanding and modifying the components most relevant for their requirements. *Syntactic matching* techniques can provide easy to use, fast and cheap, but not necessarily very accurate, search tools. On the contrary, *specification matching* can provide accurate results, while it is more difficult to use, slow and expensive (in terms of complexity and resources). In this paper, we propose a hybrid process which combines these two matching methods. At the first level, a user can perform a keyword search based on faceted classification. If results of the first level are not satisfactory, a specification based matching can be conducted among the results of the first match. In this way, the associated costs of specification matching will be dramatically dropped by the restriction of the search space (you'll pay for what you use). The proposed specification match also tries to take advantage of the characteristics of OO class libraries (i.e. inheritance and design by contract principles). We will show how these can improve both performance and accuracy of matching queries with components.

1   Introduction

Software reuse still remains an exception rather than a rule despite the simplicity of the idea and its attractive benefits [2][3]. Reuse in the traditional software development paradigms has had various levels of successes and failures [13]. In recent years, however, object-orientation (OO) has given a new hope for solving the problems in software reuse. It has been widely accepted that OO can improve modularity and abstraction levels of software products which are essential in both design with and design for reuse.

Classes are the units of software decomposition in OO Environments (OOE). A class is in fact an implementation of an ADT. Therefore, reusers need to focus only on the semantics of the behavior of the component which they want without having to worry about the actual implementations. Reuse in OO environments is typically based on systematic reuse of libraries of classes [7].

There are two types of class reuse:

1. Client-server: A class can be reused by another class (client), as a server for services which it offers. In this method, the client just needs to know the abstract interface of the server in order to use its services.
2. Inheritance: A new class can be developed as a descendent (specialisation) of other class(es) via inheritance. In this case all the data structures and operations of ancestor(s) are inherited by the descendent. The developer only needs to define additional operations and/or data structures or modify the inherited features. A class library is usually represented as a *directed acyclic graph* based on the inheritance relationships among the classes.

The notions of pre- and post-conditions have been used to provide a more clear representation of the functionality of an abstraction. Pre-conditions are the requirements of each behavior which need to be met by the client before using that behavior. On the other hand, post-conditions of each behavior are the requirements of the client which need to be met by that behavior (the supplier).

In order to make the abstraction work, designers often recommend principles for systematic reuse. The Design by Contract principle [8], for example, states that a child class may weaken the preconditions of its methods and strengthen the post-conditions, but not the other way around.

It is important to have large collections of reusable classes to make reuse possible, but at the same time, we also need to have efficient classification and retrieval tools to make effective use of the class libraries.

This paper describes a classification and retrieval tool OO-CaRE2 (Object-Oriented Classification and Retrieval Environment) based on both faceted classification and specification matching methods.

The primary use of OO-CaRE2 is to assist in the classification and retrieval of reusable class libraries. OO-CaRE2 not only finds the most relevant components that match the specified requirements, but also ranks them based on their closeness to the requirements. OO-CaRE2 can also be used in learning the contents of class libraries. Unlike in other programming environments, a significant portion of the learning curve of an object-oriented environment is mastering the class libraries that consist of several hundreds or potentially thousands of classes, and inter-relationships among them [5]. OO-CaRE2 offers a structured way of exploring the class libraries which is more effective than the usual string search and browsing mechanisms. Furthermore, the concept of closeness and the use of thesaurus help reusers to find the most relevant components based on the vocabulary which they are familiar with.

The rest of this paper is organised as follows. Section 2 is a brief introduction to the concepts of faceted classification and specification matching. Section 3 describes the components and structure of our approach. Conclusions and future work directions are discussed in Section 4. Finally, Appendix A presents proofs for all relations presented in Section 3.

2 Classification and Matching Systems

2.1 Faceted Classification

The theory of faceted classification is based on the idea of universal knowledge structures [12]. In this method, a domain is analysed into its *basic terms* (or *keywords*). Then these basic terms are conceptually arranged into *facets*. For example, a faceted classification for software components might group basic terms such as 'add', 'compare', 'compress' and 'append' into a facet called "Operations" and terms such as 'array', 'string' and 'tree' into another facet called "Collaborators" [6].

Faceted classification is a controlled vocabulary technique [4], where, each facet can only take valid values (*terms*) during the classification and retrieval process. The set of terms for a facet is called its *term space*. The term space of each facet is selected, assigned and maintained by the domain experts (and/or the librarian). Composite terms can be derived from the basic terms of different facets. For instance, the composite term 'compare string' can be created by combining the basic term 'compare' from the "Operations" facet and the basic term 'string' from the "Collaborators" facet. This ability (of deriving composite classes from the basic terms of different facets) makes this method very flexible.

A faceted scheme gives a multidimensional view of classified components based on a set of facets. Facets can be ordered by their relevance to the users. In the above example, we may consider "Operations" more relevant than "Collaborators'. This citation ordering enhances search/retrieve performance [11]. It is also easy to modify and extend the term spaces since individual facets can be changed independently of other facets. Terms can be added to, modified and deleted from the term space of each facet without the need to modify other facets. This flexibility is especially important for classifying components in a new and fast-growing field such as Computing, where the vocabulary is subject to rapid changes [11]. Another important feature of faceted schemes is the ordering of terms within each facet. Terms can be ordered in such a way as to show their conceptual closeness to each other.

Since the ordering of software components is artificial, the selection of facets is, in some sense, arbitrary. However, there are some criteria which must be met by selected facets [6]. These criteria are:

- Each facet must tell something about the component which is crucial for reuse.
- Each facet should be well defined, and as orthogonal to other facets as possible.
- All facets should be relevant for most components, regardless of the size of the component or from which phase of the development it originates.
- There must not be too many facets.

One of the first, and indeed the best known, facet based systems for software reuse is Prieto-Diaz's classification system [11]. The system distinguishes two major parts in the classification of software programs: one describing the functionality and the other describing the environment. The program's functionality is represented by a triple set of facets ⟨function, object, medium⟩ and three facets for environmental aspects of software ⟨system type, functional area, setting⟩. However, Prieto-Diaz's system has certain limitations. For instance, the citation order is fixed both for classification and for retrieval. Furthermore, the prototype system has not implemented possibilities for assigning or selecting more than one term in each facet.

Faceted classification may be considered as a very good representation method for Object-Oriented Environments [1]. However, the proposed facets by Prieto-Diaz were originally developed for functional software components and are not directly applicable to OO class libraries. Very few attempts have been made to design a faceted classification scheme for OOEs. Probably, the most comprehensive attempt to build a faceted classification scheme for reusable classes has been made as a part of the REBOOT (REuse Based on Object Oriented Techniques) project. The objective of the REBOOT project was to provide a reuse based software development environment in order to enhance productivity and quality [10]. The REBOOT researchers based their work on a life cycle oriented model of reusable components which considered information from all software life-cycle phases as potentially reusable. They developed a formal entity-relationship model of the reusable component and used this model as the database schema for storing the reusable components in a repository. This scheme has been developed and applied based on the following set of facets [6][14]:

1. **Abstraction** contains those terms (nouns) describing the classes that experts in the field can agree upon.
2. **Operations** contain the list of operations or methods (verbs) which classes may offer.
3. **Collaborators** contain those kind of objects a class manages (nouns). This facet can capture the client-server relationships among the classes.
4. **Parts** capture the data parts of the classified components.
5. **Dependencies** capture any specific dependencies which would limit the use of the class (environmental or implementation dependencies).

2.2 Specification Matching

In this method the matching process is based on the logical behavior of the components which have formally been specified, usually in the form of *pre-* and *post-conditions*. There are a number of ongoing researches in this direction, however most of them are in the non object-oriented context.

Zaremski and Wing [15] have defined a set of *exact* and *relaxed* matches for formal specifications. They have defined their matches at function and module levels. At the function level, if S is specification for a function of a component and Q is the specification for a function from the user's query, then, let S_{pre}, Q_{pre} and S_{post}, Q_{post} receptively represent pre- and post-conditions for these functions. A generic form for *pre/post matching* has been defined as: $Match_{pre/post}(S, Q) = (Q_{pre} \, \mathcal{R}_1 \, S_{pre}) \, \mathcal{R}_2 \, (Q_{post} \, \mathcal{R}_3 \, S_{post})$

The relations $\mathcal{R}_1$ and $\mathcal{R}_3$ are either equivalence ($\Leftrightarrow$) or implication ($\Rightarrow$), but they need not be the same. $\mathcal{R}_2$ is usually conjunction ($\wedge$) but may also be implication ($\Rightarrow$). Based on this generic form Zaremski and Wing have considered four kinds of pre/post matches beginning with the highest degree of match and progressively weakening it by either relaxing the relations $\mathcal{R}_1$ and $\mathcal{R}_3$ from $\Leftrightarrow$ to $\Rightarrow$, and $\mathcal{R}_2$ from $\wedge$ to $\Rightarrow$ or dropping one or more terms. (Definitions 2.1-2.6 are from [15].)

Definition 21 *ExactPre/PostMatch.*
Two functions specifications satisfy the exact pre/post match if their pre-conditions are equivalent and their post-conditions are equivalent :
$$match_{E-pre/post}(S,Q) = (Q_{pre} \Leftrightarrow S_{pre}) \wedge (Q_{post} \Leftrightarrow S_{post})$$
Exact pre/post match is a strict relation, yet two different-looking specifications can still satisfy the match.

Definition 22 *Plug-in Match.*
Both equivalence relations ($\mathcal{R}_1$ and $\mathcal{R}_3$) are relaxed to implication whilst the conjunction ($\mathcal{R}_2$) is kept as in exact pre/post match. Under plug-in match, Q matches any specification S whose pre-condition is weaker and whose post-condition is stronger :
$$match_{plug-in}(S,Q) = (Q_{pre} \Rightarrow S_{pre}) \wedge (S_{post} \Rightarrow Q_{post})$$
Plug-in match captures the notion of substitutability of S for Q.

Definition 23 *Plug-in Post Match.*
Often the user is only concerned with the effects of functions, thus a useful relaxation of the plug-in match is to consider only the post-condition part of the conjunction :
$$match_{plug-in-post}(S,Q) = (S_{post} \Rightarrow Q_{post})$$

Definition 24 *Post Match.*
Where in generic match, $\mathcal{R}_3$ is replaced with $\Rightarrow$, $\mathcal{R}_2$ is relaxed to $\Rightarrow$ and Q_{pre} is dropped :
$$match_{post}(S,Q) = S_{pre} \Rightarrow (S_{post} \Rightarrow Q_{post})$$

They have also defined a set of predicate matches that relates the entire specification predicates of the two functions, S_{pred} and Q_{pred}. A generic form for predicate match is as follows:
$$match_{pred}(S,Q) = S_{pred} \mathcal{R} Q_{pred}$$

where, the relation $\mathcal{R}$ is either equivalence ($\Leftrightarrow$), implication ($\Rightarrow$) or reverse implication ($\Leftarrow$). As with the generic pre/post match, they consider instantiations of the generic predicate match.

Definition 25 *Exact Predicate Match.*
Two functions' specifications match exactly if their predicates are logically equivalent :

$match_{E-pred}(S,Q) = (Q_{pred} \Leftrightarrow S_{pred})$ *which is less restrictive than exact pre/post match.*

Definition 26 *GeneralisedMatch. Relaxing $\mathcal{R}$ to $\Rightarrow$ in the generic predicate match :*
$match_{gen}(S,Q) = (S_{pred} \Rightarrow Q_{pred})$ *which allows the function specification to be stronger (more general) than the query.*

Zaremski and Wing's work is in the area of ADTs within the context of functional languages and does not incorporate characteristics of OO class libraries, however, it provides a good foundation for applying specification matching to OO class libraries.

3 Our Approach

We propose a hybrid process consisting of faceted and specification based matching methods. At the first level, a user can perform a keyword search based on faceted classification. If results of the first level are not satisfactory, a specification based matching can be conducted among the results of the first match. In this way, the associated costs of specification matching will be dramatically dropped because of the restriction of the search space (you'll pay for what you use). The proposed specification match also tries to take advantage of the characteristics of OO class libraries (i.e. inheritance and design by contract principles). We will show how these can improve both performance and accuracy of the matching.

3.1 First Level: Faceted Matching

As the first part of our work, we have successfully developed a search/retrieval tool (called OO-CaRE) using the same set of facets as in REBOOT project (see Section 2.1) for Eiffel class libraries (Fig. 1) [1]. Users of OO-CaRE are able to make queries (Fig. 2) consisting of a set of terms for each facet as well as assign an importance value for each facet. For a search query, OO-CaRE returns a set of components that completely or partially match the query, ordered by their closeness to the query (Fig. 3). In this system, each facet is given an importance value (weight), which is used to measure closeness and rank the matched components.

Once a set of matching components, using this process, is obtained, the reuser may want to further refine this set by matching the behavior of the desired component. Specification matching can be used at this stage.

3.2 Second Level: Specification Matching Strategy

In OO-CaRE2 we have adapted Zaremski and Wing's specification matching model into the context of object-orientation. We assume that the target class libraries

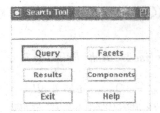

Fig. 1. OO-CaRE main window screen shot.

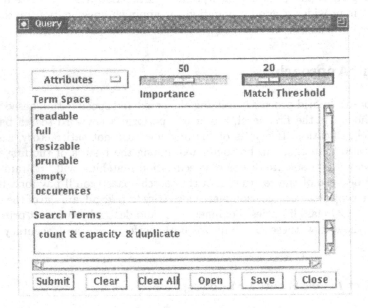

Fig. 2. OO-CaRE query screen shot.

confirm *design by contract principles* [9]. Suppose there is a weak match (e.g. *plug-in-post* or *post Match*) between specification of a method s from Class S and method q from query Q. Then the question is which of the neighboring class (in the inheritance hierarchy) is more likely to improve the match (i.e. parent, child or the sibling class)(Fig. 4). By taking inheritance into account, our strategy includes matching at both *Method* and *Class* levels.

Method Matching Strategy Let s be the specification of a matched method (from the class library) with a given method q from the query, using the faceted scheme. Also, let function $Parent(s, \downarrow s)$ represent the inheritance relation between the method s from the *parent* class and its redefined version $\downarrow s$ from the *child* class (Appendix A). Based on the above definitions for function matching,

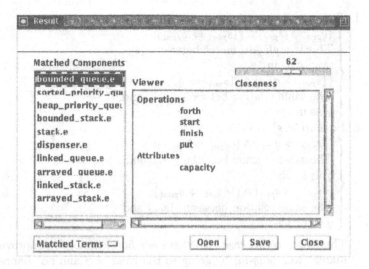

Fig. 3. OO-CaRE results screen shot.

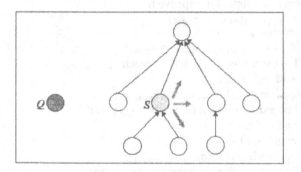

Fig. 4. Matching a query (Q) with a component specification (S) of an OO Class lib.

the relation (if any) between s_{post} and q_{post} needs to be determined first. There are four possible relations:

1. $s_{post} \Rightarrow q_{post}$: These methods can at least satisfy the *Plug-in Post Match* definition. Depending on the relations between s_{pre} and q_{pre} one of the following can be the case:

   a. $(q_{pre} \Rightarrow s_{pre}) \wedge (s_{post} \Rightarrow q_{post})$: This is a *plug-in match* (which can be considered as a strong match), so there is no need for further improvement.

   b. $(s_{pre} \Rightarrow q_{pre}) \wedge (s_{post} \Rightarrow q_{post})$

i. $Parent(s, \downarrow s) \longrightarrow$

$\begin{cases} (q_{pre} \Rightarrow \downarrow s_{pre}) \wedge (\downarrow s_{post} \Rightarrow q_{post}): \\ \text{This is a } plug\text{-}in \text{ match between } \downarrow s_{pre} \\ \text{and } q \text{ as in 1a.} \\ (\downarrow s_{pre} \Rightarrow q_{pre}) \wedge (\downarrow s_{post} \Rightarrow q_{post}): \\ \text{The same relation between } \downarrow s_{pre} \text{ and} \\ q \text{ as in 1b.} \end{cases}$

ii. $Parent(\uparrow s, s) \longrightarrow$

$\begin{cases} (\uparrow s_{pre} \Rightarrow q_{pre}) \wedge (q_{post} \Rightarrow \uparrow s_{post}): \\ \text{The same relation between } \uparrow s_{pre} \text{ and} \\ q \text{ as in 2b.} \\ (\uparrow s_{pre} \Rightarrow q_{pre}) \wedge (\uparrow s_{post} \Rightarrow q_{post}): \\ \text{The same relation between } \uparrow s_{pre} \text{ and} \\ q \text{ as in 1b.} \end{cases}$

Therefore, in this case (1b) there is a 50% chance for improving the match (to a *plug-in*) by going to the *child* of S and no chance of an improvement by moving to the *parent*.

2. $s_{post} \Leftarrow q_{post}$: This relation does not conform to any of the matching definitions, however, it might be improved.

a. $(q_{pre} \Rightarrow s_{pre}) \wedge (q_{post} \Rightarrow s_{post})$

i. $Parent(s, \downarrow s) \longrightarrow$

$\begin{cases} (q_{pre} \Rightarrow \downarrow s_{pre}) \wedge (\downarrow s_{post} \Rightarrow q_{post}): \\ \text{This is a } plug\text{-}in \text{ match between } \downarrow s_{post} \\ \text{and } q \text{as in 1a.} \\ (q_{pre} \Rightarrow \downarrow s_{pre}) \wedge (q_{post} \Rightarrow \downarrow s_{post}): \\ \text{The same relation between } \downarrow s_{post} \text{ and} \\ q \text{ as in 2a.} \end{cases}$

ii. $Parent(\uparrow s, s) \longrightarrow$

$\begin{cases} (q_{pre} \Rightarrow \uparrow s_{pre}) \wedge (q_{post} \Rightarrow \uparrow s_{post}): \\ \text{The same relation between } \uparrow s_{post} \text{ and} \\ q \text{ as in 2a.} \\ (\uparrow s_{pre} \Rightarrow q_{pre}) \wedge (q_{post} \Rightarrow \uparrow s_{post}): \\ \text{The same relation between } \uparrow s_{post} \text{ and} \\ q \text{ as in 2b.} \end{cases}$

Therefore, in this case (2a) there is a 50% chance for improving the match (to a *plug-in*) by going to the *child* of S and no chance of an improvement by moving to the *parent*.

b. $(s_{pre} \Rightarrow q_{pre}) \wedge (q_{post} \Rightarrow s_{post})$

The above relation suggests that the method specification s (from the class specification S) can be replaced by the method specification q (from the query Q). Thus, it is more likely to find a good match for q among the children of S.

3. $s_{post} \Leftrightarrow q_{post}$: This equivalence can at least satisfy the *plug-in post match* definition. It can be broken down into $(s_{post} \Rightarrow q_{post}) \wedge (s_{post} \Leftarrow q_{post})$ which may lead to a *plug-in match* by going to the child of s (as in 1a,1b, 2a, 2b and 3).

4. No relation between them. In this case, s and q can not be matched.

Thus, for weak matches (e.g. *plug-in-post* or *post Match*), there is always a better chance for a *plug-in match* by going to the child(ren) of S.

Class Matching Strategy The aim of a matching process between a classe and a query can be define as: maximising number of matched methods with the highest degree between the two. Based on the previous section, one can conclude that if a query (Q) is matched with a class specification (S) from the library in some degree, then there will be a good chance to imporve the match by trying those children (subclasses) of S with maximum number of redefined relevant methods.

4 Conclusions and future work

Object-Orientation encourages reuse by facilitating construction and use of component libraries. In this paper a two-level matching mechanism for these libraries have been proposed. In the first level, the components are matched using facets-which is fast and inexpensive. However, this is not always accurate. The second level refines the matched components from the first level, by matching their specification with the query's specification. The latter process is complex and expensive due to its need for an automated theorem prover. Reusers can choose the level of matching they need. The current prototype does not include the theorem prover. Our approach contrasts with other searching environments like REBOOT, which uses just the faceted classification mechanism [10].

References

[1] S. Araban. A faceted classification scheme for object-oriented environments. Master's thesis, Monash University, Department of Software Development, 1995.

[2] B. W. Boehm. Improving software productivity. *IEEE Computer*, 20(9):43–57, 1987.

[3] F. P. Brooks. No silver bullet: Essence and accidents of software engineering. *IEEE Computer*, 20(4):10–19, 1987.

[4] W. B. Frakes and P. B. Gandel. Representing reusable software. *Information and Software Technology*, 32(10):653–664, 1990.

[5] B. Henderson-Sellers and C. Freeman. Cataloguing and classification for object libraries. *ACM SIGSOFT, Software Engineering Notes*, 17(1):62–64, 1992.

[6] E. Karlsson, S. Sørumgard, and E. Tryggeseth. Classification of object-oriented components for reuse. In B. Meyer, editor, *TOOLS'7*. Prentice-Hall, 1992.

[7] C. W. Krueger. Software reuse. *Acm Computing Surveys*, 24(2):131–183, 1992.

[8] B. Meyer. *Object-Oriented Software Construction*. Prentice-Hall, 1988.

[9] B. Meyer. *Reusable Software, The Base Object-Oriented Components Libraries*. Object-Oriented. Prentice-Hall, 1994.

[10] J. Morel and J. Faget. The REBOOT environment. In R. Prieto-Diaz and W. B. Frakes, editors, *Advances in Software Reuse*. IEEE Computer Society press, 1993. International workshop in software reusability.

[11] R. Prieto-Diaz. *Classification of Reusable Modules*, volume 1 of *Software Reusability*, chapter 4, pages 99–123. ACM press, 1989.

[12] S. R. Ranganathan. *Prolegomena to Library Classification*. Bombay: Asia Publishing House, thierd edition, 1967.

[13] A. S. M. Sajeev. Some reusability exercises in persistent C. *Journal of Computing and Information*, 1(1):1121–1136, 1995.

[14] L. S. Sørumgard, G. Sindre, and F. Stokke. Experiences from application of a faceted classification scheme. In R. Prieto-Diaz and W.B. Frakes, editors, *Advances in Software Reuse*. IEEE Computer Society press, 1993. International workshop in software reusability.

[15] A.M. Zaremski and J.M. Wing. Specification matching of software components. *ACM Transactions on Software Engineering and Methodology*, 6(4):333–369, 1995.

Appendix A: Proofs

This appendix provides proofs for the relations in Section 3.2.

Definition 1. $Parent(P,C) = (P_{pre} \Rightarrow C_{pre}) \wedge (C_{post} \Rightarrow P_{post})$

1. $s_{post} \Rightarrow q_{post}$: These methods can at least satisfy the *Plug-in Post Match* definition. Depending on the relations between s_{pre} and q_{pre} one of the following can be the case:

   a. $(q_{pre} \Rightarrow s_{pre}) \wedge (s_{post} \Rightarrow q_{post})$: This is a *plug-in match* (which can be considered as a strong match), so there is no need for further improvement.

   b. $(s_{pre} \Rightarrow q_{pre}) \wedge (s_{post} \Rightarrow q_{post})$

   i. $$\left\{ \begin{array}{c} Parent(s, \downarrow\! s) \\ \wedge \\ (s_{pre} \Rightarrow q_{pre}) \wedge (s_{post} \Rightarrow q_{post}) \end{array} \right\} \rightarrow$$

   $$\left\{ \begin{array}{c} (s_{pre} \Rightarrow \downarrow\! s_{pre}) \wedge (\downarrow\! s_{post} \Rightarrow s_{post}) \\ \wedge \\ (s_{pre} \Rightarrow q_{pre}) \wedge (s_{post} \Rightarrow q_{post}) \end{array} \right\} \rightarrow$$

   $$(\downarrow\! s_{post} \Rightarrow q_{post}) \rightarrow \left\{ \begin{array}{c} (\downarrow\! s_{post} \Rightarrow q_{post}) \\ \wedge \\ \underbrace{[(q_{pre} \Rightarrow \downarrow\! s_{pre}) \vee (\downarrow\! s_{pre} \Rightarrow q_{pre})]}_{Tautology} \end{array} \right\} \rightarrow$$

   $$\left\{ \begin{array}{c} (q_{pre} \Rightarrow \downarrow\! s_{pre}) \wedge (\downarrow\! s_{post} \Rightarrow q_{post}) 1a \\ \vee \\ (\downarrow\! s_{pre} \Rightarrow q_{pre}) \wedge (\downarrow\! s_{post} \Rightarrow q_{post}) 1b \end{array} \right.$$

ii. $\left\{\begin{array}{c} Parent(\uparrow s, s) \\ \wedge \\ (s_{pre} \Rightarrow q_{pre}) \wedge (s_{post} \Rightarrow q_{post}) \end{array}\right\} \rightarrow$

$\qquad \left\{\begin{array}{c} (\uparrow s_{pre} \Rightarrow s_{pre}) \wedge (s_{post} \Rightarrow \uparrow s_{post}) \\ \wedge \\ (s_{pre} \Rightarrow q_{pre}) \wedge (s_{post} \Rightarrow q_{post}) \end{array}\right\} \rightarrow$

$(\uparrow s_{pre} \Rightarrow q_{pre}) \rightarrow \left\{\begin{array}{c} (\uparrow s_{pre} \Rightarrow q_{pre}) \\ \wedge \\ \underbrace{[(\uparrow s_{post} \Rightarrow q_{post}) \vee (q_{post} \Rightarrow \uparrow s_{post})]}_{Tautology} \end{array}\right\} \rightarrow$

$\left\{\begin{array}{l} (\uparrow s_{pre} \Rightarrow q_{pre}) \wedge (q_{post} \Rightarrow \uparrow s_{post}) \quad \text{2b} \\ \qquad\qquad \vee \\ (\uparrow s_{pre} \Rightarrow q_{pre}) \wedge (\uparrow s_{post} \Rightarrow q_{post}) \text{1b} \end{array}\right.$

Therefore, in this case (1b) there is a 50% chance for improving the match (to a *plug-in*) by going to the *child* of S and no chance of an improvement by moving to the *parent*.

2. $s_{post} \Leftarrow q_{post}$: This relation does not conform to any of the matching definitions, however, it may be improved.

a. $(q_{pre} \Rightarrow s_{pre}) \wedge (q_{post} \Rightarrow s_{post})$

i. $\left\{\begin{array}{c} Parent(s, \downarrow s) \\ \wedge \\ (q_{pre} \Rightarrow s_{pre}) \wedge (q_{post} \Rightarrow s_{post}) \end{array}\right\} \rightarrow$

$\qquad \left\{\begin{array}{c} (s_{pre} \Rightarrow \downarrow s_{pre}) \wedge (\downarrow s_{post} \Rightarrow s_{post}) \\ \wedge \\ (q_{pre} \Rightarrow s_{pre}) \wedge (q_{post} \Rightarrow s_{post}) \end{array}\right\} \rightarrow$

$(q_{pre} \Rightarrow \downarrow s_{pre}) \rightarrow \left\{\begin{array}{c} (q_{pre} \Rightarrow \downarrow s_{pre}) \\ \wedge \\ \underbrace{[(q_{post} \Rightarrow \downarrow s_{post}) \vee (\downarrow s_{post} \Rightarrow q_{post})]}_{Tautology} \end{array}\right\} \rightarrow$

$\left\{\begin{array}{l} (q_{pre} \Rightarrow \downarrow s_{pre}) \wedge (\downarrow s_{post} \Rightarrow q_{post}) \text{1a} \\ \qquad\qquad \vee \\ (q_{pre} \Rightarrow \downarrow s_{pre}) \wedge (q_{post} \Rightarrow \downarrow s_{post}) \quad \text{2a} \end{array}\right.$

ii. $\left\{\begin{array}{c} Parent(\uparrow s, s) \\ \wedge \\ (q_{pre} \Rightarrow s_{pre}) \wedge (q_{post} \Rightarrow s_{post}) \end{array}\right\} \rightarrow$

$\qquad \left\{\begin{array}{c} (\uparrow s_{pre} \Rightarrow s_{pre}) \wedge (s_{post} \Rightarrow \uparrow s_{post}) \\ \wedge \\ (q_{pre} \Rightarrow s_{pre}) \wedge (q_{post} \Rightarrow s_{post}) \end{array}\right\} \rightarrow$

$$(q_{post} \Rightarrow \uparrow s_{post}) \rightarrow \left\{ \begin{array}{c} (q_{post} \Rightarrow \uparrow s_{post}) \\ \wedge \\ \underbrace{[(q_{pre} \Rightarrow \uparrow s_{pre}) \vee (\uparrow s_{pre} \Rightarrow q_{pre})]}_{Tautology} \end{array} \right\} \rightarrow$$

$$\left\{ \begin{array}{c} (q_{pre} \Rightarrow \uparrow s_{pre}) \wedge (q_{post} \Rightarrow \uparrow s_{post}) 2a \\ \vee \\ (\uparrow s_{pre} \Rightarrow q_{pre}) \wedge (q_{post} \Rightarrow \uparrow s_{post}) 2b \end{array} \right.$$

Therefore, in this case (2a) there is a 50% chance for improving the match (to a *plug-in*) by going to the *child* of S and no chance of an improvement by moving to the *parent*.

Modern Avionics Requirements for the Distributed Systems Annex

Bruce Lewis[1], Steve Vestal[2], and David McConnell[3]

[1] US Army Aviation and Missile Command, Battlefield Automation Directorate,
Missile Research, Development and Engineering Center,
Redstone Aresnal AL 35898, USA
[2] Honeywell Technology Center, Minneapolis MN 55418, USA
[3] Tennessee Applied Physical Sciences, Fayetteville TN 37334, USA

Abstract. We ported an Architecture Description Language (ADL), MetaH, for automating the specification, analysis and building of Avionics/high reliability systems on top of Ada 95 and the Distributed Systems Annex (DSA). Our purpose was to explore the requirements for the DSA in such applications and to assess portability benefits. The problem domain of modern avionics will increasingly require strong partitioning of software with multilevel safety and reliability analysis to build highly complex, large, multiprocessor, predominately hard real-time software systems. This paper covers changes in the requirement driving the problem domain, the solution approach using an ADL, MetaH, on top of the DSA, and requirements for a usable DSA implementation.

1 Introduction

This work was co-funded by the Ada Joint Program Office, the Army Aviation and Missile Command, the Defense Advanced Research Projects Agency, and Honeywell.
It is part of a broader effort to develop architectural concentric approaches for the software lifecycle, providing more powerful paradigms to support system evolution. MetaH, a domain specific Architecture Description Language (ADL) developed for avionics, was used in this experiment to reflect modern avionics requirements against the Ada 95 Distributed Systems Annex (DSA). Our intent in this experiment was to provide information to implementers and users of the DSA so that it could be used efficiently in tightly coupled mission critical and safety critical systems. Although the domain of reference is avionics, the requirements stated for the DSA allow it to be used in real-time systems to isolate components. The benefits of this are: reduced verification, validation, and testing costs; efficient use of multiple partitions within a processor; and the generation of tailored, system specific executives. In addition, this approach allows strong control over partitions to enable safety and fault recovery properties.

Our paper is organized as follows:

1. A description of evolutionary trends in modern avionics.
2. ADLs as a means of building systems.
3. The resulting DSA requirements from avionics/MetaH.

2 Evolving Avionics Requirements - Driving Software Solutions

We will cite five trends that are changing the way avionics systems are being developed. Future development methods and tools must take these trends into account.

First, the amount of functionality, and the degree to which functions are integrated to take advantage of information and capabilities available from each other, is increasing. More and more functionality is being added to air vehicles: on-board maintenance and diagnostics, multimedia communications, situation awareness, mission simulation and training, higher levels of cockpit automation, greater autonomy and less dependence on central air traffic management, etc. The trend is not towards much smaller, cheaper, more dependable versions of current avionics systems, but towards avionics systems that do much more than current systems.

Second, avionics systems are changing from federated systems in which major functions (e.g. autopilot, navigation, displays) are provided by separate computer systems to more integrated systems in which many different pieces of software are integrated together on a distributed multi-processor system. This enables more efficient utilization of hardware resources, easier logistics and maintenance, easier functional and processor upgrades, and more integrated functionality. Major benefits also include reduced size, weight and power requirements. However, problems like common mode failures and error propagations require more careful attention.

Third, increased integration, efficiency and functionality can only be achieved through increased used of concurrent, multi-disciplinary development. The degree to which separate teams of engineers trained in different disciplines can work independently and with minimal interaction is decreasing. The development process and its supporting tools must allow the work of multiple teams to be easily integrated and must support trade-off decisions that cross engineering disciplines and development teams.

Fourth, there is increasing use of commercial off-the-shelf hardware components that were not specifically developed for avionics systems. This can enable reduced cost and development schedule and increased functionality. However, size/weight/power and dependability are significant issues, and commercial components must be carefully selected and used within a suitable overall avionics architecture. Commercial components may also become obsolete, unavailable and unsupported in a matter of years. Ongoing affordable upgrades are essential for avionics systems whose life cycles are measured in decades.

Fifth, assurance of correctness is becoming an increasing challenge. Testing is generally acknowledged to be inadequate to achieve very high levels of assurance when used alone. As the degree of integration and complexity increase, the effectiveness of testing becomes ever more questionable. Increased use of additional independent verification methods, such as various kinds of formal modeling and analysis methods, must occur. It is reasonable to anticipate that regulatory and certification authorities will increase their expectations and requirements in this area.

Our solution approach must handle these high level requirements changes and provide the foundation for continued evolution in the future. We need an approach that can:

1. Abstract away the increasing complexity
2. Provide software safety mechanisms to supplement hardware partitioning in increasingly tightly coupled systems
3. Provide a means of easily analyzing, integrating and replacing subsystems from multiple disciplines within and across processors
4. Allow rapid retargeting of complex multiprocessor real-time systems
5. Provide the formalisms and regular structure needed for automated analysis

All of these requirements point to an architecture concentric solution. To be sufficient, such a solution requires generation capabilities to automate building the architectural structure, automatic formal safety mechanisms, and architecture level analysis.

3 Architecture Description Languages as a Means of Building High Reliability Systems

An Architecture Description Language (ADL) provides the means to express the software and/or hardware design of a system in terms of the components, the interconnections, and system control. From this description the information required for architectural analysis is extracted. Domain Specific ADLs can provide significant leverage to develop architectures with the correct properties for a domain of application. The ADL can also provide the basis for a toolset to be used to automatically implement the architecture specified. The components within an architecture may be populated by reference using generated glue code. The toolset can provide automatic integration of the whole system, software and hardware. The ADL itself can be standardized and multiple vendors of the language can add additional analysis capabilities and can compete for targets supported, code efficiency, scheduling efficiency, etc. In the case of MetaH, discussed below, we intend to start standardizing activities this year.

3.1 MetaH, an ADL and Architecture Implementation Approach.

MetaH represents a new paradigm for the development of embedded hard real-time systems. It is based on development/evolution by architectural specification. It's a language for specifying software and hardware architectures for real-time, safely/securely partitioned, fault-tolerant, scaleable multiprocessor systems and it is also a toolset to implement/generate to that specification. MetaH provides a highly automated, formal, architecture level language approach to building and evolving software. It maintains an architecture-concentric process from the architectural specification to the implementation of the software on the hardware.

In use, the software architect/designer develops a reusable design - an architecture. He lays out the design in MetaH graphics or text and decomposes the system down to the process level, specifying the data flow, events, hardware, and scheduling. The process level is (can be incrementally) populated with functional code, some of which may be generated by domain specific generators. The system is tuned by tool-assisted analysis, then compiled, loaded and executed on the hardware. The toolset collects timing data from the system, provides signal injection, and provides easy retuning based on the target hardware results.

As a tool for system evolution, MetaH provides for significant isolation from the hardware, allowing low cost rapid upgrades to the processing platform. This isolation from the hardware also significantly extends the ease of reusability of embedded components. Process reallocation is simple as the system grows. Since it was developed for the domain of modular integrated aviation systems, it provides an environment designed to support traceability, efficiency, safety, fault tolerance and security requirements.

The specification language provides a basis for formal analysis of the system software architecture through various analysis tools. The toolset generation capabilities provide a tailored executive (including the scheduler) with all necessary calls to the Ada runtime or underlying O/S, necessary glue code to build a multiprocessor, multiprocess system from user supplied functional components, and the scripts needed to drive compilation for the target compiler and hardware. With this level of support, MetaH makes building tightly coupled multiprocessor systems relatively easy.

3.2   MetaH Language and Toolset

The MetaH language allows developers to specify how a system is composed from source modules like subprograms and packages, and hardware objects like processors and memories. MetaH is an extension to a class of specification languages variously called architecture description, module interconnect, or module composition languages. The source modules are typically produced in a variety of ways by engineers trained in a variety of disciplines, e.g., automatically generated from control block diagram specifications using tools such as ControlH[1] or MATRIX-X[2], re-engineered from existing applications[3], or hand coded.

Low-level software constructs of the MetaH language describe source components written in some traditional programming language like Ada. MetaH subprogram, package, and monitor specifications describe important characteristics of source modules such as the location of the source code, nominal and maximum compute times on various kinds of processors, stack and heap requirements, fault arrival rates, safety/certification level, etc. Events (user-specified enumeration literals used in certain service calls) and ports (buffer variables used to hold message values) can appear within source modules and must be described in the MetaH specification.

The higher-level constructs of the MetaH language are processes, macros and modes. Processes group together source modules that are to be scheduled as either periodic or aperiodic processes. A process is also the basic unit of security and fault containment, and memory protection and compute time enforcement are provided. Macros and modes group processes, define connections between events and ports, and define equivalencies between source modules that are to be shared between processes. The difference is that macros run in parallel with each other, while modes are mutually exclusive. Event connections between modes are used to define hierarchical mode transition diagrams, where mode changes at run-time can stop or start processes or change connections[4].

MetaH also allows hardware architectures to be specified using memory, processor, channel, and device components grouped into systems. Hardware objects may have ports, events or monitors in their interfaces. Software and hardware ports and events can be connected to each other, and software can access hardware monitors (hardware monitors provide hardware-dependent service calls). Hardware descriptions identify (among other things) hardware-dependent source code modules for device drivers, and code that implements the interface between the automatically generated "glue code" and the underlying run-time or real-time operating system.

Fig. 1 shows the current MetaH toolset. Both graphical and textual specification is supported, and the toolset can translate between the two different representations. In the current toolset, pieces of the specification entered graphically are first translated to text, and the text specification can be syntactically and semantically analyzed.

A simple software/hardware binding tool assigns to hardware those software objects in a specification that are not explicitly assigned, possibly subject to user-specified constraints. Processes are bound to processors in an attempt to balance loading, taking into account sharing of processes between different modes of operation. Port-to-port connections are bound to intermediate hardware channels and processors where needed, and modules shared across multiple processors are bound to specific memories physically accessible by all those processors.

An executive generator tool automatically produces the "glue" code needed to compose the various source modules to form the overall application, and an application build tool manages change propagation and compilation and linking. The glue code resembles an application-specific executive or supervisor, with code to dispatch processes, move messages, synchronize access to shared resources, vector events, perform mode changes, etc.

We currently have three formal modeling and analysis tools. A schedulability modeler and analyzer produces and solves a preemptive fixed priority schedulability model for the specified application system [5],[6]. A prototype reliability

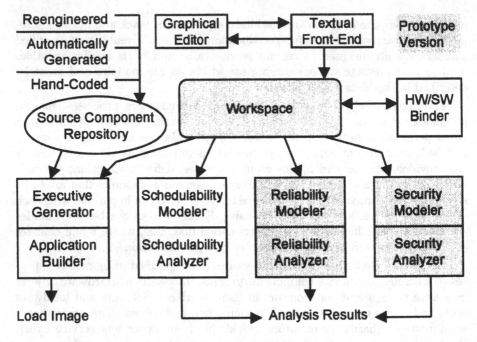

Fig. 1. MetaH Toolset

modeler generates a concurrent stochastic process reliability model, from which a traditional Markov chain is generated and solved [7]. A prototype safety/security analyzer examines the safety levels granted to various components to ensure that the operation of a component certified to a lower level cannot impact the operation of a component certified to a higher level. It will also examine component access rights to ensure that a component lacking a certain right cannot receive data from a component that has that right.

3.3 Architecture Level Analysis Approaches for Safety and Reliability

Using information contained in the MetaH specification and produced by the executive generator, the real-time modeler generates a detailed preemptive fixed priority schedulability model of the application. The model contains elements common to all applications (e.g. a dispatcher process) and elements that are application-dependent (e.g. process periods and compute times, monitor blocking times, communication times). The model includes all scheduling and communication overheads. The schedulability model is a conservative and accurate representation of the final load image structure and behavior (from the real-time scheduling viewpoint).

The schedulability analysis algorithm we currently use is an extension of the exact characterization algorithm[6]. Our analysis tool produces sensitivity analysis information describing how compute times may be changed while preserving (or in order to achieve) schedule feasibility; and it allows processes to be decomposed into component source modules and provides timing analysis data for individual source modules. The report generated by the analyzer contains listings for various application source components and also shows various executive overheads.

The MetaH language includes a construct called an error model, which allows users to specify sets of fault events and error states. An error model also includes specifications of transition functions to define how the error states of objects change due to fault, error propagation and recovery events. An individual object within a specification can then be annotated to specify the error transition function and fault arrival rates for that object.

We have a prototype reliability modeling tool that generates a stochastic concurrent process reliability model[8, 9].[1] Error propagations between objects are modeled as synchronizations or rendezvous between stochastic concurrent processes. Each such propagation synchronization in the model can be controlled using an associated consensus expression, which can conditionally mask propagations depending on the current error states of selected objects. In the MetaH specification, user-supplied consensus expressions describe the error detection protocols that are implemented by the underlying source modules for a particular application. The reliability modeler uses the MetaH error model specifications and annotations to generate the proper set of object error state machines, and uses the consensus expressions and design structure to generate the proper set of propagation synchronizations between these object error state machines. A subset of the reachable state space of this stochastic concurrent process is a Markov chain that can be analyzed using existing tools and techniques[8, 10]. We selected a stochastic concurrent process model rather than one of the more popular stochastic Petri Net[11, 12] models because it allows us to generate a reliability model whose structure can be easily traced back to the MetaH specification and vice versa (recall that maintaining good mappings between specification, formal models and code is one of our goals).

The executive code generated from a MetaH specification includes a number of security mechanisms (protected process address spaces, process criticalities, enforcement of execution time limits, capability lists for executive services). We have a prototype safety/security modeling and analysis tool to check that the mechanisms properly enforce a particular safety or security policy. We have currently identified one safety policy and one security policy to be checked.

We allow source objects to be annotated with a safety level to indicate the degree to which the code has been assured correct[13–15]. The safety policy is that proper operation of an object cannot be affected by an error in any other object having a lower safety level. For example, a higher- criticality object should not receive data from a lower-criticality object (unless the connection is explicitly annotated in the MetaH specification to allow this). A higher-criticality process

---

[1] The reliability modeler does not currently support multiple modes of operation and does not perform any Markov state space reduction optimizations.

must have a higher scheduling criticality specified than all lower-criticality processes on the same processor, or else execution times must be enforced on all lower-criticality processes on the same processor.

Objects might also be annotated with a list of security rights.[2] The security policy is that an object cannot receive or share data unless it has at least the security rights of the object that supplies the data. The connections or data accesses of an object with many security rights can be annotated in the MetaH specification to show that only some subset of these rights are needed to access information provided through that particular connection or shared data area, however. Security (and safety) properties can also be specified for hardware objects, e.g. an inter-processor channel can be flagged as low-security (or low-criticality), making it erroneous to route a high-security (or high- criticality) message over that channel.

4 Resulting DSA requirements from Avionics/MetaH

An important MetaH goal is to support integrated modular avionics systems [14, 13]. Different functions in avionics systems are typically classified to be of different levels of criticality, e.g. safety-critical, mission-critical, non-critical. The higher the criticality level is, the more extensive and expensive the certification process is. Rather than certify all software to the highest level or provide separate processors for each criticality level, each function can be certified to the level required if the system guarantees that no defect in a less-critical function can possibly disrupt the operation of a more-critical function. This is essentially a security requirement, where the executive must not only provide data protection (space partitioning) but also protection against disruption of real-time scheduling (time partitioning). An executive must provide memory protection, must limit the capabilities of certain processes to make certain service requests, and must insure that the scheduling of high-criticality processes cannot be disrupted by the behavior of a lower-criticality process.

A MetaH process is the unit of secure partitioning, and we mapped MetaH processes onto Ada 95 active partitions. MetaH allows sharing of data between processes as long as this is explicitly declared, and we mapped MetaH shared packages to Ada 95 passive partitions. Multiple active partitions must be hostable on a processor, each having its own protected address space.

MetaH is used as a software integration tool, to compose source components obtained by various methods including automatic generation. We wanted to avoid the need to hand-edit source code during integration, in particular we wanted to avoid the need to change names to avoid name conflicts. A need to hand-edit code would be particularly inconvenient, for example, if the code is automatically generated by a specialized tool. We want active partitions to have separate name spaces, and our desired partition model is probably closer to a multi-program model than a distributed single program model [16, 17]. The collective source files needed for each active partition should be compilable without

---

[2] Security checks are not currently implemented

access to any source files appearing in other active partitions (except files in shared partitions). It should be possible to have different unshared packages with the same name in different partitions.

MetaH allows multiple instances to be created of a shared package, e.g. one instance of a QUEUE package can be shared by processes A and B and a second instance of a QUEUE package can be shared by processes C and D. The MetaH toolset reads each shared package, changes its name to a unique name, and places this modified version in a special directory containing shared packages. A file containing a rename of this package back to the original name is created and compiled with the source modules of each process that accesses this instance. In the above example, two packages QUEUE_1 and QUEUE_2 would be copied into the shared package directory. Processes A and B would be compiled with QUEUE renaming QUEUE_1 while processes C and D would be compiled with QUEUE renaming QUEUE_2.

There is always a distinguished active partition on every processor called the kernel partition that contains the automatically generated "glue" code, the secure application-specific executive that typically executes in privileged mode. Remote procedure calls from an active partition to the kernel partition on the same processor should be efficient and secure, e.g. traps. Remote procedure calls between two non-kernel active partitions are not required (and in fact, for security and schedulability analysis reasons, the toolset should make it easy to verify they do not exist).

MetaH must carefully schedule all inter-processor interactions in order to ensure that hard real-time constraints are met. Consequently, we do not currently make use of features such as remote procedure calls across processors. Each processor has its own kernel partition. The generated executive code includes message-passing code that has been carefully scheduled in conjunction with the processes to meet hard real-time deadlines. We only require that an Ada 95 toolset and run-time support uni-processor systems. All multiprocessor aspects are currently handled at the MetaH level.

MetaH allows users to specify that a real-time semaphore be created for a shared data area, and the generated executive provides lock and unlock services. MetaH allows users to specify the semaphore protocol to be used, a capability analogous to the Locking_Policy pragma in the Ada 95 real-time systems annex.

Many real-time semaphore protocols require that the priority of a process holding a lock be changed at certain times. It must be possible for automatically generated executive code to dynamically set the priority of the environment task executing each active partition. Multitasking within an active partition is not required by MetaH, but if provided the partition priorities should dominate (no task from a lower-priority partition should preempt a task from a higher-priority partition). From the perspective of the generated executive code, there is a one-to-one correspondence between preemptively scheduled threads and active partitions.

It must be possible to establish a fault handler within the kernel partition for the other active partitions. The fault handler in a kernel partition should be called if any unhandled exception or fault occurs in an active partition on the same processor. Processor-wide faults (e.g. imminent loss-of-power) are also vectored to this fault handler and are logically associated with the kernel partition itself. MetaH requires that the identity of the faulting partition and the type of fault be provided as parameters to the fault handling procedure.

MetaH supports a form of dynamic reconfiguration called mode changes [18]. A mode change can alter the pattern of connections or the set of processes that are active. It must be possible to rapidly stop the Ada 95 task(s) executing in an active partition, and to rapidly restart the environment task at the main entry of an active partition. This restart must not cause the re-elaboration of any shared packages accessed by that partition.

The MetaH executive must provide time as well as space partitioning. This may be done using execution time limits or process criticalities and period transformation. It must be possible to monitor the accumulated execution time of each active partition. Execution time monitoring and controlled time- slicing is also needed for advanced scheduling techniques like slack scheduling [19, 20]. If multitasking in a partition is supported, the execution time of a partition should be the sum of the execution times of all tasks in that partition. It must be possible to set this accumulator to a desired initial value. It must be possible to optionally establish an execution time limit that, when exceeded, causes a time-out fault for that partition. It must be possible to suspend and later resume a partition following a time-out fault (e.g. by moving it off the ready queue and later putting it back on, or by setting the priority to be lower than the omni-present idle task). It must be possible to monitor the accumulated idle time (e.g. using an idle process that is monitored).

In a true real-time implementation, periodic scheduling in MetaH is driven by an external periodic hardware clock interrupt. The Real-Time Annex features would be appropriate if these are applied across partitions on the same processor (which the standard does not require).

4.1   Conclusions From a Prototype Port to GNAT/GLADE.

The following recommendations are offered concerning the implementation of the DSA. They are the result of a prototype port using the GNAT compiler and the GLADE implementation of the DSA. The prototype port was executed utilizing a five process 6DOF simulation. Only architecture level specification changes were required to port the simulation from a VME bare embedded 80960 environment to a Sun Solaris simulation environment. Regeneration of the system took about 3 hours and exhibited correct flight characteristics. The prototype did not provide full support for the MetaH language or demonstrate required performance but served to highlight the need for the following features:

Multiple active partitions should be allowed on the same processor, each with its own protected address space. Shared passive partition access should be through physical memory shared by the accessing active partitions. Remote procedure calls between active partitions hosted on the same processor should be secure but fast, e.g. traps.

It should be possible to support a "partition priority" model. Among active partitions on the same processor, tasks in a partition of higher priority should also have a higher scheduling priority than all tasks in a partition of lower priority. Real-Time Annex features should be well defined across partitions on the same processor. Execution time monitoring and controlled time-slicing (discussed shortly) is needed to transform periods when a low-rate task occurs in a high-criticality partition.

There should be some way to assure (through either development-time or run-time checks) that a designated active partition cannot perform operations at run-time that could affect another designated active partition, i.e., that it cannot change task priorities, cannot make or receive remote procedure calls.

It should be possible to establish a processor-wide fault handler for all unhandled exceptions or all possible implementation-dependent faults. It should be possible for the handler to determine if this fault is associated with and affects only a specific active partition or potentially affects the entire processor.

It should be possible to monitor the accumulated execution time of (all tasks within) active partitions, to optionally establish an exact execution time limit at which an active partition will be suspended, to establish a "handler" for execution time limit events in some other active partition, and to optionally resume a suspended partition with a new execution time limit. It should be possible to monitor the accumulated processor idle time.

It is desirable to do as much as possible off-line in order to obtain small, fast executables. It is desirable that structures like memory maps and task tables be allocated and initialized off-line. It is desirable that an appropriate optimized run-time configuration be easily constructed (e.g. remote calls on the same processor only, only the single environment task per active partition).

To the maximum extent possible, the compiler should provide separate name spaces for distinct active partitions. Identically named (but different) packages and subprograms should be allowed in distinct active partitions as long as the objects are not shared.

5 Final Conclusions

The recommended approach to implementing the DSA for real-time systems should provide an effective mechanism for the development of portable multi-processor, multi-partition systems. Our estimate on porting cost of MetaH for new target/compiler combinations was reduced by 50 percent over the typical Ada83 approach of unique multi-program runtimes. We also believe that the efficiency of the recommended approach is adequate for the avionics domains. We believe that the domain of use of this technology will go beyond avionics and safety critical systems to other large mission critical systems that need the benefit of reduced maintenance and verification and validation costs achievable through strong partitioning of software systems. We look forward to real-time DSA implementations.

References

1. Honeywell Technology Center, "Domain-Specific Software Architectures for Guidance, Navigation and Control," http://www.htc.honeywell.com/ projects/dssa, Minneapolis, MN.
2. MATRIXx User's manual, Integrated Systems, Inc., Santa Clara, CA.
3. David J. McConnell, Bruce Lewis and Lisa Gray, "Reengineering a Single Threaded Embedded Missile Application onto a Parallel Processing Platform using MetaH," *Proceedings of the 4th Workshop on Parallel and Distributed Real-Time Systems*, 1996.
4. Farnam Jahanian and Aloysius K. Mok, "Modechart: A Specification Language for Real-Time Systems," *IEEE Transactions on Software Engineering*, v20 n12, December 1994.
5. Mark H. Klein, John P. Lehoczky and Ragunathan Rajkumar, "Rate-Monotonic Analysis for Real-Time Industrial Computing," *IEEE Computer*, January 1994.
6. Steve Vestal, "Fixed Priority Sensitivity Analysis for Linear Compute Time Models," *IEEE Transactions on Software Engineering*, April 1994.
7. Andrew L. Reibman and Malathi Veeraraghavan, "Reliability Modeling: An Overview for Systems Engineers," *IEEE Computer*, April 1991.
8. Holger Hermanns, Ulrich Herzog and Vassilis Mertsiotakis, "Stochastic Process Algebras as a Tool for Performance and Dependability Modeling," *Proceedings of the IEEE International Computer Performance and Dependability Symposium* (IPDS'95), April 24-26, 1995, Erlangen, Germany.
9. Frederick T. Sheldon, Krishna M. Kavi and Farhad A. Kamangar, "Reliability Analysis of CSP Specifications: A New Method Using Petri Nets," *Proceedings of AIAA Computing In Aerospace*, San Antonio, TX, March 28-30, 1995.
10. Allen M. Johnson, Jr. and Miroslaw Malek, "Survey of Software Tools for Evaluating Reliability, Availability, and Serviceability," *ACM Computing Surveys*, v20 n4, December 1988.
11. Gianfranco Ciardo, Jogesh K. Muppala and Kishor S. Trivedi, *Manual for the SPNP Package*, version 3.1, October 18, 1992, Duke University, Department of Electrical Engineering, Durham, NC.
12. W. H. Sanders, W. D. Obal, M. A. Quershi and F. K. Widjanarko, "The UltraSAN Modeling Environment," *Performance Evaluation Journal*, vol. 25 no. 1, 1995.
13. *Software Considerations in Airborne Systems and Equipment Certification*, RTCA/DO-178B, RTCA, Inc., Washington D.C., December 1992.
14. *Design Guidance for Integrated Modular Avionics*, AEEC/ARINC 651, Airlines Electronic Engineering Committee/ Aeronautical Radio Inc., 1991.
15. Mark Johnson, "Boeing 777 Airplane Information Management System - Philosophy and Displays," Honeywell Air Transport Systems, Phoeniz AZ.
16. R. Jha, J. M. Kamrad, D. T. Cornhill, "Ada Program Partitioning Language: a Notation for Distributing Ada Programs," *IEEE Transactions on Software Engineering*, March 1989.
17. *Glade User Guide*, ftp://cs.nyu.edu/pub/gnat/glade.
18. Steve Vestal, "Mode Changes in a Real-Time Architecture Description Language," *Second International Workshop on Configurable Distributed Systems*, March 1994.
19. S. Ramos-Thuel and J. P. Lehoczky, "Algorithms for Scheduling Hard Aperiodic Tasks in Fixed-Priority Systems using Slack Stealing," *Real-Time Systems Symposium*, December 1994.
20. Pam Binns, "Scheduling Slack in MetaH," submitted *Real-Time Systems Symposium* work-in-progress session, December 1996.

A Case Study in Quantitative Evaluation of Real-Time Software Architectures[1]

José L. Fernández, Bárbara Álvarez, Francisco García,
Ángel Pérez, and Juan A. de la Puente

Departamento de Ingeniería de Sistemas Telemáticos, Universidad Politécnica de Madrid
ETSI Telecomunicación, Ciudad Universitaria s/n, E-28040 Madrid
Email: jpuente@dit.upm.es

Abstract. Generic architectures for specific domains can provide significant gains in productivity and quality for real-time systems development. In order to choose among different architectural features, a variety of qualitative criteria have been proposed in the literature. However, real-time systems require a more exact characterization based on quantitative evaluation of some architectural features related to timing properties, such as scalability. In this paper we explore a possible way of using Rate Monotonic Analysis to get a measure of scalability between alternative architectures. The technique is illustrated with a case study in a well-known real-time domain, data acquisition systems. The results show clear differences in scalability for different architectures, giving a clear indication of which one is better from this point of view. We believe that the approach can be used on other properties and domain architectures, thus opening new possibilities for quantitative evaluation of software architectures.

1. Introduction

Recent advances in software engineering show that much can be gained from developing generic software architectures for specific application domains that have some "good" properties for a family of related applications in the domain [2,10,20]. In order to find out which architectural patterns suit better for a set of properties, architecture evaluation methods are needed. Although qualitative methods may be appropriate for a large variety of systems, some properties require quantitative measures for the alternative patterns to be properly compared so that the right decision is made.

Real-time systems are special in that timing properties are part of the required capabilities. Specific timing properties, such as response time or deadline guarantees, are clearly dependent on particular system implementations. Timing analysis methods, such as Rate Monotonic Analysis [13], can be used to analyze the time

---

[1] This work has been partially supported by CICYT (projects TAP92-0001-CP and TIC96-0614).

behavior of a wide class of real-time systems, and to help detailed design and troubleshooting of these. However, if we look at more abstract properties, such as scalability, which can be applied to a range of systems with a common architecture, we find that there are no general methods applicable that can help a system architect choose among different alternative architectural patterns based on their timing properties.

In this paper we explore a possible way of dealing with this problem. We show how Rate Monotonic Analysis can be combined with prototyping in order to get a measure of scalability between alternative architectures. The technique is illustrated with a case study in a well-known real-time domain, laboratory data acquisition systems, which is mature enough for the implemented functionality and the software architectures to be well known [12]. We compare two alternative architectures based on language interface to hardware, because of the flexibility of this approach and the possibility of controlling real-time behavior. The core of both architectures is quite different because the design principles involved are also different. The first one was obtained using the structured design paradigm for real-time systems [15], while the other one is based on the object-oriented paradigm [18].

We developed instances of both architectures, and analyzed them using Rate Monotonic Analysis. This allowed us to examine how their respective timing properties scale up based on quantitative criteria that have not been considered earlier[2]. The results show clear differences in scalability for both of the architectures, which give a clear indication of which one is better from this point of view.

In the next section we describe the general approach to scalability analysis that we propose. Section 3 describes the functionality of the domain of data acquisition systems that we address, and the software architectures that we wish to evaluate. Then in section 4 we show how scalability analysis is carried out, and the main results of the analysis. We conclude by discussing the applicability of the method to other domains and the work that remains to be done for this purpose.

2. General approach

2.1 Rate Monotonic Analysis

Rate Monotonic Analysis (RMA) is a mathematical approach that helps ensuring that a real-time system meets its performance requirements. It does so through a collection of quantitative methods and algorithms that let engineers understand, analyze and predict the timing behavior of their designs, mainly in terms of their response times [16]. The methods are based on preemptive priority scheduling theory [3], which was originated by Liu and Layland in 1973 [14].

---

[2] Sanden [18] showed a way to compare real-time architectures using only indirect scalability criteria, such as the number of concurrent tasks and rendezvous.

Rate Monotonic Analysis is based on an event-response framework, and is carried out through several phases.

1. Describe real-time situations that apply.
2. Measure the execution time of actions.
3. Build the Implementation Table.
4. Build the Techniques Table.
5. Analyze the situation to determine if timing requirements are met.

Readers interested in a full description of RMA should consult the SEI RMA handbook [13].

In order to apply the method to the data acquisition systems that we have studied, we proceeded by first identifying the events which drive the system behavior, and the responses to them. The responses are decomposed into actions which use different resources. We measure the worst case execution times of the actions by means of a "dual loop" technique [6,17]. The measurements take into account the run-time system overheads and the available clock resolution. From this information, summarized in the so-called 'Implementation table', a set of analysis techniques can be applied which give information on the timing properties of the system.

2.2 Scalability analysis

Scalability is a measure of how the performance of a system varies when its size increases. The approach we have used to analyze scalability in different software architectures is based on RMA. What we do is to parameterize the size of a system by means of some quantifiable measure and then obtain estimates of some characteristic real-time properties for different system sizes. In our case, we have used the number of sensors being processed by a data acquisition system as a measure of its size, and deadline missing and response times as the real-time properties that are analyzed. An architecture is more scalable than other if it admits a larger number of sensors to be processed without missing any deadlines. The following sections describe the particular details and results of this approach for two alternative architectures for laboratory data acquisition.

3. Architectures for data acquisition systems

3.1 Data acquisition systems

In this paper we compare two different software architectures for laboratory data acquisition systems built on a simple platform, based on an Intel 486 /MSDOS configuration, with I/O boards directly connected to the computer bus (figure 1). The implementation language is Ada 83 [1].

Data acquisition is related to the reception of data from instruments or sensors. Since data from sensors are analog, I/O boards are used to sample and convert them to digital values. We decided to use software polling, as it implies the lowest level of custom programming, thus increasing the reusability of software.

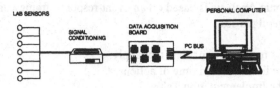

Fig. 1. System description.

Signal ID	Sensor state	Period (ms)	Next_Time_to_Read
T 308	Activated	1000	14 : 05 : 30.600
P204	Activated	500	14 : 05 : 30.100
F203	Deactivated	500	13 : 00 : 30.300
. . .	. . .	. . .	. . .

Fig. 2. Sampling Plan

Conversion to engineering units is typically required before analog data are used by the operator, by other software, or displayed in an alarm message. The software architectures that we analyze perform this conversion in real-time after each data sample is acquired.

Range checking is performed with each data sample before converting it to engineering units. Alarm checking is supported by the comparison of the engineering value of each sample with the alarm limits defined and stored in the system database.

Converted data is stored in disk to permit the engineer or scientist the analysis of data or the processing of them using more sophisticated algorithms not available for real-time processing. During the sample data processing the operator can actuate concurrently, sending commands to the system to activate or deactivate a sensor, change the gain or modify the range or alarm limits.

The core of a data acquisition system is a sampling plan which contains information related to the interval of time for recording the value of each signal. Since the interval of time is usually fixed for each signal, the period of each signal sampling is considered constant. Figure 2 shows an example of a sampling plan containing information about the sensor state, sampling period and time of the next measurement for each signal which is being read.

The sampling plan is not always implemented as a single entity. The software architecture based on the principles of structured design contains a unique sampling plan managed by a control transform that sends reading orders to the drivers connected to the I/O boards. Another approach which is typical of object oriented design, distributes the sampling plan in a collection of objects representing the problem domain and frequently known as sensor objects. The resulting architectures are different and will be described in detail in the next subsection.

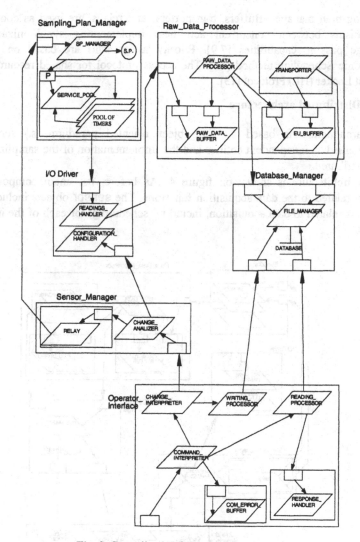

Fig. 3. Centralized software architecture.

3.2 Centralized architecture

The first architecture is based on structured design principles. The sampling plan is managed by a central component that handles the concurrent series of readings for all the sensors and schedules each reading at the appropriate instant. A special-purpose scheduling algorithm is used rather than the native task scheduling of the Ada runtime system, and thus scheduling is handled explicitly by the application.

The architecture is shown on Figure 3. Its components perform the basic functions of the data acquisition system: I/O handling, raw data processing, sensor management, operator interface, and data base management. There is also a central

218

sampling plan manager. Buffers, transporters, and relays, are used as coordination mechanisms between concurrent activities, implementing synchronization and message passing capabilities [7,9]. Priority assignments are based on the Rate Monotonic Scheduling method [14]. The access protocol for shared resources is the Highest Locker (HL) Protocol [13].

3.3 Distributed architecture

This architecture is based on the object oriented paradigm, so sensors are implemented as independent entities and the implementation of the sampling plan is also distributed.

The architecture is shown on figure 4. As before, its main components are directly related to the data acquisition functions. The sensor objects include all the functions related to data acquisition, including scheduling, for each of the input data signals.

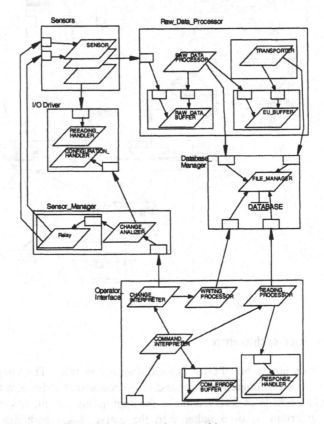

Fig. 4. Distributed software architecture.

The differences between this architecture and the centralized software architecture can be summarized as follows:

- The sampling plan does not exist as a unique entity.
- Periodic readings are managed by a set periodic tasks, each one implementing the corresponding sensor sampling interval.
- The role of each sensor task is to send reading orders, then to receive the raw data from the *I/O_Driver* and add a time tag to each sample. In the centralized solution, some of these capabilities, are implemented in the *I/O_Driver*, making it more complex.

4. Analysis of the architectures

4.1   Main event sequences

The starting point for Rate Monotonic Analysis is identifying the event sequences that act as stimuli for the system, and the responses to them, in terms of actions and used resources [5]. For the sake of brevity we will show only the main sequences related to both software architectures. The sequences having the hardest timing requirements are identified below. Readers interested in the complete description of sequences can consult the technical report describing the analysis results [8]. The event sequences are summarized in tables 1 and 2.

4.2   Rate monotonic analysis of the architectures

The analysis follows the steps described in section 2. It produces the following outputs:

Situation Table
We started building the situation tables by adding action and resource parameters to the above tables. The purpose of this form of the table is to capture the timing requirements.

Implementation Table
We derived the implementation table of the architectures using the action execution times that we obtained by the measurement method described in section 2, as well as other numeric parameters.

Techniques Table
The techniques table is a simplification of the implementation table. Its goal is to have a set of parameters that still describes the architecture but restricts assumptions to conditions where proven mathematical reasoning can be brought to bear. In this tables all the arrival patterns are approximated as periodic arrivals with hard deadlines.

The generation of the techniques table for the centralized architecture was specially difficult, and we consider it is one of the main contributions of this work.

There are several events, the reading orders, with a bursty arrival pattern, i.e. they can arrive arbitrarily on an interval defined by the sampling plan period.

Table 1. Event sequences in the Centralized Software Architecture

Event Name	Type	Arrival Pattern	Time Req.
Sensor_Reading.	Timed	Periodic, Ts	Hard, [Ts]
Timer_Assign.	Internal	Bursty [N,V]	Hard,[Ds]
RD_Processing	Timed	Periodic, Tp	Hard [Tp]
EU_Data_Storage	Timed	Periodic,Tt	Hard, [Tt]
Ch_Sensor_Gain	External	Bounded [L]	Soft [D]
Ch_Sensor_State	External	Bounded [L]	Soft [D]
Ch_Limits	External	Bounded [L]	Soft [D]
DB_Consult	External	Bounded [L]	Soft [D]
Erroneous_Comm.	External	Bounded [L]	Soft [D]

Table 2. Event sequences in the distributed software architecture

Event Name	Type	Arrival Pattern	Time Req.
Sensor_Reading_1-8	Timed	Periodic,T1-T8	Hard [T1-T8]
RD_Processing	Timed	Periodic,Tp	Hard [Tp]
EU_Data_Storage	Timed	Periodic,Tt	Hard [Tt]
Ch_Sensor_Gain	External	Bounded [L]	Soft [D]
Ch_Sensor_State	External	Bounded [L]	Soft [D]
Ch_Limits	External	Bounded [L]	Soft [D]
DB_Consult	External	Bounded [L]	Soft [D]
Erroneous_Comm	External	Bounded [L]	Soft [D]

The worst-case response time for an aperiodic event occurs just after the polling task has checked for the event arrival when all reading orders arrive at the same time. In this case, the last event has to wait for the preceding events to be processed. The first event would have to wait one polling period for its processing to begin. To model this situation we propose a scheme , where the timer tasks are considered as polling tasks which process sensor reading orders and send them to the *I/O Driver*. For the purpose of the analysis, we represent this part of the system as completely periodic, and therefore we can analyze it as if were a collection of periodic tasks. It is important to emphasize the presence of blocking due to the time interval spent by each timer task until it sends a sensor reading order to the *I/O Driver*. We estimated the blocking time considering the worst case, which is reading all the sensors in 500 ms (the sampling plan period).

The generation of the techniques table for the architecture with the distributed sampling plan is easier than the previous one, as the sensor reading tasks are periodic and there are no blocking delays.

Situation Analysis

The next step is applying analysis techniques to the event sequences using the information of the techniques table. In our case, all event responses can be modeled as periodic tasks with varying priorities, which can be analyzed using a well known technique [11,13]. The result of this analysis is the worst case response time for each event.

4.3 Results of the analysis

The main purpose of our analysis was to determine quantitatively what software design features contribute to the limitations in the performance of the real-time laboratory automation system, comparing the behavior of both design solutions. For this purpose, we start analyzing the response times for a system with 8 sensors with different frequencies, and then we scale up both software architectures by incrementing the number of sensors in groups of 8, until some of the sequences fail to meet the timing requirements.

It is important to emphasize that the timing requirements of both architectures are apparently different. In the distributed software architecture, each sensor is managed separately, implemented by a different component with an execution thread with a period and deadline determined by the sensor sampling requirements. The resulting behavior is typically periodic. The situation is quite different in the centralized software architecture, where all sensors are managed in the same way despite their sampling requirements . There is one object implementing the sampling plan, the *SP Manager*, containing a task that generates reading orders for all sensors. Due to the fact that different sensor readings are not distinguished and can occur during a very short time interval, the sequence behavior is considered bursty.

Dealing with different sensor reading requirements

Bursty arrival patterns are characterized by an event density. An event density consists of a bursty interval, the length of time over which the burst restriction applies, and a burst size, the number of events which can occur during that time interval. In the centralized software architecture, the burst interval is 500 milliseconds and the burst size 8, so the system is required to process 16 reading orders per second in the worst case. A distributed software architecture with identical sensor sampling periods as the centralized solution only requires 8 readings per second in the average. The above considerations determine the main differences in the results obtained.

For 8 sensors, the CPU total utilization is 15.41% for the centralized software architecture versus 7.86% for the distributed software architecture. This is due to the fact that the average readings of the centralized architecture for identical sensor sampling requirements duplicate the average readings of the distributed software architecture. With this number of sensors, there are no missed deadlines in either architecture.

When scaling up the centralized architecture, the first sequence to miss its deadline is *EU_Data Storage,* when the number of 48 sensors is reached.

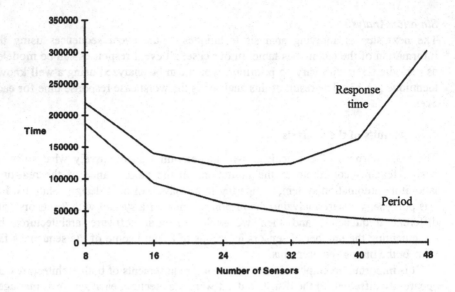

Fig. 5. Behavior of the Timer_Assignment sequence (Centralized Software Architecture)

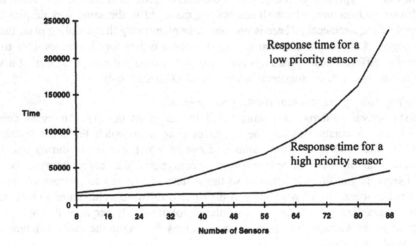

Fig. 6. Behavior of the Sensor_Readings sequence (Distributed Software Architecture)

For the distributed architecture, the first sequence missing its deadline is also *EU_Data Storage*, but this happens only when we arrive at a number of 88 sensors. The results are pessimistic for the centralized software architecture due to the bursty nature of its arrival patterns. In the analysis we are considering the worst-case when all the signals are acquired during a 500 milliseconds time interval.

Architectures Behavior

It is also interesting to describe the behavior of the sequences related to sensor readings in both architectures. Figure 5 shows the timing behavior of the *Timer Assignment* sequence for the centralized software architecture. The response time has an optimum value when 24 sensors are processed (122746 microseconds). There are two reasons to explain this behavior. When the number of sensors is lower than 24, the response time is influenced by the idle time of the timer task. When the number of sensors is greater than 24 we have to consider the increase in the processing requirements of the *Raw_Data_Processor* task (see figure 3).

Figure 6 shows the timing behavior of the *sensor reading* sequences for the distributed software architecture. We distinguish between sensors with high sampling frequency and low sampling frequency. The response time increases as the number of sensors increases. For high sampling frequency (high priority) sensors the behavior is almost linear. In contrast, the response time for low priority sensors increases abruptly as the number of sensors grow. Thus the distributed software architecture handles sensors differently with respect to their sampling time requirements, as opposed to the centralized architecture, in which all the sensors are handled in the same way in spite of their sampling time requirements.

5. Conclusions

Performance engineering using RMA allows quantitative comparison of alternative architectures, giving illustrative results about system behavior and scalability properties that cannot discovered by testing.

RMA is best suited to periodic arrival patterns, but in this study we had to deal with a bursty arrival pattern, that of the internal events generated by the *SP_Manager* task. We found a solution considering the timer tasks as polling tasks processing the internal events generated by the *SP_Manager* task and queued by the *Service_Pool* task. This modeling solution allowed us to apply seamlessly RMA.

Diverse causes of inaccuracy can be identified in the analysis techniques (Bailey 1995):

- Execution times are always assumed to be at the maximum.
- Sporadic inter-arrival intervals are always assumed to be the minimum.
- Compiler optimization has been prohibited to allow the calculation of execution times.
- Overheads associated to the Ada runtime system are simplified.

These inaccuracies imply pessimistic results in the evaluation of the architectures. Therefore, we think that the method is more suitable to compare diverse solutions as we did, than to analyze single designs at the architectural level of description, since the inaccuracies impact evenly in the evaluation of the diverse architectures.

References

1. Reference Manual for the Ada Programming Language (1983). ANSI/MIL-STD-1815A-1983; ISO/8652:1987.
2. A. Alonso, B. Álvarez, J.A. Pastor, J.A. de la Puente, A. Iborra (1997). "Software Architecture for a Robot Teleoperation System." Proc. IFAC Symposium on Algorithms and Architectures for Real-Time Control. Elsevier Science, 1997.
3. N.C. Audsley, A. Burns, R.I Davis, K. Tindell, and A.J. Wellings (1995). "Fixed Priority Pre-emptive Scheduling: An Historical Perspective." Real-Time Systems, vol. 8, no. 2/3, pp. 173-198.
4. C.M. Bailey, A. Burns,. A.J. Wellings, and C.H. Forsyth (1995). "A Performance Analysis of a Hard Real-Time System." Control Engineering Practice. Vol. 3 No 4: 447-464.
5. R.J.A. Buhr, (1990). Practical Visual Techniques in System Design. Prentice Hall.
6. R.M. Clapp and T. Mudge (1990). "The Time Problem." ACM Ada Letters, Vol. X, No. 3: 20-28.
7. J.L Fernández (1993). "A Taxonomy of Coordination Mechanisms Used in Real-Time Software Based on Domain Analysis." Technical Report CMU/SEI-93-TR-34, Software Engineering Institute, Pittsburgh, PA.
8. J.L. Fernández, A. Pérez, B. Álvarez and F. García (1995). "Performance Engineering of Real-Time Laboratory Automation Software Architectures." Technical Report DIT/UPM 1995/01.
9 J.L Fernández (1997). "A Taxonomy of Coordination Mechanisms Used by Real-Time Processes." ACM Ada Letters, vol. XVII, no. 2: 29-54.
10. D. Garlan and M. Shaw (1996). Software Architecture: Perspectives on an Emerging Discipline. Prentice-Hall.
11. M.González-Harbour, M.H. Klein and J.P. Lehoczky (1991). "Fixed Priority Scheduling of Periodic Tasks with Varying Execution Priority." Proceedings of the IEEE Real-Time Systems Symposium. Los Alamitos, C.A. pp.116-128.
12. R. House (1995). "Choosing the Right Software for Data Acquisition." IEEE Spectrum. May 1995: 24-39.
13. M.H. Klein, T. Ralya, B. Pollak, R. Obenza and M. Gonzalez-Harbour. (1993). A Practitioner's Handbook for Real-Time Analysis: Guide to Rate Monotonic Analysis for Real-Time Systems. Kluwer Academic Publishers.
14. C.L. Liu and J.W. Layland (1973). "Scheduling Algorithms for Multi-Programming in a Hard Real-Time Environment." ACM Journal. 20,1: 40-61.
15. K. Nielsen and K. Shumate (1988). Designing Large Real-Time Systems with Ada. McGraw-Hill.
16. R. Obenza (1993). "Rate Monotonic Analysis for Real-Time Systems." IEEE Computer. Vol. 26, No 3: 73-74.
17. D. Roy (1990). "PIWG Measurement Methodology." ACM Ada Letters. Vol X No 3: 72-90.
18. B. Sanden (1989). "Entity-Life Modeling and Structured Analysis in Real-Time Software Design. A comparison." Communications ACM . Vol. 32 No 12: 1458-1466.
19. L. Sha and J.B. Goodenough (1990). "Real Time Scheduling Theory and Ada." IEEE Computer. Vol. 23, No 4: 53-62.
20. B. Witt, T. Baker, and E. Merrit (1994). Software Architecture and Design. Principles, Models and Methods. Van Nostrand Reinhold.

Building Modular Communication Systems in Ada: The *Simple_Com* Approach

Jesús M. González-Barahona, Pedro de-las-Heras-Quirós,
José Centeno-González, Francisco Ballesteros

GSyC, Universidad Carlos III de Madrid
Leganés (Spain)
{jgb,pheras,jcenteno,nemo}@gsyc.inf.uc3m.es

Abstract. This paper is devoted to study the use, in the *Simple_Com* system, of several mechanisms provided by the Ada programming language (type extension, dynamic dispatching, encapsulation, generics, etc.). The *Simple_Com* system is a toolbox for building protocols of different qualities of service (both unicast and multicast). It is flexible, extensible, portable, and provides clean and simple interfaces. Many of its features are possible thanks to the extensive use of those Ada mechanisms.

The *Simple_Com* system is useful for building distributed applications (using the protocols already provided), or to design and test new protocols (either combining some of the pieces provided, or building new ones).

1 Introduction

Communication protocols (and specially multicast ones) can be designed to satisfy a wide spectrum of qualities of service (QoS), like best-effort unicast or ordered and atomic multicast delivery. Moreover, different protocol designs may be used in order to satisfy a given quality of service, each one with its own advantages and drawbacks.

When compared to unicast ones, multicast protocols introduce a wider range of possibilities with respect to useful QoS [4, 11]. In the former, usually just two different kinds of QoS are provided: reliable and ordered delivery, such as TCP; or unreliable and unordered (best-effort) delivery, such as UDP. On the other hand, the list of potentially interesting QoS currently being experimented for multicast communication protocols is quite large, and includes ordering guarantees (unordered, FIFO ordered, causally ordered, totally ordered), reliability (unreliable, atomic or reliable, uniform), special behavior in case of partitions, etc. No consensus has yet been achieved on which kind of protocol is the best one to provide a given QoS, or even on which QoS are interesting for applications.

In systems based on monolithic protocols it has been proven to be difficult and inefficient to deal with all these kinds of QoS. When tuning a certain protocol for a given quality, some other QoS suffer from performance penalties.

Extending those protocols to provide new guarantees is not easy, and they often require complete redesigns to incorporate new features. Well-known software techniques (like object oriented programming and module composition) are still not in widespread use among the multicast protocol implementors. Only in the last few years is emerging a new approach for building this kind of protocols. It pays more attention to the architectural structure, and it is based on the composition of so called *microprotocols*.

Simple_Com addresses some of these problems by proposing a modular architecture for constructing communication protocols (and in particular, multicast or group communication protocols). The proposed architecture is a clear evolution of those already existing, but at the same time introduces some new concepts, not previously identified.

This paper is devoted mainly to discuss the aspects related to the use of Ada as the programming language for the implementation of the *Simple_Com* system. In order to provide some background, the next section introduces the *Simple_Com* system, to provide some background to the reader[1]. Section 3 is the core of the paper, and discusses several aspects of the use of Ada in the system, remarking those which have proven useful for implementing some given feature. A review of related work can be found in section 4. The conclusions and further work are presented in section 5.

2   The *Simple_Com* system

The structure of the *Simple_Com* system[2] is composed of three layers:

- **Application layer** (*App_Layer*) provides interfaces suitable for applications using the *Simple_Com* system, hiding its complexities. Some of these abstractions are: remote procedure call, Isis-like *abcast* and *cbcast*, plain message passing, etc. Each application uses the interface which best fits its needs.
- **Simple communication layer** (*Simple_Com* layer) is core of the system. The protocols offered by the system (which provide different QoS) are implemented within it, by combinations of *Proto_Stages* and *Proto_Modules*. Since most of the mechanisms discussed in this paper are found in this layer, both *Proto_Stages* and *Proto_Modules* are briefly described below.
- **Lower communication layer** (*Lower_Layer*) provides access to basic communication facilities for *Simple_Com*. It hides the peculiarities of the transport protocols used, by providing an unified but flexible set of primitives for sending and receiving data between processes.

---

[1] More information on *Simple_Com* can be found in [8] (a detailed description), [9] (a preliminary presentation on the architecture) and [10] (a discussion on *Lower_Layer*, the *Simple_Com* link to transport communication).

[2] From now on, we will use the term '*Simple_Com* system' when referring to the whole system being described in this paper, and '*Simple_Com* layer' when referring to this layer, which implements the protocols offered by the system.

2.1 Proto_Stages

Protocol stages get messages, act according to the information coming within them and, eventually, pass them to other components of the layer. The information coming with a message is stored in *headers*. Usually, an up-going message which arrives at a *Proto_Stage* carries one or more headers with protocol information useful for that stage. The *Proto_Stage* studies that information, and according to it, performs some action, as defined by the protocol which it implements. That action consists of either removing the headers, storing the message for future use, delivering it to other protocol stage or just dropping it. *Proto_Stages* come in three flavors:

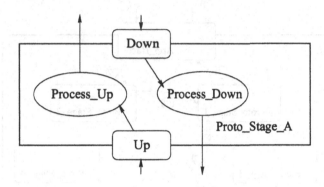

Fig. 1. Structure of a *Proto_Stage*. Rounded boxes represent the calls available in its interface. Ellipses represent the code processing up-going or down-going messages.

- **Regular protocol stages** are software units implementing some 'stage' (microprotocol or part of a protocol). They provide subprograms *Up* and *Down* for accepting messages from other components of the *Simple_Com* layer. *Up* calls are for 'up-going' messages, flowing from the lower layer towards the application layer. *Down* calls are for 'down-going' messages, which will be sent through *Lower_Layer*. An schematic overview of a regular *Proto_Stage* is shown in figure 1.
- **Application interfaces** (*App_Iface*) are units which interface to *App_Layer*. Each one offers a certain quality of service. Each *App_Iface* accepts *Send* and *Receive* calls from the *App_Layer*, and *Up* calls from other components of the *Simple_Com* layer. For specifying the destination of messages, channels are used. A channel includes both information about a transport address, and about the QoS to be used for communication with that channel.
- **Lower interfaces** (*Lower_Iface*) interface to *Lower_Layer*. They accept *Down* calls from other *Proto_Stages*, and use *Lower_Layer* services for sending and receiving messages.

228

Proto_Stages are stackable, and different QoS may be obtained by combining them. For instance, a *Proto_Stage* providing unicast FIFO order can be stacked on top of one providing reliability, thus resulting in reliable unicast ordered communication. To obtain a multicast atomic and causal QoS, a *Proto_Stage* providing multicast atomicity (messages are delivered at all destinations or at none of them) could be set under another one which provides causal order.

Proto_Stages are also interchangeable. New *Proto_Stages* with the same (or extended) functionality can be interchanged with old ones, since the interface provided by all of them is exactly the same. Thus, composability, reusability and quick prototyping of new implementations becomes easy.

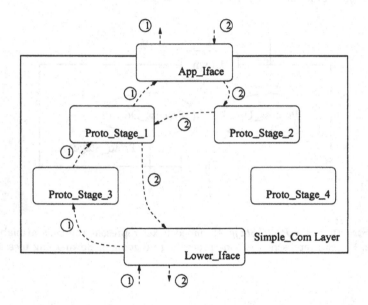

Fig. 2. Example of the structure of the *Simple_Com* layer, with several *Proto_Stages* (including one *App_Iface* and one *Lower_Iface*). An up-going message (number 1) goes through *Proto_Stage_3* and *Proto_Stage_1* before it is delivered to the application. Down-going message 2 goes through *Proto_Stage_2* and *Proto_Stage_1* before it is actually sent.

An example of the flow of messages through several *Proto_Stages* is shown in figure 2.

2.2 *Proto_Modules*

Several services useful for many *Proto_Stages* can be identified. For improving reusability and modularity, a particular element of the architecture is defined for implementing those services: the*Proto_Modules*. They may provide services local to the process (like timer management) or extended to the distributed system as a whole (like membership or token passing). Implementors can build all these services by themselves, but if already existing *Proto_Modules* suit their needs, they can concentrate in solving the problems specific to the new protocol stage they are building.

Proto_Modules are provided as (sometimes extensible) black-boxes. Their internal structure can be quite different from one to another, and may use the services provided by other *Proto_Modules*. If they need communication services, they can use the ones provided by the *Simple_Com* system itself, interfacing at the *App_Layer*.

3 Taking advantage of Ada in *Simple_Com*

Several aspects of the use of the Ada language in the *Simple_Com* system are discussed in this section.

3.1 Use of tagged types: messages are not just bytes

In most communication systems, messages are handled just as arrays of bytes, some of them corresponding to application data, some of them to protocol data. However, messages can also be handled as rich typed objects. This is the approach followed in the *Simple_Com* layer. The structure of messages in *Simple_Com* is as follows (see simplified specification of package *Messages* in code fragment 1):

- Messages in the *Simple_Com* layer are modeled as objects of type *Message*.
- *Message* type includes (among other components) a *Path*, which is used for the routing through the appropriate *Proto_Stages* (see subsection 3.2, below). The *Path* is implemented as an array of so called *Marks*. Each *Proto_Stage* declares its own *Mark* type, as a tagged type of a common hierarchy.
- The root type of the *Mark* hierarchy includes a list of headers. Headers are also types of a common hierarchy, used by the *Proto_Stages* to insert/retrieve information in/from the message. It is important to notice that no special components are provided for storing application data or the destination of the message (which are quite common in other communication systems). Instead, *App_Iface* declares types in the *Header* hierarchy for these matters, which simplifies the handling of message components.

In addition to the usual advantages of typed objects (which could be enough by themselves for justifying their use), several other benefits are obtained:

- Messages (and their components) can be handled as abstract data types. For that matter, several subprograms are declared which perform actions on *Message* objects, in child units of package *Messages*.
- Marshalling and unmarshalling of messages is done automatically, by using *Input* and *Output* attributes (see an sketch of the marshalling of a message to be sent in code fragment 2).

- Debugging is simplified, since instead of dealing with bytes in message headers, we have components in a typed structure. Displaying those components in a debugger should be enough to trace the 'life' of a message.

- Headers can be easily grouped into families, according to their relationships. Therefore, type extension is used for declaring hierarchies of *Header* types. A paramount example are the types used for application data, all of them derived from the *Data* type, which in turn is derived from the root *Header* type.

- *Proto_Stages* can use standard information hiding techniques to let other *Proto_Stages* see only the header data they may need, and not those headers only interesting for the peer *Proto_Stages* in other processes.

Code fragment 1 Simplified declaration of *Message* related types

```
-- Header root type and heterogeneous container for headers
type Header is abstract tagged null record;
type Header_CA is access Header'Class;
-- List of headers (more exactly, of Header_CA)
type Headers_List is private;
[...]
   -- Mark root type (includes headers for the corresponding Proto_Stage)
   type Mark is abstract tagged record
      Headers: Headers_List;
   end record;
   -- Dispatching Up and Down for routing messages through Proto_Stages
   procedure Up   (A_Mark: in Mark; A_Message: in out Message) is abstract;
   procedure Down (A_Mark: in Mark; A_Message: in out Message) is abstract;
[...]
   -- Heterogeneous container for marks, and array of marks.
   type Mark_CA is access Mark'Class;
   type Marks_Array is array (Natural range <>) of Mark_CA;
   type Marks_Array_A is access Marks_Array;
   type Message is private;
private
   -- Marshalling and unmarshalling for headers (Read ommited).
   procedure Write (Stream: access Ada.Streams.Root_Stream_Type'Class;
                    Item:   in Header_CA);
   for Header_CA'Write use Write;
[...]
   type Message is record
      Path:    Marks_Array_A := null;
      Current: Natural := 0;
      [...]
   end record;
```

The correct marshalling/unmarshalling done in *Simple_Com* is ensured by the redefinition of *Write* and *Read* attributes when convenient (for instance, for access types which could be included in a message).

3.2 Dynamic dispatching for selecting the proper protocol

In systems where protocols are implemented by composing some kind of protocol stages, a key characteristic is how messages are routed through them. Usually, this is done by means of 'ad-hoc' mechanisms, like tables specifying routes, or identifiers in the messages themselves. In *Simple_Com*, dynamic dispatching is used instead. This minimizes the effort devoted to maintain routing information, letting the compiler perform all the bookkeeping. The use of a standard programming technique also reduces the learning curve for programmers which implement elements within the *Simple_Com* layer.

Code fragment 2 Use of *Output* attribute for marshalling a message

```
-- Buffer for sending messages.
Send_Buffer: aliased Lower_Layer.Stream (Send_Buffer_Size);
[...]
-- Simplified version of Send. Address is the destination
-- address of the message.
procedure Send (A_Message: in Messages.Message; [...]) is
begin
   [...]
   Messages.Message'Output (Send_Buffer'access, A_Message);
   Lower_Layer.Send (Address, Send_Buffer'access);
   [...]
end Send;
```

The base of message routing in *Simple_Com* is the *Path* included in every message. Each *Proto_Stage* declares its own type in the *Mark* hierarchy, overriding subprograms *Up* and *Down*, which are declared as primitive abstract subprograms for the root *Mark* type (see code fragment 1). *Up* performs all the actions required for up-going messages, while *Down* does the same for down-going messages.

Therefore, to define a protocol stack, it is enough to declare the proper path. It should include (in the proper order) one object of the type *Mark* declared by each *Proto_Stage* in the protocol stack. When that path is included in a message (in the *Path* field), a dynamic dispatching mechanism will ensure that it will pass through the intended *Proto_Stages*.

Routing takes place every time a message is ready to leave a *Proto_Stage*. The last call before leaving is to *Up* or *Down* 'wrappers' (*Up* is shown, slightly simplified, in code fragment 3). Note that these subprograms are defined for convenience, with an object of type *Message* as parameter. In their implementa-

Code fragment 3 *Up* procedure for *Message* objects

```
procedure Up (A_Message: in out Message) is
   The_Mark: Mark_CA;
begin
   if (A_Message.Path = null) then
      raise No_Path;
   else
      A_Message.Current := A_Message.Current + 1;
      The_Mark := A_Message.Path (A_Message.Current);
   end if;
   if The_Mark /= null then
      -- Dispatching call to the proper Proto_Stage
      Up (The_Mark.all, A_Message);
   else
      raise Bad_Current;
   end if;
end Up;
```

tion, they just dispatch to the corresponding primitive subprogram of the proper *Mark* object, effectively entering the next *Proto_Stage*.

3.3   A hierarchy of types for specifying channels

The addressing mechanism used by the *Simple_Com* layer is the 'channel'. For handling channels, a hierarchy rooted at type *Channel* is declared (see code fragment 4).

Code fragment 4 *Channel* type and related declarations

```
-- Root of the Channel hierarchy
type Channel is abstract tagged record
   [...]
end record;
-- Get a path, given a channel.
function Get_Path (A_Channel: in Channel) return Messages.Marks_Array
   is abstract;
-- Heterogeneous container for Channel hierarchy
type Channel_CA is access Channel'Class;
-- Subprograms for setting or getting a transport address
procedure Set_Address (A_Channel:  in out Channel;
                       An_Address: in     Lower_Layer.Address_CA);
function Get_Address  (A_Channel:  in Channel)
                       return Lower_Layer.Address_CA;
```

The abstract type *Channel* includes a component for storing the transport address (of type *Lower_Layer.Address_CA*) corresponding to the channel. It will be used by *Lower_Iface* to send the message to its destination, using the services of *Lower_Layer*.

With regard to QoS, they are specified when a derived type of *Channel* is declared. If it is not abstract, it must provide an implementation for *Get_Path*. That function returns a path, fixing the protocol stack used for the channel type. Therefore, applications just declare channels of the appropriate types for the QoS they need. Once they are declared, all channels can be handled by using objects of type *Channel_CA*.

3.4 Generics for composing protocol stacks

It has already been shown how once a non-abstract channel type is declared, a protocol stack becomes defined. This is a common situation, which depends only on the path to be used for specifying the stack. The *Composer* generic package has been designed for helping in this situation (see code fragment 5).

Code fragment 5 Specification of *Composer* (simplified version)

```
generic
   Marks: Messages.Marks_Array;
package App_Iface.Direct.Gen is
   type Channel is new Channels.Channel with null record;
   function Get_Path (A_Channel: in Channel) return Messages.Marks_Array;
end App_Iface.Direct.Gen;
```

When a new protocol stack is to be used, it is enough to instantiate the *Composer* package, specifying the desired marks as parameters of the generic. As a result, a new channel type is available for using the new protocol stack. In code fragment 6 it is shown a package which declares two new types in the *Channel* hierarchy, in two instantiations of *Composer*. *Channels_XXX.Dummy.Channel* is a dummy channel, with its associated stack performing plain message passing. Only the mandatory *App_Iface* and *Lower_Iface* are included in its associated stack. *Channels_XXX.Reliable_Multi.Channel* provides multicast reliability, since it includes *Proto_Stage_Reliable_Multi*, which performs a simple wait-and-resend protocol, with acknowledgments.

Generics are used in many more parts of the *Simple_Com* system, but this is perhaps the most remarkable one. It is important to notice its coupling with type extension: *Composer* declares a new branch of the tree rooted at *Channel*.

3.5 Everything working together

Now, let us show how all the techniques discussed in the previous subsections work together, by describing the complete flow of messages through the *Simple_Com* layer. When an application wants to send some data, it uses one of the

---

Code fragment 6 Specification of two channel types

```
with Composer;
with Lower_Iface; with App_Iface;
with Proto_Stage_Reliable_Multi;
package Channels_XXX is
   package Dummy is new Composer
     (Marks => (1 => new Lower_Iface.Mark,
                2 => new App_Iface.Mark));
   package Reliable_Multi is new Composer
     (Marks => (1 => new Lower_Iface.Mark,
                2 => new Proto_Stage_Reliable_Multi.Mark,
                3 => new App_Iface.Mark));
end Channels_XXX;
```

---

interfaces provided by the *App_Layer*, which in turn calls *App_Iface.Send* (specifying the destination channel and the data to be sent). The resulting message flow is as follows (see also figure 2):

1. The *App_Iface*, given the destination *Channel*, builds a message with the proper *Path*, by calling *Get_Path*. The data to be sent and the destination channel will be headers of the *App_Iface Mark*, within that message.
2. *Down* is invoked, which results in a dispatching call to the primitive *Down* subprogram of the second *Mark* in the *Path*, entering the corresponding *Proto_Stage*.
3. Every *Proto_Stage* specified in the path is entered this way. Each one adds its own headers, with information relevant to its protocol stage.
4. Eventually, the message reaches the *Lower_Iface*, where it is marshalled and sent to the destination process (using the services of *Lower_Layer*).
5. On arrival at the destination process, *Lower_Layer* passes the message up to a *Lower_Iface*, where it is unmarshalled.
6. Dispatching *Up* subprograms are called for each *Mark* in the *Path* of the message, in reverse order. Each *Proto_Stage* uses information in the headers of the message for performing actions related its protocol stage.
7. Eventually, the message arrives at an *App_Iface*, which extracts the application data and delivers it to the *App_Layer*.
8. The *App_Layer* delivers the message to the application waiting for it.

4 Related work

There are some interesting examples of modular approaches for building protocols. In the unicast case, the Unix System V Streams [19] and the x-kernel [13] deserve an special mention. With respect to multicast systems, most of them are essentially monolithic (including Isis [3], Transis [5], Totem [17], RMP [21], Relacs [1], NewTop [6], and Psync [18]). However, some modular architectures do also exist. Consul [15] features a modular design [16], where each fault tolerant service is mapped to a protocol. Consul has been implemented on the x-kernel system as a *protocol graph*, where each Consul protocol is mapped to a different x-kernel protocol object. Horus [20] uses a similar approach to that of *Simple_Com*. It provides a framework for protocol development and experimentation, with group communication as its fundamental abstraction. Horus facilitates a high performance implementation of the virtual synchrony model [2], incorporating ideas both from the Unix Streams and from the x-kernel: complex protocols are partitioned in simpler microprotocols, implemented as modules that can be composed in stacks. The interfaces between modules are all uniform, providing a set of entry points for downcall and upcall subprograms. This uniformity enables the composition of microprotocols at run time. Each Horus protocol module registers its upcall and downcall handlers at initialization time. When a message enters the Horus system (i.e. for being sent), the handlers of appropriate modules are looked for (using information carried in the message headers) and invoked. Currently, Horus protocols are being reimplemented using the ML language in the Ensemble system [12].

Dynamic configurability is sought in modern industrial environments. Several industrial leaders are endorsing the Xpress Transfer Protocol (XTP) [7], which is a toolkit for building protocols (both unicast and multicast). It offers configurability by enabling the user to set option bits in a per-message basis, which simplify the implementation of protocols capable of adapting to varying circumstances.

5 Conclusions and further work

Simple_Com provides not only a communication architecture, but also an implementation and a set of useful software modules. Therefore the construction of new protocols is highly simplified. In this paper we have shown how the use of the Ada language strengths modularity, code reuse and utilization of object oriented techniques like dynamic dispatching or type extension.

The basic idea of *Simple_Com* is to divide the design and implementation of protocols into protocol stages (*Proto_Stages*), which can be composed in different orders. Each composition of *Proto_Stages* implements a protocol, providing a given QoS. We improve this model by using OO techniques for building and 'connecting' *Proto_Stages*, and by dynamically stacking them using the information carried within each message.

Summarizing, the most remarkable advantages of *Simple_Com* are:

– **Composability**: A protocol providing a given QoS, can be implemented by assembling the proper pieces (*Proto_Stages*) in the proper order. Thus, new protocols can be implemented just by reassembling existing *Proto_Stages* in new orders or in new combinations.
– **Dynamic stacking**: This assembling is done dynamically, on a per-message basis, so that a set of *Proto_Stages* implements a set of 'dynamic stacks', each one corresponding to a protocol and providing a given QoS.

- **Reusability of modules**: All the dynamic stacks share the code of common *Proto_Stages*. Thus, the improvement of a *Proto_Stage* implementation is automatically available to the set of protocols which use it.
- **Availability of reusable generic modules**: When implementing a new *Proto_Stage*, a programmer can use the services provided by existing *Proto_Modules*. This simplifies both the design and implementation of the new *Proto_Stage*.
- **Rapid prototyping**: since assembling *Proto_Stages* is quite easy, rapid prototypes of new ideas are also simple and easy to build.
- **Transparency for applications**: All the machinery is hidden from the application using *Simple_Com* by means of the *App_Layer*.
- **Portability**: The whole system is portable across different transport layer protocols, thanks to the abstractions provided by *Lower_Layer* (currently *Simple_Com* runs on top of UDP, TCP and Transis).

To test the usefulness of this system, some protocols (similar to those provided by Isis, Horus, Transis or Totem group communication systems) are now being implemented. Once this is done, performance will be measured, and compared with 'original' implementations. Some distributed computing systems will also be implemented using *Simple_Com*. As special cases, we are planning to use *Simple_Com* as one of the communication subsystem for both the *Drago* programming language [14] (a language for building distributed cooperative and replicated applications) and the Distributed Systems Annex of Ada. A membership module is currently being implemented by using the Ensemble Domain System.

We are also studying ways of improving performance while maintaining the described flow of messages through *Proto_Stages*, by collapsing path information while messages travel on the wire. Another area of research is how to define semantic relations between *Proto_Stages*, so that an implementor can specify requirements that must be satisfied by 'underlying' *Proto_Stages*. These semantic relations could be enforced at compile or run-time.

More information about *Simple_Com* can be consulted at
`http://www.gsyc.inf.uc3m.es/simple_com/`.
Simple_Com is free software, and is available under LGPL from
`ftp://ftp.gsyc.inf.uc3m.es/pub/simple_com/`.

References

[1] Ö. Babaoğlu, R. Davoli, L. Giachini, and M. Baker. Relacs: A communications infrastructure for constructing reliable applications in large–scale distributed systems. Technical Report UBLCS–94–15, Laboratory for Computer Science, University of Bologna, Italy, 1994.

[2] Kenneth Birman and Thomas Joseph. Exploiting virtual synchrony in distributed systems. In *Proceedings of the 11th ACM Symposium on Operating Systems Principles*, November 1987.

[3] K.P. Birman and T.A. Joseph. Reliable communication in the presence of failures. *ACM Transactions on computer Systems*, 5(1):47–76, 1987.

[4] George Coulouris, Jean Dollimore, and Tim Kindberg. *Distributed Systems. Concepts and Design.* Addison–Wesley, second edition, 1994.

[5] D. Dolev and D. Malki. The design of the Transis system. In *Daugstuhl Workshop on Unifying Theory and Practice in Distributed Computing*, September 1995.

[6] P.E. Ezhilchelvan, R.A. Macedo, and S.K. Shrivastava. A fault–tolerant group communication protocol. Technical report, Computer Laboratory, University of Newcastle upon Tyne, Newcastle upon Tyne, United Kingdom, August 1994.

[7] XTP Forum. *Xpress Transfer Protocol Specification. XTP Rev. 4.0.* XTP Forum, March 1995.

[8] Jesús M. González-Barahona. *Simple_Com: A Modular Communication Architecture.* PhD thesis, E.T.S.I de Telecomunicación, Universidad Politécnica de Madrid, Madrid, Spain, feb 1998.

[9] Jesús M. González-Barahona, José Centeno González, and Pedro de las Heras Quirós. Overview of the Simple_Com system. In *V Jornadas de Concurrencia*, Vigo, Spain, June 1997.

[10] Jesús M. González-Barahona, Pedro de las Heras Quirós, and José Centeno González. Lower_Layer: A family of interfaces to transport communication protocols. *Ada User Journal*, December 1997. Accepted for publication, date could change.

[11] Vassos Hadzilacos and Sam Toueg. Fault–tolerant broadcasts and related problems. In Sape Mullender, editor, *Distributed Systems*, pages 97–145. Addison–Wesley, second edition, 1993.

[12] Mark Hayden. *Ensemble Reference Manual.* Cornell University, 1997.

[13] N.C. Hutchinson and L.L. Peterson. The x-k rnel: An architecture for implementing network protocols. *IEEE Transactions on Software Engineering*, 17, January 1991.

[14] J. Miranda, A. Álvarez, S. Arévalo, and F. Guerra. Drago: An Ada extension to program fault-tolerant distributed applications. In *Ada-Europe'96*, 1996.

[15] S. Mishra, L.L. Peterson, and R.D. Schlichting. Consul: A communication substrate for fault-tolerant distributed programs. *Distributed Systems Engineering Journal*, 1(2), December 1993.

[16] S. Mishra, L.L. Peterson, and R.D. Schlichting. Experience with modularity in Consul. *Software Practice and Experience*, 23(10), October 1993.

[17] L.E. Moser, P.M. Melliar-Smith, D.A. Agarwal, R.K. Budhia, and C.A. Lingley-Papadopoulos. Totem: A fault-tolerant multicast group communication system. *Communications of the ACM*, 39(4), April 1996.

[18] L.L. Peterson, N.C. Bucholz, and R.D. Schlichting. Preserving and using context information in interprocess communication. *ACM Transactions on Computer Systems*, 7(3):217–246, 1989.

[19] D.M. Ritchie. A stream input-output system. *Bell Laboratories Technical Journal*, 63(8):1897–1910, 1984.

[20] Robbert van Renesse, Kenneth P. Birman, and Silvano Maffeis. Horus: A flexible group communication system. *Communications of the ACM*, 39(4):76–83, April 1996.

[21] Brian Whetten, Todd Montgomery, and Simon Kaplan. A high performance totally ordered multicast protocol. In *Theory and Practice in Distributed Systems*, volume LCNS 938. Springer Verlag, 1994.

Symbolic Reaching Definitions Analysis of Ada Programs

Johann Blieberger and Bernd Burgstaller

Department of Automation (183/1),
Technical University of Vienna, Treitlstr. 1/4, A-1040 Vienna
blieb@@auto.tuwien.ac.at, bburg@@auto.tuwien.ac.at

Abstract. A data-flow framework for symbolic symbolic reaching definitions analysis is presented.
It produces a more accurate solution of the reaching definitions problem than can be achieved with "classic" data-flow analysis, which is very important for safety-related applications.

1 Introduction

The *Reaching Definitions Problem* is a data-flow problem used to answer the following questions: Which definitions of a variable X reach a given use of X in an expression? Is X used anywhere before it is defined?

The underlying program presentation with data-flow problems is usually the *control flow graph (CFG)*, a directed labelled graph. Its nodes are the program's basic blocks (a basic block is a single entry, single exit, sequence of statements), whereas its edges represent transfers of control between basic blocks. *Entry* and *Exit* are distinguished nodes used to denote start and terminal node.

Traditional treatments of the Reaching Definitions Problem (confer [9]) utilise a set-based approach that aims at determining the set *Reach(B)* of variable definitions that reach a given CFG node B. We have the following equations:

$$\text{Reach}(B) = \bigcup_{B' \in \text{Preds}(B)} [(\text{Reach}(B') \cap \text{Pres}(B')) \cup \text{Gen}(B')]$$

$$\text{Reach}(\rho) = \emptyset,$$

where $\text{Reach}(B)$ is the set of definitions reaching the top of B, $\text{Preds}(B)$ is the set of *predecessors* of B, $\text{Pres}(B)$ is the set of definitions *preserved* through B (that is, not superseded by more recent definitions), and $\text{Gen}(B)$ is the set of definitions *generated* in B.

Figure 2 shows the CFG for the program fragment given in Figure 1. The comments added at statements in Figure 1 indicate in which node of the control flow graph they are contained. Note that an extraneous edge from node *Entry* to node *Exit* has been inserted which has no correspondence to the actual data-flow in procedure **Aha**, it is only present to simplify algorithms based on the CFG.

```
procedure Aha is
    h,j : integer;                          -- Node 1
begin
    if false then                           -- Node 1
        j := 0;                             -- Node 2
    end if;
    for i in 1 .. 10 loop                   -- Node 3 and 4
        h := h + i;                         -- Node 5
    end loop;
end Aha;
```

Fig. 1. Simple Example Procedure

The set of equations for the reaching definitions problem of the example program is shown in Table 1 where we have written X_i instead of Reach(B_i).

We will use this set of equations in the following to solve the reaching definitions problem with an *iteration algorithm* (confer [1]), i.e., we initialise the variables to $\emptyset$, insert these values on the right side of the equations and use the new values for the same purpose until the process stabilises.

The results are shown in Table 2. As can be seen the algorithm "converges" very fast, which is a great advantage of iteration algorithms. However, it is too optimistic in its assumptions:

- The definition of j at node 2 never occurs.
- Variable h is undefined at the beginning. Thus its value after executing procedure **Aha** is undefined too.

Both cases represent serious programming errors which cannot be detected with present data-flow algorithms. The reason for this is that "classic" data-flow analysis assumes that each edge of the CFG definitely is followed during execution of the program.

For this reason we define a data-flow framework that incorporates more information in order to allow more precise program analysis. Our data-flow framework is superior to standard techniques (compare [9]) as well as to the more involved information-flow analysis incorporated in SPADE (see [2]). Approaches like ANNA and that of [4] cannot be directly compared to ours since they are pri-

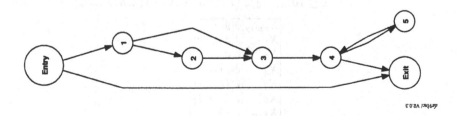

Fig. 2. Control Flow Graph of Simple Example Procedure

$$X_{\text{Entry}} = \emptyset$$
$$X_1 = (X_{\text{Entry}} \cap \{h, j\}) \cup \emptyset$$
$$X_2 = (X_1 \cap \{h, j\}) \cup \emptyset$$
$$X_3 = ((X_1 \cap \{h, j\}) \cup \emptyset) \cup ((X_2 \cap \{h\}) \cup \{j\})$$
$$X_4 = ((X_3 \cap \{h, j\}) \cup \{i\}) \cup ((X_5 \cap \{j\}) \cup \{h, i\})$$
$$X_5 = (X_4 \cap \{h, i, j\}) \cup \emptyset$$
$$X_{\text{Exit}} = (X_4 \cap \{h, j\}) \cup \emptyset$$

Table 1. Equations for Reaching Definitions Problem of Simple Example Program

marily based on annotations. In contrast our approach extracts all information from the source code alone. Note also that [4] is based on SPARK (i.e. SPADE) too.

Our approach can easily be incorporated in existing Ada compilers. In fact we have integrated a prototype into GNAT for our purposes.

2 Symbolic Evaluation of the Simple Example

According to the algorithm given in [12] we now solve the equations given in Table 3. We write "$a \to b$" for indicating that equation E_a is inserted into E_b and we write "$c \not\emptyset$" for loop-breaking equation E_c.

We denote an undefined value by "$\perp$". Furthermore we assume that an undefined value involved in an operation such as "+" or "−" results in an undefined value again. Assigning an undefined value to variable v results in v being undefined.

The equations of Table 3 are derived in a straight-forward manner. We would only like to mention that variable i is implicitly declared in the for-loop and thus does only appear at nodes 3 and 5.

In the following derivation terms with path conditions equal to *false* can be ignored, which we do sometimes without further notice.

$5 \to 4$

$$X_4 = X_3 \cup (1 \le 10) \odot X_4 \mid \{(h, h + i), (i, i + 1)\}$$

$4 \not\emptyset$

$$X_4 = \neg(1 \le 10) \odot X_3 \cup (1 \le 10) \odot X_3 \mid \{(h, h(\perp, \omega))\}$$

X_{Entry}	$\emptyset$	$\emptyset$
X_1	$\emptyset$	$\emptyset$
X_2	$\emptyset$	$\emptyset$
X_3	$\emptyset$	$\{j\}$
X_4	$\emptyset$	$\{h, i, j\}$
X_5	$\emptyset$	$\{h, i, j\}$
X_{Exit}	$\emptyset$	$\{h, j\}$

Table 2. Results of Reaching Definitions Problem of Simple Example Program

$$X_{\text{Entry}} = [\{(h, \perp), (j, \perp)\}, \text{true}]$$
$$X_1 \quad = X_{\text{Entry}}$$
$$X_2 \quad = false \odot X_1 \mid \{(j, 0)\}$$
$$X_3 \quad = true \odot X_1 \mid \{(i, 1)\} \cup true \odot X_2 \mid \{(i, 1)\}$$
$$X_4 \quad = X_3 \cup X_5$$
$$X_5 \quad = (1 \leq 10) \odot X_4 \mid \{(h, h + i), (i, i + 1)\}$$
$$X_{\text{Exit}} = true \odot X_4$$

Table 3. Set of SymEval Equations for Simple Example Program

4 → Exit

$$X_{\text{Exit}} = \neg(1 \leq 10) \odot X_3 \cup (1 \leq 10) \odot X_3 \mid \{(h, h(\perp, \omega))\}$$

3 → Exit, 1 → Exit, Entry → Exit

$$X_{\text{Exit}} = \neg(1 \leq 10) \odot [\{(h, \perp), (j, \perp)\}, true] \cup$$
$$(1 \leq 10) \odot [\{(h, h(\perp, \omega)), (j, \perp)\}, true]$$
$$= [\{(h, \perp), (j, \perp)\}, false] \cup [\{(h, h(\perp, \omega)), (j, \perp)\}, true]$$

Next we solve the recurrence relation for variable i. The recursion is

$$i(1) = 1,$$
$$i(k + 1) = i(k) + 1.$$

Clearly its solution is $i(k) = k$ for $k \geq 1$.

The recurrence relation for variable h reads

$$h(1) = \perp,$$
$$h(k + 1) = h(k) + i(k) = h(k) + k$$

Its solution is $h(k) = \perp$ for $k \geq 1$.

Hence we finally get $X_{\text{Exit}} = [\{(h, \perp), (j, \perp)\}, true]$ which correctly mirrors the fact that both j and h are undefined after procedure **Aha** has been executed.

Performing further insertions more detailed information can be derived. For example inserting Entry → 1, 1 → 3, and 3 → 4, we see that variable h is used before it is defined in Node 4.

3 Symbolic Evaluation

Symbolic evaluation is a form of static program analysis in which symbolic expressions are used to denote the values of program variables and computations (cf. e.g. [5]). In addition a path condition describes the impact of the program's control flow onto the values of variables and the condition under which control flow reaches a given program point.

Conditions and the Control Flow Graph

An edge $e = (B', B)$ of the CFG has assigned a condition $\mathrm{Cond}(B', B)$ which must evaluate to true for the control flow to follow this edge (e.g. in case of the then-branch of an if-statement Cond is the condition of the if-statement).

Program State and Context

The *state* S of a program is described by a set of pairs $\{(v_1, e_1), \ldots, (v_m, e_m)\}$ where v_i is a program variable and e_i is a symbolic expression describing the value of v_i for $1 \leq i \leq m$. For each variable v_i there exists exactly one pair (v_i, e_i) in S.

A program consists of a sequence of statements that may change S.

A *path condition* specifies a condition that is valid at a certain program point. If conditional statements are present, there may be several different valid program states at the same program point. A different path condition is associated with each of them.

States S and path conditions C specify a *program context* which is defined by

$$\bigcup_{i=1}^{k} [S_i, C_i]$$

where k denotes the number of different program states valid at a certain program point. (The $\cup$ and $\bigcup$-operators are used to enumerate different program states.) A program context completely describes the variable bindings at a specific program point together with the associated path conditions.

4   A Data-Flow Framework for Symbolic Evaluation

We define the following set of equations for the symbolic evaluation framework:

$$\mathrm{SymEval}(B_{\mathrm{Entry}}) = [S_0, C_0],$$

where S_0 denotes the initial state containing all variables which are assigned their initial values, and C_0 is true,

$$\mathrm{SymEval}(B) = \bigcup_{B' \in \mathrm{Preds}(B)} \mathrm{PrpgtCond}(B', B, \mathrm{SymEval}(B')) \mid \mathrm{LocalEval}(B),$$

where $\mathrm{LocalEval}(B) = \{(v_{i_1}, e_{i_1}), \ldots, (v_{i_m}, e_{i_m})\}$ denotes the symbolic evaluation local to basic block B. The variables that get a new value assigned in the basic block are denoted by $v_{i_1}, \ldots, v_{i_m}$. The new symbolic values are given by $e_{i_1}, \ldots, e_{i_m}$. The *propagated conditions* are defined by

$$\mathrm{PrpgtCond}(B', B, \mathrm{PC}) = \begin{cases} \mathrm{Cond}(B', B) \odot \mathrm{PC}, & \text{if } B' \text{ has } \geq 1 \text{ successors,} \\ \mathrm{PC}, & \text{otherwise.} \end{cases}$$

Denoting by PC a program context, the operation $\odot$ is defined as follows:

$$\text{Cond}(B', B) \odot \text{PC} = \text{Cond}(B', B) \odot [\mathcal{S}_1, p_1] \cup \cdots \cup [\mathcal{S}_k, p_k] =$$
$$[\mathcal{S}_1, \text{Cond}(B', B) \wedge p_1] \cup \cdots \cup [\mathcal{S}_k, \text{Cond}(B', B) \wedge p_k],$$

i.e., the $\odot$-operator is used as a placeholder for path conditions of currently unknown program contexts.

In the following we state certain rules which have to be applied to perform symbolic evaluation*:

1. If a situation like

$$\{\ldots, (v, e_1), \ldots\} \mid \{\ldots, (v, e_2), \ldots\},$$

   is encountered during symbolic evaluation, we replace it with

$$\{\ldots, (v, e_2), \ldots\}.$$

   The pair (v, e_1) is not contained in the new set.
2. If a situation like

$$\{\ldots, (v_1, e_1), \ldots\} \mid \{\ldots, (v_2, e_2(v_1)), \ldots\},$$

   where $e(v)$ denotes an expression involving variable v, is encountered during symbolic evaluation, we replace it with

$$\{\ldots, (v_1, e_1), \ldots, (v_2, e_2(e_1)), \ldots\}.$$

3. If a situation like

$$\{\ldots, (v, e), \ldots\} \mid \{\ldots, (v, v(\bot, \omega)), \ldots\}$$

   is encountered during symbolic evaluation, we replace it with

$$\{\ldots, (v, v(e, \omega)), \ldots\}.$$

   The pair (v, e) is not contained in the new set.
   The notation $v(v_0, \omega)$ is defined in Section 5.
   For the situations discussed above it is important to apply the rules in the correct order, which is to elaborate the elements of the right set from left to right.
4. If a situation like

$$[\{\ldots, (v, e), \ldots\}, C(\ldots, v, \ldots)]$$

   is encountered during symbolic evaluation, we replace it with

$$[\{\ldots, (v, e), \ldots\}, C(\ldots, e, \ldots)].$$

---

* Rules 1, 2, and 3 constitute an informal definition of the $\mid$-operator used in the SymEval equations.

5. If a situation like

$$[\{\ldots,(v,v(v_0,\omega)),\ldots\},C(\ldots,v,\ldots)]$$

is encountered during symbolic evaluation, we replace it with

$$[\{\ldots,(v,v(v_0,\omega)),\ldots\},C(\ldots,v_0,\ldots)].$$

6. If a situation like

$$[\{\ldots,(v,v(v_0,\omega)),\ldots\},C(\ldots,v(\bot,\omega),\ldots)]$$

is encountered during symbolic evaluation, we replace it with

$$[\{\ldots,(v,v(v_0,\omega)),\ldots\},C(\ldots,v(v_0,\omega),\ldots)]$$

This data-flow framework has been introduced in [3].

5 Solving the Symbolic Evaluation Data-Flow Framework

Unfortunately the definition of PrpgtCond($\ldots$) prevents the symbolic evaluation framework from being bounded. Thus it cannot be solved by iteration algorithms (compare [9, 7, 8]).

Nevertheless we can solve symbolic evaluation frameworks with help of *elimination algorithms* (see [11, 10]). Note that the set of equations ($i = 1, \ldots, n$)

$$\{E_i : x_i = W_i(x_{i_1}, \ldots, x_{i_{n_i}})\} \tag{1}$$

implies a dependency relation on the variables x_i. We say that x_i on the left side *depends* on all variables on the right side. If the corresponding dependency graph is acyclic, set ((1)) can be solved by simple insertions, thereby eliminating one variable after the other. If it contains cycles, insertions alone are not enough to obtain a solution. However, if a rule is available for replacing such an equation with one in which the left variable does not appear on the right, with a guarantee that any solution to this new equation set will satisfy the original, then it becomes possible to move the elimination process forward. Such a rule is called *loop-breaking rule*.

The loop-breaking rule for SymEval equations is defined as follows ([3]): Assume we have the following equation (we use X_i for SymEval(B_i) as a shorthand)

$$E_i : X_i = \bigcup_{1 \leq j \leq r} (C_j \odot X_i) | \{(v_{j_1}, e_{j_1}), \ldots, (v_{j_s}, e_{j_s})\} \cup$$
$$\bigcup_{1 \leq k \leq t,\ 1 \leq m \leq n,\ m \neq i} (C_k \odot X_m) | \{(v_{k_1}, e_{k_1}), \ldots, (v_{k_u}, e_{k_u})\},$$

then we replace it with

$$e_i : X_i = \neg \,\text{LoopEntryCond}_i \odot$$

$$\bigcup_{1\le k\le t,\ 1\le m\le n,\ m\ne i} (C_k \odot X_m)|\,\{(v_{k_1},e_{k_1}),\ldots,(v_{k_u},e_{k_u})\} \cup$$

$$\text{LoopEntryCond}_i \odot$$

$$\bigcup_{1\le k\le t,\ 1\le m\le n,\ m\ne i} ((C_k \odot X_m)|\,\{(v_{k_1},e_{k_1}),\ldots,(v_{k_u},e_{k_u})\})|\,\text{LoopExit},$$

where LoopEntryCond_i denotes the condition which has to be true to enter the loop body starting at basic block B_i, and

$$\text{LoopExit} = \{(v_{J_1}, v_{J_1}(\bot,\omega_\ell)),\ldots,(v_{J_t}, v_{J_t}(\bot,\omega_\ell))\}$$

for all variables v_{J_p} being contained in

$$\bigcup_{1\le j\le r} \{(v_{j_1},e_{j_1}),\ldots,(v_{j_s},e_{j_s})\}.$$

Note that the first term of e_i mirrors the case when the loop body is not executed at all, and the second term treats the case when the loop body is executed at least one times.

The purpose of our loop-breaking rule is to replace a loop by a *set of recurrence relations*. Each induction variable (cf. [1]) gives raise to an (indirect) recursion. Let v be such a variable, then $v(v_0,\omega_\ell)$ denotes the symbolic solution of the recursion, where v_0 is a suitable initial value and ω_ℓ denotes the number of iterations of loop ℓ^{**}. If no initial value is known or the initial value is irrelevant to the solution, we write $v(\bot,\omega_\ell)$.

Setting up recurrence relations during loop-breaking is described in the following. If there are nested loops in the source code of interest, we start by setting up recurrence relations from the innermost loop and proceed to the outermost*** .

Let v denote a variable, then we call $v(k)$ its *recursive counterpart*, where k is a variable that does not occur in the program being evaluated..

According to the notation above we set up a recurrence relation for all $1 \le j \le r$, $1 \le q \le s$ and for $k \ge 0$ by

$$v_{j_q}(k+1) = e_{j_q}(k) \qquad \text{if } C_j(k) \text{ evaluates to true,}$$

where $e_{j_q}(k)$ and $C_j(k)$ means that all variables contained in e_{j_q} and C_j are replaced with their recursive counterparts.

Note that we have not specified initial values for the recursion; these are supposed to be supplied by situations handled by the rules given in Section 4.

** Each loop gets assigned a unique number $\ell \in \mathbb{N}$.
*** This is guaranteed by the algorithm described in [12].

```
procedure Foo (E : in Integer; Y : out Integer) is
    Index, I, R : Integer;                    -- Node 1
begin
    Index := E;                               -- Node 1
    while Index > 0 loop                      -- Node 2
        if Index mod 2 = 0 then               -- Node 3
            I := E + 1;                        -- Node 4
        end if;
        Index := Index - 1;                   -- Node 5
        R := I + Index;                       -- Node 5
    end loop;
    Y := R + 1;                               -- Node 6
end Foo;
```

Fig. 3. Hypothetical Example Procedure

We have used and implemented an algorithm described in [12] for solving symbolic evaluation frameworks. It solves data-flow equations in $O(\log |N| \cdot |E|)$ insertions and loop-breaking operations, where $|N|$ denotes the number of nodes in the CFG and $|E|$ is the number of edges of the CFG. The CFG is supposed to be reducible, which is true for all Ada programs. Because of the undecidability of the halting problem, however, we cannot give time bounds for solving the recurrence relations produced by the loop-breaking rule.

6 A More Complicated Example

Figure 4 shows the CFG for the program fragment given in Figure 3.

The SymEval equations for this hypothetical example are shown in Table 4. Note that we can restrict our interest to the variables *Index*, *I*, *R*, and *Y* because *E* cannot be overwritten within procedure **foo** (compare [6] for semantic details).

Again we solve this set of equations according to the algorithm given in [12].

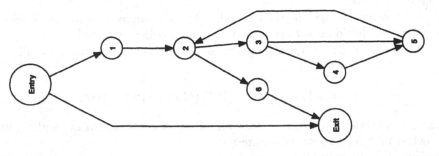

Fig. 4. Control Flow Graph of Hypothetical Example Procedure

$$X_{\text{Entry}} = [\{(Index, \bot), (I, \bot), (R, \bot), (Y, \bot)\}, \text{true}]$$
$$X_1 \quad = X_{\text{entry}} \mid \{(Index, E)\}$$
$$X_2 \quad = X_1 \cup X_5$$
$$X_3 \quad = ((Index > 0) \odot X_2)$$
$$X_4 \quad = ((Index \bmod 2 = 0) \odot X_3) \mid \{(I, E + 1)\}$$
$$X_5 \quad = (X_4 \mid \{(Index, Index - 1), (R, I + Index - 1)\}) \cup$$
$$\qquad (\neg(Index \bmod 2 = 0) \odot X_3 \mid \{(Index, Index - 1),$$
$$\qquad (R, I + Index - 1)\})$$
$$X_6 \quad = (\neg(Index > 0) \vee \neg(Index(\bot, \omega) > 0)) \odot X_2 \mid \{Y, R + 1\}$$
$$X_{\text{Exit}} = X_6$$

Table 4. Set of SymEval Equations for Hypothetical Example Program

4 → 5

$$X_5 = (((Index \bmod 2 = 0) \odot X_3) \mid$$
$$\qquad \{(I, E + 1), (Index, Index - 1), (R, I + Index - 1)\})$$
$$\qquad \cup ((\neg(Index \bmod 2 = 0) \odot X_3) \mid$$
$$\qquad \{(Index, Index - 1), (R, I + Index - 1)\})$$

5 → 2

$$X_2 = X_1 \cup (((Index \bmod 2 = 0) \odot X_3) \mid$$
$$\qquad \{(I, E + 1), (Index, Index - 1), (R, I + Index - 1)\})$$
$$\qquad \cup ((\neg(Index \bmod 2 = 0) \odot X_3) \mid$$
$$\qquad \{(Index, Index - 1), (R, I + Index - 1)\})$$

3 → 2

$$X_2 = X_1 \cup (((Index \bmod 2 = 0) \wedge (Index > 0)) \odot X_2) \mid$$
$$\qquad \{(I, E + 1), (Index, Index - 1), (R, I + Index - 1)\}) \cup$$
$$\qquad ((\neg(Index \bmod 2 = 0) \wedge (Index > 0)) \odot X_2) \mid$$
$$\qquad \{(Index, Index - 1), (R, I + Index - 1)\})$$

6 → Exit

$$X_{\text{Exit}} = (\neg(Index > 0) \vee \neg(Index(\bot, \omega) > 0)) \odot X_2 \mid \{Y, R + 1\}$$

2 ∅

$$X_2 = \neg(Index > 0) \odot X_1 \cup$$
$$(Index > 0) \odot X_1 \mid \{(Index, Index(\bot, \omega)), (I, I(\bot, \omega)), (R, R(\bot, \omega))\}$$

2 → Exit, 1 → Exit, Entry → Exit

$$X_{\text{Exit}} = [\{(Index, E), (I, \bot), (R, \bot), (Y, \bot)\}, \neg(E > 0)] \cup$$
$$\qquad [\{(Index, Index(E, \omega)), (I, I(\bot, \omega)), (R, R(\bot, \omega)),$$
$$\qquad (Y, R(\bot, \omega) + 1)\}, (E > 0)]$$

We now set up the recurrence relations involved $(k \geq 0)$. For *Index* we obtain:

$$Index(0) = E,$$
$$Index(k+1) = Index(k) - 1 \quad \text{if } Index(k) > 0$$

which has the closed form

$$Index(k) = E - k \quad \text{for } 0 \leq k \leq E,$$

from which we conclude that $\omega = E$.

For variable I we get the following recurrence relation:

$$I(0) = \perp,$$
$$I(k+1) = \begin{cases} E+1 & \text{if } (Index(k) > 0 \wedge (Index(k) \bmod 2 = 0), \\ I(k) & \text{otherwise.} \end{cases}$$

Its solution is:

$$I(1) = \begin{cases} E+1 & \text{if } (E > 0) \wedge (E \bmod 2 = 0), \\ \perp & \text{otherwise,} \end{cases} \tag{2}$$
$$I(k) = E + 1 \quad \text{for } k \geq 2.$$

For variable R we derive

$$R(0) = \perp,$$
$$R(1) = I(1) + Index(1) = \begin{cases} 2E & \text{if } (E > 0) \wedge (E \bmod 2 = 0), \\ \perp & \text{otherwise,} \end{cases}$$
$$R(k) = I(k) + Index(k) = (E+1) + (E-k) = 2E - k + 1 \quad \text{for } k \geq 2.$$

This implies

$$R(\omega) = \begin{cases} \perp & \text{if } E = 1, \\ E+1 & \text{if } E \geq 2. \end{cases} \tag{3}$$

Finally, we derive

$$Y = R(\omega) + 1 = \begin{cases} \perp & \text{if } E = 1, \\ E+2 & \text{if } E \geq 2. \end{cases} \tag{4}$$

Inserting these results into equation X_{Exit} we obtain the following context

$$X_{Exit} = [\{(Index, E), (I, \perp), (R, \perp), (Y, \perp)\}, \neg(E > 0)] \cup$$
$$[\{(Index, 0), (I, (2)), (R, (3)), (Y, (4))\}, (E > 0)],$$

where the results from equations (2), (3), and (4) are incorporated at the indicated places.

From this we see that

1. I, R, and Y are undefined if $\neg(E > 0)$, which means that the loop body has not been executed at all,
2. I, R, and Y are undefined if $E = 1$ and
3. I is undefined if $\neg(E \bmod 2 = 0)$ during the *first* iteration of the loop.

Note that case (3) is a transient fault which is propagated to Y only if $E = 1$. If for example $E = 3$, I and R are undefined during the first iteration. However this is "repaired" during the second iteration where I and R are assigned proper values.

7 Conclusion

Employing symbolic evaluation for reaching definitions analysis produces more accurate solutions than can be achieved with "classic" data-flow algorithms. We are currently investigating the implications of the *interprocedural* reaching definitions problem on our approach.

Symbolic evaluation can also be used for detecting dead paths and for improving other important data-flow properties of programs. It can also be employed for determining the *worst-case execution time* of (real-time) programs (see [3]). These properties are crucial for applications in the area of real-time, embedded, and safety related systems.

We have implemented the algorithm presented in [12] for almost all control flow affecting language features of Ada. At the current stage our implementation does not support exceptions and tasking. An implementation of the symbolic evaluation data-flow framework is under way. As already mentioned our prototype implementation is integrated into GNAT.

References

1. A. V. Aho, R. Seti, and J. D. Ullman. *Compilers: principles, techniques, and tools.* Addison-Wesley, Reading, MA, 1986.
2. J.-F. Bergeretti and B. A. Carré. Information-flow and data-flow analysis of while-programs. *ACM Trans. Prog. Lang. Sys.*, 7(1):37–61, 1985.
3. J. Blieberger. Data-flow frameworks for worst-case execution time analysis. (submitted), 1997.
4. R. Chapman, A. Burns, and A. Wellings. Combining static worst-case timing analysis and program proof. *Real-Time Systems*, 11(2):145–171, 1996.
5. T. E. Cheatham, G. H. Hollow y, and J. A. Townley. Symbolic evaluation and the analysis of programs. *IEEE Trans. on Software Engineering*, 5(4):403–417, July 1979.
6. ISO/IEC 8652. *Ada Reference manual*, 1995.
7. J. B. Kam and J. D. Ullman. Global data flow analysis and iterative algorithms. *J. ACM*, 23(1):158–171, 1976.
8. J. B. Kam and J. D. Ullman. Monotone data flow analysis frameworks. *Acta Informatica*, 7:305–317, 1977.

9. T. J. Marlowe and B. G. Ryder. Properties of data flow frameworks – a unified model. *Acta Informatica*, 28:121–163, 1990.
10. M. C. Paull. *Algorithm Design – A Recursion Transformation Framework*. Wiley Interscience, New York, NY, 1988.
11. B. G. Ryder and M. C. Paull. Elimination algorithms for data flow analysis. *ACM Computing Surveys*, 18(3):277–316, 1986.
12. V. C. Sreedhar. *Efficient Program Analysis Using DJ Graphs*. PhD thesis, School of Computer Science, McGill University, Montréal, Québec, Canada, 1995.

Looking at Code With Your Safety Goggles On

Ken Wong

Department of Computer Science, University of British Columbia
Vancouver, BC, Canada V6T 1Z4
tel (604) 822-4912 fax (604) 822-5485
kwong@cs.ubc.ca

Abstract. This paper presents a process for the refinement of safety-critical source code into a more tractable representation. For large software-intensive information systems, the safety engineering view of the system reveals a "long thin slice" of hazard-related software involving a number of different software components. The hazard-related software is documented in the system "safety verification case" which provides a rigorous argument for the safety of the source code. The refinement process creates a representation of the source code which isolates the relevant source code details. A hypothetical chemical factory information system is examined to illustrate aspects of this process and its significance.

1. Introduction

This paper presents a refinement process for the source code level implementation of a software-intensive safety-critical system. The output of the process is a model of the source code which is used in system safety verification. Details of the representation are documented in the system safety case.

The development process for software-intensive systems typically involves the refinement of functional requirements into the system design, and the refinement of the design into source code. The process often includes the creation of abstractions at each level to hide the implementation details of the lower levels. If the abstractions are sound, they can then be used with a high degree of confidence to implement the application functionality.

In the case of software-intensive systems with safety-related functionality, the development process will include the production of a safety case [16]. The safety case summarizes all the evidence that the system is safe to deploy. Included in the safety case is what we call the "safety verification case" [14] which documents the verification of the implementation with respect to previously identified hazards. The safety verification case is used to support future safety assessments of the system. These assessments are typically performed by people other than the original system developers.

This paper argues for the importance of including a representation of the safety-related aspects of the system implementation in the safety verification case. The future safety assessments of the system cannot rely with a "high degree of confidence" on the soundness of the software abstractions used to construct the system. The safety assessments will require implementation details in order to have assurance of the safety of the source code.

This paper focuses on large software-intensive information systems with modern software architectures. These systems may consist up to a million lines of production code with the equivalent of millions more in "Commercial-Off-The-Shelf" (COTS) products. Such systems are characterized by "long thin slices" of hazard-related source code involving a number of different software components. The safety verification case for these systems requires a representation of the long thin slice that isolates the relevant details.

The author has had the opportunity to examine in depth a large real-time information system with safety-related functionality through the formalWARE project [15]. The project provided access to the Ada-based implementation of the system, as well as to the safety engineering process used in system development. Some of the lessons learned from the formalWARE project are illustrated with a hypothetical chemical factory information system.

The chemical factory information system is introduced in Section 2, along with a system hazard. Section 3 discusses the differences between the safety engineering and software implementation views of the source code. Section 4 presents the need for a more tractable representation of the source code. Section 5 outlines the source code refinement process which is demonstrated on the chemical factory information system. Section 6 discusses the use of the source code representation in building a safety verification case. Section 7 provides a summary of the paper.

2. Chemical Factory Information System

For illustrative purposes, this paper focuses on a hypothetical information system for a chemical factory. The chemical factory information system is similar to other real-time information systems, like Air Traffic Management (ATM) systems, in that environmental data is received, processed and displayed to operators. The operators then make safety-critical decisions based on the information received from the system.

2.1 System Description

The factory consists of a set of reactor vessels equipped with sensors that record data such as temperature and pressure. The sensors are connected over a LAN to a central server and a set of workstations. This information system maintains and processes the vessel information it receives over the LAN and displays it on the workstation monitors.

2.2 System Hazard

There are a number of potential system hazards for the chemical factory information system. Hazards are states of the system that may contribute to a mishap [9]. For example, one system hazard is as follows:

An invalid temperature, D, is displayed for vessel V at time T.

The identification of this hazard resulted from an earlier analysis which showed that the display of an invalid temperature value for a vessel, in combination with other conditions, could lead to a mishap such as a fire or explosion.

This hazard is analogous to a typical ATM system hazard, namely, the display of an invalid altitude value for an aircraft at some particular time.

Layer 5	Human Computer Interface External Systems
Layer 4	Chemical Factory Functional Areas
Layer 3	Chemical Factory Classes
Layer 2	Support mechanisms (DVM): communications, and so on
Layer 1	Common Utilities Bindings, Low-level Services

Figure 1: The chemical factory information system static architecture.

2.3 Software Architecture

The chemical factory software architecture is based on an industrial Ada-based architecture for an ATM system [7]. The architecture can be described by a "4+1 View Model" composed of five different perspectives, or views, that include the logical, process, physical and development views. The fifth view is a set of scenarios that incorporate elements of the other four views. The software architecture is based on the use of abstraction, as well as decomposition and composition.

The logical design of the software is decomposed into a set of class abstractions. The classes capture the key domain information, as well as the common mechanisms and design elements across the different parts of the system.

The process view describes the concurrency and synchronization aspects of the design. At the highest level of abstraction, the process view can be seen as set of communicating processes (Ada programs) distributed across a set of hardware resources connected by a LAN.

The development view focuses on the organization of the software modules in the software development environment. The software is partitioned into five layers as shown in Figure 1. Each layer is decomposed into subsystems and each subsystem is further decomposed into modules (Ada packages and generics). The software development teams are then organized around the subsystems and layers.

Each layer defines a progressively more abstract machine depending only on the services of the lower layers. In particular, layer 2 is a Distributed Virtual Machine (DVM) providing services such as object distribution, a thread scheduler and tactical configuration [12]. COTS products are confined to the lowest layer.

3. Safety Engineering View of the Software

The safety engineering view of the software can be illustrated at the requirements and source code level. At both levels there are significant differences between the safety engineering and the software implementation views of the system.

3.1 Safety vs Functional Requirements

Safety engineering is often focused on what the system should **not** do, in contrast to software implementation, which is largely focused on implementing correct system functionality.

This difference is apparent when safety requirements are contrasted with functional requirements. Typical software functional requirements describe a "forward" view of system functionality, while safety requirements often involve a "backwards" look at the system.

For example, a functional requirement involving the temperature display of a vessel for the chemical plant information system, might look like this:

> *Upon receipt of a sensor update containing the information that a vessel V is at temperature D, the system shall update the displayed temperature of vessel V to D within S1 seconds.*

The focus of this requirement is the system functionality involved in the processing of sensor updates. It is a "forward" look at the system functionality, from a system input to an output.

In contrast, a safety requirement focuses on system hazards, such as the invalid temperature display hazard defined in Section 2.2. The corresponding safety requirement might be stated as:

If temperature D is displayed for Vessel V at time T, then at some time not more than S2 seconds before T, the actual temperature of Vessel V was within C degrees of D.

The safety requirement is stated in a "backwards" fashion, focusing on the desired, safe output and defining the necessary input. Such a requirement is not easily tested. It would involve determining all possible inputs that may violate this requirement.

The safety requirement is not simply a reformulation of the functional requirement. In fact, it is possible to satisfy the functional requirement, while failing to satisfy the safety requirement.

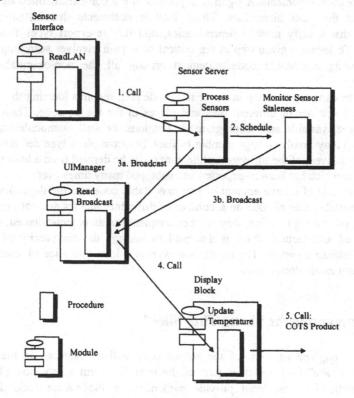

Figure 2: Temperature dataflow highlighting the key modules and subprograms.

3.2 The "Long Thin Slice" of Source Code

The software architecture uses abstractions which hide details that must be revealed for safety engineering. For software implementation, these details are relevant only to the team responsible for the module which implements a given abstraction. Safety engineering requires details from all the relevant software modules in order to evaluate the safety of the source code.

In particular, safety engineering must uncover code paths that lead to the hazard. A code path can be viewed as a sequence of steps where each step corresponds to an executable line of source code.

The relevant source code will typically be found in a number of different software components, involving only a small amount of code from each module. The result is a "long thin slice" of hazard-related software.

For the chemical factory information system, the modules related to the display of temperature data can be found in all five layers of the architecture. The modules from the upper layers of the static architecture are depicted in Figure 2.

Examination of a module from the long thin slice reveals a large number of non-executable code statements. A significant portion of the non-executable code is used to support the class hierarchies. These include statements that instantiate Ada generics, that specify module dependencies, and that re-export types from other modules. To locate a given step in the critical code path involves searching for the corresponding executable code statement among all the non-executable code statements.

To understand a given step in the critical code path requires locating the relevant details in a number of different files and places in the source code. These details include type, variable and subprogram declarations, as well as module renaming. This search may involve a large number of files. For example, a type declared in one of the upper layers of the software architecture could be derived from a base type in a lower layer which has been re-exported and subtyped many times over.

The presence of a large amount of non-executable code and the dependence of a given executable line of code on a number of different modules are not necessarily signs of a poor design. In fact, they are a consequence of an object-oriented, modular and layered architecture which is designed to manage the complexity of a large software-intensive system. The result, however, is a long thin slice of source code which is not easily documented.

4. Documenting the "Long Thin Slice"

The safety engineering view of the source code will be captured in the "safety verification case" [14], which is part of the overall system safety case [16]. The safety verification case must provide evidence that the source code does not contribute to the identified system hazards. Part of the evidence includes documentation of the hazard-related source code.

Following the long thin slice may involve looking at more than a thousand different locations in the source code merely to understand a sequence of actions of less than fifty steps. This may not present a problem to the developer who has been immersed for many months or years in the development of the software. The developer may be capable of tracing a sequence of actions across the long thin slice of code without looking up every relevant line of code from various source files.

Other people, however, must also be able follow the same sequence of actions. These people include system certifiers, system maintainers and system developers intending to reuse the software in new systems. These people must also be able to follow the long thin slice in order to carry out their own safety assessments of the system.

5. Refinement of the Source Code

A more tractable representation of the long thin slice of hazard-related code can be created through refinement of the source code. Care must be taken that the representation accurately reflects the original source code.

5.1 Refinement Properties

The refinement of the source code into a model should be documented with enough detail so that it should be easy to determine the impact of any future changes to the source code on the model. The details should also be sufficient to ensure a repeatable process.

The refinement process may make use of simplifying assumptions. These assumptions must be stated explicitly. It must also be clear where each simplifying assumption is used in the refinement.

The model should be **conservative** in the sense that every property of the model is also a property of the actual system, as long as the simplifying assumptions are true.

The model should be **complete** in the sense that the model contains enough every information to unambiguously interpret every executable statement in the model.

To the extent that the model is represented by fragments of source code, the model should be **tractable** in the sense that the ratio of executable lines of code to non-executable lines should be "reasonable". Furthermore, the number of different places in the source code required to understand a single line of executable code should also be reasonable. This is especially important if the verification depends on human comprehension of the model. If human understanding is required, "reasonable" might mean that there is no more than "7±2" lines of non-executable code, and no more than "7±2" places to look, for each executable line of code.

5.2 Refinement Process

The refinement process may be viewed conceptually as a sequence of transformations applied to a copy of the source code implementation together with a representation of the COTS products. The result of each refinement step is intended to be a conservative model of the implementation of the system.

The transformations may be carried out in an *ad hoc* manner relying on sound engineering judgment to ensure that each refinement step results in a conservative model of the implementation. To support repeatability of the safety verification case, the engineering judgment underlying each transformation must be carefully documented. The amount of documentation required to justify each step could be reduced by the use of a "standardized" set of syntax-oriented refinement rules whose soundness has been established.

Each transformation step could result in an executable model of the system in the sense that it can be compiled and executed. The refinement of the implementation into an executable model would be necessary if dynamic methods (i.e., testing) are to be used in the safety verification. But if the verification approach only uses static methods, then the refinement process can reduce size and complexity by allowing transformation steps that substitute executable aspects of the model with non-executable representations of system functionality.

These transformations might actually be applied directly to a copy of the implementation using basic editing tools. If the refinement process is based on a standardized set of transformation rules, then the entire refinement process could be documented by an executable script. It would then be possible to implement a software tool that executed the script and that checked that each transformation rule was used in a valid manner. Alternatively, these transformations may be simply be carried out "on paper" by describing the result of each transformation step.

The transformations are carried out until a tractable representation is created. This might mean that some qualitative criteria of "reasonable" has been satisfied. Alternatively, engineering judgment may be used to decide when the output of a given transformation is sufficiently tractable.

5.3 Refinement Steps

Four basic refinement steps have been identified for creating a tractable representation of the source code:

1. **Flatten** - collapse the class hierarchy.
2. **Fillet** - identify the hazard-related code.
3. **Partition** - decompose the hazard-related code into blocks.
4. **Translate** - represent the hazard-related code in a simpler notation.

Though the steps are to be carried out sequentially, they may also overlap.

5.3.1 Flatten

The class hierarchies are "flattened" to bring together the relevant lines of code and to reduce the amount of "non-executable" code. In Ada, class hierarchies are implemented with generics.

The class hierarchies are flattened by "expanding" each generic instance. A representation of each generic instance is created by substituting in the actual parameter values. It may be possible to build tools to produce this representation either directly or by extracting a compiler-intermediate form.

For the chemical factory information system, expanding the code results in, for example, a new module `SensorServer`, which is the `Server` generic with the parameter values substituted in for the parameters.

5.3.2 Fillet

Filleting involves identifying the source code which may contribute to the hazard. For the chemical factory information system, the modules and subprograms shown in Figure 2 provide a convenient starting point for the search. Further examination of the software architecture and the source code reveals that an invalid temperature has a number of potential causes, such as the corruption of the vessel temperature value, a stale sensor reading or a miscorrelation of sensors to vessels. The modules and subprograms that implement these features are identified and the relevant code is extracted.

There are a number of hazard analysis techniques [5] available which are designed to uncover system faults. These techniques include Hazard and Operability Studies (HAZOP), Failure Modes And Effects Analysis (FMEA) and Fault Tree Analysis (FTA), among others. These techniques were originally designed for mechanical systems, though there have been some attempts to adapt FTA [10, 17], HAZOP [17,19] and FMEA [17,18] to software. These techniques are useful for identifying software faults at the requirements or design level. These methods, however, are not well suited for determining which lines of code may contribute to a given hazard.

At the source code level, the search for hazard-related source code is a manual effort. The results of the hazard analysis at the requirements and design level can be used to guide the search. The search can be conducted in either a forward or backward fashion [9]. A forward search is particularly appropriate for tracing known hazard scenarios. A backward search is appropriate for identifying new scenarios.

Though the search for hazard-related code is primarily manual, the complexity of the code means that tool support is important. Software development environments, for example, provide support for module cross-referencing which is useful when tracing hazardous code paths across module boundaries. There are also other static code analysis tools, such as data flow analyzers, which would be useful in identifying critical data flows [2]. In particular, there are program-slicing tools that can be used to extract all code connected to a critical variable. Though most of these are research tools [4], there are some commercial tools that do a limited form of program slicing [11]. Program slicing for object-oriented programs is particularly difficult due to the run-time binding of methods and complex object-interaction graphs, though there is a tool that performs a limited form of object slicing [8].

5.3.3 Partition

Partitioning involves decomposing the filleted code into blocks which execute in different processes or threads (light-weight processes). Each "functional block" of code can be viewed as a procedure with input and output parameters. Partitioning the code along dynamic lines allows for the examination of certain code properties, such as the effect of block execution order on safety.

The hazard-related code is partitioned by tracing subprogram calls until a subprogram invocation results in a new process or thread. For the chemical factory information system, there are three hazard-related functional blocks: the reading and processing of a LAN message, the monitoring of stale sensor data, and updates to the temperature display.

In addition, the functional blocks can be further decomposed into existing static abstractions, such as subsystems or modules. Since system development makes use of these abstractions it would ease the fit of the safety analysis with the rest of the software development program. Unit testing and code reviews, for example, could be leveraged for the safety analysis of the functional blocks.

5.3.4 Translate

The final step of the process is to translate the hazard-related code into a simpler form. For the chemical factory information system, the hazard-related code is translated into the SPARK Ada subset [1]. SPARK is supported by program analysis and verification tools that could be used in the safety verification.

SPARK does not support generics, which are removed during the flattening stage. Though SPARK does support Ada packages, these are removed during the translation, resulting in a set of global data structures and subprograms. Many of the hazard-related modules contain only a small amount of relevant code, so the module structure is not needed for the safety analysis. In general, removal of the module structure may involve re-labeling the module subprograms and types to avoid name conflicts.

Two other approaches to representing the hazard-related code include informal English and formal mathematical notations.

The simplest approach involves extracting the hazard-related code, and annotating the code fragments in English. The annotations indicate the code's relevance to the hazard and can be supplemented by figures such as object-scenario and module diagrams to indicate the important modules and data flows [3]. The limitations of such an approach is that that the model is imprecise and not easily analyzed. The greatest virtue of a informal language notation is that it is easily understood and communicated to others.

A more precise approach would be to use a formal mathematical notation [13], which is usually more expressive than a programming language. For example, SPARK includes an annotation notation that uses the SPARK Ada subset, but is limited by not supporting quantification (i.e., "for all ..." and "there exists ..."). There are alternative machine-readable specification notations that are more expressive and which also have tool support that can aid analysis. The limitation of mathematical notations are their lack of familiarity to most developers, and their syntactic distance from the source code.

6. Safety Verification Case

The output of the refinement process is a model of the source code which is documented in the safety verification case. The safety verification case provides a detailed rigorous argument for the safety of the source code with respect to identified system hazards. Safety verification of the model can be achieved through dynamic techniques, such as testing, or static techniques, such as code inspection.

Static techniques also include the use of program verification tools such as SPARK Examiner [1]. These tools, typically, are used to verify program correctness with respect to a set of code assertions (i.e., pre- and post-conditions). Doubts have been raised about the feasibility of using these tools in safety verification [9]. The refinement of the hazard into a set of verifiable code assertions [14] is one step toward increasing the feasibility of using these tools. The refinement of the source code into a more tractable representation is another important step toward the practical use of correctness verification tools like SPARK Examiner in safety verification.

7. Summary

The safety engineering view of the software differs from the standard architectural views. This is true for the large software-intensive safety-critical information systems investigated in the formalWARE project. These systems consist up to a million lines of source code, with the equivalent to millions more in COTS products. The safety engineering view of the software reveals "long thin slices" of hazard-related software. The long thin slice consists of small amount of code in a number of different software components, spread out throughout a software architecture that may consist of hundreds of components.

The long thin slice of hazard-related code must be documented in a concise fashion in the system safety case. Though the developers may be able to locate and understand the slice, others (i.e., system certifiers, maintainers and developers intending to reuse the software) must also be able to identify and analyze the slice. The fact that a simpler representation of the source code is needed is not necessarily an indication of a poor design. It is simply the documentation that others require to conduct an independent safety assessment given the size and complexity of the system.

This paper outlines the steps necessary to create a simpler representation of the critical code for the safety verification case. The representation is created by a refinement of the source code that isolates the relevant code details. Additional work, however, is required to develop more effective techniques and tools for carrying out these steps. In particular, it would be useful to have tools for automating the code expansion and translation. As well, there is a need for more effective tool support for backward searches of the code.

8. Acknowledgments

This paper is a product of research performed in collaboration with Dr. Jeffrey Joyce of Raytheon Systems Canada Ltd. This work was partially supported by B.C. Advanced Systems Institute, Raytheon Systems Canada Ltd. and Macdonald

Dettwiler. This work is a component of the formalWARE university-industrial collaborative project.

9. References

1. John Barnes, "High Integrity Ada The SPARK Examiner Approach", Addison Wesley Longman Ltd, 1997.
2. Gregory T. Daich, Gordon Price, Bryce Raglund, Mark Dawood, "Software Test Technologies Report", Test and Reengineering Tool Evaluation Project, Software Technology Support Center, August 1994.
3. Bruce Elliott and Jim Ronback, "A System Engineering Process For Software-Intensive Real-Time Information Systems, in *Proceedings of the 14th International System Safety Conference*, Albuquerque, New Mexico, August 1996.
4. Tommy Hoffner, "Evaluation and comparison of program slicing tools. Technical Report", LiTH-IDA-R-95-01, Department of Computer and Information Science, Linkping University, Sweden, 1995.
5. Laura M. Ippolito and Dolores Wallace, "A Study on Hazard Analysis in High Integrity Software Standards and Guidelines", NISTIR 5589, National Institute of Standards and Technology, January 1995.
6. International Electrotechnical Commission, *Draft International Standard IEC 1508: Functional Safety: Safety Related Systems*, Geneva, 1995.
7. Philippe B. Krutchen, "The 4+1 View Model of Architecure", *IEEE Software*, November 1995.
8. Danny B. Lange and Yuichi Nakamura, "Object-Oriented Program Tracing and Visualization", *IEEE Computer*, pp 63 -70, May 1997.
9. Nancy G. Leveson, "Safeware: System Safety and Computers", Addison-Wesley, 1995.
10. Nancy G. Leveson, Steven S. Cha, and Timothy J. Shimall, "Safety Verification of Ada Programs using software fault trees", *IEEE Software*, 8(7), pp 48-59, July 1991.
11. "Slicer Tools List", Software Technology Support Center, October 1997.
12. Christopher J. Thompson and Vincent Celier. "DVM: An Object-Oriented Framework for Building Large Distributed Ada Systems", *Proceedings of the TRI-Ada '95 Conference*, ACM, Anaheim, November 6-10, 1995.
13. Jeanette M. Wing, "A Specifier's Introduction to Formal Methods", *IEEE Computer*, 23(9), pp. 8 -22, September 1990.
14. Ken Wong, M.Sc. Thesis, Department of Computer Science, University of British Columbia, 1997.
15. http://www.cs.ubc.ca/formalWARE/
16. Peter G. Bishop and Robin E. Bloomfield, "A Methodology for Safety Case Development", in *Safety-critical Systems Symposium*, Birmingham, UK, February 1998.
17. P. Fenelon, J.A. McDermid, et al., "Towards Integrated Safety Analysis and Design", *ACM Computing Reviews*, 2(1), p. 21-32, 1994.
18. Robyn R. Lutz and Robert M. Woodhouse, "Experience Report: Contributions of SFMEA to Requirements Analysis", in *Proceedings of ICRE'96*, 1996.
19. Francesmary Modugno, Nancy G. Leveson, Jon D. Reese, Kurt Partridge, and Sean D. Sandys, "Integrated Safety Analysis of Requirements Specifications", in *Proceedings of the 3rd International Symposium on Requirements Engineering*, Annapolis, Maryland, January 1997.

The Ravenscar Tasking Profile for High Integrity Real-Time Programs

A. Burns[1], B. Dobbing[2] and G. Romanski[2]

[1] Real-Time Systems Research Group
Department of Computer Science
University of York, UK
[2] Aonix
5040 Shoreham Place
San Diego
CA 92122 USA

Abstract. The Ravenscar profile defines a simple subset of the tasking features of Ada in order to support efficient, high integrity applications that need to be analysed for their timing properties. This paper describes the Profile and gives the motivations for the features it does (and does not) include. An implementation of the profile is then described in terms of development practice and requirements, run-time characteristics, certification, size, testing and scheduling analysis. Support tools are discussed as are the means by which the timing characteristics of the run-time can be obtained. The important issue of enforcing the restrictions imposed by the Ravenscar profile is also addressed.

1 Introduction

High-integrity systems traditionally do not make use of high-level language features such as Ada tasking. This is despite the fact that such systems are inherently concurrent. Concurrency is viewed as a 'systems' issue. It is visible during design and in the construction of the cyclic executive that implements the separate code fragments, but it is not addressed within the software production phases. Notwithstanding this approach, the existence of an extensive range of concurrency features within Ada does allow concurrency to be expressed at the language level with the resulting benefits of having a standard approach that can be analysed and checked by the compiler, and supported by other tools.

The requirement to analyse both the functional and temporal behaviour of high integrity systems imposes a number of restrictions on the concurrency model that can be employed. These restrictions then impact on the language features that are needed to support the model. Typical features of the concurrency model are as follows.

- A fixed number of activities (we shall use the Ada term *task* to denote an independent concurrent activity).

- Each task has a single invocation event, but has a potentially unbounded number of invocations. The invocation event can either be temporal (for a time-triggered task) or a signal from either another task or the environment. A high-integrity application may restrict itself to only time-triggered tasks.
- Tasks only interact via the use of shared data. Updates to any shared data must be atomic.

These constraints furnish a model that can be implemented using fixed priority scheduling (either preemptive or non-preemptive) and analysed in a number of ways:

- The functional behaviour of each task can be verified using the techniques appropriate for sequential code. Shared data is viewed as just environmental input when analysing a task. Timing analysis can ensure that such data is appropriately initialised and temporally valid.
- Following the assignment of temporal attributes to each task (period, deadline, priority etc), the system-wide timing behaviour can be verified using the standard techniques in fixed priority analysis[11, 5].

1.1 Tasking Features

The Ada95 language revision has both increased the complexity of the tasking features and provided the means by which subsets (or profiles) of these features can be defined. To all of the Ada83 features (dynamic task creation, rendezvous, abort) has been added protected objects, ATC (asynchronous transfer of control), task attributes, finalisation, requeue, dynamic priorities and various low-level synchronisation mechanisms. Subsets are facilitated by pragma Restrictions that allows various aspects of the language to be limited in scope or removed from the programmer completely.

Whilst the full language produces an extensive collection of programming aids [3], from which higher-level abstractions can be constructed [6], there are a number of motivations for defining restricted models [2]:

- increasing efficiency by removing features with high overheads
- reduce non-determinancy for safety-critical applications
- simplify run-time kernel for high-integrity applications
- remove features that lack a formal underpinning
- remove features that inhibit effective timing analysis

Of course the necessary restrictions are not confined to the tasking model – but this paper only considers concurrency. To implement a restricted concurrency model in Ada requires only a small selection of the available tasking features. At the Eighth International Real-Time Ada Workshop (1997) the following profile (called the *Ravenscar Profile*) was defined for high-integrity, efficient, real-time systems [1].

2 The Ravenscar Profile

The Ravenscar Profile is defined by the following.

- *Task type and object declarations at the library level* – that is, no hierarchy of tasks, and hence no exit protocols needed from blocks and subprograms.
- *No unchecked deallocation of protected and task objects* – removes the need for dynamic objects.
- *No dynamic allocation of task or protected objects* – removes the need for dynamic objects.
- *Tasks are assumed to be non-terminating* – this is primarily because task termination is generally considered to be an error for a real-time program which is long-running and defines all of its tasks at startup.
- *Library level Protected objects with no entries* – these provide atomic updates to shared data and can be implemented simply.
- *Library level Protected objects with a single entry* – used for invocation signaling; but removes the overheads of a complicated exit protocol.
- *Barrier consisting of a single boolean variable* – no side effects are possible and exit protocol becomes simple.
- *Only a single task may queue on an entry* – hence no queue required; this is a static property that can easily be verified, or it can lead to a bounded error at runtime..
- *No requeue* – leads to complicated protocols, significant overheads and is difficult to analyse (both functionally and temporally).
- *No Abort or ATC* – these features leads to the greatest overhead in the run-time system due to the need to protect data structures against asynchronous task actions.
- *No use of the select statement* – non-deterministic behaviour is difficult to analyse, moreover the existence of protected objects has diminished the importance of the select statement to the tasking model.
- *No use of task entries* – not necessary to program systems that can be analysed; it follows that there is no need for the accept statement.
- *'Delay until' statement but no 'delay' statement* – the absolute form of delay is the correct one to use for constructing periodic tasks.
- *'Real-Time' package* – to gain access to the real-time clock.
- *No Calendar package* – 'Real-Time' package is sufficient.
- *Atomic and volatile pragmas* – needed to enforce the correct use of shared data.
- *Count attribute (but not within entry barriers)* – can be useful for some algorithms and has low overhead.
- Ada.Task_Identification – can be useful for some algorithms and has low overhead, available in reduced form (no Abort_Task or task attribute functions Callable or Terminated)
- *Task discriminants* – can be useful for some algorithms and has low overhead.
- *No user-defined task attributes* – introduces a dynamic feature into the run-time that has complexity and overhead.

- *No use of dynamic priorities* – ensures that the priority assigned at task creation is unchanged during the task's execution, except when the task is executing a protected operation.
- *Protected procedures as interrupt handlers* – required if interrupts are to be handled.

The inclusion of protected entries allows event based scheduling to be used. For many high integrity systems only time triggered actions are employed, hence such entries and their associated interrupt handlers are not required.

The profile defines dispatching to be *FIFO within priority* with protected objects having *Ceiling Locking*. However it also allows a non-preemptive policy to be defined. Cooperative scheduling (that is, non-preemption between well defined system calls such as 'delay until' or the call of a protected object) can reduce the cost of testing as preemption can only occur at well-defined points in the code. It can also reduce the size of the run-time.

With either dispatching policy, the Ravenscar Profile can be supported by a relatively small run-time. It is reasonable to assume that a purpose-built run-time (supporting only the profile) would be efficient and 'certifiable' (i.e. built with the evidence necessary for its use in a certified system). An equivalent run-time for a constrained Ada 83 tasking model has already been used in a certified application[9].

With the profile, each task should be structured as an infinite loop within which is a single invocation event. This is either a call to 'delay until' (for a time triggered task) or a call to a protected entry (for an event triggered task).

The use of the Ravenscar profile allows timing analysis to be extended from just the prediction of the worst-case behaviour of an activity to an accurate estimate of the worst-case behaviour of the entire system. The computational model embodied by the Ravenscar profile is very simple and straightforward. It does not include, for example, the rendezvous or the abort, and hence does not allow control flow between tasks (other than by the release of a task for execution in the event triggered model). But it does enable interfaces between activities (tasks) to be checked by the compiler.

Preemptive execution, in general, leads to increased schedulability and hence is more efficient in the use of system's resources (e.g. CPU time). As preemption can occur at any time, it is not feasible to test all possible preemption points. Rather, it is necessary for the run-time system (RTS) to guarantee that the functional behaviour of a task will not be affected by interrupts or preemption. For a high integrity application evidence to support this guarantee would need to be provided by the compiler vendor (or RTS supplier). For the Ravenscar profile the RTS will be simple and small.

Not only does the use of Ada increase the effectiveness of verification of the concurrency aspects of the application, it also facilitates a more flexible approach to the system's timing requirements. The commonly used cyclic executive approach imposes strict constraints on the range and granularity of periodic activities. The Ravenscar profile will support any range and a fine level of granularity. So, for example, tasks with periods of 50ms and 64ms can be supported together. Moreover, changes to the timing attributes of activities only requires a re-evaluation of the timing analysis. Cyclic executives are hard to maintain and changes can lead to complete reconstruction.

In a control system information may be translated through several stages. Input of sensor data, may be scaled, filtered, used in control law calculations, scaled for output and finally output to a transducer. Safety critical standards e.g. DO-178B 6.4.4.2(a) requires that *"the analysis should confirm the data coupling and control coupling between the code components"*. This has been achieved in the past using cyclic executives which pass data between the code components in strict sequence. With the introduction of more sophisticated sensors, and the requirements to build more responsive systems, the data input and output rates and the rates of the computational processes may not be the same. A natural mapping for such systems is to use tasks with event triggers which enable data to be acquired, processed and output to transducers, at rates which are optimal for each processing step. Events provide a direct link between data and the code used in its processing. The Ravenscar profile facilitates the construction of concurrent programs where the code/data coupling is controlled, defined by the language and checked by the compiler (in contrast to facilities offered by run-time kernels defined independently of the language). The analysis to confirm coupling would be performed by code reviews to show that data is only accessed through synchronised or protected constructs.

Finally, note that the inclusion of a small number of event triggered activities does not fundamentally change the structure of the concurrent program or the timing analysis, but it does impose significant problems for the cyclic executive. Polling for 'events' is a common approach in high integrity systems; but if the 'event' is rare and the deadline for dealing with the event is short then the time triggered approach is very resource intensive. The event triggered approach will work with much less resources.

3 Implementing The Ravenscar Profile

Ada compiler vendor Aonix has undertaken the development of an Ada95 compilation system which implements the Ravenscar profile, known as *Raven*, hosted on Windows NT and Sparc Solaris, and targeting the PowerPC range of processors. This section describes some of the key elements of this implementation.

3.1 Development Practices

The principle goal of the implementation was to develop a runtime system for Ada95 restricted as per the Ravenscar profile, which was suitable for inclusion in:

- A safety-critical application requiring formal certification
- A high-integrity system requiring functional determinism and reliability
- A concurrent real-time system with timing deadlines requiring temporal determinism, eg. schedulability analysis

- A real-time system with execution time constraints requiring high performance
- A real-time system with memory constraints requiring small and deterministic memory usage

Consequently a rigorous set of development practices was enforced based on the traditional software development model, including:

- Documentation of the software requirements
- Definition and documentation of the design to meet these requirements, including traceability
- Formal design reviews
- Formal code walk-throughs of the runtime implementation
- Definition and documentation of the runtime tests to verify correct implementation of the design
- Documentation of the formal verification test results
- Capture of all significant items within a configuration management system

3.2 Requirements

The software requirements include the following elements:

- The runtime design shall support both the preemptive and non-preemptive implementations of the Ravenscar profile.
- The runtime design shall optimise a purely sequential (non-tasking) program by not including any runtime overhead for tasking.
- The design shall structure the runtime such that a library of additional runtime Ada packages which have not undergone formal certification can be supplied as a stand-alone 'extras', for applications which require the extra functionality but not the rigors of certification.
- The runtime algorithms shall be coded such that the worst case execution time is deterministic and as short as possible
- The runtime algorithms shall be coded such that the average case execution time is as short as possible
- The runtime algorithms shall be coded so as to minimise the use of global data, and so as not to acquire memory dynamically. (The total global memory requirement of the runtime system shall be small and deterministic.)
- The runtime algorithms shall be coded so as to conform to the certification coding standards
- The runtime algorithms shall be coded so as to conform to the Ravenscar profile plus sequential code restrictions
- A coverage analysis tool shall be provided for certification purposes
- A schedulability analyser shall be provided which supports standard algorithms used in fixed-priority timing analysis.
- Enforcement of the Ravenscar profile, plus other restrictions on sequential constructs, shall be performed at compile-time wherever possible. (This eliminates runtime code to perform the checks, and the risk of runtime exceptions being raised in the event of check failure.)

- The compilation system tools shall be verified using the Ada Compiler Validation Capability (ACVC) test suite, by coupling the tools to an alternate runtime system for the same target processor family, and which supports full Ada95. Runtime algorithms which are common to the Raven runtime and the alternate runtime shall also be verified in this way.
- The runtime kernel shall be verified using the verification tests written to validate the correct implementation of the requirements.

3.3 Design Considerations

Enforcing the Restrictions The Ravenscar profile restrictions apply only to the concurrency model. It was therefore necessary first to define the additional restrictions that apply to sequential code. These are not defined in this paper, but in essence they follow the same goals of ensuring deterministic execution, simplifying the runtime support, and eliminating constructs with high overhead.

The requirement of enforcing as many restrictions as possible at compile time was met using the Ada95 pragma **Restrictions** [RM section 13.12]. A few of the needed restrictions were already defined using standard restriction identifiers in RM sections D.7 and H.4. However, most of the restrictions required new (implementation-defined) identifiers. It is expected that if the Ravenscar profile is included in the set of language features supported by the ISO Annex H Rapporteur Group, then a standard set of restriction identifiers covering the profile will be defined at that point in time. Within the Raven implementation, the set of needed restriction pragmas are supplied in source form to facilitate compilation into the Ada program library as configuration pragmas.

A compiler that enforces a subset to satisfy safety requirements needs to be carefully constructed. The compilation algorithms should not be changed to implement a particular subset, thereby preserving the value of its maturity and testing, including ACVC validation. This is an important means of raising the trust in the correctness of the toolset being used. Instead, the changes to generate the subset compiler are confined to reporting on violations of the subset in response to the presence of pragma Restrictions.

Two of the Ravenscar profile restrictions are enforced at runtime:

1. Violation of **No_Task_Termination** is classed as a bounded error which is defined to cause permanent suspension of the task. A mechanism to invoke a user-written handler for this situation is provided, which gives a hook for the application to apply remedial action.
2. Violation of **Max_Entry_Queue_Depth=1** is a runtime check since the implementation has chosen not to restrict each protected entry to having only one statically determinable calling task, in keeping with the corresponding model which Ada95 uses for Suspension Objects [RM section D.10(10)]. Consequently violation of this restriction results in **Program_Error** exception being raised.

Runtime system code which processes bounded error conditions or raises exceptions when a restriction is violated, known as deactivated code (not dead code), is not excluded from certification considerations. DO-178B states [8] that the "software planning process should describe how the deactivated code will be defined, verified and handled to achieve system safety objectives." [DO-178B section 4.2(h)]. Coverage testing of this deactivated code is also required by DO-178B: "... additional test cases and test procedures (should be) developed to satisfy the required coverage objectives." [DO-178B section 6.4.4.3(h)]. Thus the level of trust of this error handling code is the same as that of the remainder of the runtime system.

Compilation Unit Closures The requirements for there to be no runtime overhead due to tasking in a purely sequential (non-tasking) program, and that a non-certifiable library of packages be available stand-alone, providing Ada features beyond the basic kernel functionality, are met using coding conventions regarding closures of library units, as regulated by the use of Ada context ('with') clauses.

Three runtime unit closures are defined: for the sequential program kernel, for the tasking program kernel, and for the 'extras' packages. The coding standards are such that the sequential kernel units are not allowed to 'with' tasking kernel units, and neither the sequential nor the tasking kernel units are allowed to 'with' 'extras' units. Thus the separation of concerns (sequential versus tasking and certifiable versus not-certifiable) is enforced by the compiler using Ada semantics.

Other Runtime Constraints The principle requirements governing the style of coding to be used for the runtime system are highly compatible and complementary, leadin to algorithms which are small, easy to understand, and functionally and temporally deterministic, coupled with use of simple static data structures.

Certifiability The requirements for certifiability impinge on the source code by means of specifying fixed format header comments for compilation units and all subprograms. The information in these headers includes:

- Overview of purpose or functionality
- Requirement(s) which are met
- Detailed definition of global data / parameter usage
- Detailed definition of algorithm

This description is checked against the actual code during walk-through audits, and is used to verify that the implementation conforms to the design, and that the design fully meets the requirements.

Performance Several techniques are used to improve performance of the runtime. Simple and very short runtime subprograms can be defined as having calling convention *Intrinsic*, which means that their code is built into the compiler and is used directly in place of the call. Typically this is used for immutable code sequences such as arithmetic and relational operators for types such as Time and Time_Span in package Ada.Real_Time [RM section D.8] and for highly time critical simple operations such as getting the identity of the currently-executing task.

Other short subprograms can be defined as being *inlined* [RM section 6.3.2], which gives similar performance gain by avoiding the procedure call and return overhead, but without having to actually build the generated assembler code into the compiler code generator.

In addition, since the runtime code itself must abide by the restricted Ada subset, this automatically excludes use of non-deterministic and dynamic constructs, plus those with high execution overhead or code size. Thus the code is written using simple Ada constructs which translate to equivalently simple assembler code, making it fast to execute, easy to verify, readable and maintainable.

Worst Case Execution Time In order to perform accurate schedulability analysis, it is necessary to input the runtime execution overhead[10, 4]. For hard real-time systems, in which the failure to meet a hard timing deadline is catastrophic to the entire system, worst case execution times are generally used in the computations. The user can generally either analyse the Ada code[7] or measure the worst case time for application code using tests that exercise the various code paths, but for the runtime system operations, the user has no direct way of knowing which scenario will produce the worst case time, unless the runtime source code is available and also documentation to describe the criteria which determine the execution path at each decision point.

Thus for every runtime operation with variable execution time, or whose operation can include a voluntary context switch, the vendor must provide metrics which typically define the worst case execution time either as an absolute number of clock cycles or as a formula based on application-specific data (e.g. number of tasks). For the runtime tasking kernel implementing the Ravenscar profile, this set of metrics will include:

- Entry and exit times for protected operations, including entry calls and barrier evaluation
- Entry and exit times for processing of the delay until statement
- Timer interrupt and user interrupt overheads
- Rescheduling times, such as the time to select a new task to run and the time to perform a context switch

Clearly, this imposes strict constraints on the algorithms used to implement these operations such that their worst case execution time is not overly excessive. For example, use of a linear search proportional to the maximum number of tasks in the program would be unacceptable for a program with a large number of tasks. So, the runtime contains optimisations to minimise critical worst case timings.

Runtime Size The runtime was designed and coded to minimise the size of both the code and the data. For example, an important optimisation in the Ada pre-linker tool (the 'binder') is elimination of uncalled subprograms from the executable image. But this optimisation is only fully effective if the code is structured in a very modular way. For example, the runtime treatment of user-defined interrupt handlers as protected procedures should not be included in the executable image if interrupts are not used by the program. A more extreme example of this is the requirement that no code or data which is specific to the tasking kernel should be included in the image if the program does not use tasking.

In addition to this, the coding of the runtime data and algorithms was carefully crafted to optimise on speed and space, taking advantage of the various optimisations supported by the compiler.

Regarding data usage, the runtime does not make any use of dynamically-acquired memory, which is also a restriction on the sequential code of the application, thereby eliminating the need to support a heap with its associated non-determinism during allocation. The global data which is used is as small as possible, exploiting packing of data except where poor-quality code would be generated to access it. The data is packaged so that it is eliminated if the feature that it supports is not used (eg. the interrupt handling table is eliminated when there are no interrupts in the program). The major component of the runtime data is the stack and Task Control Block (TCB) which is required for each task's execution. Each application program is required to declare the memory areas to be used for the stacks and TCBs in the Board Support Package. This provides a simple interface to tune the stack sizes to the worst case values, whilst also giving full application-level determinism on the amount of storage which is reserved for this purpose.

3.4 Additional Supporting Tools

The additional tools which have been included in the implementation to support certification and schedulability analysis include:

- Condition code and Coverage Analysis tool
- Schedulability Analyser and Scheduler Simulation tool

Coverage Analysis (AdaCover) Under the DO-178B guidelines [8], it is necessary to perform coverage analysis to show that all the object code (both the application program part and the Ada runtime system) has been executed, including all possible outcomes of conditions, by the verification tests. The entire runtime system is subjected to coverage analysis as part of its auditing process. For the user application code, the tool AdaCover is provided to assist in formal certification.

AdaCover is in two logical parts:

1. A target-resident monitor which records the execution of every instruction in the program, including the results of every decision point

2. A host-resident tool which annotates the compiler-generated assembly code listings with the results of stage 1, thereby providing the user with a report of coverage at either the object code or source code level, for the set of executed verification tests

Schedulability Analysis (PerfoRMAx) The PerfoRMAx tool embodies classic schedulability analyser and scheduler simulation functionality. Given a definition of the actions performed by the tasks in the application in terms of their priority, execution time, period and interaction with shared resources, plus certain runtime system overhead times, the tool performs analysis of the schedulability of the task set based on a user-selectable scheduling theory, for example Rate Monotonic Analysis (RMA)[11].

The tool is also able to provide a graphical view of the processor load based on a static simulation of the scheduling of the tasks by the runtime system, thereby giving clear indication of potential regions of unschedulability. If such regions exist, the tool outputs messages highlighting the cause of the unschedulability together with suggestions for corrective action.

3.5 Testing

The testing activity is split into two components:

- Use of the ACVC test suite to verify the validation status of the compiler, binder and code generator support routines
- Development of a specific test suite to certification level for the Raven runtime.

ACVC Testing Since a substantial number of ACVC tests violate Ravenscar profile restrictions, particularly relating to the tasking tests, it is not possible under current rules to validate such a subset. However by use of the same compilation system tools linked to a full Ada95 runtime system for the same target processor family, it is possible to run the full ACVC suite, thereby validating the correctness of the compiler, binder and common code generator support routines (eg. block move). The validated compiler contains all the processing to treat pragma Restrictions, but since the tests do not include these pragmas in the source code, no enforcement of the subset is performed and hence all the tests can execute.

Certification Tests A test suite has been created to verify the correctness of the kernel runtime subprograms, thereby complementing the ACVC testing (which was not able to test these), whilst also ensuring the level of reliability specified by the requirements.

Each test contains a header in the source code which includes:

- Identification of the requirement to be tested
- Identification of the runtime module under test

- Test description
- Test case definition, including inputs and expected results

The results of executing the tests against each baseline development of the runtime system are documented.

3.6 Packaging

When the Raven product is purchased, an option is available to purchase separately all the material required for formal certification. This option includes:

- Full runtime source code
- Full development documentation which is relevant to certification
- Full test pack, including sources, scripts and documentation, so that the tests can be re-executed on the runtime code during formal certification of an application.

4 Conclusion

This paper has described the Ravenscar profile, a subset of Ada95 tasking intended to model concurrency in safety-critical, high-integrity, and general real-time systems. The use of a powerful, structured, and highly-checked language such as Ada is vitally important in all market sectors demanding high reliability and efficiency.

The paper has also described a commercial-off-the-shelf implementation of the profile for the PowerPC processor family which has proved the feasibility of developing production-quality tool support and a certification-quality runtime system for the Ravenscar profile.

On-going work within the International Standards Organisation Working Group 9 exists to incorporate the profile concepts within the recommendations on the use of Ada in high integrity systems.

References

1. T. Baker and T. Vardanega. Session summary: Tasking profiles. In A.J. Wellings, editor, *Proceedings of the 8th International Real-Time Ada Workshop*, pages 5–7. ACM Ada Letters, 1997.
2. A. Burns and A.J. Welling. Restricted tasking models. In A.J. Wellings, editor, *Proceedings of the 8th International Real-Time Ada Workshop*, pages 27–32. ACM Ada Letters, 1997.
3. A. Burns and A. J. Wellings. *Concurrency in Ada*. Cambridge University Press, 1995.
4. A. Burns and A. J. Wellings. Safety kernels: Specification and implementation. *High Integrity Systems*, 1(3):287–300, 1995.
5. A. Burns and A. J. Wellings. *Real-Time Systems and Programming Languages:*. Addison Wesley, 2nd edition, 1996.

6. A. Burns and A.J. Wellings. Ada 95: An effective concurrent programming language. In Alfred Strohmeier, editor, *Proceedings of Reliable Software Technologies - Ada-Europe '96*, pages 58–77. Springer-Verlag Lecture Notes in Computer Science, Vol 1088, 1996.
7. R. Chapman, A. Burns, and A.J. Wellings. Combining static worst-case timing analysis and program proof. *Real-Time Systems*, 11(2):145–171, September 1996.
8. *Software Considerations in Airborne Systems and Equipment Certification DO-178B/ED-12B*. RTCA, December 1992.
9. B. Dobbing and M. Richard-Foy. T-SMART - task-safe, minimal Ada realtime toolset. In A.J. Wellings, editor, *Proceedings of the 8th International Real-Time Ada Workshop*, pages 45–50. ACM Ada Letters, 1997.
10. D.I. Katcher, H. Arakawa, and J.K. Strosnider. Engineering and analysis of fixed priority schedulers. *IEEE Trans. Softw. Eng.*, 19, 1993.
11. M. H. Klein, T. A. Ralya, B. Pollak, R. Obenza, and M. G. Harbour. *A Practitioner's Handbook for Real-Time Analysis: A Guide to Rate Monotonic Analysis for Real-Time Systems*. Kluwer Academic Publishers, 1993.

Guidance on the Use of Ada95 in High Integrity Systems

Steve Michell[1] and Mark Saaltink[2]

[1] Maurya Software, 29 Maurya Court, Ottawa, Ontario K1G 5S3, Canada
steve@maurya.on.ca
[2] ORA Canada, 1208-1 Nicholas St., Ottawa, Ontario, K1N 7B7, Canada
mark@ora.on.ca

Abstract. In this paper we discuss our guidance on the suitability of Ada95 for high integrity systems.
Keywords: Ada, critical systems, high integrity systems, predictable systems, HRG.

1 Introduction

High Integrity Systems, including critical systems and secure systems, are among the most demanding and expensive software development activities. Developers are faced with very high reliability requirements, stiff regulatory constraints, and personal or corporate liabilities. In response, developers apply stringent software engineering practices to design, develop, analyse, and test their systems. Because of its support for software engineering, Ada(83) has been used successfully in the development of a number of critical systems. Various approaches, including strict subsets, redundancy, code tracing, and specialized compilers, have been used.

Ada(95) [1] offers new opportunities and presents some new problems. In this paper we discuss our analysis of Ada95 as a candidate language for use in critical systems.

This paper is a report of the completion of a study done for the Canadian Department of National Defence. A paper [6] given earlier provided the framework which we used to perform the analysis, and some early results of the analysis phase. This paper gives details of the analysis that was done and the guidance on the use of Ada in high integrity systems that was developed, and discusses the use of formal Ada95 subsets for these systems.

2 The Problem

By a "critical application," we mean an application whose failure could lead to loss of life, physical injury or other untenable losses such as financial resources or privacy[1]. Consequently, critical applications must be developed to the highest

---

[1] We include both safety-critical and security-critical systems in our definition.

scientific and engineering practices. In particular, there must be solid scientific and engineering evidence that a critical application will behave in a predictable manner, and will satisfy formally-specified requirements.

Ada's support for software engineering features, support for embedded systems, and mandates by numerous organizations intent upon software engineering practices make the use of Ada for High Integrity Systems appropriate.

There are significant areas of concern with the use of any general purpose programming language for the implementation of high integrity systems. For Ada, these concerns centre on the complexity of the language and the predictability of code generated by different compilation systems. For Ada83, these concerns resulted in various groups developing subsets of Ada(83) to reduce complexity and to achieve predictability [12, 4].

Ada(95), introduces new problems and opportunities to the development of Critical Systems. It adds new programming paradigms, and therefore complexity; removes irregularities from Ada83; introduces new ways to interface to other Ada subsystems; and introduces new ways to interface to other language systems. These changes invalidated old analyses done for the Ada subsets mentioned above. The language changes and addition of new language constructs require reanalysis be done to determine Ada's suitability for this challenging environment.

One of the challenges of this research was to determine the need for a high integrity subset for Ada95. Several subsets had been developed for Ada83, such as SPARK, [12] AVA [4] and Penelope [10]. An open issue was the need to revalidate one of these subsets, develop a new subset, or develop a new approach. No matter what approach was taken, we had to determine what role the Ada95 pragma Restrictions and special needs annexes would play in this effort.

3   Ada95 Trustworthiness Study

This paper and the three documents from this project were the result of an "Ada95 Trustworthiness Study" funded by the Canadian Department of National Defence. Dan Craigen, ORA Canada, was a major participant in the development of the initial framework document and setting the parameters for this work. The main deliverable of our project is a document providing guidance on the use Ada95 for the development of the highest integrity applications. The project was assisted by members of the HRG, members of WG9, DND personnel, and critical-software experts at large through our electronic distribution and comment process. All documents and analysis are available on ORA Canada's Web site www.ora.on.ca.

The trustworthiness study had three phases: framework, language analysis, and recommendations. In the framework phase, we synthesized the critical software issues from some of the most significant standards for high integrity systems: DO-178B [8]; 00-55 [13]; and the Canadian Trusted Computer Product Evaluation Criteria [7]. From these documents we developed the requirements for Predictability, Analysability, Traceability, and Engineering. To achieve these goals, we then developed a framework containing ten criteria with which we believed that we could analyse Ada language features against.

In the language analysis phase, we analysed the Ada Reference Manual (ARM) section by section, analysing each language feature in the ten areas determined in the framework phase.

In the recommendations phase, we used the analysis done in the previous phase as well as software engineering approaches to develop guidelines for the use of Ada95 in the development of software for high integrity systems.

4 Analysis

Language features affect each other in ways that can make a feature better or worse in some of the contexts that we considered. These interactions may lead to the generation of unusually complex code for a program, may improve or reduce suport for various forms of analysis, or may change the underlying model. Any analysis must consider a language feature as devoid of interactions as possible, but also must consider what happens as features interact.

In the Analysis phase, we considered each feature and interaction in the context of the compiler technologies, models and proof technologies, static analysis technologies and dynamic analysis technologies that are currently available or on the immediate horizon. For example, we assumed that at least one ASIS (the Ada Semantic Interface Specification) [3] compliant compiler was available so that compiler analysis of the program was available to tools, even though ASIS is not yet standardized.

In order to fully rate a language feature, we considered it first with the tightest set of constraints that would give it the best ratings in the categories that we assigned. We then considered one or more alternatives where other language features (if used) would reduce our ratings. Because there could be many feature interactions, we often had to iterate the process of adding feature interactions and considering the effects.

Although the analysis was done to eventually develop the guidance for the highest integrity systems, we see the document as a living document and useful in its own right. Many high integrity software development projects will not have requirements that exactly match our assumptions. They may be developing to reduced levels of criticallity, or they may put less emphasis on some analysis methods. Furthermore, Ada95 changes slightly as WG9/ARG corrects deficiencies, and analysis technologies improve. Because of these differences, projects will often have to consider their needs in the light of additional factors. Such projects will need to review the analysis that was done and evaluate their needs in light of this analysis and the new conditions. They will also sometimes need to extend or reanalyse some portions in light of their needs.

To help understand the analysis process, we include some of the analysis that was done on arrays, and tagged types. In the next section we show the guidance that was developed from these analyses.

4.1 Feature: Arrays ARM Section 3.6

General Comments:

Arrays can be defined in anonymous type definitions with no constraints, with static constraints, and with dynamically computed constraints. In addition, they can be defined with constraints or aliases on the base type. Representation clauses ('size, 'component_size) may be applied to an array type definition. Arrays defined without explicit range constraints may not be statically sized, meaning that run-time memory allocation must be performed. Arrays defined with dynamic range constraints may be allocated within the procedure stack frame, but the amount of memory to allocate cannot be statically determined. Some implementations may use dynamic (heap) memory to allocate such arrays.

An array definition may also be a subtype of an earlier array type definition plus the (optional) inclusion of subranges.

Variant 1: Simple Case

Constraints: no unconstrained arrays; no dynamic ranges; no user-defined representation specifications; array not aliased; component not aliased.

Ratings:

Category	Rating	Comments
Run-time Support	None/Minor	
Functional Predictability	Exact	
Timing Predictability	Tightly Bounded	
Storage Usage Predictability	Exact	
Formal Definition	Existing Definition	SPARK, AVA, Penelope
Integrity and Security Issues	Enhances	Strongly typed, statically defined arrays leave almost no room for security problems.
Reliability/Engineering Support	Enhances	Work well with "for" loops, ranged subtypes, etc.
Robustness	Neutral	
Static Analysis	Tractable Analysis	
Dynamic Analysis	Neutral	

Variant: 5. Complex Case - Aliased Components of arrays

Additional Explanation: Aliased components of arrays may create special difficulties, especially when used with packed arrays, or with arrays where size or component_size has been used. The type definition for the access type expects to find an element laid out in memory in a "normal" fashion. Aliased components may be packed in ways other than that expected by the access type. This is certainly true when user-specified packing or sizes have been specified.

Ratings:

Category	Rating	Comments
Functional Predictability	Unpredictable	
Formal Definition	Unknown	
Robustness	Hinders	The use of aliased components of an array introduces possible inconsistencies between the view of an object as array element or as an aliased object

4.2 Tagged types ARM Section 3.9

There are some significant issues in the use of Ada's tagged types. We enumerate the various issues here, then we shall attempt to rate these issues below.

Class-wide Access Types To date, we do not know of any formal models of type extension and dispatching that apply to Ada's model, or close enough that we can see how such a model would be developed for Ada.

We have identified at least three significant problems with the OOP dispatching model as designed into Ada:

1. Intractability of Static Analysis. To statically analyse a module, it is imperative that the number of paths to be analysed be kept to a reasonable number. Any activity which forces us to consider transfers outside of the immediate scope increases the number of possible paths significantly. Dispatching operations, and functional programming, create N possible transfers out of an immediate scope for each class-wide object with N derived or extended types. Local analysis is not possible. Must have text of complete system. Contract model doesn't constrain enough "stuff" to limit static analysis: must revert to global reanalysis each time a new derivation is added.

2. Potential Insecurities. The basic model of object-oriented programming is that you extend a type and replace the primitive operations for that type. When an object is processed in a list, the implementation determines the basic type of the object, and transfers to the subprogram associated with that type definition. It is impossible to tell, however, from the code that calls the subprogram, which variant will be actually called at run time. All one knows is that one of the derivatives or extensions of that subprogram will be invoked. It thus becomes possible for someone to replace existing lists of objects with capricious objects, without the replacement being visible in the "executable" code. (Such set-up could be done, for example, in the elaboration code of child packages.) Static analysis, coding standards and management practices can prevent "inappropriate" addition of undesirable packages, but it cannot be done with language rules alone.

Note: This problem exists in every OOP language - not just Ada.

3. When generics and tagged types are combined to form "mixins" - a form of multiple inheritance - there are ways in which inherited operations can silently be replaced for derived types related to (but no directly descended from) the generic type.

Class_Wide and Access_to_Class_Wide types Class_Wide types passed as a parameter to a dispatchable subprogram is the mechanism to promote dispatching. If one wanted to eliminate dynamic dispatching from a system, one may try to do this by banning class_wide types. There is a fundamental approach in this technique because class_wide types and Access_class_wide types are the only mechanisms to produce heterogenous lists, and to promote extensible records. With access_class_wide types, an object of a type extended from a tagged type can automatically be placed on lists along with the parent.

Another approach to eliminating dispatching from subprograms is to place type'class in the parameter profiles instead of the "type". This will force all calls to be direct, instead of dispatching. This cannot eliminate all dispatching, however, as the primitive "=" operation will still dispatch.

Analysis of Variant: 1. Simple Case

Constraints: All type extensions occur in the same package specification or in subpackages of the ultimate parent's package specification; no discriminants; the tagged type is not part of a private declarations; no generic instantiations of the type; no aliased components; no controlled types; no rep clauses; no abstract subprograms; and no default initialization.

Ratings:

Category	Rating	Comments
Run-time Support	None/Minor	
Functional Predictability	Exact	
Timing Predictability	Loosely Bounded	
Storage Usage Predictability	Exact	
	Worst Case Analysis	
Formal Definition	Potentially Definable	
Integrity and Security Issues	Hinders	
Static Analysis	Tractable Analysis	
Dynamic Analysis	Neutral	
	Hinders	

Variant: 2. Complex Case

Additional Explanation: The permission to extend tagged types outside the package containing the root type means that analytical programs must process the complete program code to find all extensions of a type. In general this is an intractable problem.

Constraints: Extensions permitted outside same package spec as base type; no discriminants; type is not part of a private declarations; no generic instantiations of the type; no aliased components; no controlled types; no rep clauses; no abstract subprograms; and no default initialization.

Ratings:

Category	Rating	Comments
Static Analysis	Hard/Intractable	See discussion above
Integrity & Security Issues	Hinders	See discussion above

5 Guidance

After the Analysis phase we revisited the Ada95 subset issue. One logical choice was to develop an officially-sanctioned subset for high integrity systems. We rejected this approach for several reasons:

- A subset would depend on the methods of analysis to be done for the project. Other high integrity projects may use different criteria that would lead to different results, and find that our subset was inappropriate;
- There are features that are individually necessary but which should not be used together (e.g., arrays and access types). A safe subset would need to include one and exclude the other; guidance can leave the choice up to the project.
- The needs of different levels of criticality should be considered and addressed if possible;
- A subset reflects a snapshot of the technology when the subset was developed, making it less relevant as technology progresses; and
- There is an antagonism against subsets within the Ada community.

We opted instead to provide guidance on the use of individual language constructs, to show how features interact, and to show how a project or implementation could restrict usage, and what the expected effects would be.

The final product of this study is a synthesis of the analysis performed and engineering and software development. Section 5 of the document follows the ARM sections and subsections (e.g., section 5.3.3 discusses ARM 3.3). In each subsection we discuss the language feature, its applicability to high integrity software, restrictions that need to observed in the use of that feature in the highest integrity software, and alternate constructs and workarounds as applicable.

Two of the major contributions of this document are the traceability to the underlying analysis performed by these documents, and the analysis of Annex H and enforcement techniques available. The traceability to the analysis is important because clients may need to deviate from these recommendations. It then becomes crucial to understand the underlying rationale. Since all recommendations cross-refer to our analysis—right down to the case number—this analysis can be readily revisited. To assist, we also have a hypertext version of all documents commercially available.

It is impossible in a paper of this size to provide the full set of recommendations for Ada95 for high integrity systems. Each constraint has includes the analysis context, a rationale and a discussion of workarounds. This context is needed to understand the constraint and stay away from the "subset" mentality. We present below a synopsys of the guidance on two language features that we showed the analysis for above.

5.1 Array Types

Our analysis showed that Ada95's array definition is very usable and appropriate in high integrity systems in general. There are some langague interactions which necessitate care in the use of arrays. The following is an excerpt from the guidance document on the use of arrays.

Restrictions in High Integrity Systems Avoid arrays with aliased components and representation clauses Analysis Report, B.3.6(variant 5), B.13.2, and 3. It is possible that arrays with aliased components will be used in high integrity systems, together with general access types to implement storage pools. Do not place any other representations on such arrays, or their components, as it may become impossible to satisfy the conflicting requirements. This restriction could be checked by a tool or by code reviews.

Avoid the declaration of array objects with bounds that are known only at run time, i.e., arrays with bounds that are not explicitly declared named numbers, or numeric literals Analysis Report B.3.6 (variant 2). Pragma Restrictions (No_Implicit_Heap_Allocation) will cause the compiler to reject any use of this construct if it requires dynamic storage allocation. Even if dynamic storage is not used, storage requirements may be difficult to predict and may vary between implementations.

It is permissible (but not recommended) to define formal parameters of an unconstrained array type, provided that the parameter is **in out** or **out**, that no explicit subtype conversions occur as part of the call or the call return, and that there are no function returns of unconstrained arrays. Caution is advised when such a formal parameter array is manipulated as a whole, as some implementations may use temporary objects of the array subtype (which would have an unknown size at compile-time and require dynamic storage) Analysis Report, B.6.4.1 (variant 2), B.6.5 (variant 3). Pragma Restrictions (No_Implicit_Heap_Allocation) will cause the compiler to reject any use of this construct if it requires dynamic storage allocation.

Alternate Constructs and Workarounds A. Arrays with Nonstatic Bounds - Arrays with nonstatic bounds can be declared as types in any Ada95 declarative statement. Such a type could be an array with an unconstrained type as the index, or could be a constrained array where the bounds are not static. Objects of either type are not permitted under the restrictions imposed. The most effective workaround is to declare a record containing the array of the maximal size needed, and two variables to contain the bounds of the actual data. Such an object is a bounded array.

B. Aliased Arrays - Since dynamic memory is prohibited in the highest integrity systems, developers must use arrays to hold and manage collections of data. If the algorithms of the data use generalized access types, the array elements will be aliased. If arrays are used in this way, the array itself, and all subcomponents of the array, must not contain any other representation clauses (such as 'size, 'alignment, or pragma Pack).

C. Assignment of Arrays - Assignment of one array object to another array object may occur only if the arrays themselves are statically matching, i.e., that they are both statically constrained to the same bounds, have components of the same base type, and have the same representation for the components. If any of these conditions do not hold, then the array must be copied component-wise.

5.2 Tagged Types and Type Extensions

The following is an excerpt from our guidance document on Ada's tagged types.

Tagged types are Ada95's approach to extensible data types and dispatching subprograms, otherwise known as Object Oriented Programming (OOP). Ada95 separates the extensibility and the dispatching, which gives us the ability to analyse each separately.

The full OOP model, complete with type extension and primitive subprogram replacement in user code is not recommended for use in the implementation of high integrity systems. The lack of a formal model and intractability of static analysis make the full paradigm unsuitable for these high integrity systems, at least until appropriate models can be developed and validated, and possibly until analytical models and tools are developed that are tractable.

Limited usage of the OOP model is possible, as described below.

Type Extensions Tagged types, together with class-wide access values and subprogram parameters, provide the capability to build heterogeneous lists of objects with dispatching primitive subprograms. Tagged types also provide an alternative to variant records (although there is no direct analogue of an object that can hold different variants at different times).

Restrictions in High Integrity Systems All type extensions must occur in the same unit as the original parent type was defined, and in one of its subunits; i.e., avoid the extension of types in child packages, or packages that depend on the package that declares the parent type [Analysis Report, B.3.9 (variant 2)]. This restriction could be checked by a tool or by code reviews.

It is permissible to extend a type in a package that is a direct subunit (but not a child library unit) of the package that declares the parent, even if that unit is compiled separately.

Avoid the use of functions that return tagged types, unless it can be statically shown that the return type of the function is the same as the target type [Analysis Report, B.6.5 (variant 5)]. This restriction can be checked by code reviews, or possibly by formal analysis.

Alternate Constructs and Workarounds It is sometimes possible to write a normal record that contains a "parent" component, and to define non-dispatching procedures that call corresponding procedures on the "parent" field as appropriate. This is not always as convenient as extending a tagged type, but may be more easily analysed.

Dispatching Operations of Tagged Types Subprograms having a parameter of a tagged type and declared in the same package specification as the tagged type are "primitive subprograms" of the type, and can be dispatching. Such a subprogram having a parameter of tagged type T can be called with a parameter of type T'Class; in this case, the actual subprogram body called is determined by the tag of the parameter.

Ada95's dispatching mechanism offers the writer the choice of early or late binding; a call to a primitive procedure can be resolved at compile-time or the parameter can be class-wide and the call resolved at run-time.

Tagged types can also be used without dispatching. This non-dispatching usage is accomplished by making all primitive subprograms parameterized by type'class. Caution is urged, however, because equality, assignment and attributes are always dispatching for tagged types.

Applicability to High Integrity Systems Tagged types and dispatching operations provide an alternative to variant records, with the advantage that new "variants" can be added without modifying existing subprograms.

Restrictions in High Integrity Systems The prohibition of type extension outside the unit that declares the ultimate ancestor of the type also prohibits the declaration of primitive (hence dispatching) subprograms outside this context. This restriction eliminates the anomalies associated with unknown overridden dispatching operations, tractable analysis difficulties associated with uncontrolled type extension and operator overriding, and potential insecurities.

Avoid the use of private primitive subprograms for tagged types that are not also declared private. A more complete discussion is in Section 5.7.3.3 (of the guidance document).

Pragma Restrictions (No_Dispatching) prevents dispatching calls entirely.

6 Choosing and Enforcing Restrictions

The guidance document was written to provide guidance on the use of Ada95 in the highest levels of critical systems. The guidance provided and severe nature of many of the recommendations, such as no use of dynamic memory techniques, may be relaxed somewhat as the need for absolute predictability in system behaviour is reduced. The set of language features that may be used will lie somewhere between the full language, which could be used in the lowest levels of criticality, and the narrow set recommended here for the highest levels.

The recommended process for the handling of this analysis is:

- After careful review of the requirements for the system to be built, determine what the expectations are in terms of "predictability," "analysability," "traceability," and "engineering."
- Review the categories and ratings, and attempt to determine what ratings will be tolerated in each of the categories. For example, a rating of "intractable" for static analysis may be tolerated if no static analysis of the source code is to be done.
- Start with the restrictions imposed in the guidance document.
- Review the raw ratings from the analysis document for other language features to determine how it was rated, and read the discussion in this document to see why these restrictions were imposed.
- Change the restrictions to match the needs of the project and the criticality level that governs the development.

For example, consider access types and objects. For the highest levels of criticality, we have banned all dynamic objects (by prohibiting allocators and access types), and recommended that generalized access values (access all) designate only objects declared immediately in the same scope as the generalized access type. The restriction on normal access types and allocators is based on the dangers of exhausting or fragmenting dynamic storage, and on the difficulty of data-use analysis if access types are used indiscriminately; the restrictions on generalized access types are based only on the data-use analysis considerations. For less critical systems, a project may decide to add annotations to help data-use analysis, or may not perform this analysis at all. The project may therefore permit a more open use of generalized access types but still prohibit allocators and conventional access types.

6.1 Enforcement

The guidance document contains a detailed description of the ways in which its suggested restrictions can be checked or enforced. Three mechanisms are possible: language-defined pragmas or restrictions; implementation-defined pragmas or restrictions; and source tools that ensure that a given syntax is not used, or is used only in a limited way.

Annex H of the ARM specifies a set of pragmas and restrictions that can be applied to a program to make it more suitable for high integrity systems. Several of these restrictions are in complete agreement with those suggested by our analysis, and thus provide a mechanism for enforcement. For example, the Annex H restriction No_Implicit_Heap_Allocation forbids language constructs that require dynamic (heap) storage techniques for that implementation. The Guidance document recommends avoiding any use of dynamically managed storage. Because this restriction is implementation-dependent, one cannot classify those constructs that would be prohibited in a language-based document, and any enforcement tool needs intimate knowledge of the language implementation.

Use of this restriction might have the effect of permitting more language constructs (such as string function return values) than would be allowed by the general ratings of the feature in this document.

This restriction does not apply to explicit use of dynamic storage using the new operator. Such use can be prohibited by the Annex H restriction No_Allocators.

Not all of the recommended restrictions are enforcable with Ada's language-defined restrictions. For example, the Guidance document specifies the restrictions on the use of representation clauses when some of the components are designated "aliased". There is no standard pragma or restriction to enforce this prohibition. The prohibition must therefore be checked with additional static analysis, or with implementation-dependent restrictions. In this case, the necessary code analysis is not difficult or intractible.

Some restrictions are, in the general case, not checkable by a simple code analysis unless the code is augmented by assertions. For example, there are many forms of aliasing possible in Ada95, such as by "renames", aliased variables, generic in-out parameters and subprogram parameters. There is no set of Annex H restrictions that will eliminate the potential aliasing issues, so other static or dynamic checks are required.

7 Other Work

The Safety and Security Rapporteur Group (HRG) of ISO-IEC/JTC1/SC22/ WG9 Ada Working Group was a significant partner in our research. Their review, suggestions and technical contributions were invaluable in the preparation of these documents. The HRG is in the process of developing an ISO technical report on the use of Ada95 in High Integrity Systems, which is using much of the results described here and extending it to add new knowledge as it becomes available.

The United States Nuclear Regulatory Commission has developed a report on the use of many languages in Critical Systems [9]. The work on Ada95 makes extensive use of the first version of our guidance. There appear to be inconsistencies between the treatment of various languages in this report—probably reflecting different authorship of the sections on each language. These inconsistencies lead to results such as a harsh treatment of access types for Ada95, but an acceptance of pointers in C/C++, which are much less safe.

The Ravenscar tasking model for High Integrity Systems was developed at the Eighth Real-Time Ada Workshop in Ravenscar UK in 1997. This was not available in time for our work but is being considered by the HRG for its guidance document.

Various Ada95 vendors are developing their own tools and runtimes for high integrity systems.

8 Conclusion

Ada95 is and should be the language of choice when developing high integrity software on general purpose processors. It is almost certain that a subset of Ada will be used. When this subset is chosen because of analysability and verifiability, and combined with the Ada support for software engineering, it is unlikely that a better choice could be made.

There is no one set of language permissions or restrictions that will be suitable for every program, however. As a project is arriving at its requirements, it is important that management has available thorough analysis and guidance that it can rely on to make its decisions. The documents developed that we discussed in this paper should be of significant assistance in providing this guidance.

References

1. Intermetrics. The Annotated Ada Reference Manual. December 1994.
2. ANSI/ISO/IEC 8652 International Standard. Ada95 Reference Manual, Intermetrics, January 1995.
3. ISO-IEC/JTC1/SC22/WG9 ASIS Rapporteur Group. Ada Semantic Interface Specification DRAFT 2.0 (ASIS).
4. Michael Smith. The AVA Reference Manual. Technical Report 64, Computational Logic Inc., February 1992.
5. Dan Craigen, Mark Saaltink, and Steve Michell. Ada95 Trustworthiness Study: A Framework for Analysis. ORA Canada Report TR-95-5499-02, November 1995.
6. Dan Craigen, Mark Saaltink, and Steve Michell. Ada95 and Critical Systems: An Analytical Approach. Ada Europe, 1997.
7. The Canadian Trusted Computer Product Evaluation Criteria. Canadian System Security Centre, Communications Security Establishment, Government of Canada. Version 3.0e, January 1993.
8. Software Considerations in Airborne Systems and Equipment Certification (DO-178B/-ED-12B). RTCA Inc., Washington, D.C., December 1992.
9. Nuclear Regulatory Commission, NUREG/CR-6463, Rev. 1, Review Guidelines on Software Languages for Use in Nuclear Power Plant Safety Systems. Available as http://www.nrc.gov/NRC/NUREGS/CR6463/index.htm
10. David Guspari et al. Formal Verification of Ada Programs. IEEE Transactions on Software Engineering, Volume 16, Sept 1990.
11. Mark Saaltink and Steve Michell. Ada95 Trustworthiness Study: Analysis of Ada95 for Critical Systems. ORA Canada Report TR-95-5499-03, July 1996.
12. B. Carre and T. Jennings. SPARK: The SPADE Ada Kernel. Department of Electronics and Computer Science, University of Southampton, March 1988.
13. The Procurement of Safety Related Software in Defence Equipment (Parts 1 and 2). U.K. Ministry of Defence, Standard 00-55, 1997.

Ada in the JAS 39 Gripen Flight Control System

Bo Frisberg

Saab AB
SE-581 88 Linköping, Sweden
E-mail: Bo.Frisberg@saab.se

Abstract. The positive experiences from the usage of Ada in a safety critical flight control system are described in this paper. It states that preemptive scheduling implemented with tasking, can be combined with high requirements on reliability and a deterministic behaviour. How data consistency has been obtained between the periodic tasks is outlined. Also the exception handling in the system is mentioned.
Keywords: Flight control system, Safety critical, Tasking, Exception handling, Data consistency, Preemptive scheduling.

1 Introduction

The usage of Ada has been restrictive in safety critical systems. Traditionally, these systems have not trusted any high-order language at all, and they have typically been based on nonpreemptive scheduling implemented by simple cyclic executives. When Ada has been selected the usage has been limited to only a small subset. In particular the Ada tasking and exception handling have been questioned from safety aspects. For example, in the SPARK [1] subset definition (used in avionics) tasking and exception handling are excluded. Furthermore, in the Ada 95 Reference Manual [2] Annex H, Safety and Security, the restrictions "Max_Task is 0" and "No_Exception" are applied.

However, when safety critical control systems become more complex there is an increasing need to express and handle concurrency and exceptions also in this type of applications.

The flight control system in the military aircraft JAS 39 Gripen has been upgraded and is now programmed in Ada 83, which includes tasking and exception handling in a limited and controlled manner.

The test flights with the upgraded flight control system started in the beginning of 1996 (on schedule) and deliveries in production aircraft started later in the same year.

The system architecture is described in section 2, and the usage of Ada (especially the tasking and exception handling mechanisms) is described in section 3. How data consistency has been obtained between the periodic tasks when preemptive scheduling is allowed, is showed in section 4.

2 Gripen Flight Control System Architecture

The JAS 39 Gripen is a multi-role (fighter, attack and reconnaissance) aircraft. It has an electrical (fly-by-wire) flight control system, which is the most safety critical part of the avionics. The system performs input signal conditioning and voting, control law computations, functional monitoring and redundancy management, data recording, etc. Autopilot functions are also provided.

The aircraft is produced in both single- and two-seat versions. The differences between these versions are handled within the same software.

The flight control system has three redundant channels. Identical software resides in each channel, and each channel contains the following two processors:

- Primary processor (MC68040).

- Input/Output and Backup processor (TMS320C30).

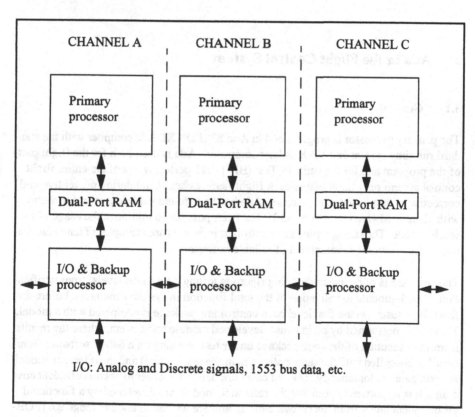

Fig. 1. Gripen digital flight control system

Typical input sources are stick and pedal position sensors, angular rate gyros, accelerometers, buttons for mode selections, etc. Outputs are sent to control surface actuators, indicators and warning lamps, etc. Communication with other subsystems in the aircraft is performed via a 1553 data bus. The Gripen avionics and bus communication system has been described in [6].

Backup control law computations are included in the I/O processor in case of primary side failures. The I/O & Backup processor is programmed in C, and the primary processor (MC68040) is programmed in Ada. Different languages were selected in order to obtain diversity. The software written in C is of significantly smaller size and is not expected to be changed very much in future updates of the system. The two processors are synchronized on software level and communicate via a Dual-Port RAM.

The execution in the three redundant channels are *not* synchronized (except during the Built-In-Test). However, as indicated by the doubled edged arrows in Fig 1, data are exchanged between the channels via a Cross Channel Data Link (CCDL), which is managed by the I/O processor.

3   Ada in the Flight Control System

3.1   General

The primary processor is programmed in Ada 83 (EDS XDAda compiler with the standard run-time system and VAX as host computer). Ada is used both for the flight part of the program and for the Built-In-Test (BIT). BIT performs test of the entire flight control system on ground before each flight (safety check) and during preventive and corrective maintenance of the aircraft. Ada has been found sufficient even for routines with close hardware interaction, and it has been possible to minimize the usage of assembler code. The strong typing and controlled interfaces are examples of language features which support development of reliable software.

The software is of course undergoing rigorous testing on various levels, from verification of each module to validation of the total function in system simulators, before the final flight tests. On the first level each control law package is compared with a model. This test is performed by an in house developed module test system, where the results from the execution of the code package under test (running on a 68040 software simulator but compiled with the same options as in the real system) and the reference model are compared automatically. The test cases are defined in order to obtain sufficient coverage. It is important to note that the reference models are developed by a functional group independent from the software group and are written in another language (FORTRAN).

3.2 Tasking

The flight control software in the primary processor is implemented in Ada with five periodic tasks. All period times are harmonic, which makes the behaviour easier to predict. The processor capacity can be utilized in full with retained schedulability. The harmonic frequencies in this application are 120, 60, 30, 15 and 7.5 Hz. The periodic tasks are assigned fixed priorities according to the rate monotonic scheduling algorithm, i.e. higher priorities to tasks with shorter periods (the general RMS theory was reviewed in [3] and [4]).

The scheduling is implemented by a separate task with the highest priority, which is activated at 120 Hz (the 8.33 ms minor frame) by an interrupt from a real time clock device. This scheduler task activates the periodic tasks in required intervals by means of conditional entry calls. It also detects if any task has missed its deadline (overrun). As this is a hard real-time application a missed deadline means that the backup control laws (basic control with only a single periodic thread) in the other processor are made active. It can be notified that it is possible to detect a missed deadline before the time for the next periodic activation of a task, i.e. the allowed execution time can be shorter than the period time (but both the allowed execution and period times have to be multiples of the minor frame).

A background task only measures and stores the computational load of the periodic tasks (the real time clock timer is read when the periodic tasks have finished its execution and the background task is resumed). Furthermore there are two tasks with lower priorities which are only executed during BIT. The main program task makes sure that the BIT tasks are only activated on ground.

Task summary in priority order:

*   Scheduler task (minor frame interrupt handler)
*   Ada main
*   120 Hz task
*   60 Hz task
*   30 Hz task
*   15 Hz task
*   7.5 Hz task
*   Background task
*   Two BIT tasks

Although tasking is allowed in this application, the following restrictions are applicable:

- All tasks are declared at library level and are created at start of the program. They are not allowed to terminate, which means that each task contains a non-terminating outer loop.

- Abort is not allowed.

- All tasks have unique and fixed priorities (no dynamic priorities).

- The Calendar package and the Delay statement are not used (not needed in this application).

3.3 Exception Handling

Exception handling is another Ada feature which have been questioned from safety aspects. The rational of SPARK [1] states: "it is easier and more satisfactory to write a program which is exception-free, and prove it to be so, than to prove that the corrective actions performed by exception-handlers would be appropriate under all possible circumstances". Another reason to use exceptions restrictively is the execution time overhead, which is hard to predict.

In the Gripen flight control system exceptions are handled, but there are no advanced recovery mechanisms designed with exceptions.

Whenever the occurrence of an exception can be foreseen, the exception should normally be avoided. For example, when converting floating-point values to 16-bits integers for analog outputs, the value is always checked and limited, if necessary, before assigned to the integer (such an error was the direct cause of the Ariane 5 first flight failure [5]). But still there may be situations where exceptions are hard to foresee, e. g. exceptions triggered by hardware failures. If an exception occurs, the type of error and program location are always recorded for diagnostic purpose. Exception event flags as well as other failure flags are stored in a non volatile memory for inspection after landing. The general action when an exception occurs is then to make the backup control laws active (similar to the periodic task overrun situation).

A special situation where exception handling has been found appropriate is to make it possible to catch failures in isolated procedures which are not critical for the result. For example, functionality may be added in such procedures only for recording purpose during flight tests. A correct normal function can still be ensured after an exception.

Another special use of the exception mechanism in this application is for exit of the BIT execution on ground when the speed of the aircraft exceeds a certain value (take-off). This is an unusual way to exit BIT, and can basically be seen as a form of asynchronous transfer of control.

So far, no exception has been raised in the air (but of course the exception handling mechanism has to be tested in system simulators).

4 Data Consistency between Periodic Tasks

In a system where preemptive scheduling is allowed, it is essential to ensure that data exchanged between the tasks are consistent, which in this system means that:

- *All* output data from one periodic task have to be computed within the same periodic activation of the task.

- *No* input data to one periodic task is allowed to be updated during the periodic activation of the task.

To obtain data consistency data buffers are used. The harmonic period times make it possible to achieve a fixed scheme of data exchanges, which is shown in Fig 2.

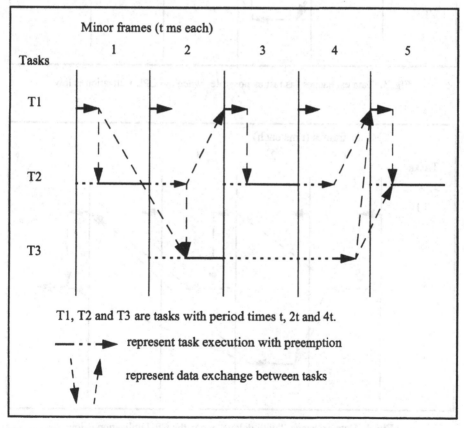

Fig. 2. Data exchange scheme between periodic tasks when the CPU utilization is high. For example, no data is exchanged between the tasks T1 and T2 when T2 is preempted by T1 in the minor frames 2 and 4

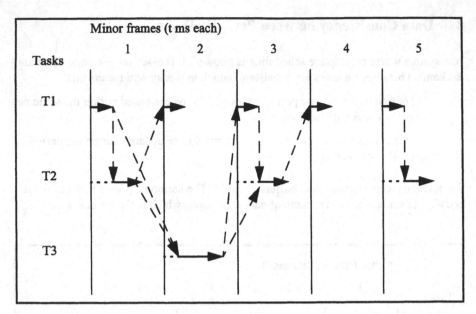

Fig. 3. Data exchanges "as fast as possible" when the CPU utilization is low

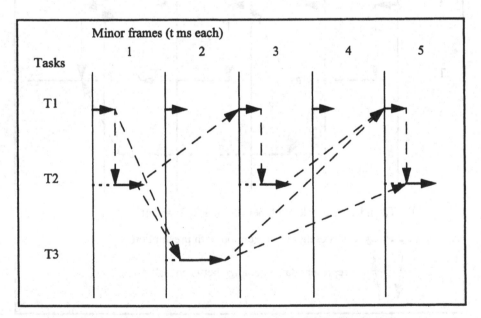

Fig. 4. Data exchanges "with delays" when the CPU utilization is low

If there is free time and the periodic task execution is not interrupted (this may be the case in the beginning of a project), the "ready" data buffers can be used as fast as possible, i.e. in the next minor frame (see Fig 3). Alternatively, the designer can choose to easily insert delays where future growth in the application is expected (see Fig 4). This means that it is possible to make the program almost independent of the actual CPU utilization, and timing concerns can be relaxed. The timing of data exchanged between the periodic tasks is identical in Fig 2 (with high CPU utilization) and Fig 4 (with low CPU utilization), i.e. preemptive scheduling can be combined with a deterministic behaviour.

The described data exchange mechanism is implemented with references (access values) to current input and output data buffers. The references are transferred from the scheduler task to the periodic tasks in the rendezvous when these are made ready for execution. The data buffers require some extra RAM space, but the execution time overhead with this technique is minimal.

As the periodic tasks are not allowed to communicate directly with each other, the risk for priority inversion, deadlock and other undesired task blocking is eliminated.

In general, all tasking and data buffering mechanisms are handled at the executive level, transparent to the application functions. The sequential parts of the program can be analyzed and tested separately. This is also an advantage from the maintenance point of view. When application functions are modified or new functionality is added, the tasking and communication framework will normally not be affected at all. This property is essential in many real-time systems (e.g. avionics) which evolve during a long period of time.

5   Conclusions

Ada with tasking can be used to implement preemptive scheduling in safety critical embedded control systems with strong requirements on reliability and a deterministic behaviour. A robust software architecture and design is necessary, including restrictions and limitations in the usage of tasking and exception handling.

The general rule that "everything should be made as simple as possible, but not simpler" is applicable. As high integrity real-time systems become more complex, there is a *need* to express and handle concurrency and exceptions in a safe and efficient way. This should be considered in future Ada guidelines and subset definitions. In this way the advantages and expressiveness of Ada can be utilized to support good software engineering also in safety critical and hard real-time systems.

The flight control system described in this paper is written in Ada 83, and no transition to Ada 95 is planned today. How the new features in Ada 95 can be utilized in this type of application is a subject for future work.

References

1. SPARK - The SPADE Ada Kernel, Edition 3.1,
    Program Validation Ltd., May 1992.

2. Ada 95 Language Reference Manual,
    International Standard ISO/IEC-8652:1995.

3. L. Sha and J. B. Goodenough,
    Real-Time Scheduling Theory and Ada,
    IEEE Computer, Apr., 1990.

4. M. H. Klein, J. P. Lehoczky and R Rajkumar,
    Rate-Monotonic Analysis for Real-Time Industrial Computing,
    IEEE Computer, Jan., 1994.

5. ARIANE 5, Flight 501 Failure,
    Report by the Inquiry Board, Paris, 19 July 1996.

6. D. Folkesson,
    Principles for Real-Time Execution in Swedish Avionics Systems (in Swedish),
    SNART 2nd Conference on Real Time Systems in Stockholm 1993.

Author Index

Lecture Notes in Computer Science

For information about Vols. 1–1332

please contact your bookseller or Springer-Verlag